Nehemiah

Focused Leadership

BIBLICAL LEADERSHIP
COMMENTARY SERIES

J. Robert Clinton, D. Miss., Ph.D.
Daniel H. Allen, D. Min.

BARNABAS
PUBLISHERS

Barnabas Publishers
P.O. Box 6006
Altadena, CA 91003-6006
ISBN No. 0-9741818-8-9

Printed in the United States of America

Series & Title Cover Design: D.M. Battermann, R&D Design Servies
Book Design & Layout: D.M. & R.D. Battermann, R&D Design Services

Table of Contents

Contents	Page

---

[1] Throughout the commentary Articles listed with numbers are included with this commentary and refer to the numbered articles listed above. Some articles, without numbers occur in other commentaries.

Abbreviations

Bible Books

Genesis	Ge	Nahum	Na
Exodus	Ex	Habakkuk	Hab
Leviticus	Lev	Zephaniah	Zep
Numbers	Nu	Haggai	Hag
Deuteronomy	Dt	Zechariah	Zec
Joshua	Jos	Malachi	Mal
Judges	Jdg	Matthew	Mt
Ruth	Ru	Mark	Mk
1 Samuel	1Sa	Luke	Lk
2 Samuel	2Sa	John	Jn
1 Kings	1Ki	Acts	Ac
2 Kings	2Ki	Romans	Ro
1 Chronicles	1Ch	1 Corinthians	1Co
2 Chronicles	2Ch	2 Corinthians	2Co
Ezra	Ezr	Galatians	Gal
Nehemiah	Ne	Ephesians	Eph
Esther	Est	Philippians	Php
Job	Job	Colossians	Col
Psalms	Ps	1 Thessalonians	1Th
Proverbs	Pr	2 Thessalonians	2Th
Ecclesiastes	Ecc	1 Timothy	1Ti
Song of Songs	SS	2 Timothy	2Ti
Isaiah	Isa	Titus	Tit
Jeremiah	Jer	Philemon	Phm
Lamentations	La	Hebrews	Heb
Ezekiel	Eze	James	Jas
Daniel	Da	1 Peter	1Pe
Hosea	Hos	2 Peter	2Pe
Joel	Joel	1 John	1Jn
Amos	Am	2 John	2Jn
Obadiah	Ob	3 John	3Jn
Jonah	Jnh	Jude	Jude
Micah	Mic	Revelation	Rev

Other

BAS	Basic English Version
CEV	Contemporary English Version
fn	footnote(s)
KJV	King James Version of the Bible
LB	The Learning Bible—Contemporary English Version
NEB	New English Bible
NLT	New Living Translation
N.T.	New Testament
O.T.	Old Testament
Phillips	The New Testament in Modern English, J.B. Phillips
TEV	Today's English Version (also called Good News Bible)
Vs	verse(s)

List of Tables

List of Figures, Charts and Lists

Introduction

This leadership commentary on Nehemiah is part of a series, **Clinton's Leadership Commentary Series.** For the past 13 years I have been researching leadership concepts in the Bible. As a result of that I (Bobby) have identified the 25 most helpful Bible books that contribute to an understanding of leadership. I have done twelve of these commentaries to date and am continuing on the rest. I originally published eight of these leadership commentaries in a draft manuscript for use in classes. But it became clear that I would need to break that large work (735 pages) into smaller works. The commentary series does that. Titus was the first in the series. Haggai was the second of the series that is being done as an individual work. Habakkuk was the third. Jonah was the fourth. And this one, Nehemiah, will be the fifth done in the series.

This is a leadership commentary, not an exegetical commentary. That means we have worked with the text to see what implications of leadership it suggests.

A given commentary in the series is made up of an *Overview Section*, which seeks to analyze the book as a whole for historical background, plan, theme, and fit into the redemptive story of the Bible. In addition, we identify, up front, the basic leadership topics that are dealt with in the book. Then we educe leadership observations, guidelines, principles, and values for each of these leadership topics. This *Overview Section* primes the reader to look with leadership eyes.

Then we have the *Commentary Proper*. We use our own translation of the text. We give commentary on various aspects of the text. A given context, paragraph size, will usually have 3 to 4 comments dealing with some suggestions about leadership items.

The *Commentary Proper* suggests *Leadership Concepts* and connects you to leadership articles that further explain these leadership concepts. The emphasis on the comments is not exegetical though we do make those kinds of comments when they are helpful for my leadership purposes.

The *Leadership Articles* (in Nehemiah there are 38 totaling 220 pages) in the series carry much of what we have learned about leadership in our years of ministry. In one sense, these articles and others in the series are my legacy. I plan to publish all of the articles of the total series in a separate work, **Clinton's Encyclopedia of Biblical Leadership Insights,** which will be updated periodically as the series expands. A leader at almost any level of leadership can be helped greatly by getting leadership perspectives from these articles.

We also include a *Glossary* which lists all the leadership concepts labeled in the comments.

Other books in the series, to be released over the next five years, include:

1,2 Timothy--Apostolic Leadership Picking Up the Mantle;
1,2 Corinthians--Problematic Apostolic Leadership;
Daniel--A Model Leader in Tough times;
Philemon--A Study in Leadership Style;
Philippians--A Study in Modeling;
John--Jesus' Incarnational Leadership.

All of the above were previously done in the large manuscript and used in classes. And they are available as the original single work on CD in pdf format. Now we will break these out as individual commentaries in the series. And then we will do other books anticipated in the series over the next five years. One of these will be,

Malachi—Renewal Lessons Needed to Face Nominality Head-On.

My long-term thinking includes developing the following:

Acts—Apostolic Leadership in Transition Times (a multi volume project)
Deuteronomy—A Study in Moses' Inspirational Leadership
Numbers—Moses, Spiritual Authority, and Maintenance Leadership
Mark—Jesus' Power Ministry
Joshua—Courageous Leadership
Mathew--A Study in Leadership Selection and Development
1,2 Samuel—Three Leaders Compared and Contrasted

I (Bobby) have already done a study of each book in the Bible from a leadership standpoint and have identified and written up a number of leadership topics for each book. This analysis is captured in my book, **The Bible and Leadership Values**.

In an age of relativity, we believe the Bible speaks loudly concerning leadership concepts offering suggestions, guidelines, and even absolutes. We, as Christian leaders, desperately need this leadership help as we seek to influence our followers toward God's purposes for their lives.

J. Robert Clinton
Daniel H. Allen
November 2002

Preface

Every Scripture inspired of God is profitable for leadership insights (doctrine), pointing out of leadership errors (reproof), suggesting what to do about leadership errors (correction), and for highlighting how to model a righteous life (instruction in righteousness) in order that God's leader (Timothy) may be well equipped to lead God's people (the special good work given in the book Timothy to the young leader Timothy) .
(2 Timothy 3:16,17—Clinton paraphrase—slanted toward Timothy's leadership situation)

The Bible--a Major Source of Leadership Values and Principles

No more wonderful source of leadership values and principles exists than the Bible. It is filled with influential people and the results of their influence—both good and bad. Yet it remains so little used to expose leadership values and principles. What is needed to break this *leadership barrier*? Three things:

1. A conviction that the Bible is authoritative and can give leadership insights
2. Leadership perspectives to stimulate our findings in the Bible—we are blind in general to leadership ideas and hence do not see them in the Bible.
3. A willful decision to study and use the Bible as a source of leadership insights

These three assumptions underlie the writing of this leadership commentary series. **Nehemiah** is one of a series of books intended to help leaders cross the *leadership barrier*.

Leadership Framework
Perhaps it might be helpful to put the notion of leadership insights from Nehemiah in the bigger picture of leadership in the Bible. Three major leadership elements give us our most general framework (cross-culturally applicable as well) for categorizing leadership insights. The study of leadership involves:

1. **THE LEADERSHIP BASAL ELEMENTS** (The *What* of Leadership)
    a. leaders
    b. followers
    c. situations

    In Nehemiah we will see:
    a. leaders—Nehemiah, Hanani, King Artaxerxes, Ezra, and other civic and religious leaders;
    b. followers—especially those who worked with Nehemiah to rebuild the wall;
    c. situations—such as crisis, conflict resolution, military threat, response to threat, approaching the king, working with limited resources, and instituting civil and religious reforms.

2. **LEADERSHIP INFLUENCE MEANS** (The *How* of Leadership)
   a. individual means
   b. corporate means

In Nehemiah we will see:
   a. individual means such as the wise selection of when and how to approach authority figures, expertise, modeling, a strong leadership style. and spiritual authority;
   b. corporate means such as celebrations, group confrontation, religious ceremonies, and covenant making.

3. **LEADERSHIP VALUE BASES** (The *Why* of Leadership)
   a. cultural
   b. theological

In Nehemiah we will see several outward indications that flow from values.
   a. We'll see Jewish cultural factors which focus on identity, motivate toward accomplishment, and give a sense of history with God. We'll see priests, Levites, and artisans—all deeply influenced by Jewish thinking. We'll see a Jewish form of administrative leadership in the city.
   b. We'll see the importance of having a secure place to worship the living God, the importance of trusting God in crises and the importance of God's Word and obedience to God. All of these will have theological roots coming from Jewish history.

It is through using these major leadership elements that we are able to analyze leadership throughout the whole Bible. Using these major notions we recognize that leadership, at different time periods in the Bible, operates sufficiently different so as to suggest leadership eras—that is, time periods within which leadership follows more closely certain commonalities than in the time preceding it and following it. This allows us to identify six such eras in the Bible.

Six Bible Leadership Eras

The six leadership eras include,

1. **Patriarchal Era**

2. **Pre-Kingdom Era**
   A. Desert Years
   B. The War Years
   C. The Tribal Years

3. **Kingdom Era**
   A. United Kingdom

    B. Divided Kingdom
    C. Southern Kingdom

4. **Post-Kingdom Era**
    A. Exilic
    B. A Foothold Back in the Land

5. **Pre-Church Era**

6. **Church Era**

For each of these major eras we are dealing with some fundamental leadership questions.[1] We ask ourselves these major questions about every leadership era. Usually the answers are sufficiently diverse as to justify identification of a unique leadership era.

Where does Nehemiah fit?
    The book of Nehemiah fits in the fourth leadership era, *The Post-Kingdom Era*, in part B of that era—*A Foothold Back in the Land*. It is a time of difficulty for God's remnant, who have gone back into the land. The message of Nehemiah deals with a courageous leader's effort to go back to Jerusalem and rebuild the defenses of the city. Once the defenses are in place Nehemiah focuses on spiritual renewal and maintenance of the renewal movement. It is a book about inspirational and focused leadership. How can a leader motivate people under difficult circumstances to accomplish a task? From Nehemiah we learn about motivational leadership. How can a leader foment a renewal and maintain its spiritual thrust? We see a leader who is at once both practical and spiritual.

What does Nehemiah say?
    Before we can look at leadership insights from Nehemiah we need to be sure that we understand why Nehemiah is in the Scriptures and what it is saying in general. Having done our homework, hermeneutically speaking, we are free then to go beyond and look for other interpretative insights—such as leadership insights. But we must remember, always, first of all to interpret in light of the historical times, purpose of, theme of, and structure of the book.

    One way of analyzing the structure, that is, the way the author of Nehemiah organizes his material to accomplish his purposes, would be:

Structure	I. (ch 1)	Receiving Direction to Rebuild in Jerusalem
	II. (ch 2-7:3)	Organizing to Rebuild the Wall
	III. (ch 7:4-10:39)	Organizing for Reform
	IV. (ch 11-13)	Organizing for Continuation

---

[1] The six questions we use to help us differentiate between leadership eras includes: 1. What is the major leadership focus? 2. What are the influence means used? 3.What are the basic leadership functions? 4. What are the characteristics of the followers? 5. What was the existing cultural forms of leadership? 6. Other? I comment on each of these in the **Clinton's Encyclopedia of Biblical Leadership Insights**.

The overall thematic intent could be represented by a subject, which permeates all of what God is doing through the book of Nehemiah and several ideas about that subject. Here is our analysis of such a theme.

Theme **NEHEMIAH'S ORGANIZATIONAL LEADERSHIP**
- was the result of God's initiation,
- made itself felt in the face of obstacles to rebuild the wall,
- was inspirational in bringing about reform and a covenant in Jerusalem, and
- included drastic steps of separation in order to insure an on-going meaningful religious atmosphere.

Purpose

It is always difficult to synthesize statements of purpose when the author does not directly and **explicitly** give them. But it seems reasonable to imply that the following are some of the purposes of this book in the Old Testament:

- to tell of the rebuilding of the walls around Jerusalem,
- to show the importance of networking power,
- to introduce a new kind of leader (a lay leader who is Bible centered and who models task oriented and organizational behavior),
- to describe task oriented inspirational leadership which has organizational issues central,
- to illustrate motivational techniques,
- to show the importance of prayer in leadership,
- to show the importance of the Word in leadership,
- to illustrate perseverance in leadership the midst of opposition and obstacles,
- to show dynamic balance between dependence upon God and activity for God.

Having done our overview of the book, hermeneutically speaking, we can now focus on Nehemiah's leadership.

General Reflections—Nehemiah

With this background in mind, we can now proceed to the leadership commentary including its *General Reflection*, *Leadership Lessons*, *Commentary Notes*, *Articles*, and *Glossary*.

Today, we live in the Church Leadership Era.[1] It is difficult to place ourselves back hundreds of years into the 4th leadership era—Post-Kingdom Leadership. God has taken a people and made them into a kingdom. But the kingdom has split into a northern segment, Israel, and a southern segment, Judah.[2] God's program using the nation of Israel has come to a halt. Both kingdoms were destroyed and the people were taken into exile. After 70 years in exile a remnant has come back into the land. Most modern day pastors and parachurch leaders do not bother to go back and study this period of time in the Bible.[3] What does this small remnant in the land have to do with anything, anyway? Why is this book of Nehemiah included in the Bible, you say? It is an example of inspirational/motivational leadership for us. As present day leaders, we need to know how to motivate people. We can study a leader who knew how to organize to accomplish a task, Nehemiah. We can learn how God uses a leader to motivate followers and catalyze renewal.[4]

Suggested Approach for Studying Nehemiah

Read through the overview to get a general feeling for what Nehemiah is about. Note particularly the *Theme* of the book and its *Plan* for developing that theme, i.e., the outline for developing that theme. Then note the various purposes we suggest that the book of Nehemiah is seeking to accomplish. Then read through each of the leadership findings that we suggest are in the book. This is all preparation for the first reading of the text.

Read the text itself, preferably at one sitting, without referring to any of the commentary notes. Just see if you can *see what of the overview information* and the *leadership lessons* are suggested to you as you read the text.

Then reread the text, probably a chapter at a time and note the comments we give.[5] From time-to-time, go back and read a leadership lesson again when it is brought to your

---

[1] See **Articles**, *13. Leadership Eras In The Bible, Six Identified; 35. Six Biblical Leadership Eras, Approaching the Bible with Leadership Eyes.* This is probably an important prerequisite for you before approaching the commentary.

[2] See **Article**, *1. Biblical Framework—The Redemptive Drama.* This is another important prerequisite giving important background information within which Nehemiah's wall-building incident happens. See also **Article**, *33. Prophetic Crises, 3 Major Biblical Times*, which pinpoints the crisis Nehemiah was facing.

[3] Except probably the book of Nehemiah. If folks teach on leadership from the Bible, Nehemiah is the favorite book to teach from—usually the only one.

[4] See **Article**, *14. Learning Vicariously From Other Leaders' Lives.*

[5] From time-to-time in the comments, we will use the abbreviation SRN. SRN stands for Strong's Reference Number. Strong, in his exhaustive concordance, labeled each word in the Old Testament

mind as you read the text and the commentary. Also feel free to stop and go to the **Glossary** for explanation of leadership terms suggested by the commentary. And do the same thing with the **Articles**. The articles capture what we have learned about leadership over the years as we have observed it, researched it, and taught it. It is these articles that will enlighten your leadership understanding. Obviously because of the uniqueness of the book, dealing primarily with a new type of leader and that leader's direct task-oriented ministry, there will be some unusual leadership articles.

Further Study

We have provided some *note space* at the conclusion of the Nehemiah commentary where you can jot down ideas for future study. Have fun as you work through Nehemiah, and by all means learn something about *motivational leadership, getting ownership in a project, perseverance against opposition and extreme focus for a limited time*. Let this book inspire you to get your work from God, plan your work, and work your plan. And also learn the important lesson of learning vicariously by studying other leaders' lives.[6]

The overview follows. It gives a summarized version of the hermeneutical background studies for Nehemiah.

(dominantly Hebrew words but also some Aramaic/Chaldean) and New Testament (Greek words mostly) with an identifying number. He then constructed an Old Testament and New Testament lexicon (dictionary). If you have a **Strong's Exhaustive Concordance** with lexicon, you can look up the words we refer to. Many modern day reference works (lexicons and word studies and Bible Dictionaries and encyclopedias) use this Strong's Reference Number.

[6] The old adage, *experience is the best teacher* is true, **if you learn from it**. Personal experience is a great way to learn. But in terms of leadership, you will never have enough time to learn, *by personal experience alone*, all you need to know for your leadership. I suppose that is why God gave us the leadership mandate—Hebrews 13:7,8. He emphatically reminds us that vicarious learning is crucial for our leadership. And we have three whole books (Job, Habakkuk, Jonah) in the Bible devoted exclusively to illustrating God's shaping of leaders. And that is their main purpose for being in the Bible. Nehemiah's leadership is in view throughout the book named after him. We can learn leadership practices vicariously from his model. See **Article**, *14. Learning Vicariously From Other Leaders' Lives.*

BOOK   **NEHEMIAH**   **Author:** Nehemiah

Characters   Nehemiah—cupbearer to the king, King Artaxerxes, numerous Jewish
                      people who went back to Jerusalem with Nehemiah, Sanballat
                      (opponent), Tobiah (opponent), Geshem (Arab opponent), Ezra (the
                      godly priest who knew the Word)

Who To/For   For Jewish people

Literature Type   Historical narrative of selected vignettes

Story Line   The time is about 12+ years after the book of Ezra's events.
                      Nehemiah, who serves in the court of Artaxerxes, hears of the need of
                      the remnant which has returned to Jerusalem to rebuild the temple.
                      After a period of fasting and prayer, seeking God on behalf of the
                      people, he asks permission of the king to return and provide
                      organizational oversight to the situation there. He organizes the
                      people to build the wall. There is opposition to this by people who
                      have vested interests in the land. Nehemiah overcomes every obstacle
                      and builds the wall in a short time. He then goes on to bring about
                      reform as the city itself is being rebuilt.

Structure   I.   (ch 1)   Receiving Direction to Rebuild in Jerusalem
              II.   (ch 2-7:3)   Organizing to Rebuild the Wall
              III. (ch 7:4-10:39)   Organizing for Reform
              IV.   (ch 11-13)   Organizing for Continuation

Theme   **NEHEMIAH'S ORGANIZATIONAL LEADERSHIP**
                 • was the result of God's initiation,
                 • made itself felt in the face of obstacles to rebuild the wall,
                 • was inspirational in bringing about reform and a covenant in
                   Jerusalem, and
                 • included drastic steps of separation in order to insure an on-going
                   meaningful religious atmosphere.

Key Words Remember (6), wall(s) (30+), build (30+), Nehemiah's spontaneous prayers (9+)

Key Events Nehemiah's prayerful response to Hanani's news, his petition to Artaxerxes, the trip to Jerusalem, examining the site of the wall, organizing to build, opposition to building, financial integrity of Nehemiah, repeated opposition against building the wall, completion of the wall, Ezra reading the Law, corporate confession, covenant making, centralizing leadership in Jerusalem, publicly dedicating the wall, final reforms in response to reading the Law

Purposes Purposes include to:

- tell of the rebuilding of the walls around Jerusalem
- show the importance of networking power
- introduce a new kind of leader (lay leader with task oriented organizational leadership)
- describe task oriented inspirational leadership which has organizational issues central
- illustrate motivational techniques
- show the importance of prayer in leadership
- show the importance of the Word in leadership
- illustrate perseverance in leadership the midst of opposition and obstacles
- show dynamic balance between dependence upon God and activity for God

Importance   A new order of leadership is seen in this book. Prophet, priest and king have come and gone and still God's work needs accomplishing. God raises up a lay person who is willing to walk by faith in the midst of darkness and opposition. Nehemiah illustrates the basic message of Habakkuk 2:4, "My righteous one shall live by faith." His attitude of persevering faith, his continued activity on the wall, and his completion of the task illustrate what leadership that mixes faith with obedience can do. Nehemiah lived out the advice of the old Bible teacher who told his students, "Pray as though everything depended on God, and act as though everything depended on you."

Where It Fits   Nehemiah occurs in Leadership Era IV, entitled Post-Kingdom Leadership, the post exilic subphase. It is a time when the work and plans of God seem minor. The people of God are few—their spirits low. They need inspirational leadership. Nehemiah provides task oriented leadership, which inspires the people.

NEHEMIAH—LEADERSHIP LESSONS/TOPICS

1. **MOTIVATIONAL LESSONS.** Nehemiah is an excellent Old Testament exemplar for motivating followers. Paul and Jesus are the New Testament exemplars. Motivational techniques for getting follower ownership seen in Nehemiah's efforts include:

   a. working with the followers
   b. sacrificing financially
   c. taking courageous stands against opposition
   d. crisis praying
   e. sensitivity to God in providential ways
   f. working for justice—reforms
   g. competitiveness, pride—each family rebuilding portion near them
   h. positional leadership
   i. networking power
   j. modeling perseverance
   k. practical advice
   l. using extreme focus for a limited time; people totally committed need to see progress
   m. affirming those who are participating in the work

Nehemiah is a strong leader. He is aware of his modeling and its impact on the people. He is aware of his seconded authority from Artaxerxes. He starts with positional authority. But it is not positional authority alone. Competency plays a strong part. He knew what he was doing. And his vision resonated with a felt need the followers had. They needed a wall to protect the city.

Leadership Observations/Principles/Values Suggested by this concept:

   a. Effective leaders are aware of motivational techniques to use with their followers.
   b. Successful change agents know their followers well. Opinion leaders should be identified and their support cultivated toward the changes involved. Nehemiah did this.
   c. Modeling perseverance in the face of difficulties is a strong motivating factor.
   d. Nehemiah uses various influence means to accomplish his task.[7]
   e. Leaders should use affirmation to motivate followers.
   f. Leaders in Christian ministries must receive their work from God, for they are called to influence followers toward God's purposes. This is the central ethic of Christian leadership. Knowing his work was from God, as evidenced through the phrase, "the Lord put it in my heart," and the phrase, "the hand of my God upon

---

[7] See **Article**, *12. Influence, Power and Authority Forms.* I have adapted Dennis Wrong's continuum. Nehemiah uses several of Wrong's power forms.

me," also gave Nehemiah the firm conviction that enabled him to motivate followers, to motivate himself, and to persevere in spite of constant opposition.

See **Articles**, *8. Getting the Job Done—Comparison of Ezra, Nehemiah and Haggai's Roles; 12. Influence, Power and Authority Forms.*

2. **PRAYERFUL SPIRIT**. The prayer macro lesson is sprinkled throughout the book of Nehemiah. A <u>macro-lesson</u> is a high level generalization of a leadership observation (suggestion, guideline, requirement), stated as a lesson, which repeatedly occurs throughout different leadership eras, and thus has potential as a leadership absolute. The prayer macro lesson is first seen in Abraham's ministry, then in Moses' and reaffirmed clearly in Samuel's ministry. The prayer macro lesson is stated as:

Leaders called to a ministry are called to intercede for that ministry.

A spirit of prayer must pervade leadership task situations, especially in the midst of crisis-like opposition. The book of Nehemiah records at least 23 instances of prayer. These use different words to emphasize the praying: (1) Pray, prayer, or prayed (11 times), see 1:4,6,11; 2:4; 4:9; 5:10,11; 11:17; (2) beseech (4 times), see 1:5, 8 (twice); (3) Think Upon (2 times), see 5:19; 6:14; (4) Remember (4 times), see 13:14, 22, 29, 31; (5) General Prayer (2 times) 6:9; 9:1. Some are more lengthy. A number of them are spontaneous prayers, where Nehemiah in his heart and thoughts in the midst of situations flings up prayers to God. A number of them are "Remember" prayers![8]

<u>Leadership Observations/Principles/Values Suggested by this concept:</u>
   a. Leaders called to a ministry are called to intercede for that ministry.
   b. Crisis times in ministry should drive a leader to prayer.[9]
   c. Nehemiah has a very balanced approach to prayer and ministry. He prayed as though everything depended on God, and he acted as though everything depended on his leadership. Prayer was backed with practical action.

See **Articles**, *Prayer Macro Lesson; 24. Nehemiah, Desperate Praying;16. Macro Lessons—Defined; 17. Macro Lessons—List of 41 Across Six Leadership Eras.*

3. **OWNERSHIP**. Ownership refers to the willing acceptance by followers of some changes being proposed by a leader. The people participate wholeheartedly because they think it is right to do so. Follower ownership is imperative for accomplishing overwhelming tasks. In the book of Nehemiah, chapter 3 lists an impressive number of people whom Nehemiah motivated to help him with his task. At least 48 people or groups of people are named. These include priests, Levites, goldsmiths, other

---

[8] These are perhaps eunuch prayers. See Lev 21:20,21 and Isa 56:3.

[9] Seen also in Habakkuk's ministry.

business men, leaders of towns, and common people. Nehemiah was able to motivate all kinds of people to willingly be a part of rebuilding the wall. A primary motivational technique he used was to have folks who lived along a wall build that portion of the wall. There was an underlying sense of competition. Each knew others would see their effort.

Leadership Observations/Principles/Values Suggested by this concept:
a. Ownership of a change project is a must for a leader seeking to bring about change.
b. Effective change agents identify opinion leaders and make a strong effort to bring them on board with the change strategy. Ideally this happens prior to introducing the change to the larger constituency of followers. Many pastors make the mistake of announcing change to their entire congregations, from their pulpits, instead of discussing the change with ever-widening circles of leaders and members at various levels of commitment to the church (e.g., pastor; pastor and his or her family; pastor and staff; pastor and chief governing board; pastor and key leaders outside of the board—especially those who will be affected by the change; pastor and leaders of all ministry areas; pastor and all those involved in ministry; then the congregation.
c. Knowledge of the change participants is a must for a leader seeking to get ownership of the change strategy—knowledge of who they are, what vested interests they hold, what cultural assumptions drive their viewpoints and behaviors, and how the change will affect them, etc.
d. People tend to be more supportive of ideas and change efforts toward which they contribute. Nehemiah wisely sought the involvement of the opinion leaders, and their response to his initiative, prior to involving larger numbers of people.
e. People from egalitarian cultures are especially resistant to change if it feels imposed to them.
f. Gathering the input and opinions of those who will be affected by the change can help a leader see the change initiative from several different perspectives, improve the change initiative, and improve how it gets presented to followers.

See *ownership*, **Glossary**. See **Articles**, *21. Nehemiah, Change Participants; 27. Nehemiah, Getting Ownership*.

4. **COSTLY CONVICTIONS.** Nehemiah was a leader with no compromise on religious convictions even though it was costly.

a. When he sensed God calling him to a renewal work in Jerusalem, he accepted the call and approached the king with his request, even though it could have been misinterpreted and could have led to his execution.
b. When first challenged by external opponents in chapter 2, Nehemiah told them outright that they had no right or place in the restoration work God had for His people and city. This too could have cost him his life.
c. When he was repeatedly rebuffed and threatened by these and additional adversaries, Nehemiah continued to hold to his conviction that God would protect

him and His people, that God would fight for His people and the work on the wall. Had his adversaries mounted a sizable opposition force, Nehemiah could have lost his life or his credibility as a leader.

d. Nehemiah continually gave credit to God for the work accomplished in the city. He seems deeply convicted about God's rightful place in the hearts and eyes of His people—He is the God of heaven who calls for a holy, wholly dedicated, and obedient people.

e. Nehemiah convenes public meetings to confront injustice and those who are oppressing their fellow Israelites. He could have incurred their opposition, hatred, and wrath by doing so. Concern for God's glory and the good of God's people seems to motivate him more than fear of what others would do or say.

f. Enforcing marriage and Sabbath regulations were costly. Homes were divided. Income was forfeited. Yet Nehemiah holds to a very high view of covenant-keeping for God's people. He understands that continued violation of the covenant was what led to their downfall in the first place.

Leadership Observations/Principles/Values Suggested by this concept:

a. Christian leadership is costly. Christian leaders are responsible to the Lord for their leadership. If they take the way of compromise, the Lord knows and will bring their true motives and deeds to light (1 Corinthians 4:5).

b. Christian leaders should lead out of their reverence (deep fear and awe) for and obedience to the Lord rather than the fear of what others might think or how they might respond. Leaders are responsible to God for influencing followers toward God's purposes. Those purposes, and acceptable ways in which they may be achieved, are rooted in biblical teachings and values.

c. Leaders should not stop their pursuit of God's purposes simply because they may be threatened or experience hardship. Since they have been called to their role by the Lord, and He has placed His purposes before them, they must persevere and endure hardship like a good soldier (2 Timothy 2:3).

d. The pulls of the flesh, the devil, and the culture are powerful. The Christian leader must crucify the flesh, resist the devil, and be transformed by the renewing of his or her mind. Following God's guidance and the revelation of the Scriptures may frequently pit the leader at odds with cultural practices and ideologies, but as surely as Nehemiah was anchored in his leadership to the covenant and his fear of the LORD, the Christian leader today must lead within the parameters of what is biblically correct (albeit in love not legalism).

5. **CONFLICT IN LEADERSHIP**. In major boundary times expect great conflict and opposition from secular people, especially where threatening change is happening.

   a. Webster defines a conflict as a sharp disagreement in positions or ideas.
   b. Nehemiah experiences conflict when he arrives in Jerusalem. Notice especially 2:10, that his opponents "were very disturbed that someone had come to promote the welfare of the Israelites." Ultimately he encounters opposition because he is advancing the purposes of God and the well-being of God's people.

c. His promotion of the welfare of the Israelites, and his re-establishment of covenant principles, will lead to a loss of position, prominence, and prosperity for those who had vested interests in perpetuating the disgraced condition of the people and the city.

d. Nehemiah faced conflict on two main fronts: externally, from the likes of Sanballat, Tobiah, Geshem, and the coalition they mustered; internally, from those in league with the external coalition. He also faced the onset of discouragement and loss of morale that accompanied the threats of attack, the reports of substandard building materials ("so much rubble"), and the problems with usury and social injustices.

e. Nehemiah faced ongoing conflict, especially during the fifty-two day period of rebuilding the wall.

f. Nehemiah took spiritual and practical steps to confront the conflict: 1) spiritually, he prayed and confessed his faith in the Lord; 2) spiritually, he rallied the people to put their trust in the Lord; 3) practically, he verbally countered the propositions of Sanballat, Tobiah, and their coalition; 4) practically, he posted guards around the city and equipped the workers with weapons as well as tools; 5) practically, he rebuked those who were guilty of charging usury and oppressing their countrymen.

Leadership Observations/Principles/Values Suggested by this concept:

a. While leaders can lead change initiatives that appear purely practical in nature, such as rebuilding walls and doors and repopulating a city, ultimately those initiatives, when tied to the purposes of God, serve to move His work forward.

b. As God's work goes forward, conflicts arise against His work and His leaders. That conflict can originate with people they lead, with secular people who are stakeholders in the status quo, or from demonic forces.[10]

c. To keep the work moving forward and the people encouraged, leaders must take action and confront the opposition.

d. God responds to His leaders who call out to Him during times of crisis and conflict.

6. **OPPOSITION LESSONS.** Opposition refers here to an opposing force or group of people. In dealing with opposition expect:

a. Ridicule. How Nehemiah handled it: 1) did not argue—first thing commit to the Lord; 2) he saw the problem in light of God.

b. Consolidation of opposing force—2 enemies become 4: Sanballat, Tobiah, Arabs, Ammonites. Nehemiah altered the plans for building and provided a military response in the midst of the working.

c. Intimidation. The opposing party sought to intimidate the workers and stop the work.

d. God's help. God gave Nehemiah insight and discernment into the false prophecies and strategies of the opposing coalition. Ultimately God gave Nehemiah and the

---

[10] No actual evidence of demonic instigation is seen in the text of Nehemiah but the New Testament does teach this (see Eph 6:10ff).

workers victory over the opposition through the completion of the wall and the renewal of civic and religious life.

Leadership Observations/Principles/Values Suggested by this concept:
a. Leaders hardly ever garner one hundred percent support for change agendas or important works for God, especially Christian leaders who promote the well-being of lost people, of believers, and the expansion of God's kingdom.[11]
b. Even well-meaning Christians find it difficult to agree at all times on what direction a particular church or ministry should take. Leaders, therefore, should expect some level of conflict and opposition. Some of it will come from personality differences, some from differing theological views, some from people with differing sets of felt needs, and some simply because people don't fully understand what is in the leader's heart and how he or she hopes to achieve it.
c. If the leader has heard from God and is following God, opposition to the vision should not halt the work. The leader should seek counsel from the Lord and from trusted advisors regarding how to respond and keep moving forward.
d. Leaders must take action toward God's vision and persevere in spite of opposition in order to see God's purposes established.

7. **BALANCE BETWEEN ACTION AND PRAYER**. Maintain balance—pray and work. Nehemiah lived out the advice of the modern teacher who told his students, "Pray as though everything depended on God, and act as though everything depended on you."

Leadership Observations/Principles/Values Suggested by this concept:
a. Leaders we've worked with are often strong in one area or the other—work or prayer, but significant works of God are divine/human partnerships.
b. Neither work nor prayer tends to be mutually exclusive. For example, leaders can pray for mechanical and technological problems in their ministries to change, but prayer alone is no substitute (as a rule) for retaining technicians who understand the nature of the problems and can provide the needed solutions. Prayer can give leaders the motivation, and perhaps even greater capacity, to become computer literate, for example, but the leaders still need to take the initiative to learn the basics of computing and a variety of software applications.
c. On the other hand, possessing advanced skills of one kind or another, and putting in 55-hour work weeks, does not guarantee that the hand of God will rest upon a leader or that God will convey spiritual authority upon that leader. Competence is needed, but intimacy with Christ is primary.

---

[11] While not seen overtly in Nehemiah, spiritual warfare often lurks behind what seems to be mere natural or human opposition. This is seen in the book of Daniel and one instance in David's life. It is more fully exposed in the New Testament.

8.   **PROCESSING.** The book of Nehemiah should be studied in light of leadership emergence theory, that is, God's processing in Nehemiah's life. Particularly the book shows the importance of conflict processing. Conflict processing can affect the character, skills, attitudes, and values of a leader. There are a number of process items in Nehemiah. Prominent ones are crises, life crises, conflict, spiritual authority discovery, prayer power, relationship insights, ministry insights and networking power.

Leadership Observations/Principles/Values Suggested by this concept:
   a.   God develops leaders throughout their lives, using important people, events and circumstances to shape their character (spiritual formation), skills (ministry formation), and calling (strategic formation).
   b.   Since God develops leaders throughout their lives, leaders can grow in their capacity to lead by responding positively to what God is trying to instill in them.
   c.   Leaders who learn to recognize God's shaping processes can gain perspective on their lives—past and present, as well as hope for their future. They can see how God shaped them in the past and grow more sensitive to how they are being shaped in the present. They can come to view present circumstances as God-given opportunities to grow in their character and their capacity to influence followers.

9.   **FINANCIAL INTEGRITY.** One of the primary barriers to leaders finishing well[12] has to do with financial integrity. Many leaders who fall and do not finish well have problems dealing with money in their ministry. Nehemiah is an exemplar in the Old Testament for careful handling of money. He did not want his handling of money to be a problem with his followers. He goes the extra mile to maintain financial integrity. Paul is the New Testament exemplar with regard to careful handling of finances.

Leadership Observations/Principles/Values Suggested by this concept:
   a.   Generally speaking, it takes financial resources to conduct ministry. Leaders don't have to be financial gurus, but they can profit from a basic understanding of financial matters, especially the basics such as cash flow, budgeting, and interpreting financial reports.
   b.   Leaders need to be able to secure the financial resources needed to fund the work God has called them to accomplish.
   c.   Leaders must set in place policies and procedures for the truthful and open accounting of the receipts and disbursements of funds.
   d.   Leaders must be aware of the temptation to greed and the misuse of finances. In particular, those who have power positions and make important decisions concerning finances can be tempted to use practices, which encourage the incorrect handling of money and tempt them with sins such as greed and the

---

[12] We have identified six major barriers to leaders finishing well: (1) abuse of power; (2) inordinate pride; (3) illicit sexual behavior; (4) inappropriate handling of finances; (5) family issues; (6) plateauing. Here we are dealing with financial integrity. Nehemiah had it.

misappropriation of funds. A character trait of greed is often deeply rooted and can lead to various types of financial impropriety.

See **Articles**, *5. Finishing Well—6 Characteristics; 6. Finishing Well—Six Major Barriers.*

10. **LEADERSHIP FUNCTIONS.** Leadership functions describe general activities that leaders must do and/or be responsible for in their influence of followers. The functions include task behaviors, relational behaviors and inspirational behaviors.

   a. Nehemiah's task behaviors include providing a workforce structure to build the wall, resolving crises, making decisions related to the completion of the work, problem solving related to the completion of the work, and transitioning work to other leaders for various civic, military, and religious functions.
   b. His relational behaviors include making decisions and solving problems based not only on the work but the people, coordinating work with subordinates and other leaders, facilitating leadership transitions, and sharing the vision and plan for completing the work.
   c. His inspiration behaviors include motivating followers toward the vision, encouraging the perseverance and faith of the workers, renewing the covenant-keeping culture of the nation, and modeling a faithful-to-God life that followers could emulate.

<u>Leadership Observations/Principles/Values Suggested by this concept</u>:
   a. High level leadership is a dynamic process that includes multiple leadership acts, over time, from three primary areas of leadership functions.
   b. Each function is important in the overall process of leading a group (people/relational) toward God's (inspirational) purposes (task) for the group.
   c. Effective leaders will employ the functions needed in a given leadership context.
   d. Leaders will serve in direct ministry in the areas of their gift-mix (evangelism, teaching, pastoring, apostleship, etc.), but will also need to do the work of a leader: task, relational, and inspirational work.
   e. The central ethic of Christian leadership is influencing followers toward God's purposes (oroverall vision) for the group. The task function discerns and structures toward the fulfillment of the vision; the relational function manages the interpersonal dynamics that arise as work on the vision progresses; the inspirational function motivates followers toward fulfillment of the vision.

See **Article** *29. Nehemiah, Leadership Functions.*

(This page deliberately blank.)

Nehemiah

CLINTON'S
BIBLICAL LEADERSHIP
COMMENTARY SERIES

Focused Leadership

Verse By Verse Commentary

(This page deliberately blank.)

Special Note:
We will not print all the Bible text, but only those passages, which have leadership comments. However, when we omit Scripture we will indicate the length of text omitted and give contextual statements for those verses.[1]

I. (1-7:3)   Organizing to Rebuild the Wall

Chapter 1

These are the memoirs[2] of Nehemiah[3] the son of Hacaliah.

In the month of Kislev[4] in the twentieth year of King Artaxerxes' reign,[5] I was at the fortress of Susa.[6] 2 Hanani, one of my brothers,[7] came to visit me with some other men who had just arrived from Judah. I asked them about the Jews who had survived the captivity and about how things were going in Jerusalem.[8] 3 They said to me, "Those who survived the exile and are back in the province are in great trouble and disgrace. The wall of Jerusalem is broken down, and its gates have been burned with fire."[9]

---

[1] See the **Article**, *23. Nehemiah, Contextual Flow—Understanding the Presentation.*

[2] Literally, the words. But usually with an Old Testament writer, like a prophet, you will have some authoritative phrase like "the Word of the Lord came" or the like. Here we have a lay leader, an administrative leader who is a spiritual man. He does not claim some authoritative word from God. He is simply recalling the events of an important time in which his leadership counted for God. We have thus chosen to render the "words" with the term memoirs. These were events well worth remembering. We wonder if perhaps Nehemiah had journaled during this critical leadership time. He has so many details about names of people, etc. It seems he might have kept a journal.

[3] See **Article**, *19. Nehemiah, Biographical Sketch*, for a quick overview of what is known about Nehemiah.

[4] Kislev would be sometime between mid-November and mid-December. For location, see comment below about winter palace. The CEV identifies this twentieth year as 446 B.C.

[5] See **Articles**, *15. Left Hand of God; 33. Prophetic Crises; 34. Restoration Leaders.* All of these give background about the timing of the book and something of Artaxerxes' involvement.

[6] Susa was the summer palace of King Artaxerxes. It was a fortified city. It was also the capital of the Elam Province. That Nehemiah was there meant he was part of King Artaxerxes' court, which traveled with the king as well as served him in the main palace. That is akin to being included in the traveling party of Air Force One. Nehemiah was part of Artaxerxes' traveling entourage.

[7] Hanani is probably a real brother, a relative. Later this same Hanani is put in charge of Jerusalem. See 7:2.

[8] These were probably folks who had returned from Babylon or descendants of some who may have stayed in the land. That Nehemiah was interested in them probably infers that he had been raised by religious parents who had instructed him in Israelite history, tradition, and probably the Law. His prayer later in this chapter shows knowledge of God's word as does his application of truth from biblical illustrations in ch 13.

[9] Gates and walls were the primary defense for a city. Without them, people in the city were prey to any kind of military force. With them, the inhabitants could withstand a siege. See **Article**, *7. Gates and Walls.*

4 When I heard this, I sat down and wept. In fact, for days I mourned, fasted, and prayed[10] to the God of heaven.[11] 5 Then I said, "O LORD, God of heaven,[12] the great and awesome God who keeps his covenant of unfailing love with those who love him and obey his commands, 6 listen to my prayer. Look down and see me praying night and day for your people Israel.[13] I confess we have sinned terribly against you. Yes, even my own family and I have sinned! 7 We have acted very wickedly toward you by not obeying the commands, laws, and regulations that you gave us through your servant Moses."

8 "Please remember what you told your servant Moses: 'If you sin, I will scatter you among the nations. 9 But if you return to me and obey my commands, even if you are exiled to the ends of the earth, I will bring you back to the place I have chosen as a dwelling for my Name to be honored.' "

10 "We are your servants, the people you rescued by your great power and might. 11 O Lord, please hear my prayer! Listen to the prayers of those of us who delight in honoring you. Please grant me success now as I go to ask the king for a great favor.[14] Put it into his heart to be kind to me."[15]

---

[10] This is the first of the instances of prayer that Nehemiah records. See 1:4, 5, 6, 8, 11; 2:4; 4:9; 5:10, 11, 19; 6:9, 14; 9:1; 11:17; 13:14, 22, 29, 31. See *vicarious praying*, **Glossary**. See **Articles**, *18. Nehemiah, And Daniel—Comparison of Vicarious Praying; 24. Nehemiah, Desperate Praying*.

[11] This reveals Nehemiah as being a person concerned with God's purposes for Jerusalem. He is not afraid to share his emotional state. He is a man of spiritual disciplines. He prayed. He fasted. Leaders who finish well exhibit the enhancement of spiritual disciplines in their lives. For other prayer references, see 1:4, 5, 6, 8, 11; 2:4; 4:9; 5:10, 11, 19; 6:9, 14; 9:1; 11:17; 13:14, 22, 29, 31. See **Articles**, *4. Finishing Well—5 Factors Enhancing; 19. Nehemiah, Biographical Sketch; Spiritual Disciplines—And On-Going Leadership*.

[12] The *God of heaven* is a title that is used 21 times in the Old Testament—two times in Genesis, once in the Psalms, once in Jonah, and the rest in the times of exile or restoration leadership. Its common thread in these usages is a title that would be recognized by people other than God's people. It is a popular term for God by the leaders in exile and restoration times.

[13] Night and day, probably a hyperbole, but intended to show the deep concern Nehemiah had. He was a leader who practiced the truth of the prayer macro lesson: **Leaders called to a ministry are called to intercede for that ministry.** A macro-lesson is a high level generalization of a leadership observation (suggestion, guideline, requirement), stated as a lesson, which repeatedly occurs throughout different leadership eras, and thus has potential as a leadership absolute. Forty-one Macro lessons have been identified in the six leadership eras. See *hyperbole*, **Glossary**. See **Articles**, *16. Macro Lessons—Defined; 17. Macro Lessons—List of 41 Across Six Leadership Eras*.

[14] The *great favor* is related to the vision Nehemiah has received from God. God has assigned to Nehemiah a restorative and renewing work—to move His people out of shame and disgrace through the restoration of the wall and gates, the restoration of civil order and proper leadership, and the renewing of the people spiritually. In 2:12 Nehemiah refers to the vision as "the plans God had put in my heart for Jerusalem (NLT). In 7:5 he will write "my God gave me the idea." What we see here is that Christian leadership is *externally* directed, that is, the vision and goals come from God. This illustrates the challenge macro lesson: **Leaders receive vision from God which sets before them challenges that inspire their leadership.** See **Article**, *17. Macro Lessons—List of 41 Across Six Leadership Eras*.

[15] Nehemiah has heard from God. He understands God's purposes for Jerusalem and its inhabitants. He now goes to influence the king and seek his permission and provision for the work the Lord has put in his heart. This is the central ethic of Christian leadership—to influence followers toward fulfillment of God's purposes for the group. See *leader*, **Glossary**.

In those days I was the king's cupbearer.[16]

Chapter 2

1 In the month of Nisan in the twentieth year[17] of King Artaxerxes' reign, I was serving the king his wine. [18] I had never appeared sad in his presence before this time. 2 So the king asked me, "Why does your face look so sad when you are not ill? You look like a man with deep troubles." [19]

Then I was badly frightened,[20] 3 but I replied, "Long live the king! Why shouldn't I be sad?[21] For the city where my ancestors are buried is in ruins, and the gates have been burned down."

4 The king said to me, "Well, how can I help you?"[22]

With a prayer to the God of heaven, 5 I replied, "If it please Your Majesty and if you are pleased with me, your servant, send me to Judah to rebuild the city where my ancestors are buried."[23]

6 The king, with the queen sitting beside him, asked, "How long will you be gone? When will you return?" It pleased the king to send me, and I set a date for my departure and return.[24]

7 I also said to the king, "If it please Your Majesty, may I have letters to the governors of the province west of the Euphrates River, instructing them to let me travel safely through their territories on my way to Judah? 8 And may I have a letter to Asaph, the manager of the king's forest, instructing him to give me

---

[16] Nehemiah has a responsible position, a position requiring the trust of the king. As cupbearer he tasted the wine for the king, to make sure there was no poison in it. Assassination was a major way of changing governments. Nehemiah has prayed for God's help. Now he states his request. Nehemiah is aware of networking power. See *networking power*, **Glossary**.

[17] The NLT translates this time phrase as *early the following spring*. See next fn.

[18] According to the CEV, Nisan, or Abib, is the first month of the Hebrew calendar. It usually is from about mid-March to mid-April. About three months have transpired between Nehemiah's receiving the news and talking to the king about it. This means Nehemiah had done a lot of praying before asking and he carefully picked his time to talk to the king. See **Article**, *31. Nehemiah, Strategic Timing*.

[19] Obviously Nehemiah was one who showed his emotions. His empathetic identification with his people in Jerusalem showed in his outward demeanor. See **Article**, *Transparency With God*.

[20] This is a critical time. Absolute rulers of empires like Assyria, Babylon, and Persia were capricious and at a whim could have those around them put to death. Nehemiah is hoping he hasn't displeased Artaxerxes.

[21] Even though frightened, Nehemiah senses this as an intervention moment. So he takes the *bull by the horns* and goes for it. See *intervention time*, **Glossary**.

[22] The intervention time is confirmed. So Nehemiah offers up a spontaneous prayer to God. He is going to ask big and wants God's blessing on his asking. For other prayers of this prayerful leader, see 1:4, 5, 6, 8, 11; 2:4; 4:9; 5:10, 11, 19; 6:9, 14; 9:1; 11:17; 13:14, 22, 29, 31. See **Article**, *24. Nehemiah, Desperate Praying*.

[23] Note, a thought prayer goes to heaven, right on the spot. Nehemiah's request could have been problematic, as Jerusalem was known for its rebellious attitude toward empires like Assyria, Babylon, and Persia. But Nehemiah has credibility with the king from his previous service, and the king trusts him.

[24] It is clear from the king's answer in verse 6 that Nehemiah knows he has the favor of the king. So he goes on in verse 7 to ask further. Notice that Nehemiah has done his homework. He knows of resources and people in influential positions throughout the king's empire. He is aware of networking power. See *networking power*, **Glossary**.

timber? I will need it to make beams for the gates of the Temple fortress, for the city walls, and for a house for myself." [25] And the king granted these requests, because the gracious hand of my God was upon me.[26]

9 When I came to the governors of the province west of the Euphrates River, I delivered the king's letters to them. The king had sent along army officers and cavalry to protect me.[27] 10 But when Sanballat the Horonite and Tobiah the Ammonite official heard of my arrival, they were very angry that someone had come to promote the welfare of the Israelites.[28]

11 Three days after my arrival in Jerusalem, 12 I slipped out during the night, taking only a few others with me. I had not told anyone about the plans God had put in my heart for Jerusalem.[29] We took no pack animals with us, except the donkey that I myself was riding. 13 I went out through the Valley Gate, past the Dragon's Spring, and over to the Dung Gate to inspect the broken walls and burned gates. 14 Then I went to the Fountain Gate and the King's Pool, but my donkey couldn't get through the rubble. 15 So I went up the Kidron Valley instead, inspecting the wall before I turned back and entered again at the Valley Gate.

---

[25] Nehemiah is open and above board about financial things. He openly requests timber for his own house. See **Leadership Topic 9: Financial Integrity.**

[26] Nehemiah asks for help with influential people along his journey (governors of provinces west of the Euphrates) and at the destination—Asaph, manager of the king's forest. The king grants this request. Note that Nehemiah gives the credit to God. *The gracious hand of my God was upon me.* He knew the <u>presence</u> <u>macro</u> <u>lesson</u> experientially. That lesson states: **The essential ingredient of leadership is the powerful presence of God in the life and ministry of a leader.** See **Article,** *17. Macro Lessons: List of 41 Across Six Leadership Eras.*

[27] Travel in these days was unsafe. King Artaxerxes sends a military escort to make sure Nehemiah will get there safely. Again this shows how highly esteemed Nehemiah was in the court.

[28] These men, Sanballat, Tobiah and another one mentioned later, Geshem, will be the primary instigators of a coalition against Nehemiah's rebuilding the wall and restoring Jerusalem. These men had vested interest in keeping the folks of Jerusalem poor. Their own holdings would be threatened by a rejuvenated presence in Jerusalem. Godly leaders with vision will usually face some determined opposition to that vision, both from within and without. Here the opposition from without makes itself known very early. The opposition from within is rooted out later in 13:4-9. See **Article,** *30. Nehemiah, Peoples and Places.*

[29] It is clear that from the very first time Nehemiah had heard of the situation in Jerusalem, he had begun to get plans for rebuilding the walls. Here he already has the plans. He needs to confirm them. Reconnaissance trips into the situation are always a powerful way to get confirmation of a ministry (see Joshua 2 and 5:13-15). We have seen this basic principle repeated in contemporary biographical studies. One noteworthy example is the life of Robert Jaffray. See Chapter 6, **Robert Jaffray** (1873-1945)—Missionary Pioneer Who Exemplifies Major Life Achievement After Age 57, from **Focused Lives—Inspirational Life Changing Lessons From Eight Effective Christian Leaders Who Finished Well,** available through Barnabas Publishers. Jaffray's survey trips into the islands of Indonesia opened the way for the Christian and Missionary Alliance to go do significant church planting there in the 1930s.

16 The city officials did not know I had been out there or what I was doing, for I had not yet said anything to anyone about my plans.[30] I had not yet spoken to the religious and political leaders, the officials, or anyone else in the administration. 17 But now I said to them, "You know full well the tragedy of our city. It lies in ruins, and its gates are burned. Come, let's rebuild the wall of Jerusalem and rid ourselves of this disgrace!" 18 Then I told them about how the gracious hand of God had been on me,[31] and about my conversation with the king. They replied at once, "Good! Let's rebuild the wall!" So they began the good work.[32]

19 But when Sanballat, Tobiah, and Geshem the Arab heard of our plan, they mocked and ridiculed us, scoffing contemptuously. "What are you doing, rebelling against the king like this?" they asked.[33]

20 But I replied, "The God of heaven will give us success. We his servants will start rebuilding. But as for you, you have no share in Jerusalem or any claim or historic right to it." [34]

---

[30] Two leadership insights need to be noted here. (1) Nehemiah is aware of the influentials in Jerusalem. They will have to be cultivated if the plans are to gain ownership among all the followers. (2) Nehemiah does not relate his plans right away. He confirms them and gives time for his own credibility to be accepted by the influentials. He is dominantly using positional authority (the king's backing). See *influentials, change participants,* **Glossary**. See **Articles**, *21. Nehemiah, Change Participants; 27. Nehemiah, Getting Ownership; 12. Influence, Power and Authority Forms*. See **Leadership Topic 3: Ownership.**

[31] Nehemiah senses intervention time with the influentials. Note how he moves from positional authority (conversation with the king) toward spiritual authority in his inspirational relating of his plans (gracious hand of God had been on me.) And he has pricked their already burdened conscience about Jerusalem (let's rebuild the wall of Jerusalem and rid ourselves of this disgrace!). See *influentials, intervention time,* **Glossary**. See **Article**, *12. Influence, Power and Authority Forms*.

[32] Nehemiah's first inspirational leadership with the influentials meets with success.

[33] The opposition threatens. Note the implication. We will inform the king of the rebellious history of Jerusalem. They are probably not aware of the close relationship that Nehemiah has with the king.

[34] This is the first of Nehemiah's persistent leadership against the opposition. See **Leadership Topic 4: Costly Convictions, Leadership Topic 5: Conflict in Leadership,** and **Leadership Topic 6: Opposition Lessons.**

Chapter 3
Contextual Statements:[35]

Nehemiah 3:1-16
Contextual statement:[36]
Nehemiah lists 22 important individuals and 3 groups of people (men of Jericho, men of Gibeon and Mizpah, inhabitants of Zanoah)[37] who built part of the wall and 4 gates (Sheep Gate, Fish Gate, Valley Gate, Dung Gate), probably along the northern part of Jerusalem.

Nehemiah 3:17-21[38]
Contextual statement:
Nehemiah singles out some Levites, naming seven specifically who worked on the next section of the wall.

Nehemiah 3:22-26[39]
Contextual statement:
Nehemiah singles out some priests, naming six individually and two groups (priests; Nethinims dwelt in Ophel—men of the plain) who worked on a wall that bordered their houses, presumably a section of the wall to the east, which contained the Water Gate.

---

[35] In this chapter Nehemiah lists all the workers who joined with him to repair the wall and gates. There are a number of leadership comments but they can be made generally and without reference to individual texts. So I will omit the actual text and simply give the contextual statements.

[36] Ownership is critical when bringing about change. Nehemiah demonstrates that he understands this. He inspires leaders and followers from a wide range of folks. This includes religious leaders, political leaders, merchants, as well as common folks. See **Leadership Topic 1: Motivational Lessons** and **Leadership Topic 3: Ownership**. See also **Articles**, *21. Nehemiah, Change Participants; 26. Nehemiah, Getting Ownership.*

[37] Nehemiah seems also to be aware of the power of affirmation. He identifies people by name and groups by name. Followers who are affirmed by leaders tend to follow those leaders. A leader who can share the credit with others will get more done than one who hogs that credit for himself/herself. The very fact that in a post-reflection recounting of this Nehemiah names these people is a good indication that he also affirmed them when the actual building was going on. See *affirmation*, **Glossary**. See also **Leadership Topic 1: Motivational Lessons.**

[38] In this context (3:17-21) and the next (3:22-26), Nehemiah specifically cultivates the religious leaders, for in his long-range plan he envisions more than just rebuilding the defenses of Jerusalem. He is interested in bringing about spiritual renewal as well. So he cultivates these religious leaders. See **Leadership Topic 3: Ownership**. They will play a big part in the actual spiritual renewal that will come and in the on-going enforcement of the followers' commitment to the covenant. See 10:28-39; 13:10-13.

[39] One motivational technique that Nehemiah used was to assign as many folks who lived along the wall to build the wall next to their abodes. This was implicitly a form of competitiveness and probably self-preservation. Each of these folks with homes bordering the wall would not want their work to be substandard, in case of attack, or inferior to their neighbors. Paul uses this competitiveness idea as a motivational methodology too. See his exhortation to giving in 2 Co 8 & 9. See **Leadership Topic 1: Motivational Lessons.**

Chapter 4

1 When Sanballat heard that we were rebuilding the wall, he became angry and was greatly incensed. He flew into a rage and mocked the Jews, 2 saying in front of his friends and the Samarian army officers, "What does this bunch of poor, feeble Jews think they are doing? Do they think they can build the wall in a day if they offer enough sacrifices? Can they bring the stones back to life from those heaps of rubble—burned as they are?"

3 Tobiah the Ammonite, who was standing beside him, remarked, "That stone wall would collapse if even a fox walked along top of it!" [40]

4 Then I prayed,[41] "Hear us, O our God, for we are being mocked. May their scoffing fall back on their own heads, and may they themselves become captives in a foreign land! 5 Do not cover up their guilt or blot out their sins from your sight, for they have provoked you to anger before the builders." [42]

6 So we rebuilt the wall to half its original height all around the city,[43] for the people had worked

---

[40] The conflict we first saw in chapter two is now intensifying. It moves from anger to intimidation to the development of a plot to attack the workers and destroy their work. Notice the progression of the anger: "angry… greatly incensed…flew into a rage…mocked the Jews." Then the opposition moves to intimidation, as evidenced again by the wording: "this bunch of poor feeble Jews…if they offer enough sacrifices…those heaps of rubble…would collapse if even a fox walked along top of it." Finally the enemies coalesce around a common plot to attack the workers and destroy the work: "plotted to come and fight…and bring about confusion…swoop down on them…kill them…end the work." See **Leadership Topic 5:Conflict,** See **Leadership Topic 6:Opposition Lessons.**

[41] Leaders respond to opposition in several ways. Some deny that it exists. Some hope it will take care of itself. Some get angry and blow up at the source of the problem. Nehemiah, on the other hand, takes the opposition to the Lord in prayer. His first response is prayer. This is similar to the response of Peter and John in Acts 4 after they were interrogated by the Sanhedrin and commanded to speak no more in the name of Jesus. What did they do? Upon their release they gathered fellow believers and took the matter to the Lord in prayer. Leaders will constantly face opposition from one or more circles—from competing agendas and interests to outright spiritual warfare. Leaders who are doing the work of the Lord can confidently take the opposition to the Lord and request divine intervention. The conflict and problems throughout the book point to the complexity macro lesson: **Leadership is complex, problematic, difficult, and fraught with risk, which is why leadership is needed.** See **Articles,** *Spiritual Warfare, Satan's Tactics; Spiritual Warfare, Two Extremes to Avoid; Spiritual Warfare, Two Foundational Axioms; 17. Macro Lessons—List of 41 Across Six Leadership Eras.* See also **Leadership Topic 6: Opposition Lessons.**

[42] This is another instance of prayer given spontaneously in response to something that just happened. See 1:4, 5, 6, 8, 11; 2:4; 4:9; 5:19; 6:9, 14; 9:1; 11:17; 13:14, 22, 29, 31. This is an imprecatory prayer. See **Article,** *24. Nehemiah, Desperate Praying.* See also **Leadership Topic 2: Prayerful Spirit.**

[43] What leaders work on gets done. Desire plus discipline plus work results in progress and productivity. Like Nehemiah's wall-building, much of the work of ministry is dusty, exhausting, and depleting. It takes place where people line up side by side, with tools and weapons in hand, take action, and persevere. While some stories of marvelous works of God sound so glamorous and inspiring, and neglect to mention the struggles that went into getting the work off the ground and moving forward, Nehemiah—to borrow from an old film title—includes the good, the bad, and the ugly.

with all their heart.[44] 7 But when Sanballat and Tobiah and the Arabs, Ammonites, and Ashdodites heard that work was going ahead and gaps in the wall were being repaired, they became furious. 8 They plotted to come and fight against Jerusalem and to bring about confusion there. 9 But we prayed to our God and guarded the city day and night to meet this threat.[45]

10 Meanwhile, the people of Judah began to complain that the workers were becoming tired. There was so much rubble to be moved that we could never get it done by ourselves.[46] 11 And our enemies were saying, "Before they know what's happening, we will swoop down on them and kill them and end their work."

12 The Jews who lived near came and told us again and again and again, "They will come from all directions and attack us!" 13 So I placed armed guards behind the lowest parts of the wall in the exposed areas. I stationed people to stand guard by families, armed with swords, spears, and bows. 14 Then as I looked over the situation, I stood up and said to the nobles, the officials and the rest of the people, "Don't be afraid of them. Remember the Lord, who is great and awesome, and fight for your brothers, your sons and daughters, your wives and homes!" [47]

---

[44] The people worked with all their heart, in part, because their leader and God's presence with their leader inspired their hope and courage. See **Leadership Topic 1: Motivational Lessons.** According to what we're learning, Christian leadership functions can be grouped into three primary categories: <u>task</u> <u>behaviors</u>, which facilitate accomplishment of the vision; <u>relational</u> <u>behaviors</u>, which address interpersonal dynamics; and <u>inspirational</u> <u>behaviors</u>, which motivate followers toward fulfillment of the vision. Inspirational leadership includes encouraging the faith and perseverance of the followers and modeling the reality of God's intervention in their lives. Nehemiah does both in this chapter. See **Leadership Topic 10: Leadership Behaviors.**

[45] Throughout the book we see how Nehemiah combines prayer with action, action with prayer. Here we have another example (see **Leadership Topic 7: Prayer and Action**). As the conflict and opposition escalate, Nehemiah responds first with prayer, then adds other actions: continuing to do the work God sent him there to do; posting guards around the city; and inspiring courage in the hearts of the people by pointing them to the Lord. While conflict and opposition can tempt even the most determined leader to despair and give up the work, Nehemiah models for us what it means to stay focused, keep working, and continue trusting God—in spite of the opposition. He neither backs down nor relinquishes his leadership role. He has been entrusted with a great work for God, as he emphasizes in chapter six, and cannot stop the work simply because of the threat of danger. We surmise that his concern for the people, his heart for God's honor, and his belief in the vision itself were part of what enabled Nehemiah to persevere. His example illustrates the <u>perseverance</u> <u>macro</u> <u>lesson</u>: **Once known, leaders must persevere with the vision God has given.** See **Article,** *17. Macro Lessons—List of 41 Across Six Leadership Eras.*

[46] For comments on internal opposition, see 6:10 and 13:4,5. See also **Leadership Topic 5:Conflict in Leadership** and **Topic 6: Opposition Lessons.**

[47] Once again Nehemiah inspires courage in the hearts of the people. His leadership points to the <u>hope</u> <u>macro</u> <u>lesson</u>: **A primary function of all leadership is to inspire followers with hope in God and in what God is doing.** See **Article,** *17. Macro Lessons—List of 41 Across Six Leadership Eras.*

15 When our enemies heard that we knew of their plans and that God had frustrated them,[48] we all returned to our work on the wall. 16 But from then on, only half my men worked while the other half stood guard with spears, shields, bows, and coats of mail. The officers stationed themselves behind the people of Judah 17 who were doing the work. The common laborers carried on their work with one hand supporting their load and one hand holding a weapon. 18 All the builders had a sword belted to their side. The trumpeter stayed with me to sound the alarm.[49]

19 Then I said to the nobles and officials and all the people, "The work is spread out, and we are widely separated from each other along the wall. 20 When you hear the blast of the trumpet, rush to wherever it is sounding. Then our God will fight for us!"

21 We worked early and late, from sunrise to sunset. And half the men were always on guard. 22 I also told everyone living outside the walls to move into Jerusalem. That way they and their servants could go on guard duty at night as well as work during the day. 23 During this time none of us—not I, nor my relatives, nor my servants, nor the guards who were with me—ever took off our clothes. We carried our weapons with us at all times, even when we went for water.

Chapter 5

1 About this time some of the men and their wives raised a cry of protest against their fellow Jews. 2 They were saying, "We have such large families. We need more money just so we can buy the food we need to survive." 3 Others said, "We have mortgaged our fields, vineyards, and homes to get food during the famine." 4 And others said, "We have already borrowed to the limit on our fields and vineyards to pay our taxes. 5 We belong to the same family, and our children are just like theirs. Yet we must sell our children into slavery just to get enough money to live. We have already sold some of our daughters, and we are helpless to do anything about it, for our fields and vineyards are already mortgaged to others." [50]

6 When I heard their complaints, I was very angry. 7 I pondered the complaints in my mind and then accused the nobles and officials. I told them, "You are oppressing your own relatives by charging

---

[48] Nehemiah gives God the credit for deliverance from their enemies. He prayed. God heard and answered. The workers and the work were spared and even moved forward, in the face of conflict and opposition. That God spared them illustrates again the primacy of the presence macro lesson: **The essential ingredient of leadership is the powerful presence of God in the leader's life and ministry.** See **Article**, *17. Macro Lessons—List of 41 Across Six Leadership Eras*.

[49] Nehemiah models flexibility as he makes needed adjustments in the implementation of his plans. His first objective is to successfully rebuild the wall. If he needs to alter work arrangements to keep the construction moving forward, he is willing to do so. In our opinion, sometimes leaders become too enamored with their plans and too inflexible themselves on strategies that may need to be altered.

[50] Nehemiah faced external (see chapters 2, 4, and 6) and internal conflict. Problems have now arisen within the Jewish community itself. And while these problems aren't directly related to rebuilding the wall, they do require Nehemiah's time and attention. Leaders can expect problems to arise from any number of sources as they carry out their God-given assignments. Here we see the relational as well as task-oriented sides of leadership. A problem has arisen that needs to be resolved (or the task will fail), but the problem revolves around how people are relating to and treating one another (relationships). See **Leadership Topic 10: Leadership Behaviors** and **Topic 6: Opposition Lessons.**

them interest when they borrow money!" Then I called a public meeting to deal with the problem.[51]

8 At the meeting I said to them, "The rest of us are doing all we can to redeem our Jewish relatives who have had to sell themselves to pagan foreigners, but you are selling them back into slavery again. How often must we redeem them?" And they had nothing to say in their defense.

9 Then I pressed further, "What you are doing is not right! Should you not walk in the fear of our God in order to avoid being mocked by enemy nations? 10 I myself, as well as my brothers and my workers, have been lending the people money and grain, but now let us stop this business of loans. 11 You must restore their fields, vineyards, olive groves, and homes to them this very day. Repay the interest you charged on their money, grain, wine, and olive oil."

12 Then they replied, "We will give back everything and demand nothing more from the people. We will do as you say." Then I called the priests and made the nobles and officials formally vow to do what they had promised.

13 I shook out the fold of my robe and said, "If you fail to keep your promise, may God shake you from your homes and from your property!"

The whole assembly responded, "Amen," and they praised the LORD. And the people did as they promised.

14 I would like to mention that for the entire twelve years that I was governor of Judah—from the twentieth until the thirty-second year of the reign of King Artaxerxes—neither I nor my officials drew on our official food allowance. 15 This was quite a contrast to the former governors who had laid heavy burdens on the people, demanding a daily ration of food and wine, besides a pound of silver. Even their assistants took advantage of the people. But because of my fear of God, I did not act that way.[52]

16 I devoted myself to working on the wall and refused to acquire any land. And I required all my officials to spend time working on the wall.[53] 17 I asked for nothing, even though I regularly fed 150 Jewish officials at my table, besides all the visitors from other lands! 18 The provisions required at my expense for each day were one ox, six fat sheep, and a large number of domestic fowl. And every ten days we needed a large supply of all kinds of wine. Yet I refused to claim the governor's food allowance because the people were already having a difficult time.[54]

---

[51] Notice the key phrase: "to deal with the problem." Once again Nehemiah confronts the problem head-on. How does he deal with it here? He feels and owns up to his anger. Nehemiah is not afraid of feeling or admitting to his emotions. But then he takes time to think through what is happening. He ponders the complaints of the people before addressing the guilty parties. Then he confronts them with their injurious behaviors, pointing them (publicly) to a higher way of living in support of their fellow Jews and in fear of the Lord. The public meeting and agreements will give him needed leverage in the on-going enforcement of the decisions made that day. Nehemiah's work to promote unity among the people illustrates the unity macro lesson: **Unity of the people of God is a value that leaders must preserve.** See **Article,** *17. Macro Lessons—List of 41 Across Six Leadership Eras.*

[52] Leadership is not about prominence and prestige, but serving the people and purposes of God. Leaders lead out of their values, which are based on assumptions and beliefs. Nehemiah believes that he is ultimately accountable to God. His belief shapes his convictions and behavior. See **Leadership Topic 4: Costly Convictions.**

[53] Nehemiah takes the lead and models the way for the people. He is a leader with integrity, a leader who himself lives in support of the vision.

[54] Nehemiah is deeply conscious about financial integrity. Holding a positional assignment from the Persian government, he could, like his predecessors, have demanded finances from the people. Many leaders who hold such positional power do abuse their people with respect to finances. One of the six barriers to finishing well concerns finances. See **Article,** *6. Finishing Well, Six Major Barriers.* See also **Leadership Topic 9: Financial Integrity.**

19 Remember,[55] O my God, all that I have done for these people, and bless me for it.

Chapter 6

1 When word came to Sanballat, Tobiah, Geshem the Arab and the rest of our enemies that I had rebuilt the wall and not a gap was left in it—though up to that time I had not set the doors in the gates—2 Sanballat and Geshem sent me this message: "Come, let us meet together in one of the villages on the plain of Ono." [56]

But they were scheming to harm me; 3 so I sent messengers to them with this reply: "I am carrying on a great project and cannot go down. Why should the work stop while I leave it and go down to you?" [57] 4 Four times they sent me the same message, and each time I gave them the same answer.[58] 5 The fifth time,[59] Sanballat's servant came with an open letter in his hand, 6 and this is what it said:

> "Geshem tells me that everywhere he goes he hears that you and the Jews are planning to rebel and that is why you are building the wall. According to his reports, you plan to be their king. 7 He also reports that you have appointed prophets to prophesy about you in Jerusalem, saying, 'Look! There is a king in Judah!' You can be very sure that this report will get back to the king, so I suggest that you come and talk it over with me."

8 My reply was, "You know you are lying. There is no truth in any part of your story." 9 They were just trying to intimidate us, imagining that they could break our resolve and stop the work. So I prayed for strength to continue the work.[60]

---

[55] Again we have a "remember" prayer. We have identified three basic types of *Remember Prayers*: One which is God-focused. One focused toward enemies. And one focused on Nehemiah's personal need for affirmation. Type I: Remember God, an exhortation for the people to remember in the past what God had done (both in blessing and punishing) or to remind God of what He has said; Type II: Remember enemies—an imprecatory prayer asking God to punish the enemies; Type III: A personal request for God to remember Nehemiah for what he had done in his leadership. We comment further on these in the final closing prayer of the book.

[56] *Sanballat, Tobiah, Geshem the Arab and the rest of our enemies* represent opposition from without. They have organized into a coalition. See **Leadership Topic 6: Opposition Lessons**.

[57] Nehemiah doesn't waste time with diplomacy with them. He sees through their plot and simply denies their request. Nehemiah is focused—dedicated to and concentrating on his God-given assignment. He is doing a work of God and does not want to be deterred from it. He will not turn aside from what he is doing. And he doesn't trust these enemies.

[58] This is determined opposition. Four times they repeat their request. Each time Nehemiah denies their request.

[59] The coalition resorts to an actual threat rather than an invitation. They resort to lies. What are the implications of an *open letter*? It seems to imply that it has been publicly voiced about.

[60] Notice Nehemiah's reply. He first denies the truth of the claims in the letter. He sees through their attempt to intimidate. He then prays and continues building the wall. Like David in 1Samuel 30:1-8, Nehemiah finds his strength in the Lord. His prayer here is one of the repeated prayer passages (1:4, 5, 6, 8, 11; 2:4; 4:9; 5:10, 11, 19; 6:9, 14; 9:1; 11:17; 13:14, 22, 29, 31). Note the phrase *imagining that they could break our resolve and stop the work*. Resolve is a key word. Leaders must have this quality if they want to carry out a vision from God. Resolve, in this context, is perseverance, which is based on dependence upon God. See Daniel 1:8 for a related type of leadership resolve. See **Leadership Topic 10: Leadership Behaviors.**

10 Later I went to the house of Shemaiah son of Delaiah and grandson of Mehetabel, who was shut in at his home. He said, "Let us meet in the house of God, inside the temple, and let us close the temple doors, because men are coming to kill you—by night they are coming to kill you." [61]

11 But I replied, "Should someone in my position run away from danger? Should someone in my position enter the temple to save his life? No, I won't do it!" 12 I realized that God had not spoken to him,[62] but that he had uttered this prophecy against me because Tobiah and Sanballat had hired him.

13 They were hoping to intimidate me and make me sin[63] by following his suggestion. Then they would be able to accuse and discredit me.

14 "Remember, O my God, all the evil things that Tobiah and Sanballat have done. And remember Noadiah the prophet and all the prophets like her who have tried to intimidate me." [64]

15 So the wall was completed on the twenty-fifth of Elul, in fifty-two days.[65] 16 When our enemies and the surrounding nations heard about it, they were frightened and humiliated. They realized that this work had been done with the help of our God.[66]

17 During those fifty-two days, many letters went back and forth between Tobiah and the officials of Judah.[67] 18 For many in Judah had sworn allegiance to him because his father-in-law was Shecaniah son of Arah and because his son Jehohanan was married to the daughter of Meshullam son of Berekiah.

---

[61] This is opposition from within, but unlike the problems in chapter 5, here the opposition has in mind to discredit Nehemiah and put an end to his work. Shemaiah, an insider, is in alliance with the outside coalition. This is another attempt to snare and discredit Nehemiah based on a religious principle—safety within the temple. See also 13:4-9, 28 for other insiders (Eliashib and Joiada) in alliance with Tobiah.

[62] How Nehemiah discerned this, we do not know. This man, Shemaiah, has the right credentials. But somehow Nehemiah sees through this as another threat from the coalition.

[63] Nehemiah is very sensitive to God and God's honor. What sin? Probably the violation of regulations specifying who could and could not enter various areas of the Temple and serve in various priestly functions (see Numbers 18:7).

[64] Another prayer instance. This is one of the remember prayers of the imprecatory type. See 1:4, 5, 6, 8, 11; 2:4; 4:9; 5:10, 11, 19; 6:9, 14; 9:1; 11:17; 13:14, 22, 29, 31. Note also that another source of opposition from within was religious. A female prophetess, Noadiah, and other prophets were bringing pressure to bear on Nehemiah by falsely prophesying. See *imprecatory prayer*, **Glossary**. See **Article**, *24. Nehemiah, Desperate Praying*.

[65] This represents an extreme focus for a limited time. That the task was done in 52 days in the midst of concerted opposition is amazing. A leader can afford extreme focus for a limited time from time-to-time. But this cannot be a way of life or the leader will burn out.

[66] This is one of the amazing statements of the book. The coalition, which had put forth determined opposition, *realized that this work had been done with the help of our God*. Nehemiah, who works hard to accomplish his task, is always careful to give credit to God. Note the dynamic balance, Nehemiah works very hard; but he also trusts very hard.

[67] There was a strong determined group within the city that was networked with the outside coalition. And note they were leaders. A leader set on making change must expect opposition even from within, from other leaders. See **Leadership Topic 6. Opposition Lessons**.

19 They kept telling me what a wonderful man Tobiah was, and then they told him everything I said. And Tobiah sent many threatening letters to intimidate me.[68]

II. (7:1-10:39) Organizing for Reform[69]

Chapter 7
Contextual Statements:[70]

Nehemiah 7:1-4
Contextual Statement:
Nehemiah appoints Hanani and Hananiah to leadership over Jerusalem and orders the gates to be watched carefully. He also appoints religious and worship leaders.[71]

---

[68] Tobiah had inside information. Nehemiah probably had no secrets. His plans were most likely divulged to Tobiah as soon as they were known to folks in the town. Note the intermarriage link between outsiders and insiders. See 13:4 where Eliashib is identified as a source of Tobiah's information. Intimidate means to make timid or afraid, to cause to cow, or to deter with threats of force or harm. The point of the intimidation, throughout the book, is to stop the work—work which was promoting the welfare of God's people.

[69] This begins a new section in the book. The crisis-like task of building the wall has been accomplished, even against determined opposition. There was tremendous motivation behind the task. But it lasted only a short time. Now Nehemiah must look to the long-term needs of the returned exiles. He turns to the notion of bringing renewal to them. He knows that they can be united only if there is good leadership and a strong religious fervor. The next 4 chapters of Nehemiah record the efforts to unite the returned exiles and to point them to worshipping and obeying God.

[70] In chapter 7 Nehemiah lays the foundation for renewing religious fervor among the people. He appoints administrative leaders over Jerusalem, men of character. He appoints worship leaders. And he registers all the returned exiles of various ilk. This registration is in line with his plan to repopulate Jerusalem. There are a number of leadership comments but they can be made generally and without reference to individual texts. So we will omit the actual texts, which for the most part give lists of the returned exiles. Instead we will simply give the contextual statements.

[71] Step 1 of Nehemiah's reform is completed. The city has its walls. It only remains to make sure there is some defensive security. Nehemiah sets the standard concerning guards and security. Regular watch schedules are to be set and kept. Folks living along the wall will have responsibility for watches too. They will have added incentive to watch. Step 2 now begins. Immediately Nehemiah sets in place leadership—military, civil, and religious. The civil and military leaders are selected based on character. Note the qualifying phrases of the military commander—*a faithful man, a man of integrity who feared God more than most.* See **Leadership Topic 12: Selecting Leaders**. Notice worship is an essential part of bringing about reform. And so too is singing a vital part of worship. Nehemiah appoints gifted leaders who have musical talent. He also appoints Levites who will administer in the temple.

Nehemiah 7:5-60
Contextual Statement:

Nehemiah registers[72] those who were the first exiles to return who had proof of their ancestry.[73]

Nehemiah 7:61-65
Contextual Statement:

Nehemiah lists those who could not prove their ancestry.[74]

Nehemiah 7:66-73
Contextual Statement:

Nehemiah sums up the total of all of the lists given previously and some of the financial resources[75] that were given to back Nehemiah's efforts.

Chapter 8

1 All the people assembled as one man in the square before the Water Gate. They asked Ezra the scribe to bring out the Book of the Law of Moses, which the LORD had given for Israel to obey.[76]

---

[72] Nehemiah knows that there must be a strong Jerusalem if reform is to happen to all of the returned exiles, many of whom live outside Jerusalem. So he has a plan for bringing in people to repopulate Jerusalem. To enact his plan he first needs to know who are all the Jews who have returned. He lists them. Note the careful taxonomy. It is lists like this that lead us to believe that Nehemiah probably journaled and/or kept accurate records of what he did. Note the categories: first exiles to return; priests with the first exiles to return; Levites who came with the first exiles to return; Nithians; descendants of Solomon's servants. Later (chapter 10) after uniting the people via strong Bible teaching and worship, Nehemiah will bring 1 out of every 10 outside the city to live in the city.

[73] He uses records that were brought with these exiles when they came with Zerubbabel and other leaders in the first return. Nehemiah lists these families by name. There are categories: people who had proof of their ancestry; priests; Levites; singers; porters; descendants of Solomon's servants; some who couldn't prove their genealogy, including some priests.

[74]This listing in ch 7, along with approval from God via the use of the Urim and Thummim, was a way of registering them for future reckonings.

[75] Evidently a number of the people had amassed financial resources, either back in exile or after they came back. Some of them were generous. This accounting also illustrates Nehemiah's financial integrity. He records the resources accurately so that all will know. See **LEADERSHIP TOPIC 9: FINANCIAL INTEGRITY**. See **Articles**, *6. Finishing Well—6 Major Barriers*; 26. *Nehemiah, Financial Integrity.*

[76] To experience and maintain renewal, God's people must know and follow God's revelation. Such is the case today. The Scriptures reveal God and God's purposes for Christian leaders. We challenge leaders today to become Bible-Centered leaders, following the example of Nehemiah and Ezra. Their knowledge of the Scriptures, and their leadership, which was informed by the Scriptures, underscores the Word centered macro lesson: **God's Word is the primary source for equipping leaders and must be a vital part of any leader's ministry.** See the **Articles,** *36. A Vanishing Breed;17. Macro Lessons—41 Across Six Leadership Eras.*

2 So on the first day of the seventh month Ezra[77] the priest brought the Law before the assembly, which was made up of men and women and all who were able to understand. 3 He read it aloud from daybreak till noon as he faced the square before the Water Gate in the presence of the men, women and others who could understand. And all the people listened attentively to the Book of the Law. 4 Ezra the scribe stood on a high wooden platform built for the occasion. Beside him on his right stood Mattithiah, Shema, Anaiah, Uriah, Hilkiah and Maaseiah; and on his left were Pedaiah, Mishael, Malkijah, Hashum, Hashbaddanah, Zechariah and Meshullam.

5 Ezra opened the scroll. The people could see him because he was standing above them; and as he opened it, the people all stood up. 6 Ezra praised the LORD, the great God; and all the people lifted their hands and responded, "Amen! Amen!" Then they bowed down and worshiped the LORD with their faces to the ground.[78]

7 The Levites--Jeshua, Bani, Sherebiah, Jamin, Akkub, Shabbethai, Hodiah, Maaseiah, Kelita, Azariah, Jozabad, Hanan and Pelaiah--instructed the people in the Law while the people were standing there. 8 They read from the Book of the Law of God, making it clear and giving the meaning so that the people could understand what was being read.[79]

9 Then Nehemiah the governor, Ezra the priest and scribe, and the Levites who were instructing the people said to them all, "This day is sacred to the LORD your God. Do not mourn or weep." For all the people had been weeping as they listened to the words of the Law. 10 Nehemiah said, "Go and enjoy choice food and sweet drinks, and send some to those who have nothing prepared. This day is sacred to our Lord. Do not grieve, for the joy of the LORD is your strength."[80] 11 The Levites calmed all the people, saying, "Be still, for this is a sacred day. Do not grieve." 12 Then all the people went away to eat and drink, to send portions of food and to celebrate with great joy, because they now understood the words that had been made known to them.

13 On the second day of the month, the heads of all the families, along with the priests and the Levites, gathered around Ezra the scribe to listen carefully to the words of the Law.[81] 14 They found written in the Law, which the LORD had commanded through Moses, that the Israelites were to live in booths during the feast of the seventh month, 15 and that they should proclaim this word and spread it throughout their towns and in Jerusalem: "Go out into the hill country and bring back branches from olive and wild olive trees, and from myrtles, palms and shade trees, to make booths"—as it is written. 16 So the people went out and brought back branches and built themselves

---

[77] Ezra is well-suited to the task, for the focus of his life was the study and observance of God's Law, and to teaching its decrees and laws in Israel. See Ez 7:10.

[78] This is the beginning of spiritual renewal. The wall has been rebuilt. The gates have been hung. Leaders have been appointed to oversee civic and military responsibilities. Now Nehemiah works with the spiritual leaders to initiate spiritual renewal. The people respond with agreement, worship, and humility as Ezra reads from the Law.

[79] In our experiences with leaders and Christian ministries, we've found it next to impossible for leaders to over-communicate. With so many distractions confronting people today, they need time to hear and process the biblical story and God's purposes for His people, repeatedly. Ezra is not content to simply read from the Law, he moves further to explanation so that people can understand what is said and then bring their lives to conform to God's revelation.

[80] Once again we see Nehemiah as a person of keen insight and understanding of the Jewish feasts and festivals. He recognizes the importance of celebration in the life of the people. He discerns and applies the reasons behind the festivals. Was he a regular synagogue participant? Were his family members devout adherents of and teachers of the law themselves? Was Ezra offering spiritual counsel to him in private sessions? However he came by it, Nehemiah moves to align the people with a proper understanding of God's revelation. Nehemiah seems to us to be a leader who walked with God and knew God's ways, a leader who walked with God and heard from God, and a leader from whom God heard in prayer.

[81] This gathering can be compared to a contemporary break-out session at a large conference. On day one a plenary session was convened. On day two a meeting was held just for family and spiritual leaders. Ezra is influencing the leaders who will in turn influence the people and their families.

booths on their own roofs, in their courtyards, in the courts of the house of God and in the square by the Water Gate and the one by the Gate of Ephraim. 17 The whole company that had returned from exile built booths and lived in them. From the days of Joshua son of Nun until that day, the Israelites had not celebrated it like this. And their joy was very great.[82]

18 Day after day, from the first day to the last, Ezra read from the Book of the Law of God. They celebrated the feast for seven days, and on the eighth day, in accordance with the regulation, they held a Solemn Assembly.[83]

Chapter 9

1 Now on the twenty-fourth day of the same month the Israelites gathered together again.[84] They were fasting, and wearing sackcloth, and threw dirt on their heads.[85] All this to show how deeply sorry they were for their sins. 2 Those of Israelite descent separated themselves from all foreigners.[86] They stood and confessed their sins and the iniquities of their ancestors.[87] 3 The Book of the law of the LORD their God was read to them for about 3 hours.[88] Then for another 3 hours they responded to what they had heard

---

[82] Godly leaders, leading from their scriptural understanding of God and God's ways, can deeply affect the condition of God's people. Renewal can happen. Hope, courage, and joy can return. The Word of God itself speaks with great power, and as people engage it for themselves, they are comforted or challenged or admonished or equipped by what it communicates. Notice the statement of result: *their joy was very great.*

[83] The Solemn Assembly deepened the experiences from the previous days and sealed the work that had taken place. It was another sacred opportunity to highlight and stress the understanding that the Jews served and represented the LORD. It reinforced the renewal work of Ezra and Nehemiah, or more accurately, of the LORD Himself among His people.

[84] Ch 8, the great spiritual revival, began on the first day of the seventh month. Now it is the 24th day of that same month. Three weeks have gone by. Nehemiah wants to capitalize on the momentum and have the people document what has happened. This will better insure follow-up. So he convenes another public meeting.

[85] The powerful response of ch 8 continues. The people have a repentant spirit as noted by the sackcloth and dirt and the fasting.

[86] They are responding to the challenges of what they heard in ch 8 and doing something specific about it (vs 9). There will be more clarification on this separating from foreigners in ch 13.

[87] They have caught on quickly. They confess their own sins and then use vicarious confession. They are clearing the air to walk in the future with God. See *vicarious praying*, **Glossary**. See **Articles**, *18. Nehemiah, And Daniel—Comparison of Vicarious Praying; 24. Nehemiah, Desperate Praying.*

[88] We wonder what was read this time. It is clear that the people have picked up a lot about God and God's dealings with them from the previous time in the word (ch 8) and this time. The following prayer is full of their understanding of God and their history with God.

by open confession of their own sins and their ancestors'.[89] In addition, they worshipped the LORD their God.[90]

4 Some Levites—Jeshua, Bani, Kadmiel, Shebaniah, Bunni, Sherebiah, Bani, and Chenani—stood on a platform and prayed publicly unto the LORD their God. 5 Then some more Levites joined them—among whom were Hashabniah, Sherebiah, Hodijah, and Pethahiah. These Levites joined to give a call to worship:

Stand up and bless the LORD your God,
    for ever and ever.
Blessed be thy glorious name,
    which is exalted above all blessing and praise.[91]

6 Then the people joined them in a long time of public prayer:[92]
You alone are LORD,
You created all the galaxies,
You created the stars in the skies.
You created land and sea,
    And everything in them.
You gave life and preserve it.
The stars praise you.[93]
7 You are the LORD our God
You chose Abram,
You called him out of Ur located in Babylon,
You changed his name to Abraham.
8 He faithfully followed you.
You made a covenant with him.

---

[89] Expression deepens impression. Allowing God's people to respond to God's word is one of the great lacks of modern public services. See material in the Titus commentary dealing with application of the Word of God. What we have here is similar to an open mike time. But also there are probably simultaneous spontaneous prayers going up. Folks are repenting, confessing, and interceding. Again vicarious praying is seen. Note the response time is equal to the input time.

[90] This probably means prostrating themselves before God. Maybe even some spontaneous singing. It is important that leaders facilitate well this kind of response. In this case, the leaders allow the spontaneity to continue for three hours and then channel it into a controlled and united time of public worship and prayer. They will move this praying toward the major application—the covenant signing.

[91] Notice that leaders are facilitating this call to worship. These leaders are probably first to share in the long prayer. But indications are that a number of people prayed.

[92] We have included this prayer in its entirety for several reasons. One, it is the longest prayer in the Bible. That alone says it should be examined. Two, it carries within it some principles of how public prayer ought to be done. Third, it illustrates vicarious praying (something leaders must know and use in their ministries). Fourth, it culminates in the signing of a covenant with God. This covenant is a major starting point for renewal for the people. They will not keep it. But Nehemiah will come back and repeatedly hold the people accountable to it. Affective learning needs to be backed with practical application, which issues in experiential learning. See *affect*, *experiential*, in **Glossary**.

[93] The prayer begins with a recognition of the greatness of God. He is the creator God. He made the galaxies and our world. He gave life to our planet. All creation praises Him. This is the starting point of prayer—a recognition of who God is.

You promised him the land of the Canaanites,
    The land of the Hittites and Amorites,
    The land of the Perizzites, Jebusites, and Girgashites.
    A land for his descendants to live in.
You kept your promise.
You are true to your word.[94]

9 You saw how our ancestors suffered in Egypt.[95]
You heard their desperate cry by the Red sea.
10 You worked powerful signs and wonders upon Pharaoh,
    and on all his servants,
    and on all the people of his land.
For you knew how they oppressed your people.
You gained great fame for this deliverance.
You still have that fame today.

11 You divided the Red sea before them,
    so that they went through the midst of the sea on the dry land.
But the persecutors who pursued them,
    drowned in the Red sea as it collapsed about them.
Like stones they sank in the raging waters.

12 Moreover you led your people,
    guiding by day with a cloudy pillar,
    and guiding by night with a pillar of fire.
13 You came down also upon mount Sinai,
    and spoke with them from heaven,
    and gave them truth to live by.
14 You taught them to keep your Sabbaths holy.
You revealed guidelines through Moses.
You made known unto them precepts and laws.[96]
15 You gave them bread from heaven for their hunger,
    and brought forth water for them out of the rock for their thirst.

----

[94] The second thrust of the prayer begins. The prayer connects this creator God with the God who chose Abraham, the ancestor of the Jewish race. The Genesis 15 unilateral covenant to Abraham, the giving of the land, is referred to. And God is honored as God the Promise Keeper. The keeping of a promise or oath is a major indicator of integrity in this culture. See **Articles**, *9. God The Promise Keeper; 32. The Promises of God.*

[95] Next the prayer traces the major event in the history of Israel, the Exodus. God is honored as a God of power who delivered first by getting the Israelites out of Egypt and then by delivering again from the military forces at the Red Sea. In this stanza God is seen for who He is in terms of intervening power. God answers prayer and delivers his people.

[96] The prayer continues tracing the highlights of the delivered Israelites. God is recognized for His guidance, provision, and revelation of truth to live by in the desert years. As in previous stanzas the Israelites are showing their familiarity with God and His interventions with them in their history.

You promised them that they should go in to possess the land,

> which you had promised under oath to give them.[97]

16 But our ancestors were a proud bunch.

They stubbornly refused to obey your commandments.

17 And not only refused to obey,

> but did not remember all the wonders you did among them.[98]

Instead they continued to resist you.

And in their rebellion they appointed a leader to take them back to Egypt.

But you are a God ready to forgive.

You are gracious and merciful, slow to anger,

> and of great kindness.

You did not forsake them.

18 They went further by making an idol shaped like a calf.

And they insulted you further by saying,

> this is our God that brought us up out of Egypt.

19 But mercifully you did not abandon them in the desert.

You continued to guide them by day.

And you continued to guide them by night.[99]

20 By your good spirit you instructed them.

You continued giving manna to eat.

You gave them water for their thirst.

21 Through forty long years in the desert you sustained them.

They lacked nothing.

Their clothes lasted.

And their shoes didn't wear out.

Nor were their feet swollen with pain.[100]

22 You gave them kingdoms and nations,

> lands that bordered their own.

They possessed the land of Heshbon, where Sihon ruled,

> and the land of Bashan, where Og was king.

23 You brought them into the land,

> the land you had promised to them.

Their descendants became numerous,

> like the stars of heaven.

---

[97] Again God is recognized for his supernatural power. He provided food and water in the desert years. And the promise of God about the land is repeated.

[98] But now the prayer intermingles history with vicarious confession. The sins of the ancestors are acknowledged. They refused to obey God. Moreover, they did not remember His powerful works on their behalf. One function of leadership is to keep God's past working in a groups' behalf alive before the people. Part of inspirational leadership involves repeated celebration to honor God's work in the past. See **Article**, *18. Nehemiah and Daniel, Comparison of Vicarious Praying.*

[99] A major failure is acknowledged—the worship of the golden calf—another aspect of the vicarious confession. Note this is mentioned in the context of God's forgiveness.

[100] The whole desert experience is summed up in the words, *You sustained them.* This is Moses' leadership covering the times of the books of Exodus, Numbers, Leviticus and Deuteronomy.

24 So the Israelites went in and possessed the land.
You subdued before them the inhabitants of the land.
You gave the Canaanites into their hands,
    with their kings, and the people of the land,
    that they might do with them as they would.
25 And they took strong cities, and a rich farm land.
They captured furnished homes with wells,
    and vineyards, and olive yards, and fruit trees in abundance.
They ate till they were full.
They delighted themselves in your great goodness.[101]

26 In spite of this they became disobedient.[102]
And they and rebelled against you.
They did away with your law.
They killed the prophets you sent.
Who warned them not to turn from you.
They insulted you.

27 So you let their enemies capture them
    and oppress them.[103]
In their time of trouble, they cried to you.
You heard their prayers.
And many times you showed your mercy,
    by sending leaders to get them out of their oppression,
    leaders who delivered them from their enemies.
28 But after a time of peace,
    they did evil again before you.
Therefore you again let their enemies conquer them,
    so that they had dominion over them.
And yet when they returned to you, and cried unto you,
    you heard them from heaven.
And repeatedly you mercifully delivered them,[104]
29 and testified against them,
    that you might bring them back to obeying your law.
But they dealt proudly, and did not obey your commandments,
    and sinned against your judgments,
        which, if a man follows, will give life.
They stubbornly refused to hear and obey.

---

[101] The conquering of the adjacent lands and the conquering of the land itself is given in this stanza. God is honored as the Promise Keeper. This is the time of Joshua.

[102] Again the vicarious confession interweaves itself along with God's repeated deliverance in the times of the judges.

[103] An oblique allusion to the *Left Hand of God*. See **Article**, *15. Left Hand of God*.

[104] The cycle, which repeatedly happens in Judges is recognized—of disobedience, given over to other nations, cry for deliverance, and deliverance. God is seen to be repeatedly merciful and forgiving when His people respond to Him.

30 Yet many years did you forbear with them,

 and testified against them by your Spirit-inspired prophets.[105]
Yet they would not give ear.
Therefore you gave them into the hand of the people of the lands.
31 Nevertheless for your great mercies' sake,

 you did not utterly destroy them,

 nor forsake them.
For you are a gracious and merciful God.

32 Now therefore, our God,[106]

 the great, the mighty, and the terrible God,

 who keeps covenant and shows mercy,

 let not all the trouble seem little before you,

 that has come upon us,

 on our kings, on our princes, and on our priests,

 and on our prophets, and on our fathers,

 and on all thy people,

 since the time of the kings of Assyria unto this day.

33 You are just in all that you brought upon us.
For you have done right,

 but we have done wickedly.
34 Neither have our kings, our princes, our priests, nor our fathers, kept thy law,

 nor hearkened unto thy commandments and thy testimonies,
Even though you did warn them.
35 For they have not served you in their kingdom,

 which in your great goodness you gave them.
 And in the large and fertile land which you gave them,

 neither turned they from their wicked works.
36 Behold, we are slaves this day,

 in the land that you gave to our fathers

 to eat the fruit thereof and the good thereof.
Behold, we are slaves in it.
37 And it yields much increase for the kings,

 whom you set over us because of our sins.
They rule over us as they please,

 and over our cattle.
We are in deep distress.[107]

---

[105] Throughout this time in the land, God is seen to be one who will reveal His will to His people. God sent prophets to correct the people. On the whole the people refused to hear and obey the prophets.

[106] Now the prayer moves to the present situation. Having traced God's working and faithfulness, the prayer vindicates God's just action throughout their history. Verse 33 captures it all: *You are just in all that you brought upon us. For you have done right, but we have done wickedly*. Verse 34 captures the guilt of the leaders—the failure to keep God's revealed law. The tracing of history and the vicarious confession have led them to this point. They are in deep need of God's work in their situation. They acknowledge this.

[107] And now the prayer concludes by expressing the petitioners' own situation. They are oppressed in their land and are in deep distress.

38 And because of all this we, the people,
     make a solemn written covenant.
Our leaders, Levites, and priests also do seal it.[108]

Chapter 10
Nehemiah 10:1-27
Contextual Statement:
The priests and Levites and leaders seal the covenant. Many (some 82) are listed individually as signing the covenant.

     28 And the rest of the people, the priests, the Levites, the porters, the singers, the Nethinims,[109] and all they that had separated themselves from the people of the lands unto the law of God, including their wives, their sons, and their daughters—every one having knowledge, and having understanding—29 joined with each other and their leaders, to enter a covenant under penalty of a curse, to walk in God's law, which was given by Moses the servant of God, and to observe and do all the commandments of the LORD our Lord, and his judgments and his statutes.[110]

---

[108] The prayer concludes with a most powerful application. They sign a covenant to follow God and return to obedience to His law. And in return they want God to work in their situation. Some observations on the prayer as a whole: 1. Leaders must capitalize on the momentum of spiritual renewal. 2. Public prayer can be structured and still meaningful. The whole prayer is in Hebrew Poetry. 3. God is recognized for who He is and for what He has done. 4. Vicarious confession involves recognition before God of wrongful acts and attitudes. 5. These people traced the highlights of their history and God's work in their people. This shows that the Bible reading and teaching times in the renewal movement have paid off. 6. The key is recognizing that God has revealed Himself and His ways to His people. They must return to following His revelation. 7. God repeatedly will respond to His people if they turn to Him. 8. The public acknowledgement and signing of the covenant to return to God and follow Him provides a benchmark that the leaders and followers can return to in the future, when the strong feelings of the renewal have waned. The benchmark, the signing of the covenant, is a major accountability factor.

[109] The TEV and LB translate the Nethinims as temple guards. The NLT as gatekeepers.

[110] All the people enter into the covenant. Eighty two of the leaders formally signed it. Notice the stipulations of the covenant, which follow. The people have been impressed deeply by Ezra's ministry.

30 And we will not give our daughters unto the people of the land, nor take their daughters for our sons.[111] 31 If the people of the land bring grain or anything else to sell on the Sabbath, we will not buy it from them. And we will follow the rule of the seventh year and let the land rest. We will cancel debts.

32 We have agreed to set aside money to help defray the expenses of temple worship. 33 We will help provide for the daily sacrifices of sacred bread and animals as well as for the special offerings needed on special days and festivals. This money will also be used to pay for the sin offerings on the day of atonement for Israel and for other expenses of the temple.[112] 34 And also yearly we will choose people from among the priests, the Levites, and the people, to provide the wood to be used for burnt offerings as required by the law. 35 And we will bring the firstfruits of our ground, and the firstfruits of all fruit of all trees, year by year, unto the house of the LORD.

36 Also we will present the firstborn of our sons, and of our cattle, as written in the law, and the firstlings of our herds and of our flocks, to bring to the house of our God, unto the priests that minister in the house of our God. 37 Likewise we will bring the firstfruits of our dough, and our offerings, and the fruit of all manner of trees, of wine and of oil, unto the priests, to the chambers of the house of our God. We will bring the tithes of our ground unto the Levites, who collect the tithes in all the farm villages. 38 And the priests, descendants of Aaron, shall be with the Levites, when the Levites take tithes.[113] The Levites shall bring up the tithe of the tithes unto the house of our God, to the chambers, into the treasure house. 39 The people of Israel and the Levites shall bring the offering of the corn, of the new wine, and the oil, unto the chambers, in which are kept

---

[111] The opening paragraph of the covenant hits two important issues. One, intermarriage with people of the conquered lands. Historically this has been a downfall of the Israelite people. Intermarriage has led them into worshipping the gods of the land—the gods of their spouses. So this important guideline is highlighted. It is true that many, many of these folks involved in the covenant have been guilty of this. This is a costly requirement. Two, the violation of the Sabbath, including the Sabbath of years and even the Jubilee time. They are returning to the principle of the Sabbath. This too is costly. No money being made on the Sabbath. Canceling debts in the 7th year. Letting the land rest for a year, etc.

[112] Ezra, Joshua, Haggai, Zerubbabel, and Nehemiah—and all the restoration leaders—have seen the necessity of centralized worship to keep the people motivated to serve God. One necessity for maintaining the centralized worship function in the temple was a budget to cover the ministry and the workers' salaries. This is emphasized strongly in this covenant. Firewood, necessary for the sacrifices, money, goods and other resources are all pledged. When Nehemiah returns from a trip back to visit Artaxerxes, in chapter 13, he finds that this part of the covenant has not been kept. He quickly admonishes and chastises the people for not keeping this part of the covenant. Without this, the temple worship stops. And with it the potential for maintaining renewal. See *restoration leaders,* **Glossary**. See **Article**, *34. Restoration Leaders.*

[113] An accountability/integrity function. Multiple people will oversee the collection and use of finances. Nehemiah is always careful with regard to finances. Misuse of finances is one of the major barriers to leaders finishing well. Nehemiah is very careful about finances. See **LEADERSHIP TOPIC 9: FINANCIAL INTEGRITY**. See **Articles**, *6. Finishing Well—6 Major Barriers*; *26. Nehemiah, Financial Integrity.*

the vessels of the sanctuary, and where the priests that minister, and the porters, and the singers are on duty. We will not forsake the house of our God.[114]

III. (11-13)   Organizing for Continuation

Chapter 11[115]
Contextual Statements:

Contextual Statement: 11:1-19[116]
Provision is made to populate Jerusalem with some folks living outside of Jerusalem. Those selected agree to move into Jerusalem.

Contextual Statement: 11:20-35[117]
Those living outside of Jerusalem in various villages and on farms are listed and instructions are given for them to help financially support those leading worship in Jerusalem.

.
Chapter 12[118]

Contextual Statement: 12:1-9
Priests and Levites who went back to Jerusalem with Zerubbabel and Joshua (official restoration leaders) are listed (including the prominent one Ezra).

Contextual Statement: 12:10-21
The descendants of the Priest, Jeshua, are listed.

12:22-26
The descendants of the Levites during the days of Eliashib, Joiada, and Johanan, and Jaddua are recorded (those up to the reign of Darius the Persian).

27 At the dedication of the wall of Jerusalem, the Levites were sought out from where they lived and were brought to Jerusalem to celebrate joyfully the dedication with songs of thanksgiving and with the

---

[114] The final sentence of the covenant stresses the importance of the centralized worship function. *We will not forsake the house of our God.* The books of 1,2 Chronicles stress repeatedly that the failure to maintain centralized worship was one of the major downfalls of the Kingdom Leadership Era.

[115] There are only a few leadership comments to be made for ch 11. They can be made generally and without reference to individual texts. So we will omit the actual texts. Instead we will simply give the contextual statements. In this section of Nehemiah (ch 11-13) we are seeing the underpinnings of organizing for continuation of renewal.

[116] A strong Jerusalem with a centralized worship set up and operating will need a well populated Jerusalem. Nehemiah had this in mind as part of his renewal efforts.

[117] The strong centralized worship in Jerusalem will need finances from more than just the Jerusalem population. Nehemiah gets commitment from those living outside of Jerusalem proper. This involvement via finances also insures they will take ownership in the centralized worship when fitting.

[118] We will skip the first 26 vs, (see the two contextual statements) and go directly to the context for which we make leadership observations.

music of cymbals, harps and lyres.[119] 28 The singers also were brought together from the region around Jerusalem—from the villages of the Netophathites, 29 from Beth Gilgal, and from the area of Geba and Azmaveth, for the singers had built villages for themselves around Jerusalem. 30 When the priests and Levites had purified themselves ceremonially, they purified the people, the gates and the wall.[120]

31 I had the leaders of Judah go up on top of the wall.[121] I also assigned two large choirs to give thanks. One was to proceed on top of the wall to the right, toward the Dung Gate. 32 Hoshaiah and half the leaders of Judah followed them, 33 along with Azariah, Ezra, Meshullam, 34 Judah, Benjamin, Shemaiah, and Jeremiah, 35 as well as some priests with trumpets, and also Zechariah son of Jonathan, the son of Shemaiah, the son of Mattaniah, the son of Micaiah, the son of Zaccur, the son of Asaph, 36 and his associates—Shemaiah, Azarel, Milalai, Gilalai, Maai, Nethanel, Judah and Hanani—with musical instruments prescribed by David the man of God.[122] Ezra the scribe led the procession. 37 At the Fountain Gate they continued directly up the steps of the City of David on the ascent to the wall and passed above the house of David to the Water Gate on the east.

38 The second choir proceeded in the opposite direction. I followed them on top of the wall, together with half the people—past the Tower of the Ovens to the Broad Wall, 39 over the Gate of Ephraim, the Jeshanah Gate, the Fish Gate, the Tower of Hananel and the Tower of the Hundred, as far as the Sheep Gate. At the Gate of the Guard they stopped.

40 The two choirs that gave thanks then took their places in the house of God; so did I, together with half the officials, 41 as well as the priests—Eliakim, Maaseiah, Miniamin, Micaiah, Elioenai, Zechariah and Hananiah with their trumpets—42 and also Maaseiah, Shemaiah, Eleazar, Uzzi, Jehohanan, Malkijah, Elam and Ezer. The choirs sang under the direction of Jezrahiah. 43 And on that day they offered great sacrifices, rejoicing because God had given them great joy. The women and children also rejoiced. The

---

[119] Once again we see the prominence of worship and music in the corporate celebration of God's goodness and intervention, as well as in the spiritual renewal of the people.

[120] Nehemiah has a sensitive spirit to God's holiness, the very heart of the purity macro lesson. The purity macro lesson, first identified in the Patriarchal Leadership Era and repeated in other eras, is stated as, **Leaders must personally learn of and respond to the holiness of God in order to have an effective ministry.** Note also ch 13 for additional reference to comments on purity and cleansing.

[121] Leaders are people of influence, and in religious circles they should be people who model the way that others are to follow. Here Nehemiah stations leaders at the front of the procession, leading the way in the worship celebration of God and God's goodness to His people.

[122] Approximately 500 years after his death, David's legacy is intact. He is still honored among the Jewish people as a man of God and a leader in the institution of corporate worship. His instructions for worship were still to be followed. Worship leaders today would do well to take note. The Bible does not instruct people to "worship the Lord in your own way", but prescribes in the Old and New Testaments guidelines for corporate worship. Worship leaders would be better served to instruct people to "worship the Lord in the way the Bible sets forth" in various locations.

sound of rejoicing in Jerusalem could be heard far away.[123]

44 At that time men were appointed to be in charge of the storerooms for the contributions, firstfruits and tithes. From the fields around the towns they were to bring into the storerooms the portions required by the Law for the priests and the Levites, for Judah was pleased with the ministering priests and Levites. 45 They performed the service of their God and the service of purification, as did also the singers and gatekeepers, according to the commands of David and his son Solomon. 46 For long ago, in the days of David and Asaph, there had been directors for the singers and for the songs of praise and thanksgiving to God. 47 So in the days of Zerubbabel and of Nehemiah, all Israel contributed the daily portions for the singers and gatekeepers.[124] They also set aside the portion for the other Levites, and the Levites set aside the portion for the descendants of Aaron.

---

[123] At least seven festivals were ordained by the Lord in the Old Testament. Festivals called people to worship and remember the Lord and His mighty works. Here the people are celebrating the completion of the wall, a work that Nehemiah and others recognized had been completed with the help of their God (see 6:16). The grand public celebration, complete with choirs, instruments, singers, and sacrificial offerings, stirred the hearts of the people and moved them to great joy. Truly God was at work in the restoration of His people back in the land. Nehemiah was providing inspirational leadership that moved the people to courage and hope. Teachers of the spiritual disciplines, such as Dallas Willard, point out the continuing benefits of celebration for believers today (see Willard's **The Spirit of the Disciplines**).

[124] What a testimony! Through the influence of these leaders, Zerubbabel and Nehemiah, provisions for worship were made and worship in the house of God was reinstated. In their days, on their watch, through their leadership, the people were renewed in their relationship with the LORD. Their attention was redirected to Him and their identity as God's people was revitalized. Once again Israel became the worshiping community the Lord intended. Christian leaders today, take note. We also have a time frame within which to influence followers. Like Luke says of David in Acts 13:36, we have a generation within which to serve the Lord and His purposes. May it be said of us that in our days, people were turned to the Lord, leaders were equipped to finish well, and churches were equipped for fruitful, God-honoring ministry.

Chapter 13[125] [126]

1 On that day when they read in the book of Moses to the people, they saw that the Ammonite and the Moabite should not come into the congregation of God forever. 2 This was because they didn't give the children of Israel bread and water, but hired Balaam against them, that he should curse them. However, our God turned the curse into a blessing.[127] 3 Now it came to pass, when they had heard the law, that they separated all the foreigners from the community of Israel.[128]

4 And before this, Eliashib the priest, was in charge of the temple storerooms. But he was in cahoots with Tobiah.[129] 5 Eliashib had prepared for Tobiah's use, a great chamber, which had been used to store the meat offerings, the frankincense, and the vessels, and the tithes of the corn, the new wine, and the oil. This was supposed to be used by the Levites, the singers, the temple guards

---

[125] In this final chapter an important macro lesson is being stressed. The one being emphasized here is the <u>stability</u> <u>macro</u>, stated as: **Preserving a ministry of God with life and vigor over time is as much, if not more of a challenge to leadership, than creating one.** A second macro-lesson is alluded to. Nehemiah is careful to have the priests and Levites purify and cleanse things—wherever some omission or sinful thing has been taking place. This occurs several times during Nehemiah's leadership—see verses 9 and 22. The <u>purity</u> <u>macro</u> <u>lesson</u>, first identified in the Patriarchal Leadership Era and repeated in other eras, is stated as, **Leaders must personally learn of and respond to the holiness of God in order to have an effective ministry.** Nehemiah seems to be deeply impressed with God's holiness. See **Article**, *17. Macro Lessons: List of 41 Across Six Leadership Eras*.

[126] Remember, these are the memoirs of Nehemiah. Whereas ch 11 and 12 look at some of the continued organizational issues that Nehemiah instituted, ch 13 seems to look back over Nehemiah's entire leadership. He seems to be selectively remembering and highlighting some critical issues he worked on in his leadership. Four things are pinpointed: 1. Separation from the Moabites and Ammonites—not allowing them to be part of the Israelite community. This was direct obedience to what they heard in the law when Ezra taught them. 2. The conflict with Eliashib about giving Tobiah a room in the temple. 3. The lack of finances to keep the temple ministry going. 4. The keeping of the Sabbath. Two of these items were part of the major covenant the people had agreed to in chapter 10. Nehemiah holds them accountable.

[127] It seems clear that Nehemiah was well versed in the Scriptures. Here he uses the Balaam illustration. And later during several of the rhetorical questions he refers to the application of Scripture drawn from several illustrations. He illustrates in this chapter that his leadership is informed from the Bible, one of the components of the definition of a Bible centered leader. See *Bible Centered Leader*, **Glossary**. See **Article**, *36. A Vanishing Breed*.

[128] Note the obedient response. However, the outworking of this probably took time.

[129] Eliashib was one of the conduits who was feeding information back to Tobiah during the building of the wall. That is certainly an implication from this incident, though it probably took place after the building of the wall.

and for storing the offerings for the priests. 6 During this time I was not at Jerusalem.[130] This was the 32nd year that Artaxerxes, king of Babylon, reigned. I had gone to report to him. After my report I obtained permission to return.[131] 7 And I returned to Jerusalem, and was shocked to find that Eliashib had allowed Tobiah to use this room. 8 I was upset and threw out Tobiah's stuff. 9 Then I commanded that the rooms be ritually cleansed and the temple equipment, meat offerings, and incense put back in this room.[132]

10 And I saw that the money promised to support the Levites had not been given them. For the Levites and the singers, that did the work, had all returned to their own farms.[133] 11 Then I

---

[130] From this passage (and the inference in 2:6) it is clear that Nehemiah was not always in Jerusalem. When he comes back from this reporting time with Artaxerxes he finds that the people have quickly forgotten their covenant vows. He holds them accountable and gets them back on track. Such is the importance of leadership. Nehemiah was a leader—a person with God-given capacity and God-given responsibility who influenced people toward God's purposes for the group. See *leader*, **Glossary**. Nehemiah demonstrates what needs to be done to keep the work of God alive—have a strong renewal ministry, organize to keep it going, get the people to publicly commit to the renewal ministry, find a way to finance it, and aperiodically hold the people accountable to their covenant vows.

[131] Back in chapter 2 Nehemiah had obtained permission and the backing of Artaxerxes to go to Jerusalem upon promise of his return. Nehemiah is a leader with integrity. An oath or promise is an important indicator of integrity. One who keeps an oath has integrity. One who does not lacks integrity. Nehemiah is a leader, whose leadership over and over again exudes integrity in his leadership. His leadership underscores the findings of the character macro lesson: **Integrity is the essential character trait of a spiritual leader.** See *integrity*, **Glossary**.

[132] Again Nehemiah deals with conflict head-on. Notice the emphasis of ritually cleansing the place. This is probably an indication of Nehemiah's awareness of the purity macro lesson,: **Leaders must personally learn of and respond to the holiness of God in order to have an effective ministry.** Some modern day spiritual warfare notes the importance of cleansing rooms in buildings and geographical places where atrocious sinful practices held sway in the past.

[133] Nehemiah knows the importance of centralized worship in keeping a work of God alive (one of the strong para-messages of 1,2 Ch). The budget for this is crucial. He gets right on this problem. This reflects his intuitive sense of the stability macro lesson: **Preserving a ministry of God with life and vigor over time is as much if not more of a challenge to leadership than creating one.**

reprimanded the leaders, and said, "Why is the house of God forsaken?" [134] And I got the Levites and singers to come back to the temple and put them to work again.[135] 12 Everyone started giving again to finance the temple work—the tithe of the corn and the new wine and the oil.[136] 13 And I appointed several to be accountable for the financial resources being given into the temple. These included: Shelemiah the priest, and Zadok the scribe, and of the Levites, Pedaiah. Others in charge included: Hanan the son of Zaccur, the son of Mattaniah. These men were trustworthy and would honestly distribute the supplies to their fellow temple workers.[137]

14 Remember me, O my God, concerning these good things I have done for the house of my God, and for the leadership of the Temple and for the worship there.[138]

---

[134] A number of rhetorical questions are used in this chapter: verses 11, 17, 18, 21, 26, and 27. A <u>rhetorical question</u> is a figure of speech in which a question is <u>not</u> used to obtain information but is used to indirectly communicate an affirmative or negative statement, the importance of some thought by focusing attention on it, and/or one's own feeling or attitudes about something. All of these rhetorical questions used by Nehemiah are devices for couching a strong reprimand. In verses 17 and 18 the three questions are interpreted as: You have broken the Sabbath and invited God to punish us again like he did when our ancestors did this. He destroyed Jerusalem. One of Nehemiah's conflictual techniques is to use rhetorical questions to emphasize Biblical precedence and principles, which convicts the people of their wrong doing and moves them toward obedience. See *rhetorical question*, **Glossary**. See **Article**, *3. Figures and Idioms in the Bible*.

[135] Strong leadership is being exerted here to get these men to return. Past promises of support have been reneged on. Nehemiah gets them back.

[136] We define a <u>leader</u> as a person with God-given gifts and a God-given responsibility who is influencing a specific group of God's people toward God's purposes for the group. The central thrust of our definition of a leader is influencing people toward God's purposes. Nehemiah does that over and over. Here is a good illustration. These workers needed to be supported financially if they were to devote their time to worship in the temple. The people have reneged on their promise to do so. Nehemiah persuades these workers to come back. He essentially has to guarantee that the finances will be there. Then he has to get the people to give. He does this too. Nehemiah influences people toward fulfillment of God's purposes.

[137] Financial integrity is important to Nehemiah. He appoints multiple people to oversee finances—people of character. See **LEADERSHIP TOPIC 9: FINANCIAL INTEGRITY**. See **Articles**, *6. Finishing Well—6 Major Barriers*; *26. Nehemiah, Financial Integrity*.

[138] This is one of the repeated prayer phrases. See 1:4, 5, 6, 8, 11; 2:4; 4:9; 5:10, 11, 19; 6:9, 14; 9:1; 11:17; 13:14, 22, 29, 31. This is a special form of prayer. We call it "The remember prayers." They occur in 1:8, 5:19; 6:14; 13:14,22,29, 31. The ones in 5:19, 13:14, 22, 29, 31 are personal remember prayers. Nehemiah is asking God to remember him personally. It is as if Nehemiah recognizes that he is a eunuch and must have special remembrance to be included in God's people. See De 23:1. It was the practice of kings, like Artaxerxes, to make the palace servants eunuchs (those of foreign nationality who served in the palace). The law excluded eunuchs from public worship. Nehemiah could be asking for special favor to be included in the congregation.

15 In those days[139] I saw people working on the Sabbath—some making wine and others loading their grain, wine, grapes, and other things on donkeys and hauling them into Jerusalem. I protested to them about selling things on the Sabbath. 16 Merchants from Tyre also were selling things in Jerusalem on the Sabbath, like fish and other wares. 17 Then I chastised[140] the leaders of Judah, and said unto them, "What are you doing allowing the Sabbath to be broken? 18 Did not our ancestors do this and were punished by God for doing so? That is why Jerusalem was destroyed. Do you want to bring such a punishment again?[141]

19 So I commanded that the gates of Jerusalem be closed at the beginning of each Sabbath. Don't open them till after the Sabbath is over. I put some of my own men to oversee[142] the shutting of the gates. I did not want the Sabbath profaned. 20 A couple of times merchants and various sellers of all kind spent the night before the Sabbath outside of Jerusalem. 21 But I warned them. Don't hang around here overnight. If you do this again I will forcibly remove you.[143] From then on they didn't return to sell on the Sabbath. 22 I ordered the Levites to purify themselves and to insure the gates were closed in order to make sure the Sabbath day was kept holy.[144]

Remember me, O my God, concerning this also, and spare me according to the greatness of your mercy.[145]

---

[139] It seems like this is a flashback to the time when Nehemiah first dealt with the Sabbath issue. This gives us more details about the Sabbath problem.

[140] This is a strong word. In the KJV, it is the word *contend* (SRN 7378). It is repeated in verse 25 where I render it even more strongly—as *quarrel*.

[141] Three rhetorical questions carrying the force of: You are violating the Sabbath! God severely punished our ancestors for this very thing! You are inviting that same punishment for us!

[142] His own men would model what must be done. It is as if Nehemiah didn't trust the people to follow the order to bar the gates.

[143] Nehemiah exercises decisive leadership. He confronts the situation. He threatens to use force. This is enough to scare away the merchants. Remember these merchants had been encouraged by people inside the city. Nehemiah wants to put a stop to this.

[144] Again we have mention of purification. The Levites must see their duty as being Holy to God, no matter how practical a task it is.

[145] Another personal remember prayer, this one strongly implying his need for God to include him.

23 In those days also saw I Jews that had married wives from Ashdod, Ammon, and Moab. 24 And the children were raised to speak their mother's tongue and not the Jewish language. 25 And I quarreled[146] with the men, calling them despicable. I punished some with beating. I embarrassed some by pulling out their hair. I forced them to make an oath to God that their children would not intermarry with foreigners. 26 Did not Solomon king of Israel sin by these things? God made him king over all Israel. There was there no king like him among all the surrounding nations. But note, these foreign women caused him to sin. 27 Shall we then follow his example and do this great evil? Shall we disobey our God by marrying foreign wives?[147]

28 Joiada was the son of Eliashib, the high priest. One of Joiada's sons married Sanballat the Horonite's daughter. I banished him from Jerusalem.[148]

29 Remember them, O my God, because they have defiled the priesthood. They have broken the covenant that all the priests and Levites signed.[149]

30 Thus I purified the people from foreign influence. I organized the priests and the Levites concerning their duties. 31 I made sure that people brought the wood for burnt offerings at the proper time. I made sure that first offerings of grain and fruit were brought in.[150]
Remember me, O my God, for the good I have done.[151]

---

[146] Notice again, this is the KJV, contend (SRN 7378). Here I give it a stronger connotation. Nehemiah is having to argue strongly that they put away foreign influence.

[147] Again we see Nehemiah's knowledge of the Scriptures informing his leadership. Further we see a second component of a Bible Centered Leader being illustrated, the dynamic application of past Scripture to a current situation. See *Bible Centered Leader*, **Glossary**. See **Article**, *36. A Vanishing Breed*.

[148] This further explains the earlier incident of forcefully removing Tobiah's things from the temple. Nehemiah had two good reasons to banish Joiada. He was married to a foreigner and evidently didn't want to obey the law. He was allied with Tobiah, an opponent of the building of the wall.

[149] Another *remember prayer*. There are three kinds of remember prayers: 1. Remember God, an exhortation for the people to remember in the past what God had done (both in blessing and punishing); 2. Remember enemies—an imprecatory prayer asking God to punish the enemies. 3. A personal request for God to remember Nehemiah for what he had done in his leadership. This last type seems to imply that Nehemiah was a eunuch who wanted God to mercifully include him with God's people (De 23:1), because he had so faithfully served God. Nehemiah is a man of prayer. See for other prayer references: 1:4, 5, 6, 8, 11; 2:4; 4:9; 5:10, 11, 19; 6:9, 14; 9:1; 11:17; 13:14,22,29,31.

[150] Nehemiah closes these special memoirs by restating how important it is to keep centralized worship going. He has solved problems that will keep the temple worship going, a final reminder to us of the stability macro, **Preserving a ministry of God with life and vigor over time is as much if not more of a challenge to leadership than creating one.**

[151] It seems fitting to us that Nehemiah, a man of prayer, concludes his memoirs with another prayer, a *remember prayer*. This is a personal remember prayer recognizing that God does reward good leadership. See Hebrews 11:6, "But without faith it is impossible to please him, for he that comes to God must believe that He is, and that He is a rewarder of them that diligently seek Him." Nehemiah is a great Old Testament leader who sought God. We, leaders today, benefit from the model this great leader left for us.

For Further Leadership Study

1. There are numerous leadership acts in chapters 1-6. Each can be analyzed using the basic principles detailed in one of the other handbooks.

2. Nehemiah goes through a major boundary[152] in his life in chapter 1. This is worth analyzing in detail.

Special Comments

Notice in particular the notion of closure (4:6, 6:15 & 16, 12:27). Nehemiah finished what he started out to do. He built the wall, organized the people, brought about reform and sought to make it a long-lasting.

---

[152]Analysis over the lifetime of a leader identifies major periods of time called development phases. Movement from one development phase to another represents a critical transition and is called a boundary which usually has three stages: entry, evaluation, expansion. See position paper, "Boundary Processing," available through Barnabas Publishing.

Nehemiah

CLINTON'S
BIBLICAL LEADERSHIP
COMMENTARY SERIES

Focused Leadership

Commentary Articles

(This page deliberately blank.)

Leadership Articles[1] (bold faced articles appear in other commentaries as well).

   1. Biblical Framework—The Redemptive Drama
   2. Biographical Study in the Bible, How To Do
   3. Figures and Idioms in the Bible
   4. Finishing Well—Five Enhancements
   5. Finishing Well—Six Characteristics
   6. Finishing Well— Six Major Barriers
   7. *Gates and Walls*
   8. *Getting the Job Done—Comparison of Ezra, Nehemiah and Haggai's Roles*
   9. God The Promise Keeper
  10. *God's Shaping Processes with Leaders*
  11. Haggai—Leadership Coalition
  12. Influence, Power and Authority forms
  13. Leadership Eras In The Bible, Six Identified
  14. Learning Vicariously From Other Leaders' Lives.
  15. Left Hand of God, The
  16. Macro Lessons—Defined
  17. Macro Lessons: List of 41 Across Six Leadership Eras
  18. *Nehemiah, And Daniel—Comparison of Vicarious Praying*
  19. *Nehemiah, Biographical Sketch*
  20. *Nehemiah, Calendar and Dating*
  21. *Nehemiah, Change Participants*
  22. *Nehemiah—Civil Leadership With A Spiritual Twist*
  23. *Nehemiah, Contextual Flow—Seeing the Flow*
  24. *Nehemiah, Desperate Praying*
  25. *Nehemiah, Eight Ideas to Communicate*
  26. *Nehemiah, Financial Integrity*
  27. *Nehemiah, Getting Ownership*
  28. *Nehemiah, In the Trenches*
  29. *Nehemiah, Leadership Functions*
  30. *Nehemiah, Peoples and Places*
  31. *Nehemiah, Strategic Timing*
  32. Promises of God, The
  33. Prophetic Crises—Three Major Biblical Times
  34. Restoration Leaders
  35. Six Biblical Leadership Eras, Approaching the Bible with Leadership Eyes
  36. Vanishing Breed

In addition to these numbered articles, which are included in the Nehemiah commentary, I mention other articles which occur in other commentaries. Those will be unnumbered. All numbered articles, those relating to Nehemiah specifically, are included in this commentary.

---

[1] Throughout the commentary Articles listed with numbers are included with this commentary and refer to the numbered articles listed above. Some articles, without numbers occur in other commentaries.

1. Biblical Framework—The Redemptive Drama

Introduction

In each of the overviews on the various individual books in the leadership commentary series I have a section called **Where It Fits**. In that section, I try to deal with the application of my first general hermeneutical principle,[2]

Language Principle 1 Book and Books
In The Spirit, Prayerfully Study The Book As A Whole In Terms Of Its Relationship To Other Books In The Bible (i.e. the Bible as a whole) **TO INCLUDE:**
- a. its place in the progress of redemption (both as to the progress of revelation, what God has said, and also the notion of what God has done in redemptive history)
- b. its overall contribution to the whole or Bible literature (i.e. *its purposes —why is it in the Bible?*) and
- c. its abiding contribution to present time.

I seek to find **Where It Fits** using two basic overall frameworks:

1. *The Unfolding Drama of Redemption*—that is, telling the story of what God has said and done in the Bible.[3]

2. *The Leadership Framework*. Since this is a leadership commentary series, I want to trace the contribution of a book to leadership. The leadership era it fits in helps inform us as to how to interpret its leadership findings.

This article is concerned with the first of these two frameworks: *The Unfolding Drama of Redemption*. I have previously dealt with the second framework in several articles.[4]

I will first introduce the overall framework with a diagram. Then I will give a brief synopsis for each chapter of the redemptive drama. Finally, I will list the Bible books in terms of the chapters of the redemptive drama.

---

[2] See Appendix G in **Having A Ministry That Lasts** for the whole hermeneutical system I use.

[3] I am deeply indebted to a teaching mentor of mine, James M. (Buck) hatch who introduced me to this framework in his course, Progress of Redemption, given at Columbia Bible College. I have used his teaching and adapted it in my own study of each book in the Bible in terms of the Bible story as a whole. I have also written in depth on this in my handbook, **The Bible and Leadership Values**. This article is a condensed version of that larger explanation.

[4] See **Articles**, 35. *Six Biblical Leadership Eras--Overviewed; 16. Macro Lesson Defined; 17. Macro Lessons--List of 41 Across Six Leadership Eras.*

Overall Framework—Redemptive Drama Pictured

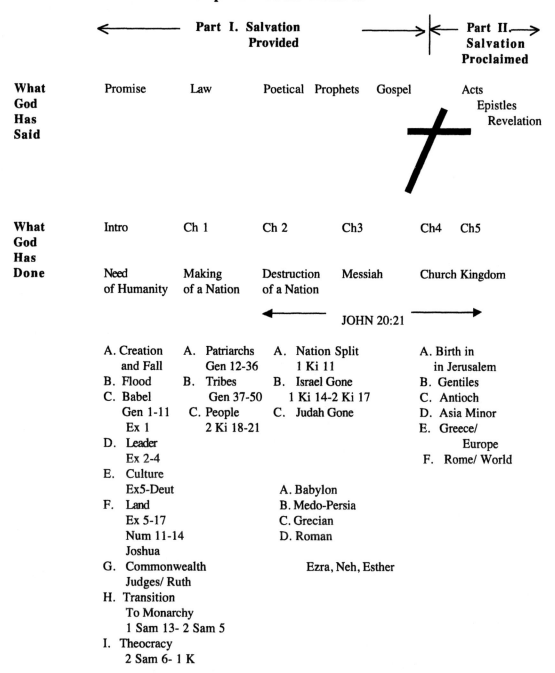

Figure Ne 1-1. Overview of Redemptive Drama Time Line

The **Time-Line of the Redemptive Story** contains six sections,
              Introduction,
              Chapter 1. The Making of A Nation,
              Chapter 2. The Destruction of A Nation,
              Chapter 3. Messiah,
              Chapter 4. The Church, and
              Chapter 5. The Kingdom.

This story is briefly explained in a Running Capsule of the Redemptive Story. The story traces **what God does** and **what He says** throughout the Bible. And it shows that there is a progressive revelation of God throughout the whole drama. The Bible is unified around this salvation history. Once this is recognized then the notion of intentional selection becomes important. Each book in the Bible is there for a purpose and contributes something to this salvation story.

It is this framework, which provides the macro context for studying each book of the Bible. Where is the book in the progress of redemption time-line? What does it contribute to it? Why is it there? What would we miss if it were left out? Understanding each book in terms of its own purpose is a preliminary first step that must be done before we can interpret it for leadership findings.

The Running Capsule for the Redemptive Story
I will first give an overview and then give more detail from each part of the redemptive drama.

Overall
At the center of the Biblical revelation is the concept of a God who has intervened in human history. He created the human race. He has revealed himself to that race. That race rebelled against His desires. In its fallen state it continually rebels against His wishes and desires and for the potential that it could accomplish.

So He started again and selected specifically a people through whom He could reveal Himself to the world. God moves unswervingly toward His purpose which is to redeem people and relate to them. He moves toward His purposes whether or not the people He has chosen follow them or not. They can willingly be a part in which they enjoy the blessings of God or they can be by-passed and He will find other ways to accomplish His purposes. He patiently works with them to include them in His purposes. But when all is said and done He moves on with or without them.

All the time He is increasingly revealing more of Himself and His purposes to His people. They come to know Him as a mighty God, all powerful and controlling, yet allowing human beings their choices. He is a holy God, that is, a being of perfection. He reveals His purposes as that of having a Holy people following Him. People who are becoming Holy as He is holy. They learn that to fall short of His demands or standards is to sin against Him and is deserving of retribution if justice is to be satisfied.

Part I of the redemption drama, **SALVATION PROVIDED,** is His selection of a people, which will prove foundational to accomplishing His purposes. Out of that people will come one who is central in the decrees of God. Not an afterthought but mysteriously beyond our thinking, known to God. Look at Revelation 13:8, the Lamb slain before the foundation of the world. In terms of what we know of God today, we see this Part I as revealing to us, God the Father, that is, the God who is source of all that we are and to whom we relate, infinite, eternal, powerful, a spirit.

God protects that line through which He will come over a period of many years and in times of failure on their part to know Him and obey Him as they should.

His incarnation into the world begins Part II of the Redemptive Drama, **SALVATION PROCLAIMED.** Galatians 4:4, in God's time. That incarnate God, manifest in the flesh, to communicate directly with the human race, to be a part of it, to share in its joys and sorrows, finally pays the supreme price of rejection, by a world who wanted to call its own shots, the death of the Cross, perfection paying the perfect price to satisfy God's Holy just demands. The great dilemma was solved, how God could be absolutely just and yet lovingly receive to Himself, those for whom justice demanded the harsh penalty of death. That time in which Jesus lived and walked and taught and did so many things to reveal God to us is the time, as we now know it of God the Son, God revealed to a human race as one of that race. Having accomplished the first portion of His work, the Cross, He ascended to heaven and will yet come again. Having ascended, He sent the Holy Spirit into the world, the intimation of what is to come, the Spirit who indwells those people He has chosen.

In the meantime while we wait we are involved in **Part II Salvation Proclaimed**, which shows that this message was more than just for the Jews but for a whole world. And that is what we are about today, the proclamation of that reconciling message, that God has provided a way in which sinful human beings can be rightly related to Him and progress to live a satisfying and fruitful life, in harmony with His purposes. And as they live this purposeful life, demonstrating the power and presence of God in their time on earth, they know that God is going to make all things right someday—there is a justice coming; the Lord Jesus, now a risen Savior, a life-giving Spirit will return to claim His own. There will be a time of His reigning on earth and then there will be eternity. And we who have been called out, as a people to His name, will reign with Him for all eternity. In terms of what we know today, this is the Age of God, the Spirit.

Introduction
  Genesis tells us of many beginnings. It tells of the beginning of the creation, the human race, of sin in the world, of the spread of the race, of judgment on the race and a new beginning for the race. It does not satisfy all our questions. We would ask more and want more. But it does give us the backdrop for the salvation story. Humanity is in need. It can not get along with itself. It has alienated itself from God. Left to itself it will be destructive at best. There is a need. And the salvation story, which begins in Genesis chapter 12 will give God's response to meet that need.

Chapter 1. The Making of a Nation
  God's basic plan is to choose a people and to reveal Himself and His plans for reconciling the world to Himself through that nation. Chapter 1 tells of the story of God's building of the nation.

  If I were to pick out the most important events in the making of a nation, Chapter 1 of the redemptive drama I would say the following would certainly be a part of it.
1. The call of Abraham—the Abrahamic Promise
2. The renewal of the covenant with Isaac
3. The renewal of the covenant with Jacob
4. The deliverance of Jacob and sons through Joseph
5. The call of Moses
6. The power encounters in Egypt and the Exodus
7. The Red Sea deliverance
8. The Spies in the Land/corporate failure of a faith check
9. The Giving of the 10 Commandments/covenant
10. Moses' failure—striking the rock
11. Moses' outstanding leadership in the desert years with a rebellious followership and his transition of Joshua into leadership
12. Crossing of Jordan
13. Circumcision at Gilgal
14. Joshua meets the Captain of the Hosts
15. Capture of Jericho
16. Failure at Ai

17.   Success at Ai
18.   Gibeonite deception
19.   Capture of Land (lack of total obedience)
20.   Repetitive Failure—moving from dependence to independence. The Cycle of the Judges (need for centralized influence)
21.   Samuel's unifying influence
22.   Saul's anointing and failure
23.   David's anointing and success
24.   David's failure and discipline
25.   David's preparation for building the temple

Lets examine some of the Bible books, which present these events.

<u>From Genesis</u>
From the introduction we know that humanity is not in good shape and is in need of intervention by God. And God has a plan thought out in eternity past.

God chooses one man, Abraham, and Promises (*The First Great Revelation—The Promise*) to make of him a great nation and to give them land and to bless the world through his offspring. (Gen 12:1-3, 7; 15:4,18, et al) Now God plans to use the nation He will bring forth to be a channel of redemption and revelation of Himself. So He begins to build a nation. For a nation you need people (including numbers) a coherent culture, a land, and a leader.

God begins to work on these things—the people first (the land has people on it who will be judged eventually when they are too evil to be redeemed). From this one man, who exemplifies faith in God's promise, comes a son, Isaac. Isaac has two sons, one of whom, Jacob, becomes the successor of the family line through which God will work—the 12 heads of the tribes: Reuben, Simeon, Levi, Judah, Zebulun, Issachar, Dan, Gad, Asher, Naphtali, Joseph, Benjamin.

Joseph, a son of Jacob's old age and his favorite, is sold into slavery by his jealous brothers (Acts 7:9). Because the patriarchs were jealous of Joseph they sold him as a slave into Egypt. But God was with him and rescued him from all his troubles. He gave Joseph wisdom and enabled him to gain the goodwill of Pharaoh king of Egypt; so he made him ruler over Egypt and all his palace.) Joseph, a person of proven integrity, rises to power through a series of providential appointments in which he shows wisdom from God upon several occasions. God gives some dreams to Pharaoh, the ruler of Egypt, which predict some good years followed by famine years. Joseph gives a wise plan to Pharaoh on how to prepare for it. He is put in charge and is right on target to protect his own family when the famine hits. The family comes to Egypt and rides through the famine years. It stays and expands in the land. Joseph , never losing sight of God's promise, exacts a promise from his brothers and fellow Israelites that they will take him back into the land when God takes them back. That is how Genesis ends.

<u>From Exodus</u>
Exodus opens many years later. There are many Israelite descendants, so many in fact, that the Egyptian King is fearful of them so he subjugates them. They are slaves and being ill-treated. Persecution takes the form of enforced labor and attempts to cut down the population (executing the boy babies).

God, having fulfilled the first part of his plan, getting a people, now works on the second part—getting a leader. Moses, an Israelite baby is preserved providentially and taken into the palace and educated as an Egyptian royal class person. As he reaches adulthood he recognizes that his people by blood relationship are in great bondage. So he wants to free them. His first attempt to help them is a disaster. He kills an Egyptian and has to flee Egypt. He goes to Midian, settles down, marries a Midianite woman, and has a family. After forty years, God selects him via a miraculous revelation, to go back to Egypt to lead God's people out of Egypt and into the promised land. Moses goes back and after 10 major confrontations with the Egyptian ruler (in which God-given power is seen—Moses certainly has spiritual authority) the people are freed to leave. But on the way the Egyptian ruler has second thoughts and pursues with his military. The military should overtake the Israelites who will be trapped by the Red Sea. God miraculously intervenes and they escape across the Red Sea on dry ground. The sea moves back as the military forces start to cross and they are wiped out. This is the heart of *the Exodus*.

From Exodus and Leviticus

God next begins to build the people culturally into what He will need. He gives them the LAW, the second great revelation and reveals more of Himself, His standards, and His purposes. The tabernacle, which He gives the plans for reveals more of who God is in terms of access and revelation. The rest of EXODUS is given to that, revealing who God is as is the whole of LEVITICUS. It is especially in Leviticus that the holiness of God is developed—an understanding of sin and its implications; what atonement is (that is, being made right with God by making up for wrong against Him).

From Numbers

After disobedience and a lack of faith prevent the people from going in to the land (see NUMBERS) they wander for 40 years in the Sinai desert until the older rebellious people die off. During the desert years they learn to trust in God's provision. God reveals Himself primarily through his leader Moses. Near the end of the 40 years they are again ready to go into the land. God has a people, a culture, a leader, Moses, and a leader to take his place, Joshua. Moses prepares them for that push into the land by giving them a series of addresses (DEUTERONOMY—second law). These messages, his final words to them, reflect warnings drawn from their desert experience, remind them of standards of obedience which reflects what they have learned of God, and gives encouragement in the form of expectations as they enter the land. He closes his final words to them with songs of warning and blessing that portend the future. And thus we are ready for the third part of God's plan to build Himself a people—getting them into the land.

From Joshua

Joshua transitions into leadership with some sterling miraculous interventions by God, which give him the spiritual authority he will need to follow Moses (a hard act to follow) as leader. Joshua seizes Jericho, after following a supernaturally revealed plan for its capture. He proceeds after an unexpected failure, which teaches an important corporate lesson on obedience, to the people, to split the land in two militarily and then begins to mop up in the north and south. The land is allotted. Each tribe has a portion, just as Moses had planned. They decentralize and begin to settle into their spots—with much trouble. After having been so long in a centralized authoritarian mode, they enjoy being decentralized and having autonomy. But this decentralization eventually leads to spiritual deterioration. This brings us up into the times of the judges.

From Judges

For a long period of time, longer than we in the United States have been a nation, the twelve tribes live scattered. There is frequent civil war in specific locales and much fighting with various surrounding nations and peoples who were not totally destroyed when the land was taken.

In short there is an oft repeated cycle: the people deteriorate spiritually getting far from God, God brings judgment upon them, they finally recognize that their problem is relationship with God—they repent and cry out for God's help. He sends along leaders, very charismatic who usually lead a volunteer army to defeat their enemies. There are at least 13 of these including: Othniel, Ehud, Shamgar, Deborah (Barak), Gideon, Abimelech, Tola, Jair, Jephthah, Ibzan, Elon, Abdon, and Samson. Some of these are more well known than others. Gideon and Samson for example. These are evil times and few there are who follow God.

In a section of the Judges (Judges 2:7) the writer sums it up well, "After Joshua had dismissed the Israelites, they went to take possession of the land, each to his own inheritance. The people served the Lord through out the lifetime of Joshua and of the elders who outlived him and who had seen all the great things the Lord had done for Israel." And then again in the closing portion a repeated phrase haunts us—Judges 21:25, "In those days Israel had no king; everyone did as he saw fit." These are the pre-kingdom years. Corporately the people are negatively prepared for the kingdom, which will come.

From Ruth

There is a spark of life during those dreadful times. Ruth introduces us to that life by showing that there were some people of integrity who honored the Lord. This little romantic book shows how God provides and also allows us to see how the line through which the redeemer will later arise progresses.

The Judges and Ruth are pre-kingdom times. They prepared the Israelites to want a centralized structure after so much independence and autonomy. The Israelites were dependent upon voluntary armies raised up in times of crisis. Many times, other of the tribes than the one threatened, were not interested in their local squabbles and would not fight for them. Thus the entire commonwealth of tribes comes to the place where it needs, wants, and will accept a kingdom. Again God steps in and provides a transition leader—Samuel.

From 1 Samuel

The first thirteen chapters show how Samuel was providentially raised up as a leader. His ministry as judge was not just a momentary deliverance but a continual one. He visited the different tribes and judged them—that is, established law and justice for them. Samuel paves the way for a centralized kingdom. Crises around the people spur the need; Samuel's own sons are not able to replace him. The people demand a king—showing their need for one but also showing that they basically did not trust the unseen King. God gives them one king, Saul, who outwardly is what they would expect. But he fails repeatedly to follow God. His kingdom is spiritually bankrupt. God replaces him with David, whom God describes as *a man after my own heart*. The last part of 1 Samuel describes Saul's fall and David's early pre-kingdom years, in which David is gaining military expertise as a guerrilla warfare leader with a para-military band.

From 2 Samuel and 1 Chronicles and the Psalms

2 Samuel and 1 Chronicles give David's story—one written earlier to it and one written later. David is a long time in getting the kingdom as Saul's descendants try to hold on to the kingdom. After seven years of civil war, David is ruling a smaller part of Israel, the kingdom is united. God gives a covenant to David concerning his descendants. The poetical literature, particularly the Psalms, emerge more solidly from this era. David is an artistic person who spends time alone with God in worship. Many of the Psalms come out of those times alone with God, many spurred on by crises in David's kingdom. The kingdom is established under David and expands. In mid-life David has a major sin which

tarnishes his lifetime. He has one of his military leaders killed in order that he might take his wife for himself. It and failure to manage his family well lead to a rebellion by one of his sons Absalom. David is deposed briefly but comes back winning a strategic battle. He is reinstated. Most of the rest of his kingdom is downhill. David's son, Solomon, after some manipulation and political intrigue succeeds David.

A number of the Psalms are ascribed to David. They reveal something of the personal touch—what that great leader was feeling during some of the more important times of his kingdom. They particularly show his need for God and why God calls him a "man after my own heart."

From Proverbs and Ecclesiastes

Solomon has the best start of any king in all the history of Israel. There is peace in the land. The borders have expanded almost to the full extent of God's promise. There is money and resources in the kingdom as well as a good military. Times are stable. Solomon builds the temple for God—a symbol of the centralized importance of religious worship in the capital. Solomon's early years are characterized by splendor. Most likely during the early and middle part of his reign many of the Proverbs were collected. These sayings embody truth that has been learned over the years (times of the Judges, times of the kingdom) about how to live harmoniously with others. Toward the end of his reign, he slips and falls away from following God. In this latter part of his reign, he writes Ecclesiastes which sums up much that he has learned over his lifetime. Its cynical tone shows need for an intimate relationship with God that is missing.

The nation is there. There are people. They know of God and his desires for them. There is a land. But they continually fail to live up to what God wants. During the reigns of David and Solomon the kingdom reaches its zenith. And thus ends Chapter 1, the making of a nation. In it all, God is seen to weave His purpose all around a people who frequently rebel against Him. They freely choose to live as they do, whether following after God or not. But even so He manages to move unswervingly forward to His purposes.

Chapter 2. The Destruction of a Nation

The story-line of chapter 2 hinges around the following major events:
1. Solomon goes away from the Lord, great warning—had the best start of any king yet did not finish well.
2. Rehoboam (1 Kings 12) makes unwise decision to increase taxes and demands on people—kingdom splits as prophecy said. 10 tribes go with the northern kingdom, Judah with the southern.
3. The northern kingdom under Jereboam quickly departs from God. Jereboam is used as the model of an evil king to whom all evil kings are likened; He had a good start also—God would have blessed him.
4. The southern kingdom generally is bad with an occasional good Kings and partially good kings: Asa, Jehoshaphat, Joash, Amaziah, Uzziah, Jotham, Hezekiah, Josiah. But the trend was always downward. The extended length of life of the southern kingdom, more than the northern kingdom, is directly attributed to the spiritual life of the better kings. Spiritual leadership does make a difference.
5. During both the northern and southern kingdoms God sent prophets to try and correct them—first the oral prophets (many—but the two most noted were Elijah and Elisha) and then the prophets who wrote.

Now in order to understand this long period of history you should know several things:
1. The History books that give background information about the times.

2. The Bible Time-Line, need to know when the books were written.
3. Need to know the writing prophets: northern or southern kingdom, which crisis, direct or special.

<u>The History Books</u>

The history books covering the time of the destruction of a nation include 1, 2 Samuel, 1,2 Kings, and 1,2 Chronicles. The following chart helps identify the focus of each of these books as to major content.

Chart Ne 1-1 The History Books—Major Content

1 Samuel	2 Samuel 1 Chronicles	1,2 Kings 2 Chronicles
Samuel, Saul, David	David	1,2 Kings: Solomon to Zedekiah 2 Chronicles exclusively on line of Judah

There are four categories of prophetical books. Prophetical books deal with three major crises: the Assyrian crisis which wiped out the northern kingdom; the Bablonian crisis, which wiped out the southern kingdom; the return to the land after being exiled. There are also prophetical books not specifically dealing with these crises but associated with the time of them. The prophetical books dealing with these issues are:

A. Northern—Assyrian Crisis
Jonah, Amos, Hosea, Nahum, Micah
B. Southern—Babylonian Crisis
Joel, Isaiah, Micah, Zephaniah, Jeremiah, Lamentations, Habakkuk, Obadiah
C. In Exile
Ezekiel, Daniel, Esther
D. Return From Exile
Nehemiah, Ezra, Haggai, Zechariah, Malachi

In addition, to knowing the crises you must know that prophets wrote:

A. Direct to the Issue of the Crisis either Assyrian, Babylonian, or Return To The Land
Amos, Hosea, Joel, Micah, Isaiah, Jeremiah, Ezekiel, Haggai , Zechariah, Malachi
B. Special
Jonah, Nahum, Habakkuk, Obadiah, Zephaniah, Daniel.

The special prophets, though usually associated with one of the crisis times, wrote to deal with unique issues not necessarily related directly to the crisis. The following list gives the special prophets and their main thrust.

1. Jonah—a paradigm shift, pointing out God's desire for the nation to be missionary minded and reach out to surrounding nations.
2. Nahum—vindicate God, judgment on Assyria.
3. Habakkuk—faith crisis for Habakkuk, vindicate God, judgment on Babylon.
4. Obadiah—vindicate God, judgment on Edom for treatment of Judah.
5. Zephaniah—show about judgment, the Day of the Lord.

6. Daniel—give hope, show that God is indeed ruling even in the times of the exile and beyond, gives God's plan for the ages.

The Destruction of A Nation—The Return From Exile (see page 32)

Several Bible books are associated with the return to the land from the exile. After a period of about 70 years (during which time Daniel ministered) Cyrus made a decree which allowed some Jews (those that wanted to) to return to the land. Some went back under Zerrubabel, a political ruler like a governor. A priest, Joshua, also provided religious leadership to the first group that went back. This group of people started to rebuild the temple but became discouraged due to opposition and lack of resources. They stopped building the temple. Two prophets, after several years, 10-15, addressed the situation. These two, Haggai and Zechariah, were able to encourage the leadership and the people to finish the temple.

Another thirty or forty years goes by and then we have the events of the book of Esther, back in the land. Her book describes the attempt to eradicate the Jewish exiles—a plot which failed due to God's sovereign intervention via Esther, the queen of the land and a Jewish descendant going incognito, and her relative Mordecai.

Still another period of time passes, 20 or so years and a priest, Ezra, directs another group to return to the land. The spiritual situation has deteriorated. He brings renewal.

Another kind of leader arrives on the scene some 10-15 years later. Nehemiah, a lay leader, and one adept at organizing and moving to accomplish a task, rebuilds the wall around Jerusalem. He too has to instigate renewal.

Finally, after another period of 30 or so years we have the book of Malachi, which again speaks to renewal of the people. The Old Testament closes with this final book.

A recurring emphasis occurs during the period of the return. People are motivated to accomplish a task for God. They start out, become discouraged, and stop. They must be renewed. God raises up leadership to bring renewal.

Preparation for the Coming of Messiah—The Inter-Testamental Period

I do not deal with this in detail, that is, in terms of the various historical eras.[5] Some 400+ years elapse between the close of the Old Testament and the Beginning of the New Testament. There are significant differences in the Promised Land. The following chart highlights these differences.[6]

Chart Ne 1-2 Differences in Palestine—Close of O.T., Beginning of N.T.

The End of the Old Testament	The Beginning of the New Testament
1. Palestine was part of a Persian satrapy, since Persian, an eastern nation was the greatest governmental power in the world at the time.	1. Palestine was a Roman province, since the entire world had come under the sway of the western Nation of Rome.
2. The population was sparse.	2. One of the most dense parts of the Roman empire.
3. The cities of Palestine as a whole were	3. There was general prosperity throughout

---

[5] In **Leadership Perspectives**, I do deal more in a detailed way with the various historical sub-phases of this period of history. A number of books in the Catholic canon occur during this period of time.

[6] These notes are adapted from material studied with Frank Sells at Columbia Bible College in his Old Testament survey course.

heaps of rubbish.	Palestine.
4. The temple of Zerubbabel was a significant structure.	4. The temple of Herod the Great was a magnificent building.
5. There were no Pharisees or Sadducees, although the tendencies from which they developed were present.	5. The Pharisees and Sadducees were much in evidence and strong in power.
6. There were no synagogues in Palestine.	6. Synagogues were located everywhere in the Holy Land. There was no hamlet or village so small or destitute as to lack a synagogue.
7. There was little extra-biblical tradition among the Jews.	7. There was a great mass of tradition, among both the Jews of Palestine and those of the dispersion.
8. The Jews were guilty of much intermarriage with the surrounding nations.	8. There was almost no intermarriage between Jews and non-Jews.
9. Palestine was under the rule of a Hebrew.	9. Palestine was under the rule of an Edomite vice-king, Herod the Great.
10. The Hebrew governor was regarded by the Jews as their spiritual leader.	10. The scribes and priest were regarded by the Jews as their spiritual leaders.

In addition to differences, there were some similarities between end of O.T. times and beginning of N.T. times.

1. **Freedom from idolatry**. God had used the Babylonian Captivity to free His people from their oft-repeated tendency to idolatry.
2. **Israel in two great divisions**, the Jews of the Homeland (Isolation) and the Jews of the Dispersion (who were scattered throughout the world). In the time of Malachi a relatively small proportion of God's chosen people was located in Palestine, while by far the larger part was still in exile. Although Palestine was much more thickly populated in the time of Christ than in the time of Malachi, the same general situation prevailed as to the two-fold division of Israel into Palestinian Jews and Jews of the Diaspora (Dispersion), with a far greater number in exile than in the land of Canaan.
3. **Externalism and dead orthodoxy**. A comparison of Malachi (the last prophetical book of the Old Testament) and Nehemiah (the last historical book of the Old Testament) with the Gospels indicates that the outward conformity of the Pharisees to the law which they inwardly revolted from, was but an advanced step of the hypocritical conformity which had marked many Israelites at the end of Old Testament days.

It was during the inter-testamental period that these changes occurred. Daniel had foretold of the various empires that would emerge after Babylon: the Medo-Persian, the Grecian, and the Roman. Each of these were used by God to prepare the way for the coming of Messiah, the next chapter in the redemptive drama.

Galatians 4:4 states that Messiah came at the "fullness of time." That is, the time was ready. Some have suggested a fivefold preparation for Christ's Coming.

1. Religious Preparation—both negative and positive
2. Political Preparation—world at peace

3. Cultural Preparation—lack of meaning; cultural vehicle through
   which to spread the Gospel
4. The Social Preparation—great needs; life under bondage
5. The Moral Preparation

Chapter 3. Messiah

At the right moment in time—Jesus was born. His miraculous birth attested to his uniqueness.

He was the fulfillment of the Old Testament as to many of its prophecies, types, and symbols. He was the seed of the woman who dealt a fatal blow to the seed of the serpent (Genesis 3:15); he was the tabernacle who lived among us (Exodus 25-40); he was the archetype of the brazen serpent, lifted up that people might look, see and be healed (Numbers 21); he was the archetype of the Levitical offerings , the perfect sacrifice (Leviticus 1-5); he was that prophet like unto Moses (Deuteronomy 18); he was the ultimate fulfillment of the Davidic covenant (2 Samuel 7); he was the Messianic Sufferer (Psalm 22); he was the one who was anointed to preach good news to the poor, to proclaim freedom for the captives, and release from darkness those who are prisoners, to proclaim the year of the Lord's favor (Isaiah 61:1ff) and the Suffering Servant (Isaiah 53); he was the righteous branch from David's line (Jeremiah 23); he was the one shepherd, the servant David, the prince of Ezekiel (Ezekiel 37); he was the one greater than Jonah, the sign after three days he arose (Jonah 2:1ff; Matthew 12:39,40); he was the proper leader coming out of obscure Bethlehem (Micah 5:2); and we could go on.

Matthew showed he was the Messiah King, rejected. Mark showed him to be vested with divine power, a person of action and authority. Luke showed him to be the perfect representative of the human race: one of courage, ability, social interests, sympathy, broad acceptance. And John showed him to be Immanuel, God with us, revealing God to us and acting to demonstrate grace and truth, the heartbeat of the divine ministry philosophy.

The bottom line of the story line is given in a quote taken from John, "He was in the world, and though the world was made through him, the world did not recognize him. He came unto his own, but his own did not receive him. Yet to all who received him, to those who believed in his name, he gave the right to become children of God, children born not of natural descent, nor of human source but born of God. The Word became flesh and made his dwelling among us. We have seen his glory, the glory of the One and Only, who came from the Father, full of grace and truth." (John 1:10-14).

The story of this chapter of the redemptive drama ends abruptly. But there is a postscript. Each of the Gospel stories and the Acts tell us of Jesus Christ's resurrection. After His death He arose and was seen for a period of about 40 days upon various occasions. During those days He gave the marching orders for the movement He had begun. The great commissions repeated five times, Matthew 28:19,20, Luke 24:46,47, Mark 16:15, John 20:21, and Acts 1:8. Each of these carry the main thrust which is to go into the world and tell the Good News of salvation, that people can be reconciled to God. Each also carries some special connotation. It is these marching orders, which set the stage for Chapter 4, The Church, in the redemptive story.

Chapter 4. The Church

The essence of the story line of chapter 4, is contained in the book of Acts. Its central thematic message is the essence of the story line.

Theme: **The Growth Of The Church**
- which spreads from Jerusalem to Judea to Samaria and the uttermost parts of the earth,
- is seen to be of God,
- takes place as Spirit directed people present a salvation centered in Jesus Christ, and
- occurs among all peoples, Jews and Gentiles.

This basic phenomenon reoccurs as the Gospel spreads across cultural barriers throughout the world. Though the message of the book of Acts covers only up through the first two thirds of the first century its basic essence reoccurs throughout the church age until the present time in which we live.

About half of the book of Acts tells of the formation of the church in Jerusalem and its early expansion to Jews, Samaritans, and finally to Gentiles. The latter half of the book traces the breakout of the Gospel to Gentiles in Asia and Europe. The structure of the book highlighted by the linguistic discourse markers (the Word of the Lord grew) carries the notion of a God-given church expanding.

Structure: There are seven divisions in Acts each concluding with a summary verse. The summary verses are: 2:47b, 6:7, 9:31, 12:24, 16:5, 19:20, 28:30,31

I.	(ch 1-2:47)	The Birth of the Church in Jerusalem
II.	(ch 3-6:7)	The Infancy of the Church in Jerusalem
III.	(ch 6:8-9:31)	The Spread of the Church into Judea, Galilee, Samaria
IV.	(ch 9:32-12:24)	The Church Doors Open to the Gentiles
V.	(ch 13-16:5)	The Church Spreads to Asia Minor
VI.	(ch 16:6-19:20)	The Church Gains a Foothold in Europe
VII.	(ch 19:21-28)	The Travels of the Church's First Missionary To Rome (The Church on Trial in Its Representative Paul)

As to details there are many important pivotal events in the Acts, many of which have similarly reoccurred in the expansion of the Gospel around the world and throughout church history. Acts begins with Jesus' post resurrection ministry to the disciples and his Ascension to heaven. Then the disciples are gathered at Jerusalem praying when the Pentecost event, the giving of the Holy Spirit to the church, as promised in Luke's version of the Great Commission, happens and Peter gives a great public sermon which launches the church.

Early church life is described. Peter and John imbued with power heal a lame man at the temple gate and are put in prison. They are threatened and released. An incident with Ananias and Sapphira shows the power and presence of the Holy Spirit.

Stephen an early church servant has a strong witness and is martyred for it. General persecution on the church breaks out. The believers are scattered and preach the gospel where ever they go. Phillip, another early church servant leads an Ethiopian palace administrator to Christ and has ministry in Samaria.

Saul, the persecutor of Christians, is saved on the road to Damascus. Peter demonstrates Godly power in several miraculous events. Peter is divinely chosen to preach the Gospel to a Gentile, Cornelius. Herod kills James and imprisons Peter. Peter is miraculously delivered.

The story line now switches to follow the missionary efforts of Barnabas and Paul (formerly Saul) to Cyprus and Asian minor. It then goes on to follow Paul's efforts which go further into Asia minor and Greece. Paul makes a return visit to Jerusalem where he is accused by the Jewish opposition in Jerusalem. Eventually after several delays and hearings he is ordered to Rome. The book ends with the exciting journey to Rome, including a shipwreck.

The books of the New Testament were written to various groups during the church chapter. Many were written by Paul. These generally were letters to the various churches which had resulted from his missionary efforts. Each was contextually specific—written at a certain time, written at a certain stage of Paul's own development as a leader, and dealing with a specific situation—either an individual in a church or to a corporate group, some church at a location or in a general region.

Other New Testament books were not written by Paul. The book of Hebrews, author uncertain, John's three letters, Jude's one letter and Peter's two letters all are of a general nature. With the exception of possibly 2nd and 3rd John, these letters were written to believer's in general in scattered regions—probably Asia minor.

All of these, Paul's letters, and the general books, deal with the church. They give us insights into church problems, church situations at that time, and the essence of what the church is and how Christians ought to live. These New Testament books are filled with leadership information. Each of them represents a major leadership act of a leader seeking to influence followers of Christ. Many of them have actual details that reflect leadership values, leadership problem solving, and leadership issues. All of them have important modeling data.

We would have an unfinished story if we were left only with *just these* New Testament books. We would have a task. And men and women would be out and about the world attempting to fulfill that task. But where is it leading? What about those Old Testament prophecies yet to be fulfilled about *that day?* Our story is incomplete. We need to know how this redemptive drama is going to end. And so the Revelation.

Chapter 5. The Kingdom
The final book of the Bible is aptly named. The Revelation (unveiling, revealing, making clear) of Jesus Christ (the unveiling of Jesus Christ) brings closure to the redemptive drama. This final book in the Bible has among others these purposes:

1 . to reveal future purposes of Jesus Christ and graphically show the power He will unleash in accomplishing His purposes, which include bringing about justice and bringing in His reign,
2 . to show those purposes and power to be in harmony with His divine attributes, and
3 . to bring a fitting climax to the redemptive story developed throughout Scripture.

The theme statement of the book of Revelation highlights the fitting climax of the redemptive drama.

Theme: **God's Ultimate Purposes For His Redemptive Program**
- center in the Person of His Son,
- involve His churches,
- will take place in a context of persecution and struggle—as described cryptically by many visions,
- will focus on the triumph of Jesus and his judgment of all things in harmony with his divine attributes, and
- will be realized in final victory for His people and ultimate justice accomplished in the world.

God's intent from the first of Genesis on has been to bless His people with His eternal presence. Ezekiel closes his book with that thought in mind. Numerous of the prophets point to a future day in which things would be made right and God would dwell with His people. The plan has had many twists and turns but through it all God has sovereignly moved on to His purpose.

Some have followed hard after God and were included in His purposes. Others refused to follow God. They were cast aside. God moved on.

In the New Testament God prepares a way where He can reveal Himself in justice and love and reconcile all people unto Himself. The Cross climaxes all of God's preparation to bless the world. The message of the Cross is seen to be for all. The church goes out into all the world. It has its problems. But always it seeks to be part of God's future purposes looking forward to Christ's return. Were there no Revelation, the Redemptive Story would be incomplete. The Revelation brings to a fitting climax all of God's working to bless the world. There is an ultimate purpose in history! Justice is meted out! And then a final blessing—God's eternal presence with His people.

Suggested Chronological Writing of New Testament Books
When we study a given book of the Bible we should know where it occurs in the redemptive drama. We should be familiar with what God has revealed to that point in time and what God has done redemptively up to that time. Table Ne 1-1 below lists each book of the Bible in terms of the Chapter in the redemptive story in which it falls. I have attempted to list each book in chronological order though there is not scholarly consensus on when some of these books were written.

Table Ne 1-1. Bible Books Related To Chapters of the Redemptive Drama

The Bible Books: Chapter 1. The Making of a Nation

Exodus	Joshua	2 Samuel	Ecclesiastes
Leviticus	Judges	1 Chronicles	Song of Songs
Numbers	Ruth	Psalms	
Deuteronomy	1 Samuel	Proverbs	

The Bible Books: Chapter 2. The Destruction of a Nation

1,2 Kings	Hosea	Zephaniah	Daniel	Nehemiah
2 Chronicles	Micah	Jeremiah	Haggai	Malachi
Jonah	Isaiah	Lamentations	Zechariah	
Joel	Nahum	Obadiah	Esther	
Amos	Habakkuk	Ezekiel	Ezra	

The Bible Books: Chapter 3. Messiah

Matthew	Mark	Luke	John

1. Biblical Framework—The Redemptive Drama   page 67

The Bible Books: Chapter 4. The Church

James	2 Corinthians	Colossians	Titus	2 John
Acts	Galatians	Philemon	2 Timothy	3 John
1 Thessalonians	Romans	1 Peter	Hebrews	
2 Thessalonians	Ephesians	2 Peter	Jude	
1 Corinthians	Philippians	1 Timothy	1 John	

The Bible Book   Chapter 5. Kingdom
Revelation

2. Biographical Study in the Bible, How To Do

Introduction

Biographical data represents the single most important leadership source in the Scriptures. There is much biographical information.

Definition   Biographical data refers to that large amount of information in the Scriptures which is made up of small narrative slices of life about a person.

These narrative slices or vignettes give information about Bible characters , which allows us to perceive processing, pivotal points, leadership acts or other such interpretations from this source material. The more slices there are the more we can build to a more complete biography.

Sometimes God allows us a glimpse into the inner life of His servants as he develops them. Some books in the Bible are given dominantly just for that purpose. Some do that but have another more important or at least as important other message.

Three such glimpses into God's shaping processes with leaders include Job, Habakkuk, and Jonah. In fact, the major reason for inclusion of these books in the Scriptures is to give us God's ways of working with leaders. Consider the main leadership insights from these three.

1. Job   Isolation processing—most comprehensive treatment of it in the Scriptures; theological delving into the nature of suffering. A paradigm shift concerning the nature of suffering.

2. Habakkuk   Doubting the nature and activities of God. A faith challenge. A paradigm shift about God and his activities.

3. Jonah   Major paradigm shift—how God views others; obedience.

These three books illustrate one of the four types of biographical information in the Scriptures—the critical incident type.

Four Types of Biographical Information

There are four major categories. There is some overlap in these at the borders between them. Table **Ne** 2-1 describes these four sources.

Table Ne 2-1. Four Types of Biographical Sources

Type	Explanation
1. Critical Incident Source.	A single incident or series of incidents taking place in a very short time. There may actually be a large amount of information but all focused on a short time-interval. The information can be interpreted for processing or for a leadership act or other such findings. *example: Job, Habakkuk, Jonah*
2. Mini-Sources.	Multiple incidents over a period of time which allows the creation of an abbreviated time-line and the possibility to see some patterns over time. *example: Asa, Jehoshaphat, Hezekiah*
3. Midi-Sources.	Multiple incidents over the whole lifetime, which allow not only the creation of an abbreviated time-line but some processing from the various time periods. *example: Barnabas, Joseph, Daniel, Joshua, Peter, Jeremiah*
4. Maxi-Sources.	There is much information in the Scripture on the character. *example: Moses, David, Jesus, Paul, Jeremiah*

Biblical Leaders To Study
     I list here those Biblical leaders who should be studied because they will give information essential or very helpful for leadership.   Some of these lessons will be positive encouragement. Some will present warnings. There are four groupings that should be studied. I have not listed all that I could. You may want to add to these different lists.

List Ne 2-1 All Who Finished Well (Mini, Midi, Maxi Types)

1. Abraham	6. Samuel	11. Jesus	16. Isaac
2. Joseph	7. Elijah	12. Paul	
3. Moses	8. Elisha	13. Peter	
4. Joshua	9. Daniel	14. John	
5. Caleb	10. Jeremiah	15. Jacob	

By finished well I mean that at the end of their lifetime they:
1. were enjoying intimacy with God,
2. were still growing, had a learning posture,
3. left behind a legacy—achieved things for God that contributed to his on-going redemptive plan,
4. realized potential, achieved their destiny: a. fully; b. limited; c. somewhat,
5. had Godly character,
6. had lived out convictions about God's truth and promises and demonstrate them to be real.

List Ne 2-2. Some—Not Sure About Their Finish (Mini, Midi, Maxi Types)
1. Nehemiah
2. Jephthah

List Ne 2-3. Some Who Did Not Finish Well (Mini, Midi, Maxi Types)

1. Gideon	6. Hezekiah	11. Others—you add them on:
2. Saul	7. Asa	
3. David	8. Jehoshaphat	
4. Solomon	9. Josiah	
5. Uzziah	10. Samson	

List Ne 2-4. Critical Incident Types

1. Job	6. Abigail	11. Deborah
2. Habakkuk	7. Mordecai	12. Barak
3. Jonah	8. Isaiah	13. Timothy
4. Ezra	9. Ezekiel	14. Titus
5. Esther	10. Hosea	

The basic approach to the study of Biblical leaders includes 12 steps. But depending on which type you are studying you may or may not be able to use all the steps. Such is the case especially with the first three types of biographies. The commentaries on Habakkuk and Jonah illustrate the benefit of studying critical incidents.

12 Steps For Studying Bible Leaders

The following outline gives a basic approach to biographical study in the Bible. Not all 12 steps can be done with each leader but they provide the ideal framework that should be attempted. Do as many of the 12 steps as you can, depending on the material available for a leader.

<u>Step 1</u>. **Identify All The Passages That Refer To The Leader.**
  a. Use an exhaustive concordance to help you identify all such passages.
  b. There are two kinds of passages:
    (1) *Direct,* which refers to actual historical vignettes—a short literary sketch of a given slice of life, which gives raw data about the person and his/her actions. This is data that can be interpreted for leadership findings.
    (2) *Indirect,* not actual vignettes but references to the leader or accomplishments usually in retrospect such as summary passages, intentional selection which groups several important names, etc.
  c. For the *Direct*—actual historical vignettes—Number and label each vignette separately for reference.
  d. For the *Indirect*—note the commentary on the leader. What was said? Why important? Why remembered? Why selected? Ultimate contribution? Some trait or characteristic?
  e. Books written by the leader or prophecies made by the leader.

<u>Step 2</u>. **Seek To Order The Vignettes Or Other Passages In A Time Sequence.**
  a. Bible dictionaries or encyclopedias usually have articles on most Bible characters. These articles usually help in establishing time of events in the life. Actual vignettes as given in the Bible may be out of chronological order (e.g. Jeremiah).
  b. Remember the time period in the progress of redemption in which the leader is acting. Put the leadership in the broader time framework.
  c. Remember the leadership era in which the leader is acting. Remember what is expected of a leader in that era. Remember the kind of leader he or she is and the basic thrust of leadership for that kind of leader at that time.
  d. Note how the leader fits those stereotypes or doesn't.
  e. Notice if the leader is breaking new ground.

<u>Step 3</u>. **Construct A Time-Line If You Can. At Least Tentatively Identify Major Development Phases.**
  a. See **Article,** *Time Line Defined for Biblical Leaders.* See also examples of time-lines. See Joseph, Barnabas, and Joshua for examples.
  b. Sometimes not enough information is given to fill out the time-line completely. You can tentatively construct to fill in gaps as long as you know it is only suggestive.

    c. Be especially alert to how the leader finished.

    d. Check for the six major barriers to finishing well: sex, family, money, pride, power, plateauing and locate along the time-line.

    e. Check for any of the five major enhancements to finishing well: life time perspective, renewal experiences, guarding of the inner life with God—spiritual disciplines, mentoring, learning posture. Locate along the time-line.

    f. See if the person's life illustrates or sheds light on any of the seven major leadership lessons: lifetime perspective, power base, ministry philosophy, learning posture, leadership emergence, relational empowerment, sense of destiny.

<u>Step 4</u>. **Look For Process Items (Critical Events, People, Happenings) In The Life.**

    a. **The Making of A Leader** by Clinton or **Leadership Emergence Theory** defines process items in-depth, that is, shaping activities used by God. Usually a critical incident can be viewed through several process item grids. *See process item definitions,* **Glossary.**

    b. But even if you do not know the names of processes you can analyze what happened in some critical situation.

<u>Step 5</u>. **Identify Pivotal Points From The Major Process Items.**

    a. Seek to identify the kind of pivotal point it is. See *pivotal point,* **Glossary.**

    b. Seek to determine what might have happened or the after effects of the pivotal point. Various kinds of lessons can be learned from this analysis.

    c. How can knowing about this pivotal point be of aid to other leaders or emerging leaders? See **Article,** *Pivotal Points.*

<u>Step 6</u>. **Seek To Determine Any Lessons You Can From A Study Of These Process Items And Pivotal Points. Use The Certainty Continuum To Help You Identify The Level Of Authority For Using The Lessons You Find.** See **Article,** *Principles of Truth.*

    a. Seek to identify specific lessons first (use wording of the specific situation, time, place, and person concerned).

    b. Seek to abstract the specific lessons into wording that could apply more broadly.

    c. Assess the level of authority for application of the lesson. See **Article,** *Principles of Truth.*

<u>Step 7</u>. **Identify Any Response Patterns** (or unique patterns).

    a. The **Leadership Emergence Theory** Manual identifies 23 patterns. The *Destiny Pattern* is especially helpful. Use the patterns to help you see ideas and lessons in the leader's life. See *patterns; destiny processing; destiny patterns, Four Types;* **Glossary.** See **Article,** *Destiny Pattern.*

    b. Look for unique patterns that only fit the leader's life.

<u>Step 8</u>. **Study Any Individual Leadership Acts In The Life. Use The Approach Demonstrated In This Chapter.** See *leadership act,* **Glossary.**

    a. Identify leadership style(s).

    b. Identify the situation—look for any dynamics, micro or macro that shed light on the situation.

    c. Study the followership. See **Article,** *Followership—10 Commandments.*

<u>Step 9</u>. **Use The Overall Leadership Tree Diagram To Help Suggest Leadership Issues To Look For.** See Article, *Leadership Tree Diagram.*
  a. Use the basal elements to suggest things to look for.
  b. Use the influence means (individual) to help you suggest things to look for, i.e. look at the leader in terms of leadership style theory.
  c. Use the influence means (spiritual power) to help you suggest things to look for.
  d. Use the influence means (corporate) to analyze the power situations wrapped up in institutions, or tradition, or cultural family patterns.
  e. Use the value bases to help you identify values—philosophical or cultural or theological that are worth noting.

<u>Step 10</u>. **Use The List Of Major Functions (Task Functions, Relationship Functions And Inspirational Functions) To Help Suggest Insights. Which Were Done, Which Not.** See Article, *Leadership Functions.*
  a. Were there relational functions in view?
  b. Were there task functions in view?
  c. Were there inspirational functions in view? Usually you will always have something on this function.

<u>Step 11</u>. **Observe Any N.T. Passages Or Commentary** (indirect source—anywhere in Bible) **On The Leader. Especially Be On The Lookout For** *Bent Of Life* **Evaluation.**
  a. For example, Ezekiel refers to Daniel three times. This is actually a contemporary evaluation of Daniel. See Eze14:14,20; 28:3. Three names are listed in the first two: Noah, Daniel, and Job. These are intentionally selected—the focus is righteousness. The third commends Daniel's wisdom. This is bent-of-life testimony. This is what stands out as an important thing to be remembered about the character. These kinds of hints can then lead you back to the direct data for focused study. That is, now go back and study these three characters for ideas on righteousness. Study Daniel for ideas about wisdom in a leader.
  b. The N.T. references are usually bent of life types. See Ro 4:20,21 about Abraham and his faith. See Ac 7 for Stephen's comments. All of these indirect type of references give us focuses with which to go back and search the direct data. See *bent of life*, **Glossary**.

<u>Step 12</u>. **Use The Presentation Format For Organizing Your Display Of Findings For Steps 1-11.**
  a. The presentation format is a technical layout for presenting the highlights of your data. The order of presentation is logically arranged.
  b. This standardized approach to presenting findings is used by me and by all that I teach in workshops, seminars, and classes. It makes for ease of referencing material.
  c. For popular consumption (articles, booklets, books, public preaching, etc.) you would not use this technical format but take out of it that which you want to use.

Presentation Format—Findings On Bible Leaders

The following is a logical order of presenting data. It is standardized for reference purposes. When doing an actual study, the information available on the character and the nature of the findings will actually determine which of these categories are actually filled. Attempt to do them all.

1. *Biblical Name(s)*—Primary: Other:

2. *Biblical Data*:
   Here list the direct contextual material on the leader studied, the indirect references to the leader, and note especially any summary passages on the leader (if an O.T. leader look especially for N.T. references or assessment on that leadership).

3. *Abbreviated Time-Line*:
   Construct a time-line with development phases—as much as possible from the data given. Recognize that the time-line is incomplete (if more data were given—more phases or sub-phases probably could be distinguished).

4. *Giftedness Indications*:
   If O.T., then list areas of natural abilities, acquired skills or special anointings seen in the leader's life. If N.T., attempt to identify gift-mix or gift-cluster.

5. *Sphere of Influence*:
   Here give the followership being influenced. If possible note direct, indirect or organizational categories.

6. *Major Contributions*
   Assess the leader's achievements in God's on-going redemptive program in the Bible.

7. *Biblical Context*
   Here use the overview of Biblical Leadership Time-line. You want to place this leader, contextually, in terms of kind of leadership expected during that time period.

8. *Capsule*
   Give a narrative overview of the leader's life in paragraph format based on a linear time organization of Bible vignettes or data. This narration should follow the time-line and give information that allows one to put the major findings in context.

9. *Major Lessons*
   A. Pivotal Points
   B. Major Processing
   C. Barriers to finishing
      Well
   D. Here include lessons learned from leadership acts
      —Give actual analysis in an Appendix attached to the presentation.
   E. General/ Other
   F. Major Lessons Stated

10. *Ultimate Contribution Set*
    Here use the categories from the ultimate contribution explanation to assess the long term achievement of this leader. See *ultimate contribution set*, **Glossary**. See **Article**, *Leaving Behind a Legacy*.

11. *Appendices*:
    Here you would include any leadership acts analyzed or any other pertinent information such as family tree diagrams, etc.

Conclusion
   You will not have enough time in your lifetime to learn all you can about leadership through your direct experience or even observation of it around you. You will need to learn vicariously, that is, study and learn from the lives of others. The Bible is probably one of the richest sources for leadership study. And biographical information is the largest single leadership genre. Make the most of it.

3. Figures and Idioms In The Bible

Introduction to Figures

All language is governed by law—that is, it has normal patterns that are followed. But in order to increase the power of a word or the force of expression, these patterns are deliberately departed from, and words and sentences are thrown into and used in unusual forms or patterns which we call figures. A figure then is a use of language in a special way for the purpose of giving additional force, more life, intensified feeling and greater emphasis. A figure of speech is the author's way of underlining. He/She is saying, "Hey, take note! This is important enough for me to use a special form of language to emphasize it!" And when we remember the fact that the Holy Spirit has inspired this product we have—the Bible—we are not far wrong in saying figures are the Holy Spirit's own underlining in our Bibles. We certainly need to be sensitive to figurative language.

Definition   A figure is the unusual use of a word or words differing from the normal use in order to draw special attention to some point of interest.

For a figure, the unusual use itself follows a set pattern. The pattern can be identified and used to interpret the figure in normal language. Here are some examples from the Bible. I will make you fishers of people. Go tell that fox. Quench not the Holy Spirit. I came not to send peace but a sword. As students of the Bible we need to be sensitive to figures and know how to interpret and catch their emphatic meaning.

Definition   A figure or idiom is said to be captured when one can display the intended emphatic meaning in non-figurative simple words.

One of the most familiar figures in the Bible is Psalm 23:1. The Lord is my shepherd. I shall not lack. *Captured*: God personally provides for my every need.

E.W. Bullinger, an expert on figurative language, lists over 400 different kinds of figures. he lists over 8000 references in the Bible containing figures. In Romans alone, Bullinger lists 253 passages containing figurative language. However, we do not need to know all of those figures for the most commonly occurring figures number much less than 400. Figure Ne 3-1, below, lists the 11 most common figures occurring in the Bible. If we know them we are well on our way to becoming better interpreters of the Scripture. In fact, you can group these 11 figures under three main sub-categories, which simplifies learning about them.

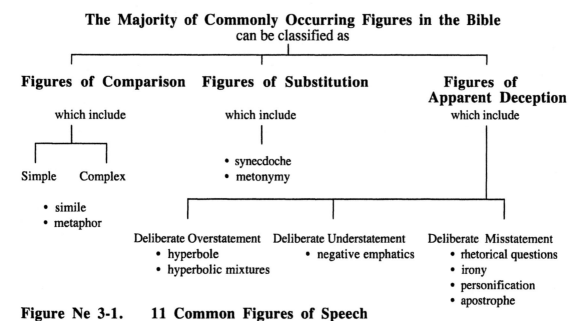

Figure Ne 3-1.   11 Common Figures of Speech

Table Ne 3-1 below gives these 11 figures of speech, a Scriptural reference containing the figure, and the basic definition of each of these figures.

Table Ne 3-1. 11 Figures in the Bible Defined

Category/ Figure	Scriptural Example	Definition
Figures of Comparison: 1. Simile 2. Metaphor	simile—Isa 53:6 metaphor—Ps 23:1	A <u>simile</u> is a stated comparison of two unlike items (one called the real item and the other the picture item) in order to display one graphic point of comparison. A <u>metaphor</u> is an implied comparison in which two unlike items (a real item and a picture item) are equated to point out one point of resemblance.
Figures of Substitution 3. Metonymy 4. Synecdoche	metonymy—Ac 15:21 Moses for what he wrote synecdoche— Mt 8:8 roof for the whole house.	A <u>metonymy</u> is a figure of speech in which (usually) one word is substituted for another word to which it is closely related in order to emphasize something indicated by the relationship. A <u>synecdoche</u> is a special case of metonymy in which (again usually) one word is substituted for another to which it is related as, a part to a whole or a whole to a part.
Figures of Apparent Deception— Deliberate Overstatement: 5. Hyperbole 6. Hyperbolic mixtures	hyperbole—1 Co 4:14-16 ten thousand instructors hyperbolic mixture—2 Sa 1:23 swifter	A <u>hyperbole</u> is the use of conscious exaggeration (an overstatement of truth) in order to emphasize or strikingly excite interest in the truth. Hyperbole is sometimes combined with other figures such as comparison and substitution. When such is the case it is called a <u>hyperbolic mixture</u> figure.

	than eagles, stronger than lions	
Figures of Apparent Deception— Deliberate understatement: 7. Negative emphatics	negative emphatics—Mk 12:34 not far = very near	A figure of <u>negative emphasis</u> represents the deliberate use of words to diminish a concept and thus call attention to it or the negating of a concept to call attention to the opposite positive concept (I have deliberately merged two figures, litotes and tapenosis into one because of the basic sameness of negative emphasis).
Figures of Apparent Deception— Deliberate Misstatement: 8. Rhetorical questions 9. Irony 10. Personification 11. Apostrophe	rhetorical question—1Ti 3:5 irony—2Co 12:13 personification —Heb 4:12 apostrophe—1 Co 15:55	A <u>rhetorical question</u> is a figure of speech in which a question is not used to obtain information but is used to indirectly communicate, (1) an affirmative or negative statement, or (2) the importance of some thought by focusing attention on it, or (3) one's own feeling or attitudes about something. <u>Irony</u> is the use of words by a speaker in which his/her intended meaning is the opposite of (or in disharmony with) the literal use of the words. <u>Personification</u> is the use of words to speak of animals, ideas, abstractions, and inanimate objects as if they had human form, character, or intelligence in order to vividly portray truth. <u>Apostrophe</u> is a special case of personification in which the speaker addresses the thing personified as if it were alive and listening.

I have developed in-depth explanations for all of the above figures. I have developed study sheets to aid one in analysis of them. Further I have actually identified many of these in the Scriptures and captured a number of them.[7]

Introduction to Idioms

Idioms are much more complicated than figures of speech.

Definition An <u>idiom</u> is a group of words, which have a corporate meaning that can not be deduced from a compilation of the meanings of the individual words making up the idiom.

What makes idioms difficult is that some of them follow patterns while others do not. For the patterned idioms, like figures, you basically reverse the pattern and capture the idiom. Table Ne 3- 2 lists the patterned idioms I have identified in the Bible.

Table Ne 3-2. 13 Patterned Idioms

Idiom	Example	Definitive principle/ Description
Three Certainty Idioms: 1. Double certainty (pos/neg) 2. Fulfilled (promised/proposed)	double certainty— 1Ki 18:36 fulfilled— Ge 15:18 prophetic past—Jn	<u>double certainty</u>—a negative and positive statement (in either order) are often used to express or imply certainty. <u>fulfillment</u>—in the fulfillment idiom things are spoken of as given, done, or possessed, which are only promised or proposed. <u>prophetic past</u>—in the prophetic past idiom the

---

[7] See my self-study manual, **Interpreting the Scriptures: Figures and Idioms.**

3. Prophetic past	13:31	past tense is used to describe or express the certainty of future action.
4. Superlative (repetitive superlative)	Ge 9:25 servant of servants Isa 26:3 peace, peace = perfect peace 2Ti 4:7	The Hebrew superlative is often shown by the repetition of the word. Paul uses a variation of this by often using the noun form and a verb form of the same word either back to back or in close proximity. (the good struggle I have struggled).
5. Emphatic comparisons	1Pe 3:3,4	This takes three forms: absolute for relative: one thing (importance or focus item) is emphasized as being much more important in comparison with the other thing (the denial item). The form not A but B really means A is less important than B. relative for absolute: One thing is positively compared to another when in effect it is meant to be taken absolutely and the other denied altogether. abbreviated emphatic comparisons: Half of the comparison is not given (either the focus item or denial items). Half of the statement is given. The half missing is an example of ellipsis and is to be supplied by the reader.
6. Climactic arrangement	Pr 6:16-19 Ro 3:10-18	To emphasize a particular item it is sometimes placed at the bottom of a list of other items and is thus stressed in the given context as being the most important item being considered.
7. Broadened kinship	Ge 29:5	Sometimes the terms son of, daughter of, mother of, father of, brother of, sister of, or begat, which in English imply a close relationship have a much wider connotation in the Bible. Brother and sister could include various male and female relatives such as cousins; mother and father could include relatives such as grandparents or great-great-grandparents, in the direct family line; begat may simply mean was directly in the family line of ancestors.
8. Imitator	Ge 6:2, 11:5	To indicate that people or things are governed by or are characterized by some quality, they are called children of or a son of or daughter of that quality.
9. Linked noun	Lk 21:15	Occasionally two nouns are linked together with a conjunction in which the second noun is really to be used like an adjective modifying the first noun.
Indicator Idioms: 10. City indicator 11. List indicator 12. Strength Indicator	city indicator La 1:16, daughter of Zion list indicator Pr 6:16, these 6 yea	City indicator—idiomatic words, daughter of or virgin of or mother of. List indicator—2 consecutive numbers—designates an incomplete list of items of which the ones on the list are representative; other like items could be included. Strength indicator—a horn denotes aggressive strength or power or authority.

	7 Strength indicator 1Sa 2:1,10	
13. Anthropomorphism	Lk 11:20	In order to convey concepts of God, <u>human passions, or actions, or attributes are used to describe God.</u>

In addition, to the patterned idioms there are a number of miscellaneous idioms, which either occur infrequently or have no discernible pattern. I have labeled 32. Their meaning must be learned from context, from other original language sources, or from language experts' comments, etc.

Table Ne 3-3.   15 Body Language Idioms

Name	Word, Phrase, Usually Seen	Example	Meaning or Concept Involved
1. Foot gesture	shake off the dust	Mt 10:14, Lk 9:5 et al	have nothing more to do with them
2. Mouth gesture	gnash on them with teeth; gnashing of teeth	Ps 35:16; 37:12 Ac 7:54 et al	indicates angry and cursing words given with deep emotion and feeling
3. Invitation	I have stretched forth my hand(s)	Ro 10:21; Pr 1:24; Is 49:22	indicates to invite, or to receive or welcome or call for mercy
4. New desire	enlighten my eyes, lighten my eyes	Ps 13:3; 19:8; 1Sa 14:29; Ezr 9:8	to give renewed desire to live; sometimes physical problem, sometimes motivational inward attitude problem
5. Judgment	to stretch forth the hand; to put forth the hand	Ex 7:5; Ps 138:7; Job 1:11	to send judgment upon; to inflict with providential punishment
6. Fear	to shake the hand, to not find the hand, knees tremble	Is 19:16; Ps 76:8	to be afraid; to be paralyzed with fear and incapable of action.
7. Increase punishment	to make the hand heavy	Ps 32:4	to make the punishment more severe
8. Decreased punishment	to make the hands light	1Sa 6:5	to make punishment less severe
9. Remove punishment	to withdraw the hands	Eze 20:22	to stop punishment
10. Repeat punishment	to turn the hand upon	Is 1:25	to repeat again some punishment which was not previously heeded
11.	to open the	Ps 104:28;	to generously give or bestow

Generosity	hand	145:16	
12. Anger	to clap the hands together	Eze 21;17; 22:13	to show anger; to express derision
13. Oath	to lift up the hand	Ex 6:8; 17:16; De 32:40; Eze 20:5,6	to swear in a solemn way; take an oath; an indicator of one's integrity to consider worthy to be accepted; to accept someone or be accepted by someone
14. Promise	to strike with the hands (with someone else)	Pr 6:1; Job 17:3	become a co-signer on a loan; to conclude a bargain
15. Accept	to lift up the face	Nu 6:26; Ezr 9:6; Job 22:26	to consider worthy to be accepted; to accept someone or be accepted by someone

Table Ne 3-4. 14 Miscellaneous Idioms

Name	Word, Phrase, Usually Seen	Example	Meaning or Concept Involved
1. Success	tree of life	Pr 3:18; 11:30; 13:12; 15:4	idea of success, guarantee of success, source of motivation to successful life
2. Speech cue	answered and said	Mt 11:25; 13:2 and many others	indicates manner of speaking denoted by context; e.g. responded prayed, asked, addressed, etc.
3. Notice	verily, verily	Many times in Jn	I am revealing absolute and important truth; give close attention (this is a form of the superlative idiom)
4. Time	___ days and ___ nights	Jn 1:17; Mt 12:40; 1Sa 30:11; Est 4:16	any portion of time of a day is indicated by or represented by the entire day
5. Lifetime	forever and ever	Ps 48;14 and many others	does not mean eternal life as we commonly use it but means all through my life; as long as I live
6. Separation	what have I to do with you	Jn 2:4; Jdg 11;12; 2Sa 16:10; 1Ki 17;18; 2Ki 3;13; Mt 8:29; Mk 5:7; Lk 8:28	an expression of indignation or contempt between two parties having a difference or more specifically not having something in common; usually infers that some action about to take place should not take place
7. Reaction	heap coals of fire	Ro 12:20; Pr 25:21	to incur God's favor by reacting positively to a situation in which revenge would be normal
8. Orate	open the mouth	Job 3:1	to speak at great length with great liberty or freedom

9. Claim	you say	Mt 26:25,63,64	means it is your opinion
10. Excellency	living, lively	Jn 4:10,11 Ac 7:38; Heb 10:20; 1Pe 2:4,5; Rev 1:17	used to express the excellency of perfection of that to which it refers
11. Abundance	riches	Ro 2:4; Eph 1:7; 3:8; Col 1:27; 2:2	used to describe abundance of or a great supply
12. Preeminence	firstborn	Ps 89:27; Ro 8:29; Col 1;15, 18; Heb 12:23	special place of preeminence; first place among many others
13. Freedom	enlarge my feet; enlarge	2Sa 22:37; Ps 4:1; 18:36	freed me; brought me into a situation that has taken the pressure off, taken on to bigger and better things
14. Reverential respect for	fear and trembling	Ps 55:5; Mk 5:33; Lk 8:47; 1Co 2:3; 2 Co 7:15; Eph 6:5, Php 2:12	describes an attitude of appropriate respect for something. The something could be God, could be a person, or could be a combination including some process. Sometimes indicates confronting a difficult situation or thing with a strong awareness of it and possible consequences

Again I would recommend you refer to my manual **Figures and Idioms** to see the approach for capturing the patterned idioms.

Figures and Idioms should be appreciated, understood, and should be interpreted with emphasis. Hardly any passage, which is any one of the seven leadership genre, will be without some figure or idiom.

Closure
This article is included in the Nehemiah commentary for two reasons. One, you need to be aware of the importance of figures and idioms when studying the Bible and this article gives a rather complete source (relatively, that is,) for help in that direction. Two, Nehemiah uses rhetorical questions as a confrontational device. And you might just discover other figures.

4. Finishing Well— Five Factors That Enhance It

Introduction

In 1989 in an article entitled, *Listen Up Leaders! Forewarned is Forearmed!* I summarized my research on Biblical leaders with the following opening comments.

A repeated reading of the Bible with a focus on leadership reveals four crucial observations fraught with leadership implications:

Observation 1. Few leaders finish well.
Observation 2. Leadership is difficult.
Observation 3. God's enabling presence is the essential ingredient of successful leadership.
Observation 4. Spiritual leadership can make a difference.

And what is true of Biblical leaders is equally true of historical and contemporary leaders.[8] It is the first observation to which this article speaks. Identifying the fact that few leaders finish well was a breakthrough warning for me. This led to further study. Why do few leaders finish well? What stops them? What helps them?

Five Enhancements

Comparative study of effective leaders who finished well has identified five commonalities. Not all five always appear in leaders who finish well but at least several of them do. Frequently, effective leaders who finish well will have four or five of them seen in their lives. What are these enhancements?

Enhancement 1. Perspective.

We need to have a lifetime perspective on ministry. Effective leaders view present ministry in terms of a lifetime perspective.[9] We gain that perspective by studying lives of leaders as commanded in Hebrews 13:7,8. I have been doing intensive study of leaders' lives over the past 13 years. Leadership emergence theory is the result of that research. Its many concepts can help us understand more fully just how God does shape a leader over a lifetime.[10]

---

[8] At the time of this article I have studied nearly 1300 cases with about 50 Bible leaders, perhaps 100 historical leaders and the rest contemporary leaders. The findings for enhancements and barriers generally hold true.

[9] This is one of seven major leadership lessons derived from comparative studies. See **Article**, *Seven Major Leadership Lessons.*

[10] My findings are available in two books, **The Making of A Leader**, published by Nav Press in 1988 and a lengthy detailed self-study manual, **Leadership Emergence Theory**, that I privately publish for use in classes and workshops. In addition, my latest research is available in position papers published by Barnabas Publishers. See **For Further Study Bibliography** for full listings of these books.

Enhancement 2.   Renewal.

Special moments of intimacy with God, challenges from God, new vision from God and affirmation from God both for personhood and ministry will occur repeatedly to a growing leader. These destiny experiences will be needed, appreciated, and will make the difference in persevering in a ministry. All leaders should expectantly look for these repeated times of renewal. Some can be initiated by the leader (usually extended times of spiritual disciplines). But some come sovereignly from God. We can seek them, of course, and be ready for them.

Most leaders who have been effective over a lifetime have needed and welcomed renewal experiences from time to time in their lives. Some times are more crucial in terms of renewal than others. Apparently in western society the mid-thirty's and early forty's and mid-fifty's are crucial times in which renewal is frequently needed in a leader's life. Frequently during these critical periods discipline slacks, there is a tendency to plateau and rely on one's past experience and skills, and a sense of confusion concerning achievement and new direction prevail. Unusual renewal experiences with God can overcome these tendencies and redirect a leader. An openness for them, a willingness to take steps to receive them, and a knowledge of their importance for a whole life can be vital factors in profiting from **enhancement 2** for finishing well. Sometimes these renewal experiences are divinely originated by God and we must be sensitive to his invitation. At other times we must initiate the renewal efforts.

Enhancement 3. Disciplines.

Leaders need discipline of all kinds. Especially is this true of spiritual disciplines. A strong surge toward spirituality now exists in Catholic and Protestant circles. This movement combined with an increasingly felt need due to the large number of leadership failures is propelling leaders to hunger for intimacy. The spiritual disciplines are one mediating means for getting this intimacy. Such authors as Eugene Peterson, Dallas Willard, and Richard Foster are making headway with Protestants concerning spirituality.[11] Leaders without these leadership tools are prone to failure via sin as well as plateauing.

I concur with Paul's admonitions to discipline as a means of insuring perseverance in the ministry. When Paul was around 50 years of age he wrote to the Corinthian church what appears to be both an exhortation to the Corinthians and an explanation of a major leadership value in his own life. We need to keep in mind that he had been in ministry for about 21 years. He was still advocating strong discipline. I paraphrase it in my own words.

> **I am serious about finishing well in my Christian ministry. I discipline myself for fear that after challenging others into the Christian life I myself might become a casualty.** 1Co 9:24-27

Lack of physical discipline is often an indicator of laxity in the spiritual life as well. Toward the end of his life, Paul is probably between 65 and 70, and he is still advocating discipline. This time he writes to Timothy, who is probably between 30 and 35 years old.

> **...Instead exercise your mind in godly things. 8 For physical exercise is advantageous somewhat but exercising in godliness has long term implications both for today and for that which will come.** (1Ti 4:7b,8)

---

[11] See also my section on spiritual guides and the appendix on the disciplines in **The Mentor Handbook,** available through Barnabas Publishers. See **Article,** *Spiritual Disciplines and On-Going Leadership.*

Leaders should from time to time assess their state of discipline. I recommend in addition to standard word disciplines involving the devotional life and study of the Bible other disciplines such as solitude, silence, fasting, frugality, chastity, secrecy. My studies of Foster and Willard have helped me identify a number of disciplines which can habitually shape character and increase the probability of a good finish.

Enhancement 4. Learning Posture.

The single most important antidote to plateauing is a well developed learning posture. Such a posture is also one of the major ways through which God gives vision. I will describe more about how to do this in the commentary which follows.

Another of the seven major leadership lessons is *Effective leaders maintain a learning posture all their lives.* It sounds simple enough but many leaders don't heed it. Two Biblical leaders who certainly were learners all their lives and exemplified this principle were Daniel and Paul. Note how Daniel observed this principle. In Da 9 when he is quite old we find that he was still studying his Bible and still learning new things from it. And he was alert to what God wanted to do through what he was learning. Consequently, Daniel was able to intercede for his people and become a recipient of one of the great messianic revelations. Paul's closing remarks to Timothy show he was still learning. "And when you come don't forget the books Timothy!" (2Ti 4:13).

There are many non-formal training events available such as workshops, seminars, and conferences covering a variety of learning skills. Take advantage of them. A good learning posture is insurance against plateauing and a helpful prod along the way to persevere in leadership. An inflexible spirit with regards to learning is almost a sure precursor to finishing so-so or poorly.

Enhancement 5. Mentoring.

Comparative study of many leaders lives indicates the frequency with which other people were significant in challenging them into leadership and in giving timely advice and help so as to keep them there. Leaders who are effective and finish well will have from 10 to 15 significant people who came alongside at one time or another to help them. Mentoring is also a growing movement in Christian circles as well as secular.

The general notion of mentoring involves a relational empowerment process in which someone who knows something (the mentor) passes on something (wisdom, advice, information, emotional support, protection, linking to resources) to someone who needs it (the mentoree, protégé) at a sensitive time so that it impacts the person's development. The basic dynamics of mentoring include attraction, relationship, response, accountability and empowerment. My observations on mentoring suggest that most likely, any leader will need a mentor at all times over a lifetime of leadership. Mentoring is available if one looks for specific functions and people who can do them (rather than an ideal mentor who can do all). God will provide a mentor in a specific area of need for you if you trust Him for one and you are willing to submit and accept responsibility.

Simply stated a final suggestion for enabling a good finish is find a mentor who will hold you accountable in your spiritual life and ministry and who can warn and advise so as to enable you to avoid pitfalls and to grow throughout your lifetime of ministry.

Conclusion

A leader ought to want to finish well. I never give this warning, few leaders finish well, and this challenge, do you want to finish well?, without an overwhelming response. Yes, I do. Then heed these five factors. Proactively take steps to get these factors working in your life. Finish well!!!

See **Articles**: *5. Finishing Well--Six Characteristics; Leadership Lessons—Seven Major Lessons Identified.*

5. Finishing Well—Six Characteristics

Introduction to Research on Finishing Well

In 1989 in an article entitled, *Listen Up Leaders! Forewarned is Forearmed!* I summarized my research on Biblical leaders with the following opening comments.

A repeated reading of the Bible with a focus on leadership reveals four crucial observations fraught with leadership implications:

Observation 1. Few leaders finish well.[12]
Observation 2. Leadership is difficult.
Observation 3. God's enabling presence is the essential ingredient of successful leadership.
Observation 4. Spiritual leadership can make a difference.

And what is true of Biblical leaders is equally true of historical and contemporary leaders.[13] It is the first observation to which this article speaks. Identifying the fact that few leaders finish well was a breakthrough warning for me. This led to further study. Why do few leaders finish well? What stops them? What helps them? What does it mean to finish well? This article identifies six characteristics of those finishing well.

Six Characteristics

Comparative study of effective leaders who finished well has identified six characteristics. While there may be other characteristics that I have not seen, certainly these are important ones. Not all six always appear but at least several of them do in leaders who finish well. Frequently, effective leaders who finish well will have four or five of them seen in their lives. And some, like Daniel in the O.T. and Paul in the N.T. demonstrate all of them. What are these six characteristics of those finishing well.

Characteristic 1.
They maintain a personal vibrant relationship with God right up to the end.

Example: Daniel is the classic O.T. leader who exemplifies this. In the N.T., Peter, Paul and John all demonstrate this. See their last writings—the tone, the touch with God, the revelation from God, their trust in enabling grace for their lives.

---

[12] There are around 800 or so leaders mentioned in the Bible. There are about 100 who have data that helps you interpret their leadership. About 50 of these have enough data for evaluation of their finish. About 1 in 3 finished well. Anecdotal evidence from today indicates that this ratio is probably generous. Probably less than 1 in 3 are finishing well today.

[13] At the time of this article I have studied nearly 1300 cases with about 50 Bible leaders, perhaps 100 historical leaders and the rest contemporary leaders. The findings for enhancements and barriers generally hold true.

Characteristic 2.
They maintain a learning posture and can learn from various kinds of sources—life especially.

This characteristic is also one of the enhancement factors for finishing well.

Example: Daniel is the classic O.T. leader who exemplifies this. See Daniel chapter nine for a late in life illustration of one who continues to study and learn from the Scriptures. Paul and Peter are the classic N.T. leaders with a learning posture (see 2Pe 3:18 and 2Ti 4:13).

Characteristic 3.
They manifest Christ-likeness in character as evidenced by the fruit of the Spirit in their lives.

Example: Daniel is the classic O.T. leader who exemplifies godliness (See the summary references to him in Eze 14:14,20). In the N.T. note the evidence of character transformation in Paul's life (2Ti 2:24 and an illustration of it—the book of Phm). These were men who over a lifetime moved from strong personalities with roughness in their leadership styles to strong personalities with gentleness in their leadership styles.

Characteristic 4.
Truth is lived out in their lives so that convictions and promises of God are seen to be real.

Example: Joshua's statement about God's promises never having failed him in his closing speech demonstrate this characteristic of someone believing God and staking his life on God's truth (Jos 23:14). See the many aside truth statements that Paul weaves into his two letters to Timothy. See his famous stirring convictions echoed in Ac 27:22-25.

Characteristic 5.
They leave behind one or more ultimate contributions.

In a study on legacies left behind by effective leaders who finished well I have identified the following categories:

Table Ne 5-1. Categories of Lasting Legacies

Category	Explanation
saint	a model life that others want to emulate
stylistic practitioners	a ministry model that others want to emulate
family	Models a godly heritage and sees that godliness reproduced in own biological family (or closely related spiritual family).
mentors	extensive personal ministry; end product changed lives
public rhetoricians	extensive public ministry; end product changed lives
pioneers	start new works for God; end product is new churches, new movements, new works for God

crusaders	those who correct wrongs, end product, changed institutions, societies, etc. which reflect justice, fairness, etc.
artists	those who introduce creative ways of doing things; end products—whatever is created— as well as a model for how to do things differently
founder	a special category of pioneer who starts a new Christian organization; end product, the organization
stabilizers	those who can work in churches, movements, and other organizations to improve them and keep them alive and consistent; end product the organization revitalized and efficient
researchers	those who find out why things happen the way they do in Christian endeavor; end product an, understanding of the dynamics of things that can help others in Christian work
writers	those who can capture ideas in writing in order to help others in Christian work; end product, the writing produced
promoters	those who can motivate others and inspire them to use ideation, to join movements, etc.; end product people committing themselves to new ventures

Examples: Daniel's ultimate contributions include: saint, (mentor), writer, stabilizer. Paul's ultimate contributions include: saint, mentor, pioneer, crusader, writer, promoter.

Of course, in addition to these standard categories there are also unique legacies that leaders also leave behind. These have to be described individually for each leader.

Characteristic 6.
They walk with a growing awareness of a sense of destiny and see some or all of it fulfilled.

Definition   A sense of destiny is an inner conviction arising from an experience or a series of experiences in which there is a growing sense of awareness that God has His hand on a leader in a special way for special purposes.

Over a lifetime a leader is prepared by God for a destiny, receives guidance toward that destiny, and increasingly completes that destiny. No Biblical leader who accomplished much for God failed to have a sense of destiny, one that usually grew over his/her lifetime.

Examples: Joseph's dreams and his saving of the embryonic nation; Moses' saving of the nation; Paul's vision to take the Gospel to the Gentiles.

Conclusion
The classic example in the O.T. of a good finish is Daniel who manifests all six characteristics. The classic example in the N.T. other than Christ is Paul. There are gradations of finishing well. Some finish well but not quite having all six or lesser intensity on one or the other major characteristics. This list of characteristics is probably not complete. Others may not agree totally with them. In that case, they should at least provide an alternate list. But these are certainly evident in many leaders who have finished well.

See **Article,** *Leaving Behind a Legacy.*

6. Finishing Well— Six Major Barriers

Introduction to Research on Finishing Well

In 1989 in an article entitled, *Listen Up Leaders! Forewarned is Forearmed!* , I summarized my research on Biblical leaders with the following opening comments.

A repeated reading of the Bible with a focus on leadership reveals four crucial observations fraught with leadership implications:

Observation 1.   Few leaders finish well.
Observation 2.   Leadership is difficult.
Observation 3.   God's enabling presence is the essential ingredient of successful leadership.
Observation 4.   Spiritual leadership can make a difference.

And what is true of Biblical leaders is equally true of historical and contemporary leaders.[14] It is the first observation to which this article speaks. Identifying the fact that few leaders finish well was a breakthrough warning for me. This led to further study. Why do few leaders finish well? What stops them? What helps them?

Six Barriers To Finishing Well

Comparative study of effective leaders who finished well has identified six. barriers that hindered leaders from finishing well. It only takes one of them to torpedo a leader. But frequently a leader who fails in one area will also fail in others. What are these barriers? We can learn from those who didn't finish well. We can be alerted to these barriers. We can avoid them in our own lives. Pr 22:3 tells us that,

> **Sensible people will see trouble coming and avoid it, but an unthinking person will walk right into it and regret it later.** Pr 22:3

Let me share with you six barriers to finishing well that I have identified. We need to look ahead in our lives and not walk right into these barriers. We need to avoid being entrapped by them.

Barrier 1.   Finances—Their Use And Abuse

Leaders, particularly those who have power positions and make important decisions concerning finances, tend to use practices which may encourage incorrect handling of finances and eventually wrong use. A character trait of greed often is rooted deep and eventually will cause impropriety with regard to finances. Numerous leaders have fallen due to some issue related to money.

Biblical Examples: O.T.: Gideon's golden ephod. N.T.: Ananias and Sapphira.

---

[14] At the time of this article I have studied nearly 1300 cases with about 50 Bible leaders, perhaps 100 historical leaders and the rest contemporary leaders. The findings for enhancements and barriers generally holds true.

Barrier 2. Power—its Abuse
Leaders who are effective in ministry must use various power bases in order to accomplish their ministry. With power so available and being used almost daily, there is a tendency to abuse it. Leaders who rise to the top in a hierarchical system tend to assume privileges with their perceived status. Frequently, these privileges include abuse of power. And they usually have no counter balancing accountability.

Biblical **Example**: Uzziah's usurping of priestly privilege.

Barrier 3. Pride--which Leads To Downfall
Pride (inappropriate and self-centered) can lead to a downfall of a leader. As a leader there is a dynamic tension that must be maintained. We must have a healthy respect for our selves, and yet we must recognize that we have nothing that was not given us by God and He is the one who really enables ministry.

Biblical Example: David's numbering.

Barrier 4.   Sex--illicit Relationships
Illicit sexual relationships have been a major downfall both in the Bible and in western cultures.[15] Joseph's classic integrity check with respect to sexual sin is the ideal model that should be in leaders minds.

Biblical Example: David's sin with Bathsheba was a pivotal point from which his leadership never fully recovered. It was all downhill from there on.

Barrier 5. FAMILY--Critical Issues
Problems between spouses or between parents and children or between siblings can destroy a leader's ministry. What is needed are Biblical values lived out with regard to husband-wife relationships, parent-children, and sibling relationships. Of growing importance in our day is the social base profiles for singles in ministry and for married couples.

Biblical Example: David's family. Amnon and Tamar. Absalom's revenge.

Barrier 6. Plateauing.
Leaders who are competent tend to plateau. Their very strength becomes a weakness. They can continue to minister at a level without there being a reality or Spirit empowered renewing effect. Most leaders will plateau several times in their life times of development. Some of the five enhancement factors for a good finish will counteract this tendency (perspective, learning posture, mentor, disciplines). There again is a dynamic tension that must be maintained between leveling off for good reasons, (consolidating one's growth and/or reaching the level of potential for which God has made you) and plateauing because of sinfulness or loss of vision.

Biblical Example: David in the latter part of his reign just before Absalom's revolt.

Forewarned is forearmed. There are many other reasons why leaders don't finish well—usually all related to sin in some form. But at least the six categories are major ones that have trapped many leaders and taken them out of the race. Leaders who want to finish well, Take heed!

---

[15] This is probably true in other cultures as well though I do not have a data base to prove this.

6. Finishing Well— Six Major Barriers page 89

See **Articles**: *5. Finishing Well—Six Characteristics; 4. Finishing Well—Five Enhancements.*

7. Gates and Wall

Introduction
Two of the most repeated words in the book of Nehemiah are gates (31 times) and wall (35 times). Note the first instance of each.

> In the month of Kislev in the twentieth year of King Artaxerxes' reign, I was at the fortress of Susa. 2 Hanani, one of my brothers, came to visit me with some other men who had just arrived from Judah. I asked them about the Jews who had survived the captivity and about how things were going in Jerusalem. 3 They said to me, "Those who survived the exile and are back in the province are in great trouble and disgrace. The wall of Jerusalem is broken down, and its gates have been burned with fire."
>
> Ne 1:1-3

Note the answer given to Nehemiah concerning how the people who had returned to the land were doing. One, two words describe their personal status—trouble and disgrace. The connotation of these words involve the notions of distress and scorned. Then note the second description—referring to the city itself. There is no wall. The gates, entrances through the wall, are destroyed. Gates and walls were the primary defense for a city. Without them, people in the city were the prey of any kind of military force. With them, the inhabitants could withstand a siege.

Nehemiah's first reaction to this news is to grieve before God—fasting and praying. He prays for this situation. And out of this time of fasting and praying a plan emerges. Nehemiah begins to formulate a plan, the first step of which is to rebuild the wall and gates. Later in ch 2:12 we see that God had initiated this plan in Nehemiah's heart.

What was the significance of this message to Nehemiah? Why were the people in trouble and disgrace? Why were the wall and gates important? An understanding of the concepts of wall and gates are needed.

Wall
From the very beginning of their history as a nation, the Israelites were acquainted with fortified cities. The spies who returned to give their report to Moses describe the cities as being great and fortified up to heaven—inhabited by descendents of Anak, Amalekites, Hittites, Jebusites, Amorites and Canaanites. You will remember that this struck terror in the hearts of the Israelite followers. To a people who were basically a large mass of fugitives just getting accustomed to camp life in the desert and who had no knowledge of warfare involving siege weapons the task was daunting. No wonder they did not want to fight.

Walls, sometimes wide enough to be a small road[16] and high enough, 20 or more feet high, protected the towns. Towers were often built at the corners or at points on the wall where attack was to be expected. These were manned by warriors who had spears, bows and arrows, slings and rocks, boiling water and the like. Walls were important as means of defense. Even surrounding farmers of a walled city would work their farms in the daytime and spend the night in the walled city.

Jerusalem's walls were destroyed—piles of rubble here and there along the location of the old wall—were all that was left. Indeed, the people who had returned were in trouble. A people without means of safety or defense. How could they last long? Who would respect them? Hanani had it right. "Those who survived the exile and are back in the province are in great trouble and disgrace."

Nehemiah wanted to correct that. He wanted to replace the wall—make it a strong means of defense. Jerusalem would be a place of refuge. The temple and worship of God would have a centralized location that was defensible. God would be honored for who He was.

Nehemiah knew also that Hanani's description (trouble and disgrace) was probably deeply felt by the people who had returned to the land. This was a lever he would use to motivate them to rebuild the wall. Note in Nehemiah's report to the leaders in the city after his night reconnaissance around the city. He uses this sense of "trouble and disgrace" to motivate the people.

> 16 The city officials did not know I had been out there or what I was doing, for I had not yet said anything to anyone about my plans. I had not yet spoken to the religious and political leaders, the officials, or anyone else in the administration. 17 But now I said to them, "You know full well the tragedy of our city. It lies in ruins, and its gates are burned. Come, let's rebuild the wall of Jerusalem and rid ourselves of this disgrace!" 18 Then I told them about how the gracious hand of God had been on me, and about my conversation with the king. They replied at once, "Good! Let's rebuild the wall!" So they began the good work. Ne 2:16-18

Two leadership insights need to be noted here. (1) Nehemiah is aware of the influentials in Jerusalem. They will have to be cultivated if the plans are to gain ownership among all the followers. (2) Nehemiah does not relate his plans right away. He confirms them and gives time for his own credibility to be accepted by the influentials. He is dominantly using positional authority (the king's backing). Nehemiah senses intervention time with the influentials. Note how he moves from positional authority (conversation with the king) toward spiritual authority in his inspirational relating of his plans (gracious hand of God had been on me.) And he has pricked their already burdened conscience about Jerusalem (let's rebuild the wall of Jerusalem and rid ourselves of this disgrace!). Nehemiah's first inspirational leadership with the influentials meets with success.

Nehemiah has gained ownership from the leaders. These leaders will motivate others to join in the project of rebuilding the wall. And remember we are talking about a big wall, like an on-ramp of an interstate. Wide and high. A big work force will be needed. Nehemiah knows the importance of this wall to the people. He will assign portions of the wall to people who live near it. They will be motivated to do a good job—one, for their

---

[16] Notice in the celebration of the completion of the wall in 12:27-43 that the parade of people, broken up into two groups, going in two directions, are doing so upon the wall. It is a very wide wall indeed.

own safety and two, because those to the right and left of them are building also and they want their wall to be at least as good. No shirking here. Nehemiah is a master motivator.

The building of the wall will take resources. Nehemiah has already made arrangements for part of those resources. The workers on the wall, under stressful conditions (threatened attacks from opponents to the building of the wall), work long hours. The amazing thing is that the wall was completed in 52 days. Nehemiah has recruited a large working force, that worked hard.[17] No wonder there was such a great celebration.

Gates

Gates controlled access to the city. A large city would have several gates. Such was the case with Jerusalem. Depending on the size of a given gate, it might consist of an outside gate and an inside gate and sometimes even 3 or 4 doors. The doors were generally wood, though often covered metal. They were secured by great bars, often of iron. The gate complex often had rooms to the sides for guards and towers for military forces. The city gate was more than just a defensive access way. It played an extremely important part in the social life of the people. Often there was a market place just inside the gate. Administrative interaction as well as business ventures took place at the gate. So the gates were symbolic of the life of the people as well as practical for defensive purposes.

Jerusalem had several gates. Nehemiah's night reconnaissance describes several gates. Table Ne 7-1 lists the gates mentioned by Nehemiah.

Table Ne 7-1 Jerusalem Gates[18] as Indicated in Nehemiah

Verse(s)	Name of Gate/ Descriptive Comments	Who Worked on It or Near It
2:13; 3:13	Valley Gate/ Gate of the Gai, a gate opening into the Gai Hinnom;	Hanun, and the inhabitants of Zanoah
2:13; 3;14	Dung Gate/ southeastern corner of city	Malchiah the son of Rechab
2:14; 3:15	Fountain Gate/ probably source of running water	Shallum the son of Colhozeh
3:1, 32	Sheep Gate	Eliashib the high priest and fellow priests
3:3	Fish Gate	sons of Hassenaah
3:6	Old Gate	Jehoiada the son of Paseah, and Meshullam the son of Besodeiah
3:26	Water Gate	Nethinims from Ophel
3:28	Horse Gate	Probably the Priests
12:39	Gate of Ephraim/ probably on the western wall	This is mentioned in the celebration parade but is not referred to in the ch 3 section on rebuilding the wall.

The names of the gates are probably suggestive of a function they played.

Closure

Nehemiah wanted a centralized worship established again in Jerusalem. Haggai's work had earlier rebuilt the temple. Now what was lacking was a strong Jerusalem. Nehemiah

---

[17] As far as I can see this was a voluntary work force. They were not paid to do this.

[18] A lot of archeological work has been done to find and identify the gates and trace the wall. I am not going into detail. I simply want to show that multiple gates were involved. This was a fairly large wall with several gates.

correctly saw that for a strong Jerusalem there would be need for a strong fortification wall, including towers. This was a felt need of the people in and around Jerusalem. He thus used the wall and gates as a first step in motivating the people to gain ownership in the changes he was to bring about. These changes included a renewed people, seeking to follow God—a people who would apply God's word to their lives and who would want public worship. Thus the changes included a strong temple worship with financial backing for priests, Levites, singers, temple workers, and guards. A strong Jerusalem would be needed if Nehemiah was to repopulate Jerusalem. And Nehemiah had plans to bring more people into Jerusalem. Walls and gates were important—as a rallying point, as a return to tradition, as an incentive for repopulation. Nehemiah wisely used this as his starting point in motivating the people.

8. Getting the Job Done—Comparison of Ezra, Nehemiah and Haggai's Roles

Introduction

Every Christian leader has an assignment from the Lord, some group she or he has been called to influence toward God's purposes. Each leader is also accountable to the Lord for the work he or she does and for getting the job done.

But what does it take to get the job done? Does each leader get the job done in the same way? To what leaders would you look for insights on getting the job done?
In this article we'll compare the work of Haggai, Ezra and Nehemiah. We'll look at what they had in common as they got the work done that God assigned to them. We'll look in particular at the following seven commonalities that characterize their work.

1. They served in the same chapter of redemptive history—the return to the land.
2. Each received a specific assignment from the Lord and contributed something to God's overall plan for His people.
3. Each was gifted to complete his assignment from the Lord.
4. Each motivated the leaders and/or followers toward fulfillment of God's purposes.
5. Each depended on the Lord in the accomplishment of his assignment.
6. Each worked as part of a coalition for the rebuilding and/or renewal of physical structures and/or the people of God.
7. Each worked at a specific time and place with a specific group of people.

Let's take a look now at each of the seven commonalities.

1. They served in the same chapter of redemptive history—the return to the land.

Several key events occurred during this chapter, from 538 to 445 B.C. (a span of about 93 years). Here are a few of the highlights: return, rebuilding, renewal, and reform. More than 42,000 people returned to Israel when the exile ended (2 Chr 36:22-23). The altar of the Temple of the LORD was rebuilt in 536 B.C. (Ezra 3:8); the temple itself was completed between 520 and 516 (Ezra 4:24; 6:15); the walls of Jerusalem were rebuilt in 445 B.C. (Nehemiah 6:15); and Ezra and Nehemiah fostered spiritual renewal and reforms from 458-445 B.C. (and beyond).

2. Each received a specific assignment from the Lord and contributed something to God's overall plan for His people.

Haggai was a prophet who delivered God's messages to Zerubbabel, Jeshua and the people of Israel. He encouraged them to resume and complete the reconstruction of the temple.

Ezra was a priest and teacher of the Law of Moses. He taught the law to the people and helped to catalyze spiritual renewal.

Nehemiah was cupbearer to King Artaxerxes. In Jerusalem he was a civil leader who provided organizational and inspirational leadership to the rebuilding of Jerusalem's wall, to the repopulation of Jerusalem, and worked with Ezra to catalyze spiritual renewal.

3. Each was gifted to complete his assignment from the Lord.

Haggai was gifted to prophesy, that is, to deliver timely messages from the Lord to His people.

Ezra was gifted to teach. He had committed himself to study and obey the Law of the LORD, and to teach God's laws and regulations to the people of Israel (Ezra 7:10).

Nehemiah was gifted to discern, to organize and administrate, to lead, and to believe God (faith).

4. Each motivated the leaders of the people and/or the people toward fulfillment of God's purposes.

Haggai was a prophet (peripheral religious leader[19]) and primarily a task-oriented leader who motivated the leaders of the people, Zerubbabel and Jeshua, as well as the people themselves, in a number of different ways. He met each stage of the task, with its discouraging feature, with a positive solution that inspired his followers to rejoin the effort. Of the suggested nine leadership functions of inspirational leadership,[20] the book of Haggai focuses on five of them. But note who of the leadership team (Haggai, Joshua, Zerubbabel, Zechariah) is essentially involved with the function. The five functions seen in the book of Haggai include:

- must motivate followers toward vision (all three but Haggai dominant)
- must encourage perseverance and faith of followers (Haggai dominant)
- are responsible for the financial welfare of the effort (Zerubbabel dominant, implied)
- are responsible for direct ministry along lines of giftedness, which relate to inspirational functions (Haggai dominant; prophetic gift/received revelation)
- must model (knowing, being, and doing) so as to inspire followers toward the reality of God's intervention in lives. (Haggai dominant but Joshua very supportive in this).

Note some of the details of this inspirational leadership. In response to the people's obedience and as part of this renewing, God stirs up the spirit of the people. This stirring begins with the leaders (at least in the order mentioned in verse 14) and extends to all the people.

> So the Lord stirred up the spirit of Zerubbabel son of Shealtiel, governor of Judah, and the spirit of Joshua son of Jehozadak, the high priest, and the spirit of the whole remnant of the people. They came and began to work on the house of the Lord Almighty, their God (Haggai 1:14).

---

[19] See **Article**, *11. Haggai—Leadership Coalition*, in the Clinton Biblical Leadership Commentary on Haggai.

[20] See **Leadership Perspectives**, chapter 1 for the functions listed for task oriented leadership, relationally oriented leadership and inspirationally oriented leadership. See also **Article**, *29. Nehemiah, Leadership Functions*.

Leaders can expect God to stir the hearts of others to join in the task. God speaks to the mind, but He also moves the spirit. This is one form of guidance that God will use to direct people to take part in a project. This principle occurs in other parts of Scripture as well.[21] God is in the business of moving people's hearts. Consider this: if your ministry project does not stir people's hearts, you better reconsider whether God is in it or not.

Consider also these principles:
- Inspirational leadership is complex and will usually require a range of giftedness not residing in only one leader.
- The heart of inspirational leadership is the final function—motivating followers to see the hand of God in their situation. The recognition of the reality of God's intervention in a situation is the essential ingredient of restoration.
- When leading a God-given project in God's timing, expect Got to stir up people to assist. The assistance may take the form of direct work or indirect support—finances, prayer, etc.

Ezra was a mainstream religious leader who motivated the people primarily through the life of hope and obedience he modeled before them, which led to God's hand upon his life (see Ezra 7:6; 27-28), and by calling the people back to the standards of the Law of Moses. In terms of the sub-set behaviors of the inspirational leadership function[22], Ezra:
- encouraged the faith and perseverance of his followers
- sought to develop and maintain the corporate (religious) culture of his
- organization (country)
- conducted direct ministry along the lines of his giftedness—teaching
- was accountable to God for the organization in which he operated
- (most important of all) modeled a personal relationship with God (holistically—knowing, being and doing) so as to inspire followers toward the reality of God's intervention in their lives.

Nehemiah was a civic leader who was especially adept at inspiring a shared vision, believing God for the fulfillment of the vision, focusing on and working toward the fulfillment of the vision, and organizing and inspiring others in that work. Like Haggai, Nehemiah models a number of motivational strategies:
- working with the followers
- sacrificing financially
- taking courageous stands against opposition
- crisis praying
- sensitivity to God in providential ways
- working for justice—reforms

---

[21] In 1 Samuel 10:26, we see the newly anointed King Saul "accompanied by valiant men whose hearts God had touched". In a related book, Ezra (related to Haggai), we see that "everyone whose heart God had moved—prepared to go up and build the house of the Lord in Jerusalem" (Ezra 1:5). All the way back in Exodus, we see God stirring hearts, "everyone who was willing and whose heart moved him came and brought an offering to the Lord for the work on the Tent of Meeting, for all its service, and for the sacred garments." (Exodus 35:21).

[22] See **Article**, *29. Nehemiah, Leadership Functions.*

- competitiveness, pride—each family rebuilding portion near them
- positional leadership
- networking power
- modeling perseverance
- practical advice
- using extreme focus for a limited time; people totally committed need to see progress
- affirming those who are participating in the work

Nehemiah is a strong leader. He is aware of his modeling and its impact on the people. He is aware of his seconded authority from Artaxerxes. He starts with positional authority. But it is not positional authority alone. Competency plays a strong part. He knew what he was doing. And his vision resonated with a felt need the followers had. They needed a wall to protect the city.

Nehemiah also, more than the Biblical record reveals of any other Old Testament leader, affirmed the people. To affirm is to give power to a person. It may be physical, spiritual or emotional power. Nehemiah affirms Hanani and Hananiah when he appoints them to leadership over the city and the citadel, respectively, and when he writes of Hananiah that he was a faithful man who feared God more than most (7:2). He affirms the workers when he lists so many of them by name (ch 3), as well as those who served in the ceremonies for the dedication of the wall (ch 12). Leaders today can affirm people by:

- thanking them verbally as they are serving
- asking them what they think
- writing cards or emails to say they are praying for them
- appreciate them in front of other people
- sending inexpensive gifts of appreciation
- approving study leaves for full-time staff
- providing tools needed to do the job

Notice that:

- Effective leaders are aware of motivational techniques to use with their followers.
- Modeling perseverance in the face of difficulties is a strong motivating factor.
- Nehemiah uses various influence means to accomplish his task.[23]
- Leaders should use affirmation to motivate followers.

5. Each depended on the Lord in the accomplishment of his assignment.

Ministry originates in the heart of God the Father. Ministry happens because of him. But ministry is also a divine-human partnership (1 Co 3:5-9), and when God's leaders are dependent upon Him, they have developed the correct posture. Knowing their work was from God:

- Haggai could write (1:1, 3, 5, 7, and 13; 2;1, 6, 11, and 20) that the LORD gave him a message (or a similar phase);

---

[23] See **Article**, *12. Influence, Power and Authority Forms.* I have adapted Dennis Wrong's continuum. Nehemiah uses several of Wrong's power forms.

- Ezra could say how the hand of his God was upon him and point out how the Lord had brought them safely on their journey from the Ahava Canal to Jerusalem (in response to their fasting and prayer, 8:15ff);
- Nehemiah could say that the Lord had put certain ideas or plans into his heart, note how the gracious hand of his God had been upon him, point out how God had turned back their adversaries, and emphasize how the work had been completed with the help of their God (2:17-18; 4:15; 6:15-16).

When leaders plateau in their relationship with the Lord and the ministry they do flows out of past experiences alone rather than a fresh touch from God, they are losing a vital connection with Jesus the True Vine who is the source of all fruitfulness and effectiveness in ministry (John 15:1-8).

6. Each worked as part of a coalition for the rebuilding and/or renewal of physical structures and/or the people of God.

Coalition is a French word that originated from a Latin participle having to do with growing together. Having crossed over into English, its meaning is as follows:

Definition   Coalition refers to an alliance, especially a temporary one, of people, factions, parties, or nations.

Taking this definition a bit further, we arrive at our Biblical leadership definition,

Definition   A leadership coalition in Biblical literature refers to

- a partnership, whether formal or informal,
- which exists between civil leaders, mainstream religious leaders and/or peripheral religious leaders,
- for a temporary period of time

in order to accomplish some God-directed task(s).

The more formal and deliberate the coalition is and the more specifically the task is defined, the more effective is the leadership and the coalition.

Some Possible Coalitions Throughout The Leadership Eras

Table Ne 8-1 Possible Coalitions in the Leadership Eras

Leadership Era	Partnership	Formal (F) Informal (I)	God-Directed Task	Time Span of Coalition
I. Patriarchal	None seen		None seen	None seen
2. Pre-Kingdom a. Desert	a. Moses, Aaron, Miriam, Joshua	I	Survival in Desert	40 years
2. Pre-Kingdom b. Conquering the Land	Joshua, Eleazar	F	Conquer the Land; Parcel it out to the Tribes	10 years or so???
2. Pre-Kingdom b. Conquered by the Land	Deborah, Barak Samuel, Saul	I I	Military Defense Transition to Kingdom	Very Short (less than a year) Relatively Short

				(year or so??)
3. Kingdom	Frequently you will see some king in a coalition with a military leader and/or some religious priest	I (military part more formal)	Self-preservation	Varied—some for several years
4. Post-Kingdom a. As Kingdom was crumbling	Not clear; except that some kings allied themselves with some priests against the peripheral ministry of prophets	I	Reject God's Corrective Ministry Through Prophets	Relatively short
b. In exile	Mordecai, Esther	I at first but increasingly became more deliberate, F	Preservation of Jewish exiles	Relatively short
c. Return to Land	Haggai, Zechariah, Joshua and Zerubbabel	I at first but increasingly became more deliberate, F	Rebuilding of Temple	Relatively short
	Nehemiah, Ezra	Appears to be F	Building of Wall Around Jerusalem for Protection; Instituting spiritual reforms	Relatively Short, initially, but could have lasted up to 12 years

Coalitions are dominantly an Old Testament concept having to do with the various leadership needs of the people of God.

Some Observations

The two most effective coalitions were that of Haggai, Zechariah, Joshua and Zerubbabel and that of Ezra and Nehemiah. Some commonalities include:

1. Both of these coalitions were for relatively short times.
2. Both of these coalitions were very specific, one to rebuild the temple, the other to rebuild the wall around Jerusalem and then initiate further spiritual reforms.
3. In both cases, all of the leaders were spiritually alive—civil, formal religious, and peripheral religious.

Some differences include:

1. Ezra operated in the role of formal religious (was a priest) and informal religious leader (calling for reform and renewal). Haggai, the major motivator, was a peripheral religious leader. The religious leader, Joshua, was supplementary to Haggai's leadership.
2. Ezra's informal religious ministry was focused on renewal—via the revealed word of God—getting people back to knowing and obeying God's word. Haggai's informal religious ministry was focused on motivating the people to rebuild the temple.
3. Nehemiah was the inspirational leader, though a civil leader. He was the practical, get it done kind of person. Haggai was the inspirational leader, though not in the formal religious structure.
4. Nehemiah, though very practical, was a man of dependence upon God in prayer. Haggai was the practical point person in the rebuilding of the temple. Zechariah was probably the spiritual motivator.
5. The obstacles that Nehemiah and Ezra faced were primarily external (coming from opposition from without though there were some internal obstacles in terms of resources). The obstacles that Haggai, Zechariah, Joshua, and Zerubbabel faced were dominantly internal—in the hearts and minds of the followers.
6. Nehemiah's connections into the power structure provided a source of resources. Zerubbabel had to raise resources from the people themselves, who were going through major times of depression.

7. Each worked at a specific time and place with a specific group of people.

Two items are of note here. First, each of these leaders *worked*. They met with leaders, raised resources, communicated vision, inspired people, solved problems, functioned in their gifts, made decisions, and surmounted obstacles. Their ministry was fraught with the same kind of frustrations and complications, joys and victories, that characterize the ministries of leaders today. But it was mostly work not glamour. Mostly a lot of prayer and teaching, motivating and modeling, confronting and clarifying. Sometimes it was three steps forward and two steps back. But these leaders trusted God and persevered in their work and ultimately saw the completion of their assignments, especially Haggai and Nehemiah, whose work of rebuilding is easier to evaluate than the impact of Ezra's teaching ministry.

Second, each leader worked at a specific time and place with a specific group of people. We don't see them wishing they were elsewhere, working with this group or that group, in that place or this place. We see them settling in to the place and with the people God has called them to serve. Leaders today would do well to imitate their example and get to work on leading when, where and with the particular group God has already called them to serve.

Closure

Now, how about you, our fellow leader? How are you getting along in the work the Lord has given you? Are you getting the job done? Here are several questions to help you apply the seven commonalities between Haggai, Ezra and Nehemiah.

1. Are you aware of the times in which you live, the macro and micro contexts, and what God is doing? Is your ministry in sync with His?

2. Can you articulate your specific assignment from the Lord and show how your daily and weekly schedule contribute to the accomplishment of that assignment?

3. Are you functioning in and developing your giftedness in order to maximize your potential for impact?

4. Are you motivating followers toward God's purposes for the group? Do they sense the touch of God on your life and ministry?

5. Are you attempting ministry projects that will only succeed if God is in them?

6. Are you working with a coalition or team of like-minded leaders? Do you need to ask the Lord to send other leaders your way?

7. Are you settled where you are and are you at peace with serving the people God has placed you with?

We know how Haggai, Ezra and Nehemiah would answer these questions. They got the job done. How would you answer them?

9. God The Promise Keeper

Introduction

Have you been to a *Promise Keepers'* event? That is an oft asked question these days. I smile and answer that question with another one. Do you know **The Promise Keeper**? Great as those Promise Keepers' events are they are nothing when compared to **The Promise Keeper** meeting with you.

Promises of God

When I was a little boy my friends and I would often say, "I promise." And the other person would say, "Cross your heart and hope to die?" The meaning was, "Do you really mean it?" Now little boys make and break promises about as fast as can be. But with God it is not so. One, He does not promise helter-skelter-like. And when He does promise He can be trusted. Our problem is learning to hear Him promise and being sure what we heard was a promise from Him, for us.

Definition   A <u>promise from God</u> is an assertion from God, specific or general or a truth in harmony with God's character, which is perceived in one's heart or mind concerning what He will do or not do for that one and which is sealed in our inner most being by a quickening action of the Holy Spirit and on which that one then counts.

There are three parts to the promise:

1. the cognitive part which refers to the assertion and its understanding, and
2. the affective part which is the inner most testimony to the promise, and
3. the volitional act of faith on our part which believes the assertion and feelings and thereafter counts upon it.

A leader can err in three ways, concerning promises. One, the leader may misread the assertion. That is, misinterpret what he/she thinks God will do or not do. Or two, the leader may wrongly apply some assertion to himself/herself which is does not apply. It may even be a true assertion but not for that leader or that time. Or the leader may misread the inner witness. It may not be God's Spirit quickening of the leader.

Sometimes the assertion comes from a command, or a principle, or even a direct statement of a promise God makes. The promise may be made generally to all who follow God or specifically to some. It may be for all time or for a limited time. Commands or principles are not in themselves promises. But it is when the Holy Spirit brings some truth out of them that He wants to apply to our lives that they may become promises. Such truths almost always bear on the character of God.

One thing we can know for certain, if indeed we do have a promise from God, then He will fulfill it. For Titus 1:2 asserts an important truth about God.

God can not lie.

He is **The Promise Keeper**. This is an image of God that all leaders need.

Examples of God As The Promise Keeper

God keeps his promises. He is the Promise Keeper. Table Ne 9-1 gives some examples to shore up our faith in **The Promise Keeper**. I could have chosen hundreds of promises.[24]

Table Ne 9-1. God The Promise Keeper—Examples

To Whom	Vs	Basic Promise/ Results
Abraham	Gen 12:1,2	Bless the world through Abraham. Give descendants. Spawn nations. Give a land. / This has happened and continues to happen.
Nahum	Whole book	Judgment on Nineveh/ Assyria. Promises fulfilled.
Obadiah	Whole book	Judgment on Edom. Promises fulfilled.
Habakkuk	Ch 2	Judgment on Babylon. Promises fulfilled. See Da 5.
Zechariah	Lk 1:13	Birth of John the Baptist. Promise fulfilled.
Mary	Lk 1:35	Birth of Jesus. Promise fulfilled.
Hezekiah	Isa 39:1ff, especially vs 5-7	Babylonian captivity. Royal hostages taken (Daniel was one of these). Promise fulfilled.
Daniel	Ch 2	The broad outlines of history/ nations and God's purposes. Promise fulfilled in part with more to come.
Daniel	Ch 9	Messiah and work of cross. Promise fulfilled.
Daniel	Ch 10-11:35	Again the broad outline of history particularly with reference to Israel. Everything up to 11:35 has taken place in detail as promises. The rest is yet to come.

Conclusion

The dictionary defines a promise as giving a pledge, committing oneself to do something, to make a declaration assuring that something will or will not be done or to afford a basis for expectation. Synonyms for promise include: covenant, engage, pledge, plight, swear, vow. The central meaning shared by these verbs is *to declare solemnly that one will perform or refrain from a particular course of action.* God is **The Promise Keeper**. As children of His we should learn to hear His promises and to receive them for our lives. As a leader you most likely will not make it over the long haul if you do not know God **as The Promise Keeper**.

One of the six characteristics[25] of a leader who finishes well is described as,

---

[24] Over the years I have kept a listing of promises I felt God has made to me and my wife. Many of these have been fulfilled. In December of 1997 I reviewed all of these—an encouraging faith building exercise.

[25] The six characteristics include: 1. They maintain a personal vibrant relationship with God right up to the end. 2. They maintain a learning posture and can learn from various kinds of sources—life especially. 3.

> **Truth is lived out in their lives so that convictions and promises of God are seen to be real.**

A leader who has God's promises and lives by them will exemplify this characteristic.[26] Paul did. Paul, the model N.T. church leader knew God as **The Promise Keeper**. Do you?

They manifest Christ-likeness in character as evidenced by the fruit of the Spirit in their lives. 4. Truth is lived out in their lives so that convictions and promises of God are seen to be real. 5. They leave behind one or more ultimate contributions. 6. They walk with a growing awareness of a sense of destiny and see some or all of it fulfilled.

[26] One of the symptoms of a plateaued leader is failure to get new fresh truth from God—especially failure to get new promises from God. Such a leader will also lack faith to see old promises fulfilled.

10. God's Shaping Processes With Leaders

Introduction

One major leadership lesson derived from comparative study of effective leaders states,

> **Effective leaders see present ministry in light of a life time perspective.[27]**

This article deals with God's shaping processes with a leader.[28] It gives important aspects of perspective that all leaders need. Six observations of God's shaping processes with leaders include the following.

1. God first works in a leader and then through that leader.
2. God intends to develop a leader to reach the maximum potential and accomplish those things for which the leader has been gifted.
3. God shapes or develops a leader over an entire lifetime.
4. A time perspective provides many keys. When using a time perspective, the life can be seen in terms of several time periods, each yielding valuable informative lessons. Each leader has a unique time-line describing his/her development.[29]
5. Shaping processes can be identified, labeled, and analyzed to contribute long lasting lessons.[30]
6. An awareness of God's shaping processes can enhance a leader's response to these processes.

Figure Ne 10-1. Describes a generalized time line and some of the processes used by God over a lifetime.

---

[27] I have identified seven which repeatedly occur in effective leaders: 1. Life Time Perspective—Effective Leaders View Present Ministry In Terms Of A Life Time Perspective. 2. Learning Posture—Effective Leaders Maintain A Learning Posture Throughout Life. 3. Spiritual Authority—Effective Leaders Value Spiritual Authority As A Primary Power Base. 4. Dynamic Ministry Philosophy—Effective Leaders Who Are Productive Over A Lifetime Have A Dynamic Ministry Philosophy Which Is Made Up Of An Unchanging Core And A Changing Periphery Which Expands Due To A Growing Discovery Of Giftedness, Changing Leadership Situations, And Greater Understanding Of The Scriptures. 5. Leadership Selection And Development—Effective Leaders View Leadership Selection And Development As A Priority Function In Their Ministry. 6. Relational Empowerment—Effective Leaders See Relational Empowerment As Both A Means And A Goal Of Ministry. 7. Sense Of Destiny—Effective Leaders Evince A Growing Awareness Of Their Sense Of Destiny. See the **Article**, *Leadership Lessons—Seven Major Identified*.

[28] See also the **Article**, *Leadership Selection* which gives an overview across time of the major benchmarks of God's development of a leader.

[29] See **Article**, *Time-Lines: Defined for Biblical Leaders*.

[30] See **For Further Study Bibliography**, Clinton's **Leadership Emergence Theory**, a self-study manual which gives detailed findings from research on God's shaping processes with leaders. This manual describes 50 shaping processes in detail. This article touches on only a few of these shaping processes.

I. Ministry Foundations	II. Early Ministry	III. Middle Ministry	IV. Latter Ministry	V. Finishing Well

• character shaping	• leadership committal • authority insights • giftedness discovery • guidance	• ministry insights • conflict • paradigm shifts • leadership backlash • challenges	• spiritual warfare • deep processing • power processes	• destiny fulfillment

Figure Ne 10-1. Some Major Shaping Processes Across The Time-Line

Shaping in Early Ministry —In and Then Through

Most younger emerging leaders in their initial exuberance for ministry feel they are accomplishing much. But in fact, God is doing much more in them than through them. The first years in ministry are tremendous learning years for a young leader who is sensitive to God's working in his/her life. God works on character first, even before a leader moves into full time leadership. Table Ne 10-1 lists four major shaping processes dealing with character and four major shaping processes dealing with early ministry.

Table Ne 10-1. Early Shaping Processes Identified and Defined

Type	Name	Explanation/ Biblical Example
Character	Integrity Check	A shaping process to test heart intent and consistency of inner beliefs and outward practice./ Daniel 1:3,4.
Character	Obedience Check	A shaping process to test a leader's will for obedience to God. /See Abraham, Ge 22.
Character	Word Check	A shaping process to test a leader's ability to hear from God./ See Samuel ch 3.
Character	Ministry Task	A shaping process to test a leader's faithfulness in performing ministry./ See Titus, Corinth trip (references in both 1,2Co).
Foundational Ministry	Leadership Committal	A shaping process, part of Guidance, to recruit a leader into ministry and to continue to engage that leader along the ministry path destined for him/her. /See Paul, Ac 9,22,26.
Foundational Ministry	Authority Insights	A shaping process to help leaders learn how to deal with leaders over them and folks under them./ See Ac 13 Barnabas and Paul.
Foundational Ministry	Giftedness Discovery	A shaping process in which a leader learns about natural abilities, acquired skills, and spiritual gifts that God wants to use through that leader./ See Phillip, Ac 8.
Long Term Ministry	Guidance	A shaping process in which God intervenes in the life of a leader at critical points to direct that leader along the ministry path destined for him/her./ See Paul, Ac 16.

Shaping in Middle Ministry —Efficient Ministry

During middle ministry the leader now sees God working through as much as in the leader. Leaders identify giftedness. They learn how to influence; they are learning to lead. They gain many perspectives that channel their ministry toward effectiveness. Table Ne 10-2 lists some of the more important shaping processes that happen during this developmental phase.

Table Ne 10-2. Middle Ministry Shaping Processes—Identified, Defined

Type	Name	Explanation/ Biblical Example
Character/ Ministry	Conflict	A shaping process in which a leader learns perseverance, surfaces defects in character, gets new perspective on issues, and learns how to influence in less than ideal conditions./ See Paul, Ac 19 Ephesus.
Breakthroughs in Ministry	Paradigm Shifts	A shaping process in which God gives breakthrough insights that allow a broadening of perspective so as to propel the leader forward in ministry. /See Paul, Ac 9.
Character/ Ministry	Leadership Backlash	A shaping process in which a leader learns about follower reactions and about perseverance, hearing from God, and inspirational leadership./ See Moses, Ex 5.
Renewal/ Long Term	Challenges	A shaping process in which a leader is induced along the lines of new ministry; a part of the guidance process to take a leader along the life path. /See Paul and Barnabas, Ac 13.

Latter Ministry And Finishing Well—Effective Ministry

The essential difference between middle ministry and latter ministry has to do with focus.[31] In middle ministry the leader learns to be efficient in ministry—that is, to do things well. In latter ministry and the finishing well time the leader learns to be effective—that is, to do the right things well. There is a further deepening of character which enhances the leader's spiritual authority. There is a growing awareness of spiritual warfare. The leader learns to minister with power. Table Ne 10-3 lists some of the shaping processes that take place in the latter part of a leader's lifetime.

Table Ne 10-3. Latter Ministry Shaping Processes—Identified and Defined

Type	Name	Explanation/ Biblical Example
Deep Processing	Crises	A shaping process in which a leader's person or ministry is threatened with discontinuation; an overwhelming time in which the leader feels intense issues which could torpedo his/her whole ministry./ See Paul, 2Co.
Deep Processing	Isolation	A shaping process in which a leader is set aside from ministry and goes through a searching time about identity and a deepening trust of God./ See Paul, Php.
Long Term Guidance	Negative Preparation	A shaping process in which an accumulative effect of a number of negative things in the life and ministry of a leader is used by God to release that leader from some previous ministry and give freedom to enter another ministry./ See Paul, 2Co.
Long Term Guidance	Divine Contacts	A shaping process in which God uses some person in a timely fashion to intervene in a leader's life to give perspective—could be directed toward personhood, ministry, or long term guidance./ See Paul and Barnabas, Ac 9:27.

---

[31] See **Article**, *Focused Life.*

Long Term Guidance	Double Confirmation	A shaping process in which God gives clear guidance by inward conviction and by external conviction (unsought)./ See Paul and Ananias, Ac 9.
Effective Ministry	Power Issues	A group of shaping processes including power encounters, gifted power, networking power and prayer power. The leader learns balance between own effort and God's enabling through him/her. The leader learns to minister effectively with God's power./ See Elijah, 1Ki 18 et al.

Conclusion

Awareness of these shaping processes allows a leader to combat the usually overwhelming attitude of *why me*? By seeing that these shaping processes occur in many leaders lives, leaders are affirmed that they are not way off base. It is part of God's way of developing a leader. A leader who understands what is happening in his/her life stands a better chance of responding to the processes and learning the lessons of God in them than one who is blindsided by these processes.

See *Integrity Check; Obedience Check; Word Check; Ministry Task; Leadership Committal; Authority Insights; Giftedness Discovery; Guidance; Conflict; Paradigm Shifts; Leadership Backlash; Faith Challenge; Leadership Challenge; Crises; Isolation; Negative Preparation; Divine Contacts; Double Confirmation; Power Encounters; Prayer Power; Gifted Power; Networking Power;* **Glossary**. See **Articles**, *Sovereign Mindset; Isolation Processing—Learning Deep Lessons from God; Spiritual Authority—Defined, Six Characteristics*. See **For Further Study Bibliography—The Making of A Leader; Leadership Emergence Theory;** *The Life Cycle of a Leader*.

11. Haggai—Leadership Coalition

Introduction

In the article on civil leadership I defined several important terms. Several of these definitions are important to the thrust of this article on leadership coalition. To have impact on a society, a broad spectrum is needed which includes civil leadership, mainstream religious leadership, and peripheral religious leadership. Several of these definitions will be used in this article.

Definition   <u>Civil leadership</u> refers to people of God, sold out on following God, yet impacting the society via two types of roles often needed—1. Governmental or political roles sanctioned by the society and 2. Military roles sanctioned by the society.

They are not considered religious workers.

Definition   <u>Mainstream religious</u> leadership refers to officially recognized religious roles sanctioned by the society and religious structures.

Priest and various ordained ministry roles (e.g. pastor) would be mainstream religious roles.

Definition   <u>Peripheral religious</u> leadership refers to those roles, mostly outside the mainstream religious structures, which attempt to speak for God to bring about change in religious groups, structures, and society in general.

These sometimes fringe leaders are frequently needed because mainstream religious leaders go nominal in their pursuit of God. God raises these types of leaders up in an *ad hoc sort of manner*, as and when needed. The oral and writing prophets of the O.T. and those exercising prophetic ministries and some apostolic ministries in the present *Church Leadership* Era typically would be examples of peripheral religious leaders.

Typically, all three of the above types of leadership are needed to accomplish God's work in our world. Table Ne 11-1 lists the six Biblical leadership eras and shows how these roles played out in the various eras.

Coalition is a French word that originated from a Latin participle having to do with growing together. Having crossed over into English its meaning is as follows:

Definition   <u>Coalition</u> refers to an alliance, especially a temporary one, of people, factions, parties, or nations.

Taking this definition a bit further, we arrive at our Biblical leadership definition,

Definition   A leadership coalition in Biblical literature refers to

- a partnership, whether formal or informal,
- which exists between civil leaders, mainstream religious leaders and/or peripheral religious leaders,
- for a temporary period of time

in order to accomplish some God-directed task(s).

The more formal and deliberate is the coalition and the more specifically the task is defined, the more effective is the leadership.

Some Possible Coalitions Throughout The Leadership Eras

Table Ne 11-1 Possible Coalitions in the Leadership Eras

Leadership Era	Partnership	Formal (F) Informal (I)	God-Directed Task	Time Span of Coalition
I. Patriarchal	None seen		None seen	None seen
2. Pre-Kingdom a. Desert	a. Moses, Aaron, Miriam, Joshua	I	Survival in Desert	40 years
2. Pre-Kingdom b. Conquering the Land	Joshua, Eleazar	F	Conquer the Land; Parcel it out to the Tribes	10 years or so???
2. Pre-Kingdom b. Conquered by the Land	Deborah, Barak	I	Military Defense	Very Short (less than a year)
	Samuel, Saul	I	Transition to Kingdom	Relatively Short (year or so??)
3. Kingdom	Frequently you will see some king in a coalition with a military leader and/or some religious priest	I (military part more formal)	Self-preservation	Varied—some for several years
4. Post-Kingdom a. As Kingdom was crumbling	Not clear; except that some kings allied themselves with some priests against the periphereal ministry of prophets	I	Reject God's Corrective Ministry Through Prophets	Relatively short
b. In exile	Mordecai, Esther	I	Preservation of Jewish exiles	Relatively short

c. Return to Land	Haggai, Zechariah, Joshua and Zerubbabel	I at first but increasingly became more deliberate, F	Rebuilding of Temple	Relatively short
	Nehemiah, Ezra	I at first but increasingly became more deliberate, F	Building of Wall Around Jerusalem for Protection	Relatively Short

Coalitions are dominantly an Old Testament concept having to do with the various leadership needs of the people of God.

Some Observations

The two most effective coalitions were that of Haggai, Zechariah, Joshua and Zerubbabel and that of Ezra and Nehemiah. Some commonalities include:

1. Both of these coalitions were for relatively short times.
2. Both of these collations were very specific, one to rebuild the temple, the other to rebuild the wall around Jerusalem.
3. In both cases, all of the leaders were spiritually alive—civil, formal religious, and peripheral religious.

Some differences include:

1. Ezra operated in the role of formal religious (was a priest) and informal religious leader (calling for reform and renewal). Haggai, the major motivator was a peripheral religious leader. The religious leader, Joshua, was supplementary to Haggai's leadership.
2. Ezra's informal religious ministry was focused on renewal—via the revealed word of God—getting people back to knowing and obeying God's word. Haggai's informal religious ministry was focused on motivating the people to rebuild the temple.
3. Nehemiah was the inspirational leader, though a civil leader. He was the practical, get it done kind of person. Haggai was the inspirational leader, though not in the formal religious structure.
4. Nehemiah, though very practical, was a man of dependence upon God in prayer. Haggai was the practical point person in the rebuilding of the temple. Zechariah was probably the spiritual motivator.
5. The obstacles that Nehemiah and Ezra faced were primarily external (coming from opposition from without though there were some internal obstacles in terms of resources). The obstacles that Haggai, Zechariah, Joshua, and Zerubbabel faced were dominantly internal—in the hearts and minds of the followers.

6. Nehemiah's connections into the power structure provided a source of resources. Zerubbabel had to raise resources from the people themselves, who were going through major times of depression.

Closure

Coalitions worked because various leadership functions were needed to pull off the accomplishments that God was challenging them to. And leaders who were gifted in the various areas (civil, main stream religious, military, and peripheral religious) were willing to work together and respect the necessary leadership of the others in the coalition. It is the cooperative effort and respect for others leadership that made the two most effective coalitions so successful (Nehemiah's—the building of the wall; Haggai's—the rebuilding of the temple).

Because of the dispersed nature of local churches in various geographical and cultural areas all over the world there is no formal coalition leadership made up of civil political, military, formal religious and peripheral religious leadership. Instead, what is seen in the New Testament expansion of the church into different cultures and geographical areas is the concept of a team, which takes the Gospel into these new regions. It is a diverse gifted team. And the same kind osf cooperation and respect are needed for a Gospel expansion team to pull off its ministry.

Probably, several important lessons can be learned from the study of these effective coalitions. (1) God brings together diverse leadership people in order to carry out specific tasks. (2) The more these diverse leaders can recognize the other leaders' functions and respectfully cooperate with them the more effective will be the accomplishment of God's task. (3) For short periods of time—various leaders can contribute their efforts jointly to see something accomplished.

12. Influence, Power and Authority Forms

Introduction

A major lesson concerning how a leader ought to influence states:

Effective leaders value spiritual authority as a primary power base.

To understand this important principle we need to define some terms. The terms that are used to describe leadership make a difference in how we see leadership. Three important terms are influence, power, and authority. Sometimes these important terms are used interchangeable in leadership literature. I use a simplified adaptation of Dennis Wrong's[32] basic schema for relating these concepts—though I have adapted it to fit my understanding of spiritual authority. Influence is the most embracing of the concepts. Power is intended use of influence. And authority is one kind of power usually associated with tight organizations.[33]

---

[32] See Dennis Wrong, **Power--Its Forms, Bases, and Uses**. San Francisco, CA: Harper and Row, 1979. This is a brilliant treatment involving definitions of power concepts as well as recognition of how these forms change over time. His analysis gave a complicated taxonomy which I have simplified and adapted.

[33] Christian organizations operate on a continuum from tight to loose. The more loose an organization is the more it is characterized by voluntary workers who are not paid to do some job but do it because they want to. Therefore leaders in loose organizations do not have as much authority as those in tight organizations which are characterized by paid workers, structures levels of leadership, and supervisory responsibility (that is, people have bosses who can fire them if they don't submit to authority).

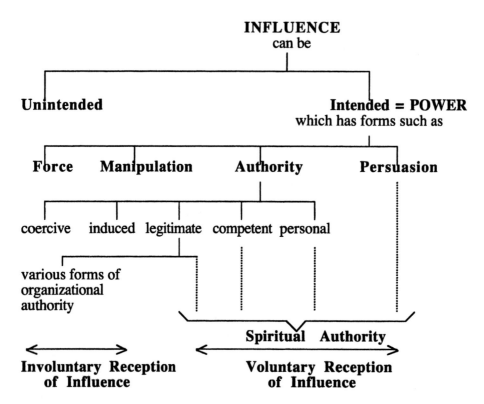

Figure Ne 12-1. Leadership Influence Components—(Adapted from Wrong)

Explanation

Leaders are people with God-given capacities and God-given responsibilities who are influencing specific groups of people toward God's purposes for them. They are intentional in their use of means to influence, meaning using deliberate power forms. When we describe such leaders we are coming down the right side of the diagram in Figure Ne 12-1. Leaders have a right to influence. The ability to influence comes through the control of power bases.

Definition   Power base refers to the source of credibility, power differential, or resources which enables a leader (*power holder)* to have authority to exercise influence on followers (*power subjects*).

Definition   Authority refers to the right to exercise leadership influence by a leader over followers with respect to some field of influence.

Power is manifested in power forms which bring about compliance. The four major power forms in our tree diagram include FORCE, MANIPULATION, AUTHORITY, AND PERSUASION. Authority is further sub-divided into coercive, induced, legitimate, competent, and personal. Spiritual authority is a hybrid combination of persuasion and legitimate, competent, and personal authority.

Power forms depend upon power bases. Bases come from power resources—those individual and collective assets such as organization, money, reputation, personal appeal, manipulative skills, interpersonal skills, kinds of knowledge, information, indwelling Holy Spirit, giftedness.

The central concept of authority is the right to exercise influence. That right is recognized both by leader and follower. It is based upon common assumptions about the *field of influence*. For a spiritual leader the *field of influence* has to do with God's purposes and His directions for accomplishing specific aims that He reveals. Morality, corporate guidance, and clarification of truth are three aspects within the *field of influence* which define the leader's range of use of authority.

Table Ne 12-1 details a number of important concepts that help clarify how a leader influences.

Table Ne 12-1. Influence, Power, Authority Concepts Defined

Influence, Power, Authority Concepts	Description
Power forms	Power forms refer to four general terms of influence means: force, manipulation, authority, and persuasion.
Force	A force power form refers to the use of physical and psychic influence means to gain compliance. This form is now rarely used by spiritual leaders though historically it has been used.
Manipulation	A manipulative power form refers to any influence means whereby a leader gains compliance of a follower where the follower does not have awareness of the leader's intents and therefore does not necessarily have freedom to exert moral responsibility in the situation.[34]
Authority	An authority power form refers to influence means such as: coercive authority, induced authority, legitimate authority, competent authority, personal authority and spiritual authority. See definitions which follow in this Table.
Persuasion	A persuasive power form refers to any influence means such as arguments, appeals or exhortations whereby the leader gains compliance of the follower yet protects the freedom of the follower to exercise moral responsibility.
Coercive Authority	Coercive authority is the form of power in which a leader obtains compliance by using influence means such as threat of force or of punishment.
Induced Authority	Induced authority is the form of power in which a leader obtains compliance by using influence means of promise of reward or some gain for the follower.
Legitimate Authority	Legitimate authority is the form of power in which a leader obtains compliance by using influence pressure consonant with common expectations of the role or positions held by the follower and leader.
Competent Authority	Competent authority is the form of power in which a leader obtains or can expect (but not demand) compliance by virtue of acknowledged expertise in some field of endeavor. The authority is limited to that field of endeavor.
Personal Authority	Personal authority is the form of power in which a leader obtains or expects compliance (but can not demand it) by virtue of the follower's recognition of the leader's personal characteristics.

---

[34]Manipulation in general usually has only negative connotations in western societies since it usually implies influencing against one's wishes. While it is true that manipulation is usually bad, it does not have to be so. The definition above is neutral. It is the motivation behind and the ultimate purpose of the influence that is the key.

Machiavelli[35] posited two real ultimate motivations: fear and love. For him, fear was the stronger of the two and hence a vital part of effective leadership. Jesus advocated love as the stronger. On the power continuum, those forms to the left of inducement all utilize the motivation of fear—they are categorized by the notion of involuntary reception of influence. Those from induced authority to the right all have in essence love as the primary motivation. They are categorized by the notion of voluntary reception of influence.

Hersey and Blanchard[36] give terms which help us understand further the *competent* authority form. They use the term *expert* to indicate a person who has expertise, skill and knowledge about something so as to command respect from followers. In addition, they define *information* to indicate the leader's possession of information that is valuable to followers. Competent power includes this as well. From a Christian standpoint, giftedness—a God-given capacity—fits under competent power.

Two terms from Hersey and Blanchard help us understand further the *personal* power sub-form. *Referent* power is a type of power based on the leader's personal traits. Such a leader is usually liked and admired by others because of personality, sincerity, or the like. *Modeling* describes the Christian equivalent of this form. Follower are influenced by leaders they admire. They want to emulate them. *Connection* power refers to a type of power that arises because a leader has connections to influential or powerful people. In leadership emergence theory this is called networking power.

Leaders will need the entire range of power forms and authority forms in order to lead followers. It is helpful to know this as well as the negative and positive aspects of these forms.[37]

Seeing Spiritual Authority Via Influence, Power, and Authority Concepts
Now we can examine that major trans-Biblical lesson I stated earlier.

Effective Leaders Value Spiritual Authority As A Primary Power Base.

While it will take a whole range of power forms to accomplish God's purposes to take immature followers to maturity, it should be the goal of spiritual leaders to move people toward the right on the power continuum so that they voluntarily accept leadership and follow for mature reasons.[38] So, leaders who are concerned with developing followers should be continually using spiritual authority whenever possible. From our diagram in Figure 1, spiritual authority is defined as a hybrid power form which includes influence via persuasion and authority, especially competent and personal. Legitimate authority frequently helps supplement spiritual authority but does not guarantee it. Notice the voluntary aspect of the spiritual authority definition.

Definition   Spiritual authority is the right to influence conferred upon a leader by followers because of their perception of spirituality in that leader.

---

[35] His views were published in the classic, **The Prince.**

[36] See Paul Hersey and Ken Blanchard, **Management of Organizational Behavior--Utilizing Human Resources.** Englewood Cliffs, N.J.: Prentice-Hall, 1977.

[37]See Dennis Wrong, **Power--Its Forms, Bases, and Uses.** New York: Harper and Row, 1979. He gives an excellent treatment of definitions as well as the dynamics of the forms. When certain forms are overused they tend to change to other types of forms.

[38] This is the model God uses with us as believers. He can force us to do things and sometimes does, but He always prefers for us to willingly obey.

An expanded clarification of this definition describes spiritual authority further as that characteristic of a God-anointed leader, which is developed upon an experiential power base that enables him/her to influence followers through:

1. Persuasion (a major power form),
2. Force of modeling (fits under the personal authority form) and
3. Moral expertise (fits under the competent authority form).

Spiritual authority comes to a leader in three major ways. As leaders go through deep experiences with God they experience the sufficiency of God to meet them in those situations. They come to know God. This *experiential knowledge of God and the deep experiences with God* are part of the experiential acquisition of spiritual authority. A second way that spiritual authority comes is through a life which *models godliness*. When the Spirit of God is transforming a life into the image of Christ, those characteristics of love, joy, peace, long suffering, gentleness, goodness, faith, meekness, temperance carry great weight in giving credibility that the leader is consistent inward and outward. Both of these sources of spiritual authority reflect themselves dominantly via the personal authority form. A third way that spiritual authority comes is through *gifted power*. When a leader can demonstrates gifted power—that is, a clear testimony to divine intervention in the ministry—there will be spiritual authority. This source of spirituality buttresses the competent authority form. While all three of these ways of getting spiritual authority should be a part of a leader, it is frequently the case that one or more of the elements dominates.

Conclusion

Some closing observations on spiritual authority are worth noting:

1. Spiritual authority is the ideal form of influence that should be used by leaders.
2. Because of the responsibility of leaders, that is, they must influence—it will require more than just spiritual authority as a power base because of immature followers who cannot recognize spiritual authority.
3. Leaders must develop followers in maturity so that they can more sensitively see God's use of spiritual authority in a leader.
4. Leaders who do not develop followers in maturity will find they have to use the less ideal forms of power (coercive, inducive, legitimate) more often.
5. These forms tend to degenerate toward the left on the continuum becoming less effective over time. This in turn often drives a leader to abuse his/her authority because of the need to force influence.
6. Spiritual authority, like any of the authority forms, can be abused.
7. Mature leaders never abuse spiritual authority.
8. Spiritual authority is ideally used to build up followers and carry out God's purposes for them.
9. Leaders should treasure deep processing with God, knowing that God will use it to develop their spiritual authority.
10. Giftedness alone, even when backed by unusual power, is not a safe source of spiritual authority. Giftedness backed by godliness is the more balanced safe source of spiritual authority.

Jesus led almost totally by spiritual authority. Paul, having to deal frequently with immature believers, uses almost the whole range of authority forms. However, whenever Paul can he uses spiritual authority. Both of these models set the pattern for Christian leaders.

An awareness of what spiritual authority is and how it relates to the basic ways a leader influences forms a solid foundation upon which to move toward spiritual authority.

Effective Leaders Value Spiritual Authority As A Primary Power Base.

Do you value spiritual authority? Are you using it to influence specific groups of God's people toward His purposes for them?

See **Articles**, *Pauline Leadership Styles, Spiritual Authority—Defined, Six Characteristics*.

13. Leadership Eras In The Bible, Six Identified

Introduction

A <u>Bible Centered leader</u> refers to a leader whose leadership is informed by the Bible, who has been personally shaped by Biblical values, has grasped the intent of Scriptural books and their content in such a way as to apply them to current situations and who uses the Bible in ministry so as to impact followers. Notice that first concept again—

whose leadership is informed by the Bible.

Two of the most helpful perspectives for becoming a Bible centered leader **whose leadership is informed by the Bible** include:

(1) recognizing the differences in leadership demands on leaders throughout the Bible, i.e. seeing the different leadership eras, and

(2) Recognizing and knowing how to draw out insights from the seven genre of leadership sources in the Bible.

This article overviews the first of these helpful perspective—seeing the leadership eras in the Bible.

The Six Leadership Eras

Let me start by giving you one of the most helpful perspectives, a first step toward getting leadership eyes, for recognizing leadership findings in the Bible. That first helpful perspective involves breaking down the leadership that takes place in the Bible into leadership eras which on the whole share common leadership assumptions and expectations for the time period. These assumptions and expectations differ from one leadership era to the next, though there are commonalties that bridge across the eras.

Definition A <u>leadership era</u> is a period of time, usually several hundred years long, in which the major focus of leadership, the influence means, basic leadership functions, and followership have much in common and which basically change with time periods before or after it.

An outline of the six eras I have identified follows.

I. Patriarchal Era (Leadership Roots)—Family Base
II. Pre-Kingdom Leadership Era—Tribal Base
 A. The Desert Years
 B. The War Years--Conquering the Land,
 C. The Tribal Years/ Chaotic Years/ Decentralized Years--Conquered by the Land
III. Kingdom Leadership Era—Nation Based
 A. The United Kingdom

B. The Divided Kingdom
C. The Single Kingdom--Southern Kingdom Only
IV. **Post-Kingdom Leadership Era—Individual/ Remnant Based**
A. Exile--Individual Leadership Out of the Land
B. Post Exilic--Leadership Back in the Land
C. Interim--Between Testaments
V. **New Testament Pre-Church Leadership—Spiritually Based in the Land**
A. Pre-Messianic
B. Messianic
VI. **New Testament Church Leadership—Decentralized Spiritually Based**
A. Jewish Era
B. Gentile Era

I have used the following tree diagram[39] to provide an overview of leadership. The three overarching components of leadership include: the leadership basal elements (leader, follower, situation which make up the What of leadership); leadership influence means (individual and corporate leadership styles which make up the How of leadership); and leadership Value bases (Biblical and cultural values which make up the Why of leadership).

The Study Of Leadership
involves

Leadership Basal Elements	Leadership Influence Means	Leadership Value Bases
including	such as	including
• Leader	• Individual Means	• Cultural
• Followers	• Corporate Means	• Theological
• Situation	• Spiritual Means	

Figure Ne   13-1. Tree Diagram Categorizing the Basics of Leadership

It was this taxonomy which suggested questions that helped me see for the first time the six leadership eras of the Bible. Table Ne 13-1 below gives the basic questions/subjects/categories that helped me identify the different leadership eras. It is these categories that allows comparison of different leadership periods in the Bible.

Table Ne   13-1. Basic Questions To Ask About Leadership Eras

1. **Major Focus**—Here we are looking at the overall purposes of leadership for the period in question. What was God doing or attempting to do through the leader? Sense of destiny? Leadership mandate?
2. **Influence means**—Here we are describing any of the power means available and used by the leaders in their leadership. We can use any of Wrong's categories or any of the leadership style categories I define. Note particularly in the Old Testament the use of force and manipulation as power means.
3. **Basic leadership functions**—We list here the various achievement/ responsibilities expected of the leaders: from God's standpoint, from the leader's own perception of leadership, from the followers. Usually they can all be

---

[39] This was derived in a research project, the historical study of leadership in the United States from the mid 18th century to the present—for further study see **A Short History of Leadership Theory**, 1986, by Dr. J. Robert Clinton. Altadena, CA: Barnabas Publishers. See **Further Study Bibliography**.

categorized under the three major leadership functions of task, relational, and inspirational functions. But here we are after the specific functions.

4. **Followers**—Here we are after sphere of influence. Who are the followers? What are their relationship to leaders? Which of the 10 Commandments of followership are valid for these followers? What other things are helpful in describing followers?

5. **Local Leadership**—in the surrounding culture: Biblical leaders will be very much like the leaders in the cultures around them. Leadership styles will flow out of this cultural press. Here we are trying to identify leadership roles in the cultures in contact with our Biblical leaders.

6. **Other**—Miscellaneous catch all: such things as centralization or decentralization or hierarchical systems of leadership; joint (civil, political, military, religious) or separate roles.

   Thought Questions—Here try to synthesize the questions you would like answered about leaders and leadership if you could get those answers. We are dealing here with such things as the essence of a leader (being or doing), leadership itself, leadership selection and training, authority (centralized or decentralized), etc.

Using these leadership characteristics I studied leadership across the Bible and inductively generated the Six Leadership Eras as given above.[40] Table Ne 13-2 adds some descriptive elements of the eras.

Table Ne 13-2. Six Leadership Eras in the Bible—Brief Characterizations

Leadership Era	Example(s) of Leader	Definitive Characteristics
1. Foundational (also called patriarchal)	Abraham, Joseph	Family Leadership/ formally male dominated/ expanding into tribes and clans as families grew/ moves along kin ship lines
2. Pre-Kingdom	Moses, Joshua, Judges	Tribal Leadership/ Moving to National/ Military/ Spiritual Authority/ outside the land moving toward a centralized national leadership
3. Kingdom	David, Hezekiah	National Leadership/ Kingdom Structure/ Civil, Military/ Spiritual/ a national leadership—Prophetic call for renewal/ inside the land/ breakup of nation
4. Post-Kingdom	Ezekiel, Daniel, Ezra	Individual leadership/ Modeling/ Spiritual Authority
5. Pre-Church	Jesus/ Disciples	Selection/ Training/ spiritual leadership/ preparation for decentralization of Spiritual Authority/ initiation of a movement/
6. Church	Peter/ Paul/ John	decentralized leadership/ cross-cultural structures led by leaders with spiritual authority which institutionalize the movement and spread it around the world

---

[40] I have a short form of answers to each of these questions for each of the six leadership eras. See **Article 35. Six Biblical Leadership Eras,** *Approaching the Bible With Leadership Eyes,* where I answer these questions for each era.

13. Leadership Eras In The Bible, Six Identified   *page* 122

When we study a leader or a particular leadership issue in the Scriptures we must always do so in light of the leadership context in which it was taking place. We cannot judge past leadership by our present leadership standards. Conversely, we will find that major leadership lessons learned by these leaders will usually have broad implications for our leadership. By using these lessons we are taking initial steps of Bible Centered Leadership.

See **Articles**: *Leadership Genre—Seven Types; 16. Macro Lessons Defined; 17. Macro Lessons —List of 41 Across Six Leadership Eras; 35. Six Biblical Leadership Eras, Approaching the Bible With Leadership Eyes.*

14. Learning Vicariously From Other Leaders' Lives—Using the Leadership Mandate, Heb 13:7,8

Introduction

I like to refer to Hebrews 13:7,8 as *The Leadership Mandate*. That is, we have the right and duty to study leaders and in fact are commanded to do so. Note my paraphrase of this famous contextual unit in Hebrews 13.

> Remember your former leaders. Imitate those qualities and achievements
> that were God-Honoring, for their source of leadership still lives -- Jesus!
> He, too, can inspire and enable your own leadership today.
> Hebrews 13:7,8 Clinton paraphrase

The Leadership Mandate carries a two-fold whammy. One, you can study leaders—biblical, historical, and contemporary—for God-honoring qualities and achievements, that is, learning leadership lessons from their lives. And you can expect Jesus to enable you to get these same things in your own life and leadership. Two, you can model leadership qualities and achievements in your own life and expect God to use them in other lives. This leads me to identify an important leadership observation.

EFFECTIVE LEADERS LEARN VICARIOUSLY FROM OTHER LEADERS' LIVES.

Passages like 1 Co 10:6, 11 and Ro 15:4 exhort us to learn from the examples of the Old Testament in general. And Hebrews 13:7,8 exhort us to learn from the examples of leaders specifically. Biblical leaders' biographical information should be studied to learn lessons vicariously.

Vicarious Learning Defined

Let me define vicarious learning and give two reasons why it is important.

Definition   Vicarious learning refers to the method of learning from someone else's life.

Reason 1. The principle of intentional selectivity plays a vital role here. That something of a biographical nature is included in Scripture, out of all that could be included, signifies something special about the entry. It should be studied carefully. The Holy Spirit superintended the shaping of what is put in the Bible and what is left out. We can be assured that things are included in the Bible for important reasons. Such is the case with biographical information. It is there for a reason. The book of Jonah was important enough to be included. It has some very important lessons for us. This book is not about what a prophet prophesied. It is about the shaping of that prophet.

Reason 2. You will not have enough time nor experiences to learn first hand all of the leadership lessons you will need to have an effective ministry. You must learn to learn second hand in order to get the leadership lessons you will need for your ministry.

Biography Leadership Genre

Biographical data represents the single most important leadership source in the Old Testament and a large source in the New Testatment.[41] There is much biographical information in the Bible.

Definition   <u>Biographical</u> data refers to that large amount of information in the Scriptures, which is made up of small narrative slices of life about a person.

These narrative slices or vignettes gives information about Bible characters, which allows us to perceive processing, pivotal points, leadership acts or other such interpretations from this source material. The more slices there are the more we can build to a more complete biography. Examples of biographical information include the biblical material on Joseph, Moses, Joshua, Caleb, Jephthah, Habakkuk, and Jonah. In fact, some 288 biblical leaders are named in the Old Testament and 112 are named in the New Testament. Not all these leaders named have sufficient information for profitable biographical study.Of these 400 leaders, there is enough information to do helpful leadership studies of about 75.

Four Different Kinds of Biographical Sources

Depending on the kind and amount of information available, biographical studies can be broken into four major categories.[42]

1. **CRITICAL INCIDENT SOURCE.** A single incident or series of incidents taking place in a very short time. There may actually be a large amount of information but all focused on a short time-interval. The information can be interpreted for processing or for a leadership act or other such findings.

   example: Job, Habakkuk, Jonah

2. **MINI-SOURCES.** Multiple incidents over a period of time, which allows the creation of an abbreviated time-line and the possibility to see some patterns over time.

   example: Asa, Jehoshaphat, Hezekiah

3. **MIDI-SOURCES.** Multiple incidents over the whole lifetime, which allow not only the creation of an abbreviated time-line but some processing from the various time periods.

---

[41] Seven types of leadership source materials have been identified in the Bible. These include: 1. Biographical like Joseph, Moses, Joshua, Caleb, Jephthah, etc.; 2. Historical Leadership Acts—e.g. Samuel's final leadership act 1Samuel 12; 3. Actual leadership contexts like1 Peter 5:1-5; 4. Parabolic leadership literature like the Stewardship parables and many others; 5. Indirect—passages dealing with Christian character or behavior, which also apply to Christian leadership as well; 6. The study of Bible books as a whole—placing them in their context hermeneutically and in terms of leadership development; 7. The Study across Books for common themes and lessons on leadership (macro lessons). See the **Article**, *Leadership Genre—7 Types.*

[42] These four categories are not exclusive. There is some overlap in these at the borders between them.

example: Barnabas, Joseph, Daniel, Joshua, Peter, Jeremiah

4. **MAXI-SOURCES**. There is much information in the Scripture on the character.

example: Moses, David, Jesus, Paul, Jeremiah

Jonah—Critical Incident Source

Jonah is typical of a critical incident source of biographical information. Our study of Jonah in this commentary includes only a very few scenarios from his life that represent perhaps a few months. Yet this information has in it a number of leadership lessons.

Values of Vicarious Learning Through Biography

You can learn negative lessons, hard lessons, without going through the deep processing or tragic things the leader you are studying did to learn them.

You can learn through the positive things, the blessings, the gains the good things that leader experienced.

You can gain valuable long-term perspective that you cannot get until you have lived a whole lifetime.

In fact, as a leader, you will never learn enough leadership lessons, just from what you experience personally, to have an effective and successful ministry. You need to learn from other leaders.

How To Do Biographical Study

The **Article**, *Biographical Study in the Bible, How To Do* lists 12 steps for doing biographical study. I list them below to indicate what is involved in studying to learn vicariously. But you should study that article in depth. It is not the purpose of this article to teach you how to do biographical study, but to exhort you of its importance.

Step 1. **Identify All The Passages That Refer To The Leader.** e.g. Jonah is mentioned once outside the book of Jonah and then a number of times in the book of Jonah. Nehemiah is mentioned only in the books of Nehemiah and Ezra.

Step 2. **Seek To Order The Vignettes Or Other Passages In A Time Sequence.** e.g. for a critical incident source like Jonah, the book itself orders what happened. This step is very helpful in the study of Nehemiah.

Step 3. **Construct A Time-Line If You Can. At Least Tentatively Identify Major Development Phases.** e.g. this can't be done for Jonah or Habakkuk. We simply know that the critical incidents take place during the mature portion of their ministry. Only partially, can a time line be done for Nehemiah.

Step 4. **Look For Process Items (Critical Events, People, Happenings) In The Life.** e.g. Jonah has 5 identifiable process items: ministry task; obedience check; life crisis; isolation; paradigm shift. Habakkuk has four: crisis; faith challenge; isolation; paradigm shift. See **Glossary** for definitions of these process items. There are a number of process items in Nehemiah. Prominent ones are crises, life crises, conflict, spiritual authority discovery, prayer power, relationship insights, ministry insights and networking power.

<u>Step 5</u>. **Identify Pivotal Points From The Major Process Items.** e.g. for both Habakkuk and Jonah the series of critical incidents describe a pivotal point in their ministries. Dealing with the peoples concerns about loans and interest was probably a pivotal point for Nehemiah. See **Article**, *Pivotal Points*.

<u>Step 6</u>. **Seek To Determine Any Lessons You Can From A Study Of These Process Items And Pivotal Points. Use The Certainty Continuum To Help You Identify The Level Of Authority For Using The Lessons You Find.** See **Article**, *Principles of Truth*. e.g. The study of Jonah and Habakkuk results in numerous leadership observations. See the **Articles**, *Jonah, Eight Important Ideas to Communicate; Habakkuk, Eight Important Ideas to Communicate;Nehemiah, Eight Important Ideas to Communicate*.See also the leadership topics and text comments which contain many leadership observations.

<u>Step 7</u>. **Identify Any Response Patterns** (or unique patterns). e.g. for Jonah, the negative and positive test patterns are seen.

<u>Step 8</u>. **Study Any Individual Leadership Acts In The Life. Use The Approach Demonstrated In This Chapter.** See *leadership act*, **Glossary**. e.g. for Jonah, this step is not applicable. Several leadership acts occur in Nehemiah, one of the most significant is when he challenges the leaders to build the wall.

<u>Step 9</u>. **Use The Overall Leadership Tree Diagram To Help Suggest Leadership Issues To Look For.** See **Article**, *Leadership Tree Diagram*. e.g. for Jonah, this step is not applicable. This is important for Nehemiah both in terms of recognizing the followers and for analyzing leadership styles.

<u>Step 10</u>. **Use The List Of Major Functions (Task Functions, Relationship Functions And Inspirational Functions) To Help Suggest Insights. Which Were Done, Which Not.** See **Article**, *Leadership Functions*. e.g. for Jonah, this step is not applicable. Nehemiah was dominantly a task oriented leader with powerful inspirational leadership. He applied relational leadership when it was desperately needed (loans and interest).

<u>Step 11</u>. **Observe Any N.T. Passages Or Commentary** (indirect source—anywhere in Bible) **On The Leader. Especially Be On The Lookout For** *Bent Of Life* **Evaluation.** e.g. for Jonah, Jesus validates the historicity of Jonah and the important lesson concerning truth and its response and degrees of judgment. The New Testament is silent on Nehemiah.

<u>Step 12</u>. **Use The Presentation Format For Organizing Your Display Of Findings For Steps 1-11.** e.g. for Jonah or Nehemiah, this step is not applicable.

Closure

The difference between leaders and followers is perspective. The difference between leaders and effective leaders is better perspectives. Vicarious learning affords a leader a chance to get better perspectives. Yet, many leaders have never done any biographical study of biblical leaders, historical Christian leaders or contemporary Christian leaders. You must learn how to learn second hand.

15. Left Hand of God

Introduction

Vertical verses in a horizontal book like Proverbs demand our attention.[43] Note Proverbs 21:1 in the several translations given below.

21:1 The king's heart [is] in the hand of the LORD, [as] the rivers of water: he turneth it whithersoever he will. KJV

21:1 The king's heart is in the hand of Jehovah as the watercourses: He turneth it whithersoever he will. ASV

2:1 The king's heart is [like] channels of water in the hand of the LORD; He turns it wherever He wishes. NASB

21:1 The king's heart is in the hand of the LORD; he directs it like a watercourse wherever he pleases. NIV

21:1 The king's heart [is] in the hand of the LORD, [Like] the rivers of water; He turns it wherever He wishes. NKJV

21:1 The king's heart is a stream of water in the hand of the LORD; he turns it wherever he will. RSV

21:1 The Lord controls rulers, just as he determines the course of rivers. CEV

21:1 The Lord controls the mind of a king as easily as he directs the course of a stream. TEV

21:1 The king's heart is like a stream of water directed by the Lord; he turns it wherever he pleases. NLT

The terms used—rivers, watercourses, channels, stream, course could refer to a canal or channel of water such as an irrigation ditch. Just as the farmer directs the irrigation ditch so as to bring water where he wants it, so God directs kings and other rulers to do what He wants done.

---

[43] Psalms is a vertical book. That is, most of the Psalms are dealing with humans talking and/or hearing from God (vertical communication). Proverbs is dealing for the most part with humans relating to each other (horizontal relationships or activity). So then in a book dealing with horizontal relationships or activity it behooves us to note those few vertical passages. They demand our attention.

Every missionary better learn this verse and its view of God very quickly. For missionaries operate in countries controlled by others. They must abide by decisions made by political rulers—usually not in favor of their being in the country. Missionaries learn to trust God to move in the affairs of these pagan rulers.

Glasser Phrase

Dr. Arthur Glasser uses the phrase, the *Left Hand of God*, to call attention to God's use of non-believers to accomplish His purposes. This *Left Hand of God* is seen numerous times in the Old Testament. Table Ne 15-1 depicts just a few of them.

Table Ne 15-1. Some Occurrences of the Left Hand of God

Passage	Persons Involved	Explanation
Genesis 20, 21	Abraham, Sarah, Abimelech	Abraham lied to Abimelech about Sarah his wife. God protects her while she is with Abimelech and gives Abimelech a dream to let him know who Sarah is.
Genesis	Joseph, Pharaoh	God sends two dreams to Pharaoh, which need to be interpreted. Joseph comes to the forefront by interpreting these dreams and suggesting a wise course of action. Joseph is elevated to high position and is in place to deliver his people when the famine hits hardest.
Daniel	Nebuchadnezzar	Daniel ch 4 is one of the clearest examples of the king's heart being in the hand of Jehovah. God humbles Nebuchadnezzar, a very powerful ruler.
Isa 45	Cyrus; Daniel et al	God predicts He will use Cyrus and He does as noted in Table Ne 15-2 below.
Hag 1:1,2	Darius, Haggai	It is clear that Darius was used by God to help the remnant back in the land.
Ne ch 1 et al	Artaxerxes	Artaxerxes not only wrote decrees allowing the Jews to go back in the land, but he also helped fund their return.

Restoration Leaders

All the restoration leaders were very much aware of the Left Hand of God. They were rebuilding the work of God back in the land. They were there because God had moved in the hearts of pagan rulers, very powerful ones. Those rulers—particularly Cyrus, Darius, Xerxes, Artxerxes—were moved to aid God's people. Esther, Mordecai, Ezra, Nehemiah, Haggai, Zechariah, and Malachi were all aware of the Left Hand of God.

One of the astounding things is God's prediction that He will use these rulers to accomplish His purposes. A beautiful illustration of this is Isaiah's famous passage, Isa 45. Table Ne 15-2 below illustrates just a few of the passages referring to Cyrus.

Table Ne 15-2. God's Left Hand Working Through Cyrus

Passages Predicting	Passages Fulfilling
Isa 44:28 That saith of **Cyrus**, [He is] my shepherd, and shall perform all my pleasure: even saying to Jerusalem, Thou shalt be built; and to the temple, Thy foundation shall be laid. Isa 45:1 Thus saith the LORD to his anointed, to **Cyrus**, whose right hand I have holden, to subdue nations before him; and I will loose the loins of kings, to open before him the two leaved gates; and the gates shall not be shut; Isa 45:13 I have raised him (Cyrus) up in righteousness, and I will direct all his ways: he shall build my city, and he shall let go my captives, not for price nor reward, saith the LORD of hosts.	2Ch 36:22,23 Now in the first year of **Cyrus** king of Persia, that the word of the LORD [spoken] by the mouth of Jeremiah might be accomplished, the LORD stirred up the spirit of **Cyrus** king of Persia, that he made a proclamation throughout all his kingdom, and [put it] also in writing, saying, Thus saith **Cyrus** king of Persia, All the kingdoms of the earth hath the LORD God of heaven given me; and he hath charged me to build him an house in Jerusalem, which [is] in Judah. Who [is there] among you of all his people? The LORD his God [be] with him, and let him go up. Ezr 1:2, 7, 8 Thus saith **Cyrus** king of Persia, The LORD God of heaven hath given me all the kingdoms of the earth; and he hath charged me to build him an house at Jerusalem, which [is] in Judah. 7 Also **Cyrus** the king brought forth the vessels of the house of the LORD, which Nebuchadnezzar had brought forth out of Jerusalem, and had put them in the house of his gods; 8 Even those did **Cyrus** king of Persia bring forth by the hand of Mithredath the treasurer, and numbered them unto Sheshbazzar, the prince of Judah.

Closure

Most of us as leaders know something of the *Right Hand of God*. We have experienced God's intervention in our lives and ministries in such a way as to be awed by His power. But can we see His *Left Hand* working today. We need to be aware of this facet of God's power. And we need discernment, maybe even prophetic voices, to point out to us the *Left Hand of God*. It is especially comforting to believe we have a sovereign God in our world controlled by the most part by non-godly political leaders. May we see God turn the heart of the kings to accomplish His purposes.

See *Sovereign Mindset*; **Glossary**.

16. Macro Lessons—Defined

Introduction to Macro lessons

Macro Lessons inform our leadership with potential leadership values that move toward the absolute. We live in a time when most do not believe there are absolutes. In my study of leadership in the Bible, I have defined a leadership truth continuum which recognizes the difficulty in deriving absolutes but does allow for them.[44] Figure Ne 16-1 depicts this.

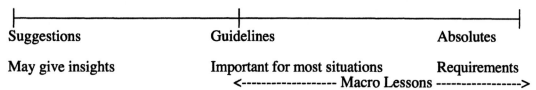

Suggestions   Guidelines   Absolutes

May give insights   Important for most situations   Requirements
<------------------- Macro Lessons ----------------->

Figure Ne 16-1. Leadership Truth Continuum/Where Macro Lessons Occur

In the *Complexity Era* in which we now live,[45] the thrust of leadership theory has moved, toward the importance of leadership values. The questions being asked today are not as much what is leadership (the leadership basal elements—leader, followers, and situations) and how does it operate (leadership influence means—corporate and individual) as it is why do we do what we do (leadership value bases). The first three eras (Great Man, Trait, and Ohio State) answered the question, "What is leadership?" The Contingency and early part of the Complexity Era answered the question, "How do we do it?" Now we are grappling with, "Why do we lead? or What ought we to do?" We are looking for leadership values. A leadership value is an underlying assumption which affects how a leader behaves in or perceives leadership situations. They are usually statements that have *ought* or *must* or *should* in them. Macro-Lessons are statements of truth about leadership which have the potential for becoming leadership values. These macro-lessons are observations seen in the various leadership eras in the Bible. Many of these became values for numerous Bible leaders. These macro-lessons move toward the right (requirement, value) of the leadership truth continuum.

What is a macro lesson?

Definition A <u>macro-lesson</u> is a high level generalization
- of a leadership observation (suggestion, guideline, requirement), stated as a lesson,

---

[44] See Clinton, **Leadership Perspectives** for a more detailed explanation of the continuum and for my approach to deriving principles from the Scriptures. See **Article**, *Principles of Truth*.

[45] A study of leadership history in the United States from 1850 to the present uncovered 6 Eras (an era being a period of time in which some major leadership theory held sway): 1. Great Man Era (1840s to 1904); 2. Trait Theory (1904-1948); 3. Ohio State Era (1948-1967); Contingency Era (1967-1980); Complexity Era (1980-present). See Clinton, **A Short History of Leadership Theory**. Altadena, Ca.: Barnabas Publishers.

- which repeatedly occurs throughout different leadership eras,
- and thus has potential as a leadership absolute.

Macro lessons even at their weakest provide strong guidelines describing leadership insights. At their strongest they are requirements, or absolutes, that leaders should follow. Leaders ignore them to their detriment.

examples **Prayer Lesson**: If God has called you to a ministry then He has called you to pray for that ministry.
Accountability: Christian leaders minister ought always with a conscious view to ultimate accountability to God for their ministry.
Bible Centered: An effective leader who finishes well must have a Bible centered ministry.

Macro Lessons are derived from a comparative study of leadership in the Six Leadership Eras. These Six Leadership Eras and number of macro lessons identified are shown in Table Ne 16-1.

Table Ne 16-1. Leadership Eras and Number of Macro Lessons

Leadership Era	Number of Macro Lessons
1. Patriarchal Era	7
2. Pre-Kingdom Era	10
3. Kingdom Era	5
4. Post-Kingdom Era	5
5. Pre-Church Era	9
6. Church Era	5

I have identified 41 macro lessons, roughly 5 to 10 per leadership era. When a macro-lesson is seen to occur in varied situations and times and cultural settings and in several leadership eras it becomes a candidate for an absolute leadership lesson. When that same generalization becomes personal and is embraced by a leader as a driving force for how that leader sees or operates in ministry, it becomes a leadership value.

The top three Macro Lessons for the four O.T. Leadership Eras are listed in Table Ne 16-2.

Table Ne 16-2. Top Three Macro Lessons in O.T. Leadership Eras

Priority	Leadership Era	Label	Statement
1	Pre-Kingdom	Presence	The essential ingredient of leadership is the powerful presence of God in the leader's life and ministry. (*Therefore a leader must not minister without the powerful presence of God in his/her life.*)
2	Patriarchal	Character	Integrity is the essential character trait of a spiritual leader. (*Therefore, a leader must maintain integrity and respond to God's shaping of it.*)
3	Pre-Kingdom	Intimacy	Leaders develop intimacy with God which in turn overflows into all their ministry since ministry flows out of being. (*Therefore a leader must seek to develop intimacy with God.*)

The top three Macro Lessons for the two N.T. Leadership Eras are listed in Table Ne 16-3.

Table Ne 16-3. Top Three Macro Lessons in N.T. Leadership Eras

Priority	Leadership Era	Label	Statement
1	Church	Word Centered	*God's Word must be the primary source for equipping leaders and must be a vital part of any leader's ministry.*
2	Pre-Church	Harvest	*Leaders must seek to bring people into relationship with God.*
3	Pre-Church	Shepherd	*Leaders must preserve, protect, and develop those who belong to God's people.*

You will notice that some of these macro lessons are already described in value language (should, must, ought) while others are simply statements of observations. I have put in italics my attempt to give the value associated with the observation.

Comparative study across the six leadership eras for macro lessons makes up one of the seven leadership genres, i.e. sources for leadership findings from the Bible.

See **Articles**, *17. List of Macro Lessons; Leadership Genre—Seven Types (Macro Lessons, Biographical Material, Books as A Whole, Direct Context, Indirect Context, Leadership Acts, Parabolic).* See Clinton, **A Short History of Leadership Theory.** Altadena, Ca.: Barnabas Publishers. See also Clinton, **Leadership Perspectives.** Altadena, Ca.: Barnabas Publishers.

17. Macro Lessons: List of 41 Across Six Leadership Eras

Introduction

Macro Lessons inform our leadership with potential leadership values that move toward the absolute. The following are the 41 lessons I have identified as I comparatively studied the six different leadership eras for leadership observations.

No.	Label	Leadership Era	Statement of Macro Lesson
1.	Blessing	Patriarchal	God mediates His blessing to His followers through leaders.
2.	Shaping	Patriarchal	God shapes leader's lives and ministry through critical incidents.
3.	Timing	Patriarchal	God's timing is crucial to accomplishment of God's purposes.
4.	Destiny	Patriarchal	Leaders must have a sense of destiny.
5.	Character	Patriarchal	Integrity is the essential character trait of a spiritual leader.
6.	Faith	Patriarchal	Biblical Leaders must learn to trust in the unseen God, sense His presence, sense His revelation, and follow Him by faith.
7.	Purity	Patriarchal	Leaders must personally learn of and respond to the holiness of God in order to have effective ministry.
8.	Intercession	Pre-Kingdom	Leaders called to a ministry are called to intercede for that ministry.
9.	Presence	Pre-Kingdom	The essential ingredient of leadership is the powerful presence of God in the leader's life and ministry.
10.	Intimacy	Pre-Kingdom	Leaders develop intimacy with God which in turn overflows into all their ministry since ministry flows out of being.
11.	Burden	Pre-Kingdom	Leaders feel a responsibility to God for their ministry.
12.	Hope	Pre-Kingdom	A primary function of all leadership is to inspire followers with hope in God and in what God is doing.
13.	Challenge	Pre-Kingdom	Leaders receive vision from God which sets before them challenges that inspire their leadership.
14.	Spiritual Authority	Pre-Kingdom	Spiritual authority is the dominant power base of a spiritual leader and comes through experiences with God, knowledge of God, godly character and gifted power.
15.	Transition	Pre-Kingdom	Leaders must transition other leaders into their work in order to maintain continuity and effectiveness.
16.	Weakness	Pre-Kingdom	God can work through weak spiritual leaders if they are available to Him.

17.	Continuity	Pre-Kingdom	Leaders must provide for continuity to new leadership in order to preserve their leadership legacy.
18.	Unity	Kingdom	Unity of the people of God is a value that leaders must preserve.
19.	Stability	Kingdom	Preserving a ministry of God with life and vigor over time is as much if not more of a challenge to leadership than creating one.
20.	Spiritual Leadership	Kingdom	Spiritual leadership can make a difference even in the midst of difficult times.
21.	Recru-descence	Kingdom	God will attempt to bring renewal to His people until they no longer respond to Him.
22.	By-pass	Kingdom	God will by-pass leadership and structures that do not respond to Him and will institute new leadership and structures.
23.	Future Perfect	Post-Kingdom	A primary function of all leadership is to walk by faith with a future perfect paradigm so as to inspire followers with certainty of God's accomplishment of ultimate purposes.
24.	Perspective	Post-Kingdom	Leaders must know the value of perspective and interpret present happenings in terms of God's broader purposes.
25.	Modeling	Post-Kingdom	Leaders can most powerfully influence by modeling godly lives, the sufficiency and sovereignty of God at all times, and gifted power.
26.	Ultimate	Post-Kingdom	Leaders must remember that the ultimate goal of their lives and ministry is to manifest the glory of God.
27.	Perseverance	Post-Kingdom	Once known, leaders must persevere with the vision God has given.
28.	Selection	Pre-Church	The key to good leadership is the selection of good potential leaders which should be a priority of all leaders.
29.	Training	Pre-Church	Leaders should deliberately train potential leaders in their ministry by available and appropriate means.
30.	Focus	Pre-Church	Leaders should increasingly move toward a focus in their ministry which moves toward fulfillment of their calling and their ultimate contribution to God's purposes for them.
31.	Spirituality	Pre-Church	Leaders must develop interiority, spirit sensitivity, and fruitfulness in accord with their uniqueness since ministry flows out of being.
32.	Servant	Pre-Church	Leaders must maintain a dynamic tension as they lead by serving and serve by leading.
33.	Steward	Pre-Church	Leaders are endowed by God with natural abilities, acquired skills, spiritual gifts, opportunities, experiences, and privileges which must be developed and used for God.
34.	Harvest	Pre-Church	Leaders must seek to bring people into relationship with God.
35.	Shepherd	Pre-Church	Leaders must preserve, protect, and develop God's people.
36.	Movement	Pre-Church	Leaders recognize that movements are the way to penetrate society though they must be preserved via appropriate ongoing institutions.

37. Structure	Church	Leaders must vary structures to fit the needs of the times if they are to conserve gains and continue with renewed effort.
38. Universal	Church	The church structure is inherently universal and can be made to fit various cultural situations if functions and not forms are in view.
39. Giftedness	Church	Leaders are responsible to help God's people identify, develop, and use their resources for God.
40. Word Centered	Church	God's Word is the primary source for equipping leaders and must be a vital part of any leaders ministry.
41. Complexity	All eras	Leadership is complex, problematic, difficult and fraught with risk—which is why leadership is needed.

Conclusion—Macro Lessons Illustrated in Nehemiah's Leadership
   More macro lessons are observed in Nehemiah's leadership than any other single leader in the Old Testament. Some are seen explicitly in his leadership. Some are strongly implied. And then many are seen in seed form—that is, there are intimations of the core idea seen though certainly not known by Nehemiah.

Table Ne 17-3 Macro Lessons Overtly Seen In Nehemiah's Leadership

Number	First Seen--Leadership Era	Label/Statement of Macro Lesson
3	Patriarchal	Timing/ God's timing is crucial to accomplishment of God's purposes.
5	Patriarchal	Integrity/ Integrity is the essential character trait of a spiritual leader.
6	Patriarchal	Faith/ Biblical Leaders must learn to trust in the unseen God, sense His presence, sense His revelation, and follow Him by faith.
7	Patriarchal	Purity/ Leaders must personally learn of and respond to the holiness of God in order to have effective ministry
8	Pre-Kingdom	Intercession/ Leaders called to a ministry are called to intercede for that ministry.
9	Pre-Kingdom	Presence/ The essential ingredient of leadership is the powerful presence of God in the leader's life and ministry.
10	Pre-Kingdom	Intimacy/ Leaders develop intimacy with God which in turn overflows into all their ministry since ministry flows out of being.
11	Pre-Kingdom	Burden/ Leaders feel a responsibility to God for their ministry.
13	Pre-Kingdom	Challenge/ Leaders receive vision from God which sets before them challenges that inspire their leadership.
14	Pre-Kingdom	Spiritual Authority/ Spiritual authority is the dominant power base of a leader and comes through experiences with God, knowledge of God, godly character and gifted power.

17	Pre-Kingdom	Continuity/ Leaders must provide for continuity to new leadership in order to preserve their leadership legacy.
19	Kingdom	Stability/ Preserving a ministry of God with life and vigor over time is as much if not more of a challenge to leadership than creating one.
20	Kingdom	Spiritual Leadership/ Spiritual leadership can make a difference even in the midst of difficult times.
21	Kingdom	Recrudescence/ God will attempt to bring renewal to His people until they longer respond to Him.
27	Post-Kingdom	Perseverance/ Once known, leaders must persevere with the vision God has given.
30	Pre-Church	Focus/Leaders should increasingly move toward focus in their ministry—focusing on their calling and ultimate contribution.
35	Shepherd	Shepherd/ Leaders must preserve, protect, and develop God's people.
41	All Eras	Complexity/ Leadership is complex, problematic, difficult and fraught with risk—which is why leadership is needed.

An amazing thing is that a number of macro lessons, which are discovered explicitly in later leadership eras, are seen in early seed form in Nehemiah's leadership.

Table Ne 17-4 Macro Lessons Seen In Seed Form in Nehemiah's Leadership

Number	First Seen--Leadership Era	Label/Statement of Macro Lesson
4	Patriarchal	Destiny/ Leaders must have a sense of destiny.
25	Post Kingdom	Modeling/ Leaders can most powerfully influence by modeling godly lives, the sufficiency and sovereignty of God at all times, and gifted power.
26	Post Kingdom	Ultimate Goal/ Leaders must remember that the ultimate goal of their lives and ministry is to manifest the glory of God.
28	Pre-Church	Selection/ The key to good leadership is the selection of good potential leaders which should be a priority of all leaders.

31	Pre-Church	Spirituality/ Leaders must develop interiority, spirit sensitivity, and fruitfulness in accord with their uniqueness since ministry flows out of being.
32	Pre-Church	Servant/ Leaders must maintain a dynamic tension as they lead by serving and serve by leading.
36	Pre-Church	Movement/ Leaders recognize that movements are the way to penetrate society though they must be preserved via appropriate ongoing institutions.
39	Church	Giftedness/ Leaders are responsible to help God's people identify, develop, and use their resources for God.
40	Church	Word Centered Ministry/ God's Word is the primary source for equipping leaders and must be a vital part of any leaders ministry.

See Also **Article** *16. Macro Lessons—Defined.*

18. Nehemiah, And Daniel—Comparison of Vicarious Confession Prayers

Introduction

Even a cursory reading of the books of Daniel and Nehemiah reveal that the two men for whom the books are named were men of prayer and believed in prayer. Table Ne 18-1 reveals incidents from the book of Daniel, which show Daniel's prayer fervor. Table Ne 18-2 reveals incidents from the book of Nehemiah, which show Nehemiah's repeated reliance upon prayer.

Table Ne 18-1 Incidents of Prayer Times Important to Daniel

Number	Verse(s)	Label	Description
1	Da ch 2	Survival Praying	Daniel relies on friends to pray through the night while he seeks the King's hidden vision.
2	Da 6:10	Habitual Prayer	Daniel prayed three times a day. This was his normal habit.
3	Da 9:	Vicarious Praying	Daniel prays one of the great vicarious confessions of the Old Testament in this passage.
4	Da 10	Fasting/ Seeking God's Perspective	Daniel fasts and prays to understand future perspectives that have come to him in visions.

Table Ne 18-2 Incidents of Prayer Times Important to Nehemiah

Number	Verse(s)	Label	Description
1	Ne 1:4, 5, 6, 8, 11	Burdened Prayer for Jerusalem	Vicarious confession by Nehemiah seen here. Remember prayer Type I[46].
2	Ne 2:4-11	Vicarious Praying	Vicarious confession by Nehemiah seen here.
3	Ne 4:4,9	Thought Prayer	Prayed for protection as they guarded the city.
4	Ne 5:19	Thought	Remember prayer Type III. Nehemiah

---

[46] Type I. Remember God, an exhortation for the people to remember in the past what God had done (both in blessing and punishing) or to remind God of what He has said; Type II. Remember enemies—an imprecatory prayer asking God to punish the enemies. Type III. A personal request for God to remember Nehemiah for what he had done in his leadership.

		prayer	asking God to remember himself.
5	Ne 6:9	Thought Prayer	Nehemiah asks for strength to continue the work in light of the threats received
6	Ne 6:14	Though Prayer	Remember prayer Type II. Nehemiah asking God to punish enemies.
7	Ne 9:5-38	Longest Prayer in the Bible	Vicarious confession occurs here. Nehemiah a part of this but not only one praying.
8	Ne 13:14	Thought Prayer	Remember prayer Type III. Nehemiah asking God to remember himself.
9	Ne 13:22	Thought Prayer	Remember prayer Type III. Nehemiah asking God to remember himself.
10	Ne 13:29	Thought Prayer	Remember prayer Type II. Nehemiah asking God to punish enemies.
11	Ne 13:31	Thought Prayer	Remember prayer Type III. Nehemiah asking God to remember himself.

This article is concerned with number 3 from the Daniel list and numbers 1 and 6 from the Nehemiah list. Here are two great Old Testament Leaders. They both are aware of vicarious confession.[47] What can we learn about vicarious confession from a comparison of these passages?

Vicarious Confession Defined

Vicarious confession,[48] involves the confession of pasts sins, even many generations ago, by a present day leader as if he/she had committed those sins. The confession is done on the behalf of people in the past who did not confess these sins. The result is the on-going work of God, which may have been blocked in some way or other due to this unrepentant sin.

It is not clear why present-day leaders need to confess corporate past sins. The two prominent Old Testament leaders who do this, Daniel and Nehemiah, were burdened because they had read or studied the history of their people and they knew God had disciplined Israel for rebellion and failure to obey His commandments, etc. They saw their own situation in terms of what God could do to restore His people and they somehow sensed that they should intercede for God to work in their day to restore His people. As part of this restoration, they sensed the need to worship God for who He is, recognize Him for past work, vindicate His just actions in the past—even the discipline that was so tragic, sending His people into exile—and to ask God for His forgiveness for those past wrongdoings, as well as His blessings upon the restoration of His people. They were aware of promises God had made which said He would bring his people back if they would repent and turn to Him. Daniel and Nehemiah, as representative leaders took this repentance seriously. The vicarious confession was part of their serious attempt to demonstrate a repentant spirit.

Structure of Daniel's Vicarious Confession

Both Daniel and Nehemiah knew the history of their people. They knew that disobedience to God in the past had brought about the discipline of the fall of Jerusalem

---

[47] Ezra's prayer found in Ezra 9:5-10:1 is possibly another example of vicarious praying. I will deal with it in the Ezra leadership commentary.

[48] See Kraft (2002:177, 229-30) who along with Wagner and others use the term *identificational repentance* somewhat like I do vicarious confession. They go a bit further and apply this confession specifically to spiritual warfare.

and the resulting exile. Daniel recognized that the timing was such that God would take back a group of Israelites to the land. He had been reading in Jeremiah and saw that the time was right to go back in the land. He partners with God to see this happen. His prayer wants to see that happen. Read carefully his prayer given below.

Chapter 9

1 It was the first year of the reign of Darius the Mede , the son of Ahasuerus, who was king over Babylon. 2 In that first year of his reign I, Daniel, was studying the writing of the prophets—in particular Jeremiah's prophecies about the 70 years captivity in Babylon—explaining that Jerusalem would be desolate for 70 years. I saw that it was time for the 70 years to be completed. 3 So I fasted and prayed earnestly to the Lord God pleading with Him and interceding about this fulfillment of the 70 years prophecy. 4 In my prayer I confessed to the LORD my God.

"O Lord, you are great and are an awesome God. You keep your solemn promises and show loving mercy to those who love you, and obey you. 5 We have sinned. We have done wrong. In our wickedness we have rebelled against you forsaking your commands and guidelines. 6 We have refused to listen and obey what your servants the prophets, who have spoken in your name to our kings and our rulers, to our ancestors and all the people of the land. 7 Lord, you always do right. But we have brought disgrace and shame upon ourselves even to the very present. This is true of all of us including those who live in Judah and in Jerusalem and to those you have scattered to other countries. You have done this because they were unfaithful to you. 8 Our kings, rulers, and ancestors have acted shamefully and sinned against you. 9 You, O Lord our God show mercy and forgiveness, even though we have rebelled against you. 10 We have not obeyed your voice O LORD our God. We have not obeyed your laws, which you gave by your servants the prophets. 11 All Israel has broken your law, and has turned away, refusing to listen to your voice. So now, the curse s written in the Law of Moses, the servant of God, have been fulfilled toward us because of our sin. 12 You have done exactly what you said you would do to us and to our rulers. 12, Never in all history has such a disaster occurred like the one that affected Jerusalem. 13 All the punishment described by Moses has happened. Yet we have not turned from our sins. We have refused to understand your truth. We have not turned in prayer to you, O Lord. 14 Therefore you, O LORD, were prepared to punish us with this disaster. And you did it. And you were right in doing so. We did not listen to you." 15 "O Lord our God, you rescued your people from Egypt with mighty acts of power. You brought lasting honor to your name. But we have sinned and have done wickedly! 16 O Lord, you have delivered us in the past, I pray, let your furious anger against Jerusalem abate. It is your holy mountain. Everyone in the neighboring countries all look down on Jerusalem and on your people because of our sins, and the evil our ancestors did. 17 O our God, hear my prayer. You know I serve you. For your own sake fulfill my requests and again fill your sanctuary with your presence. 18 O my God, please listen to me. Please open your eyes and see our distress. See the city which is called by your name. We don't deserve to have our prayers answered. But we do so want your mercy. 19 O Lord, hear! O Lord, forgive! O Lord, listen and act! In order that people might know you are God, don't delay. These people and this city are yours."

20 I went on praying confessing my sin and the sin of my people. I
continued to plead with God asking for deliverance for Jerusalem, God's
own city.

And then in verses 21 through 27 the Angel Gabriel interrupted Daniel's prayer and
gave him the Messianic vision foreshadowing the Cross and the atonement for sin.

Daniel got more than he bargained for in this prayer. He was concerned with the sins of
his people and wanting God's forgiveness for them. Daniel was relying on Moses' words
and Solomon's words that if God's people would repent God would take them back into
the land. God gives Daniel an answer about not only Israel's sins but how He is going to
take care of the sins of the world. God reveals to Daniel one of the great Messianic
prophecies in the Old Testament. This prophecy foreshadows the Cross and the solution for
sins of the world.

Table 18-3 analyzes the structure of Daniel's prayer.

Table Ne 18-3 Structure of Daniel's Confessional Prayer

Number	Verse(s)	Structural Form/ Descriptions of Structured Item
1	vs 3	**Preliminary—Burdened Response/** Following vs 1,2 which give the time indicator and setting for the prayer we have Daniel's Response to the situation. He fasted and prayed earnestly to God about what he had just studied in Jeremiah—that is the return to the land.
2	vs 4a	**Prayer Indicator/** I confessed to the Lord, My God.
3	vs 4b	**Worship/** Daniel honors God as the awesome god, the promise keeping God, the merciful God to those who love God and obey them.
4	vs 5a	**Vicarious Confession, Who/** Daniel uses the inclusive we (ancestors—he has just been reading about their disobedience in his Bible study in Jeremiah).
5	vs 5b, 6	**Vicarious Confession, What/** Here Daniel confesses that his ancestors failed to listen and obey the prophets sent by God—forsaking God's commands and guidelines.
6	vs 7	**Vindication of God's Judgments/** Here Daniel contrasts God's just actions with his ancestors wrongful actions.
7	vs 8	**Vicarious Confession, Who and What/** Daniel includes the leaders as well as people and declares they were all unfaithful to God.
8	vs 9	**Vindication of God's Judgments/** Again Daniel contrasts God's just actions with his ancestors wrongful actions. God shows mercy and forgiveness. We (ancestors) rebelled.
9	vs 10-14	**Vicarious Confession, Who and What/** Daniel elaborates on who sinned and what they did; again contrasted by God's just actions in bringing on the disaster, the exile.
10	vs 15-16a	**Honoring of God, Why/** God has delivered in the past and can do so with mighty acts.

11	vs 16b-20	**The Request/** Hear my prayer. I serve you. For your own character, Bless Jerusalem; fill it with your presence so that people may know you as God; show mercy; forgive;
12	Vs 21ff	**Closure/** Daniel continues praying and confessing until interrupted by Gabriel.

Structure of Nehemiah's Personal Illustration of Vicarious Confession

Nehemiah, like Daniel, is aware of God's promises to be with and for His people if they repent and turn toward Him to obey His word. Note Nehemiah's personal vicarious confession:

Nehemiah 1:4-11 (see especially 6,7)

4 When I heard this, I sat down and wept. In fact, for days I mourned, fasted, and prayed to the God of heaven. 5 Then I said, "O LORD, God of heaven, the great and awesome God who keeps his covenant of unfailing love with those who love him and obey his commands, 6 listen to my prayer. Look down and see me praying night and day for your people Israel. **I confess we have sinned terribly against you. Yes, even my own family and I have sinned! 7 We have acted very wickedly toward you by not obeying the commands, laws, and regulations that you gave us through your servant Moses."**
8 "Please remember what you told your servant Moses: 'If you sin, I will scatter you among the nations. 9 But if you return to me and obey my commands, even if you are exiled to the ends of the earth, I will bring you back to the place I have chosen as a dwelling for my Name to be honored.'"
10 "We are your servants, the people you rescued by your great power and might. 11 O Lord, please hear my prayer! Listen to the prayers of those of us who delight in honoring you. Please grant me success now as I go to ask the king for a great favor. Put it into his heart to be kind to me."

Note the structure of his prayer as shown in Table Ne 18-4.

Table Ne 18-4 Structure of Nehemiah's Confessional Prayer

Number	Verse(s)	Structural Form/ Descriptions of Structured Item
1	vs 4	**Preliminary—Burdened Response/** Following vs 1-3 which give the time indicator and surrounding immediate situation (Nehemiah has just heard about the Jerusalem situation), we have Nehemiah's Burdened Response—Mourning, fasting, praying for days.
2	vs 5	**Worship/** Honoring of God for Character Traits: God of Heaven; great and awesome God; God who keeps covenant with those who love him and obey him
3	vs 6a	**Prayer Indicator/** Listen To My Prayer
4	vs 6b	**Prayer Indicator-Explanation/** See my Burden
5	vs 6c	**Vicarious confession, Who/** Note the inclusive we (ancestors) and also his own family
6	vs 7	**Vicarious confession, What/**

		The sin; not obeying commands, laws, regulations that came through Moses
7	vs 8,9	**Honoring of God, Why/** Character trait that will be basis for request—promise given to Moses about scattered people returned and being blessed by God in Jerusalem,
8	vs 10, 11	**The Request/** Again based on character of God; Give success to me as I ask the King for a great favor—with a view toward blessing the people in the land; give me favor with him; let him show me kindness.
9	( )	**Closure/** Missing from Nehemiah's prayer.

Structure of Corporate Illustration of Vicarious Confession from Nehemiah

The corporate vicarious confession was carefully orchestrated by Nehemiah, Ezra, priests, and other worship leaders, so that it would lead to a major committal. Chapter 9 gives the prayer. Chapter 10 gives the covenant that was the goal of the prayer. I am not going to include the prayer here. I suggest you go back and read it in the commentary text. Instead I will give a condensed version of the structure of this prayer in Table Ne 18-5. This prayer is not from an individual but from a people who are corporately turning back to God. But it does contain many of the same elements seen in Daniel and Nehemiah's vicarious confessions.

Table Ne 18-5 Structure of Public Confessional Prayer, Nehemiah Ch 9

Number	Verse(s)	Structural Form/ Descriptions of Structured Item
1	vs 1-5a	**Preliminary—Burdened Response/** Gives time indicator and occasion. A large public gathering has been called as a follow-up to the tremendous revival in ch 8 due to Ezra's ministry. The people are Worshipping God.
2	vs 5b-6	**Call to Worship/** Opening prayers phrases honoring God who is worthy of praise.
3	vs 7-25	**Worship of God Tracing Historical Interventions/** The people recognize God as the one who chose Abraham and formed the nation of Israel and led it; delivered from Egypt; and took it into the land and gave it the land. This is a tremendous time of recognizing God's work in their past.
4	vs 26-31	**Vicarious confession, Who, What, and Vindication of God/** The vicarious confession takes place in this section and details who sinned and what they did along with vindicating God for his just actions.
5	vs 32-37	**Honoring of God and Vindication of God Preliminary To Request/** Character traits that will be basis for their request. They also vicariously confess and vindicate God.
6	vs 38 and ch 10	**Implied Request and Closure/** The people present a covenant that they want to make with God. It indicates their turning to God and following Him. Implied is their asking God to accept this covenant and bless them as His people.

Observations

From a comparison of the three confessional prayers I have drawn the following observations.

Observation 1. Leaders Sensitive to God Timing
Both Daniel and Nehemiah were leaders who were very sensitive to God in terms of what God wanted to do in their situations. They both sensed an intervention time in which God was going to work.

Observation 2. Leaders Responding to The God-Given Burden
Both Daniel and Nehemiah responded to God's inner promptings. They used cultural means of expressing their response—mourning, fasting, praying.

Observation 3. Leaders Worshipping God
Both Daniel and Nehemiah recognize God and worship Him. Different attributes of God are praised.

Observation 4. Worship, Recognition of God Prior
Both Daniel and Nehemiah worship and recognize God prior to asking God for anything.

Observation 5. Vindication of God
Both Daniel and Nehemiah vindicate God. This vindication is often mixed with worshiping God and vicariously confessing to Him.

Observation 6. Vicarious Confession
Both Daniel and Nehemiah confess as if they were part of the sinning people and in some representative fashion represent the past.

Observation 7. Vicarious Confession a Pre-Requisite for Requests
Both Daniel and Nehemiah somehow, intuitively see that this vicarious confession is a necessary pre-requisite for going to God and asking for His restorative work and blessing in what they are to do for Him or want from Him.

Observation 8.   Requests
Both Daniel and Nehemiah have requests for God. They both want God's blessing upon restorative work—taking the people back into the land and restoring them as God's witness in Jerusalem.

Observation 9. Absence of Comments
The Bible is silent about this vicarious praying. Neither of these leaders are referred to in terms of their vicarious confession. There are no commandments saying other leaders must use vicarious confession.

Observation 10. Spiritual Warfare
The Old Testament in general says very little about spiritual warfare. Neither of these vicarious confession/prayers are contextually connected to spiritual warfare praying or activity.

Observation 11. No New Testament Examples
We have no clarification teaching in the New Testament nor illustrations of vicarious praying or nor commands that leaders should do this.

Observation 12. It Worked For Daniel and Nehemiah
Both Daniel and Nehemiah were obviously model leaders. This powerful praying worked for them. They were sensitive to God and what God was doing. Their prayer worked hand-in-hand with what God was doing.

On Deriving Principles of Truth[49] From Scripture—Like These Two Illustrations
I have found it helpful to define notions about principles of truth and to use a continuity continuum to help me evaluate how to apply something seen in the Bible.

Principles of truth are attempts to generalize specific truths for wider applicability and will vary in their usefulness with others and the authoritative degree to which they can be asserted for others.

description   The <u>certainty continuum</u> is a horizontal line moving from suggestions on one extreme to requirements on the other extreme which attempts to provide a grid for locating a given statement of truth in terms of its potential use with others and the degree of authority with which it can be asserted.

The basic ideas are that:
1. Principles are observations along a continuum.
2. We can teach and use with increasing authority those principles further to the right on the continuum.

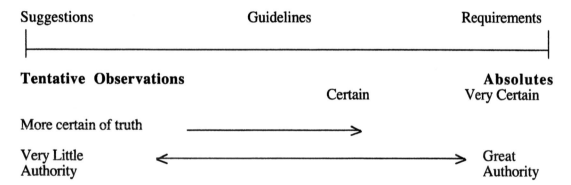

Suggestions   Guidelines   Requirements

Tentative Observations   **Absolutes**
                                        Certain   Very Certain

More certain of truth

Very Little   Great
Authority   Authority

Figure Ne 18-1. The Certainty Continuum

I am identifying principles as a broad category of statements of truth, which were true at some instance of history and may have relevance for others at other times. The more Biblical evidence there is for something, the further to the right on the continuum it goes.

There is little difference between *Suggestions* and *Guidelines* on the continuum. In fact, there is probably overlap between the two. Some *Guidelines* approach *Requirements*. But there is a major difference from going from *Suggestions* to *Requirements*—the difference being *Suggestions* are optional but *Requirements* are not. They must be adhered to.

Definition   <u>Suggestions</u> refers to truth observed in some situations and which may be helpful to others but they are optional and can be used or not with no loss of conscience.

---

[49] See the **Article**, *Principles of Truth*, where I explain this basic notion in much more detail.

Definition   <u>Guidelines</u> are truths that are replicated in most leadership situations and should only be rejected for good reasons though there will be no loss of conscience.

Definition   <u>Absolutes</u> refer to replicated truth in leadership situations across cultures without restrictions. Failure to follow or use will normally result in some stirrings of conscience.

Absolutes are principles, which evince God's authoritative backing. All leaders everywhere should heed them.

Suggestions are the most tentative. They are not enjoined upon people. They may be very helpful though.

Remember that a *Suggestion* or *Guideline* may move to the right or left if more evidence is found in the Bible to support such a move. If a *suggestion* or *guideline* identified in one place in the Scriptures is found to be abrogated, modified or somehow restricted at a later time in the progressive flow of revelation then it will move most likely to the left. However, if later revelation gives evidence of its more widespread usage or identifies it more certainly for everyone then it will move to the right.

Closure

What about vicarious confessional prayer today? Should leaders today use it? My answer may not seem very strong but it is based on my understanding of deriving principles of truth from the Bible. I would assess the notion of a leader using vicarious prayer in his/her ministry as being at the suggestion location on the continuum.[50] That means that by all means it is certainly usable by leaders today. However, I do not believe that we must enjoin this truth on leaders, saying they must use it.

Leaders who are sensitive to God may, like Daniel or Nehemiah, recognize that God is burdening them to use vicarious praying. They may or may not know the historical situation leading to the present (Daniel and Nehemiah did). And they may be led to pray vicariously for the situation. I, personally would have no problem with that.

My sense is that leaders engaged in spiritual warfare—especially those having power gifts of discernings of spirits, workings of miracles, and word of knowledge or word of wisdom—will frequently be led into vicarious praying. This I know, I admire Daniel and Nehemiah. I see them as Heb 13:7,8 kind of people. And I know that examples from the Old Testament are valid to instruct us and warn us and encourage us (1 Cor 10:6,11; Rom 15:4).

---

[50] However, should more Biblical evidence be found to move the truth along the continuum to the right, so be it. I am open to this. Particularly any New Testament truth clarifying vicarious praying.

19. Nehemiah, Biographical Sketch

Introduction

Nehemiah is a modified type 1 biographical source. This type is called a *Critical Incident Source*.[51]

Definition   A type 1 biographical source of leadership information is labeled a <u>Critical Incident Source</u> when its source material is comprised of a single incident or series of incidents taking place in a very short time. That is, there is limited information (span wise over a leader's entire life) available about the leader being studied.

There may actually be a large amount of information but all focused on a short time-interval. The information can be interpreted for processing or for a leadership act or other such findings. Other examples besides Nehemiah include Jonah, Job and Habakkuk. Though information is minimal in critical incident sources, valuable lessons can be learned.

What is Known About Nehemiah

Nehemiah is mentioned by name only 5 times in the Scriptures. All of these are in the book of Nehemiah. Table Ne 19-1 gives the basics about these references.

Table Ne 19-1. References to Nehemiah in the Scripture

Reference	What is Seen About Nehemiah/Implications
Ne 1:1	<u>Ne 1:1</u> The words of **Nehemiah** the son of Hachaliah. And it came to pass in the month Chisleu, in the twentieth year, as I was in Shushan the palace./ Nehemiah was in the summer palace at the court of a Persian king. Time indicator.
Ne 8:9	<u>Ne 8:9</u> And **Nehemiah**, which is the Tirshatha, and Ezra the priest, the scribe, and the Levites that taught the people, said unto all the people, This day is holy unto the LORD your God; mourn not, nor weep. For all the people wept, when they heard the words of the law./ Nehemiah held an official governorship post. He was part of a renewal team that instigated a spiritual renewal among the exiles. Note Ezra described as a Priest and Scribe. This is one of the first instances of the notion of the role of a scribe, one who preserved and copied the Old Testament. Referred to this way again in 12:26.
Ne 8:10	<u>Ne 8:10</u> Then he said unto them, Go your way, eat the fat, and drink the sweet, and send portions unto them for whom nothing is prepared: for this

---

[51] See **Article**, 2. *Biographical Study In The Bible, How to Do* which gives 4 categories of biographical source material: 1. Critical Incident Source; 2. Mini-Source; 3. Midi-Source; 4. Maxi-Source.

	day is holy unto our Lord: neither be sorry; for the joy of the LORD is your strength./ There was an affective impact on the people who were saddened at the recognition of disobedience to God's law.
Ne 10;1	<u>Ne 10:1</u> Now those that sealed were, **Nehemiah**, the Tirshatha, the son of Hachaliah, and Zidkijah./ Prominent leaders in the spiritual renewal movement are modeling *what they believe in* by signing the covenant. The people will now follow along and sign also.
Ne 12:26	<u>Ne 12:26</u> These were in the days of Joiakim the son of Jeshua, the son of Jozadak, and in the days of **Nehemiah** the governor, and of Ezra the priest, the scribe./ Again asserts Nehemiah's official leadership post and connects him to Ezra.
Ne 12:47	<u>Ne 12:47</u> And all Israel in the days of Zerubbabel, and in the days of **Nehemiah**, gave the portions of the singers and the porters, every day his portion: and they sanctified holy things unto the Levites; and the Levites sanctified them unto the children of Aaron./ Nehemiah is at the heart of providing finances to keep worship going in the Temple. He knows the importance of music and centralized worship.

In addition to the actual references to Nehemiah by name, which reveal special things about Nehemiah, all throughout the book of Nehemiah we have actual vignettes[52] in which Nehemiah exerted influence. All of these give information about Nehemiah. These vignettes are sources of processing, leadership acts, macro lessons and other leadership observations. Table Ne 19-2 lists the vignettes in time sequence, that is, when they most likely occurred in real time over against when Nehemiah includes the vignette in his presentation.

Table Ne 19-2 Ordered[53] Vignettes

Number	References	Descriptive Label
1	1:1-11	Nehemiah Burdened About Jerusalem and the Returned Exiles
2	2:1-8	Nehemiah Before Artaxerxes
3	2:9-20	To Jerusalem—Reconnaissance Around the City; Opposition; Challenge to Rebuild the Wall
4	Ch 3	Nehemiah Affirms Workers on the Wall
5	Ch 4	Opposition from Sanballat Et Al
6	Ch 5	Financial Needs of People; Nehemiah's Financial Integrity
7	6:1-14	Alliance for Opposition Increases Pressure
8	6:15-19	Wall Completed
9	12:27-43	Celebration of Completion of Wall
10	13:4-9	Tobiah's Information Network Discovered
11	7:1-4	Nehemiah Appoints Civil Leaders of Character
12	7:5-73	People Are Registered
13	11:1-19	Provision to Repopulate Jerusalem Made
14	12:1-26	Priests and Levites Registered
15	8:1-13	1st Big Renewal Gathering (Law of Moses Proclaimed to People—Spiritual Renewal Movement Instigated)

[52] A <u>vignette</u> when referring to a biographical source is a mini-narrative source, which describes some happening in a single period of time in a brief but elegant way.

[53] It is clear from chapter 13 that vignettes described there take place earlier in real time. Careful reflection on other vignettes reveals that some of them probably take place earlier in real time. This ordering may not be exactly right. It cannot be affirmed nor denied. But it is at least plausible and does have a logical order.

16	8:14-18	Feast of Tabernacles Kept
17	Ch 9, 10	2nd Big Renewal Gathering (Vicarious praying; signing of the covenant)
18	13:1-3	Flashback to Separation Issue
19	13:23-31	Further Flashback to Separation Issue
20	13:15-22	Flashback to Sabbath Issue
21	Ch 11	Administrative Leadership--Provision for Ongoing Renewal
22	13:10-14	Flashback to Incident Restoring Financing of Temple

What We Can Learn About Nehemiah From the Book Itself—The Vignettes
Biographical study is important. Books like Nehemiah, Job, Habakkuk, and Jonah are included in the canon of Scripture. That they are there is important. There are lessons to be found in them. As leaders, we can learn vicariously leadership lessons from such study. Let me briefly suggest several lessons that can profit leaders today. Below I list each vignette[54] and some suggested leadership observations from each.

Vignette 1. Ch 1— Nehemiah Burdened For Jerusalem and Returned Exiles
In ch 1 we see Nehemiah receiving the news about the situation in Jerusalem concerning those who have returned from exile. He feels the burden of the situation. He lets us know later, 2:11, that God had touched his heart not only with a call to go to Jerusalem but an initial plan of what to do when he got there. Essentially then, this chapter describes Nehemiah's call to ministry. Technically that shaping activity is called a leadership committal. And by implication there is the evidence of sovereign guidance. God has sovereignly placed Nehemiah in the court and given favor with Artaxerxes. He has him positioned for the events of vignette 2, Before Artaxerxes. Destiny Preparation[55] is evidenced in this sovereign guidance. And this vignette also illustrates Destiny Revelation. God is opening up to Nehemiah His purposes for the major contribution of Nehemiah's life.

What We Learn About Nehemiah from this Vignette
- a. Nehemiah is a detailed/careful person. Note the phrase, "These are the memoirs of Nehemiah." He has jotted down a basic historical record, probably journalled as well as kept detailed records of registry, from which he constructed these memoirs.
- b. Nehemiah is concerned about God's work in Jerusalem. This is in contrast to many other exiles who were concerned only with survival and prosperity in the exile.
- c. Nehemiah receives a call from God about this work in Jerusalem. His prayer burden becomes a call[56] as he realizes that he may be able to do something. Note his immediate first reaction is to go to God about what he has heard.

---

[54] I would suggest that you read through the text of the vignette before reading my interpretive leadership insights. I assume you have done that in my comments.

[55] One of the seven major leadership lessons we have identified from comparative study of effective leaders is: *Effective leaders evince a growing awareness of their sense of destiny over their lifetimes.* All biblical leaders who accomplished things for God have a sense of destiny. A sense of destiny is an inner conviction arising from an experience or a series of experiences in which there is a growing sense of awareness that God has His hand on a leader in a special way for special purposes. Sense of destiny usually unfolds over a lifetime via a three-fold pattern: destiny preparation, destiny revelation, destiny fulfillment.

[56] This is a frequent observation in contemporary case studies of leaders. In contrast to spectacular calls like Jeremiah, Isaiah and Paul which illustrate overt supernatural awe-inspiring kinds of sense of destiny experiences, Nehemiah's call is an inward realization. He recognizes that as he prays about the situation in Jerusalem and gets under the burden of that situation, God is actually calling him to do something about it. This has frequently happened to people today who study the Perspectives Courses that have radiated out

d. Nehemiah is a person who can exercise spiritual disciplines (mourn, fast, pray). These are basic skills and habits that have been built into Nehemiah during his sovereign foundations stage of his life. Leaders need these skills. See **Article**, *Spiritual Disciplines—And On-Going Leadership.*

e. Nehemiah is in a position that has potential to do something about the situation in Jerusalem. This didn't happen by accident. God has put him there.

f. While the book of Nehemiah does not highlight God's shaping activities[57] of the leader Nehemiah as does Job, Jonah, and Habakkuk[58] it does, however, illustrate a number of process items (shaping activities of God). In this vignette four[59] are illustrated, two by implication only: 1. Leadership Committal; 2. Sovereign Guidance (by implication); 3. Destiny Preparation (by implication); 4. Destiny Revelation.

g. This vignette illustrates one of the macro lessons[60] that Abraham learned and that every leader in the Bible who significantly contributed to God's purposes learned: 6. Faith Macro Lesson—*Biblical Leaders must learn to trust in the unseen God, sense His presence, sense His revelation, and follow Him by faith.* Nehemiah's favorite name for this unseen God is, The God of Heaven.[61]

h. One component of the definition for a leader is in focus in this vignette and two others are alluded to. *Definition—A leader is a person with God-given capacity and God-given responsibility who is influencing a specific group of God's people toward God's purposes.* In focus is the notion of God-given responsibility and specific group of God's people. Alluded to are God-given capacity and God's purposes. God-given responsibility involves a vertical upward and vertical downward aspect. The vertical downward is the notion that God is initiating this leadership responsibility. The vertical upward aspect is that Nehemiah will be held responsible for leadership involving this call.

---

from the U.S. Center for World Mission in Pasadena. Many lay people have been turned on to missions and got their call when studying this course and seeing the needs.

[57] See the **Article**, *10. God's Shaping Processes With Leaders.* A <u>process item</u> is the technical name in leadership emergence theory describing actual occurrences in a given leader's life including providential events, people, circumstances, special divine interventions, inner-life lessons and other like items which God uses to develop that leader by shaping leadership character, leadership skills, and leadership values. We call process items by the more popular phrase, shaping activities. Biographical Bible books like Job, Habakku, and Jonah are written to expose God's shaping activities as prominent in the book. Nehemiah's story reveals them incidentally or by implication. His leadership is what is prominent in the book.

[58] These books actually focus on the shaping activities themselves for Job, Habakkuk, and Jonah.

[59] See *leadership committal, sovereign guidance, destiny preparation and destiny revelation,* **Glossary**.

[60] A <u>macro-lesson</u> is a high level generalization of a leadership observation (suggestion, guideline, requirement), stated as a lesson, which repeatedly occurs throughout different leadership eras, and thus has potential as a leadership absolute. Macro lessons even at their weakest provide strong guidelines describing leadership insights. At their strongest they are requirements, or absolutes, that leaders should follow. Leaders ignore them to their detriment. 41 Macro Lessons have been identified. These macro lessons are numbered. This faith macro is number 6 one of the early macro lessons discovered in the Bible. See the list of macro lessons. See **Articles**, *16. Macro Lessons—Defined; 17. Macro Lessons: List of 41 Across Six Leadership Eras.*

[61] The *God of heaven* is a title that is used 21 times in the Old Testament—two times in Genesis, once in the Psalms, once in Jonah, and the rest in the times of exile or restoration leadership. Nehemiah uses it 4 times: 1:4,5; 2:5,20. Its common thread in these usages is a title that would be recognized by people other than God's people. It is a popular term for God by the leaders in exile and restoration times.

Vignette 2. 2:1-8—Nehemiah Before Artaxerxes[62]

In this vignette Nehemiah is given the chance to ask Artaxerxes for help in rebuilding the walls of Jerusalem. Nehemiah has the favor of Artaxerxes, presumeably by competent service as a cupbearer. About three months have transpired between Nehemiah's receiving the news in ch 1 and talking to the king about it. This means Nehemiah had done a lot of praying before asking. He has studied into resources available in the Persian empire that could be helpful in the Jerusalem situation. And he carefully picked his time to talk to the king. The king grants him his request. Nehemiah will be allowed to take a leave of absence and return to Jerusalem to build the walls. Note that Nehemiah researching allows him to be ready with requests for timber, for protection, and other resources. The king grants these also. Note also that the request involves more than the temporary visit, which was approved. The king granted him lumber to rebuild the gates and Nehemiah's own personal residence. It was clear that Nehemiah would make a visit and return and report and then go back for permanent service. Later in the book we see that Nehemiah was appointed as Governor of Jerusalem and its surrounding environ.

<u>What We Learn About Nehemiah from this Vignette</u>

    a. Again we see that Nehemiah is a detailed/careful person. He has done his homework. He knows about the various provinces and governors in Artaxerxes empire. He is ready to ask the king for resources from the king's forests in a province near Jerusalem. He also asks for safe conduct through neighboring provinces on the way to Jerusalem.

    b. Nehemiah is sensitive as to timing. About three months have transpired between Nehemiah's receiving the news and talking to the king about it. This means Nehemiah had done a lot of praying before asking and he carefully picked his time to talk to the king. He is waiting for the opportune moment. Nehemiah has an intuitive awareness of intervention time. That is, he senses this opportunity before the king as one in which God will intervene for him in a timely fashion that will mean a very positive advance in his leadership. See *intervention time*, **Glossary**. See **Article**, *31. Nehemiah, Strategic Timing*.

    c. Obviously, Nehemiah was a person who showed his emotions. Such a person is more likely to be openly transparent with God than one who covers these outward symptoms. And that is the case with Nehemiah. See his prayers: Ne 1:4, 5, 6, 8, 11; 2:4; 4:9; 5:10, 11, 19; 6:9, 14; 9:1; 11:17; 13:14,22,29,31. Habakkuk, Jonah, Job and Nehemiah are leaders whose emotions are open before God. See **Article**, *Transparency with God*.

    d. Nehemiah is courageous. He is willing to risk his life for something important to him. This moment before the king is a critical time. Absolute rulers of empires like Assyria, Babylon, and Persia were capricious and at a whim could have those around them put to death. Nehemiah is hoping he won't displease Artaxerxes by his show of emotions and the requests he will make. This could have been problematic as Jerusalem was known for its rebellious attitude toward empires like Assyria, Babylon, and Persia. But Nehemiah has credibility with the king from his previous service. And the king trusts him.

    e. Nehemiah knows the value of spontaneous-on-the-spot praying. He utters a thought prayer to God for help as he faces this intervention moment. This kind of praying occurs throughout the book.

---

[62] Persia was one of the greatest empires in biblical times and dominated the Middle East for nearly 200 years. At its greatest it extended from the Aegean Sea in the west to the Indus Valle in the east and from what we call Turkey today in the north to Egypt in the South. That Nehemiah is part of the court of Artaxerxes means he has information about a very large part of the then known world. He is aware of political maneuvers and rulers all over. God has him in a place where networking power is known. See *networking power*, **Glossary**.

    f. Nehemiah is open and above board about financial things. Note he openly asks for timber for his own house. Later we will see how very careful Nehemiah is about financial things. He was a person of financial integrity.

    g. Nehemiah recognizes God's sovereign working behind the scenes. Notice his statement, which gives the credit to God. *And the king granted these requests, because the gracious hand of my God was upon me.* He personally knows the reality of the *9. Presence Macro Lesson. The essential ingredient of leadership is the powerful presence of God in the life and ministry of a leader.*

Vignette 3. 2:9-20— To Jerusalem—Reconnaissance Around the City; Opposition; Challenge to Rebuild the Wall

In this vignette, Nehemiah travels to Jersualem under the king's protection and gets aid along the way from Governors of provinces to whom he shows his credentials from Artaxerxes. He meets opposition from Sanballat, the Governor of Samaria, a neighboring province to Jerusalem and its surrounding environ. Nehemiah also conducts a secret reconnaissance around Jerusalem to size up the rebuilding task. Finally, he challenges the leaders of Jerusalem and other exile leaders to the challenge of rebuilding the wall and providing for a secure walled city of Jerusalem.

<u>What We Learn About Nehemiah from this Vignette</u>

    a. Again we see that Nehemiah is a detailed/careful person. Nehemiah is a careful planner. Very shortly after arriving he personally surveys the destroyed remains of the wall around Jerusalem. It is clear that from the very first time Nehemiah had heard of the situation in Jerusalem, he had begun to get plans for rebuilding the walls. Here he already has the plans. He needs to confirm them. Reconnaissance trips into the situation are always a powerful way to get confirmation of a ministry.

    b. Nehemiah is a person of change. He is a catalyst and process helper.[63] He is going to implement some major changes in the situation. That requires knowledge of the change participants—those who will be for the change, those neutral to the change, and those opposing it. Note his challenge is the the influentials—those who must be motivated to own the change. Note two things about Nehemiah as a person of change. (1) Nehemiah is aware of the influentials in Jerusalem. They will have to be cultivated if the plans are to gain ownership among all the followers. (2) Nehemiah does not relate his plans right away. He confirms them and gives time for his own credibility to be accepted by the influentials.

    c. Nehemiah again shows sensitivity to timing. Nehemiah senses intervention time with the influentials. Note how he moves from positional authority (appointment from the king) toward spiritual authority in his inspirational relating of his plans (gracious hand of God had been on me.) And he has pricked their already burdened conscience about Jerusalem (let's rebuild the wall of Jerusalem and rid ourselves of this disgrace!).

    d. Again Nehemiah shows that he is a person of courage. He basically ignores the threat from Sanballat (rebelling against the king). One reason, Nehemiah has positional authority roughly the equivalent of Sanballat. Both are governors of small provinces in the Persian Empire—both appointed by higher ups in the Persian administration. But Nehemiah also holds a trump card. He has a personal relationship with Artaxerxes.

Vignette 4. Ch 3—Nehemiah Affirms Workers on the Wall

In this chapter Nehemiah lists all the workers who joined with him to repair the wall and gates. And he tells where they worked. This listing of them in itself is an act of affirmation.

---

[63] See *catalyst, process helper*, **Glossary**. See **Article**, *21. Nehemiah, Change Participants.*

<u>What We Learn About Nehemiah from this Vignette</u>
  a. Again we see Nehemiah as a person of change. He is a catalyst and process helper. He is implementing the first major step in his bridging strategy toward a renewed Jerusalem serving God. Ownership is critical when bringing about change. Nehemiah demonstrates that he understands this. The various persons and groups represented in these lists show the complexity of the change process that Nehemiah faced. He inspires leaders and followers from a wide range of folks. This includes religious leaders, political leaders, merchants, as well as common folks. He was an able leader.
  b. Nehemiah knows the value of affirmation of followers, an important relationship insight.[64]
  c. Nehemiah is a motivational leader.[65] One technique, wall assignments that have a touch of competitiveness. See **Article**, *8. Getting the Job Done—Comparison of Ezra, Nehemiah and Haggai's Roles*.

Vignette 5. Ch 4— Opposition from Sanballat Et Al
Ch 4 vividly points out the first major crisis that Nehemiah faced in step 1 of his renewal effort. As Nehemiah unified the work force, assigned areas of the wall and began the actual work on the wall, opposition from without—the alliance between Sanballat, Gesham, and Tobiah—threatens military intervention. Nehemiah counters by:

  1. Overt dependence on God via prayer,
  2. having workers armed,
  3. setting up an alert system set up that could call all workers to defend at a needed location, and
  4. bringing in surrounding workers to stay in Jerusalem overnight during the duration involved in building the wall.

Nehemiah is at once spiritual, courageous, and practical. As one old Bible teacher used to repeatedly say, "What we are in a crisis is what we really are!" Nehemiah shows forth what he really is in this crisis.

<u>What We Learn About Nehemiah from this Vignette</u>
  a. Nehemiah is a spiritual leader at core. In the midst of this external threat he goes to God in prayer and trusts God to work.
  b. Nehemiah is very practical. Having prayed to God asking that the enemies be thwarted and reminding the people of who God is, he takes very practical steps. He arms the workers and has some working and some ready to do battle. He also sets up a communication system that can bring all together at a threatened point. He also has the people who lived outside of Jerusalem and commuted to work on the wall come and stay in Jerusalem for the duration of the project. He makes provision for night time guards. Extreme conditions call for extreme measures. Nehemiah knew that the wall could be done in a relatively short time. He therefore asks for sacrificial efforts from all concerned. They practically lived in the same clothes for this work time on the wall. They probably were sleep deprived due to night time security watches. They worked on the wall with military weapons at the ready. They ate on the run. Nehemiah inspired them to do this.

---

[64] <u>Relationship Insights</u> is a technical name of one of the shaping processes of God seen across comparative study of leaders developing over time. It is certainly implied that Nehemiah had learned a good deal about realitionship insights. Ch 3 verifies this.

[65] See also, **Haggai Commentary**. Haggai is a strong motivational leader.

c.   Nehemiah is courageous. He goes on with step 1 of the renewal project, building the wall, despite the repeated threats and rumors that were continually being kept before the people by the Alliances contacts in the city.

Vignette 6. Ch 5— Financial Needs of People; Nehemiah's Financial Integrity

Loyalty goes two ways. If a leader expects loyalty upward toward his/her leadership needs then that leader must give loyalty downward toward followers' needs. Nehemiah shows that in this vignette which brings up an extreme financial need the common people were facing. They did not have enough money to live in their daily situations. They had hocked all they could and borrowed all they could. But they were not making it. They appeal to Nehemiah who recognizes the high rate of interest problem people with loans were having. He applies a Biblical principle to the situation. And he himself models what ought to be done. People with resources must learn to be generous. Nehemiah is generous.

What We Learn About Nehemiah from this Vignette
   a.   Again as in ch 1, we see that Nehemiah was a person who showed his emotions. He was angered at the rich Jews exploiting their fellow poorer Jews. And he reprimands them strongly as he corrects the situation.
   b.   Nehemiah exhibits loyalty to his followers in their need. Loyalty goes two ways up and down. A leader who expects followers to give loyalty to his leadership situation and decisions must also show loyalty to the followership in terms of their situations and needs.
   c.   Nehemiah models generosity with his resources and financial integrity. He is above board about his finances. He does not exploit the people under his rule. Previous governors have.

Vignette 7 & 9 Ch 6:1-14—Alliance for Opposition Increases Pressure; The Wall is Completed

The project is almost done. The wall is completed but the gates have not been put in place. The alliance against Nehemiah's project realizes this. They have solidified into a real coalition. Repeated threats finally culminate in a letter which accuses Nehemiah of rebelling against the Persian empire. Nehemiah denies the accusations made in the letter as being untrue. He ignores the invitation to dialog over the issue (really an invitation to be assassinated). He prays to God for vindication. He discerns an inward plot to have him assassinated. And he goes on with the completion of the project.

What We Learn About Nehemiah from this Vignette
   a.   Nehemiah is focused. He refused to be sidetracked from completing the project. He completes the wall project. He has resolve. Resolve is a key word. Leaders must have this quality if they want to carry out a vision from God. Resolve is perseverance, which is based on dependence upon God.
   b.   Nehemiah has spiritual discernment. He recognizes the efforts of Shemaiah as not from God.
   c.   Nehemiah is again courageous.
   d.   Again, we see Nehemiah's dependence upon God. He prays for strength to continue the work (probably indicating that he needed it; it is easy to be discouraged in a project when continued opposition occurs).

Vignette 9.   Ch 12:27-43—Celebration of Completion of the Wall

This vignette stresses how important closure is to a project which has required intense sacrificial effort. It describes the celebration of the completion of the wall, which was a parade around the wall led by Levites and singers and leaders and workers.

<u>What We Learn About Nehemiah from this Vignette</u>
- a. Nehemiah knows the value of celebration as part of closure on an important project. Music, pomp, a parade, recognition of God, and good food are all a part of the celebration that Nehemiah organized.
- b. Nehemiah is inclusive in his closure celebration. Workers from surrounding villages, religious leaders—especially singers and musical instrument people—as well as leaders and workers from within the city and spouses and children are all part of the joyful celebration.

Vignette 10. Ch 13:4-9—Tobiah's Information network Discovered

This vignette is a flashback. In ch 13 Nehemiah relates this story, which shows that during this wall project time there was inward opposition to the wall project. All leaders who instigate change must recognize that both inward and outward opposition to the change is very likely.

<u>What We Learn About Nehemiah from this Vignette</u>
- a. Nehemiah faced conflict head on. He was not afraid to take action, if he felt he was right, even if it meant opposing the top religious leadership.
- b. When the cat is away the mice will play. Nehemiah learned a valuable lesson. Absence allows inroads for opposition to undo what has been done. Under leaders need to be in place who can exercise influence authoritatively in the absence of a top leader.

Vignette 11. 7:1-4 Nehemiah Appoints Civil Leaders of Character

Nehemiah knows that for an on-going continuation of his renewal efforts there must be leaders of character on location. The crisis-like task of building the wall has been accomplished, even against determined opposition. There was tremendous motivation behind the task. But it lasted only a short time. Now Nehemiah must look to the long-term needs of the returned exiles. He turns to the notion of bringing renewal to the exiles who have returned. He knows that they can be united only if there is good leadership and a strong religious fervor.

<u>What We Learn About Nehemiah from this Vignette</u>
- a. Nehemiah selects leaders based on character as a primary ingredient.
- b. Again we see that Nehemiah is a detailed/careful person. He selects on-going leadership and he makes sure that security watches are set up for manning the wall watches and gate watches.

Vignette 12, 13, & 14 Efforts to Organize for Continuance (7:5-73; 11;1-19; 12;1-26)

I am going to group the next several vignettes. All deal with Nehemiah's efforts to build a renewal base that will be on-going. Nehemiah knows that there must be a strong Jerusalem if reform is to happen to all of the returned exiles, many of whom live outside Jerusalem. So he has a plan for bringing in folks to repopulate Jerusalem. To enact his plan he first needs to know who are all the Jews who have returned. He thus lists them. Later (ch 10) after uniting the people via strong Bible teaching and worship, Nehemiah will bring 1 out of every 10 outside the city into live in the city.

<u>What We Learn About Nehemiah from these Vignettes</u>
- a. Again we see that Nehemiah is a detailed/careful person. In preparation for repopulating Jerusalem he takes a census of people. Later after motivating them, he will assign people living outside of Jerusalem to relocate into the city.
- b. Nehemiah is aware of resources. Note how Nehemiah identifies the wealth of the folks with means.

Vignette 15, 16 & 17—The Spiritual Emphases Underlying Renewal Efforts
     In these three vignettes we see the powerful spiritual dynamics involved in Nehemiahs efforts to renew God's work in Jerusalem. Nehemiah uses mass events with strong application. In vignette 15 there is the first big renewal gathering, like a modern national bible conference. There is a long plenary session in which Ezra and his co-workers read and explain the word of God. This is one of the crowning moments of Ezra's life and one for which he has prepared all his life. The then known written Word of God is read and explained to the people. This is the first time that most of these people have ever heard of God's Word. This causes a response by the people. They grieve that they and their ancestors have disobeyed God. A spiritual renewal movement is born. It is clear that this is more than a momentary reaction. There is actual application and follow-up to what was heard. The people keep the feast of tabernacles. This involved publishing about it to the surrounding areas of Jerusalem. Time was involved. People were invited and came. The actual feast of tabernacles lasted for eight days. During this time the Word of God was read each day. People were being informed not only of God's demands for their lives but also of the history of their ancestors. And then some time later[66] another large conference was called. Clearly Nehemiah and the leaders wanted to take advantage of the spiritual momentum. The conference had as its aim the signing of a covenant, which would nail firmly into place the gains of the past weeks. It would provide a base for accountability. The conference did just that. The people respond well to God's word in worship, repentance, and genuine desire to follow God. The leaders model by signing the covenant. The people do also. This is the spiritual highlight of Nehemiah and Ezra's ministry. But Nehemiah knows that to maintain this spiritual movement he will have to organize. He has laid the groundwork well in appointing leaders of character and in registering people—priests, Levites, people of means, common people. He knows his resources and plans to follow this last major conference with actual organized efforts to maintain it.

<u>What We Learn About Nehemiah from these Vignettes</u>
     a. Again we see that Nehemiah is a detailed/careful person. The building of the wall was part of a bigger plan in which a renewed people of God in Jerusalem was the end result. Nehemiah, has planned well for the whole thing, not just the building of the wall.
     b. Nehemiah is a team player. He knows that the spiritual impact needed to move the hearts and minds of the people will take a person like Ezra, gifted for that, and the men that Ezra has trained. Nehemiah
     c. Nehemiah uses two effective methodologies which he is aware of from experience, Scripture and understanding of his culture. (1) He uses a mass gathering and the reading of the Word. (2) He uses a covenant to nail down specific results from the spiritual fervor. This will be an accountability tool for later use in maintaining the spiritual movement.
     d. Nehemiah, the top civil leader, Ezra, the top spiritual leader and other leaders model what they want the people to do. They sign the covenant first.
     e. Nehemiah, a man of prayer, is part of the public prayer, the longest in the Bible. While it does not state that he was by name, it certainly flows with what we have seen of his prayerful spirit throughout the whole book. It is in harmony with his vicarious praying elsewhere and his knowledge of the Word.

---

[66] The time is not exactly clear, 9:1 24th day of the month. Probably several weeks after the feast of tabernacles.

Vignette 18, 19 & 20—Flashbacks Showing Detailed Application of Truth
In the vignettes of ch 13, vs 1-3 and vs 23-31 on separation issues and vs 15-22 on Sabbath issues, we see that Nehemiah was a stickler on follow-through. The people had agreed to follow God's law. Nehemiah holds them to it.

<u>What We Learn About Nehemiah from these Vignettes</u>
    a. Again we see that Nehemiah is a detailed/careful person. He applies in a detailed manner the truth that has been revealed. He does not compromise even when his stand is going to bring on conflict with influential religious leaders.
    b. Nehemiah is a person of integrity. Promises to God must be kept.
    c. Nehemiah is a leader who knows the value of accountability.
    d. Nehemiah will not compromise on a truth, even if financial pressure to do so is involved (Sabbath issues).

Vignette 22 & Final Remarks—Administrative Leadership for Renewal; Flashback Application
In ch 11 Nehemiah takes steps to make Jerusalem strong so that it can help move the spiritual movement into a more permanent ongoing institution involving centralized worship. He makes certain that adequate financing is there for this effort. The flashback of ch 13 showed just how important centralized worship was in Nehemiah's thinking. He goes to a lot of effort to re-institute the financial commitments to keep the centralized worship going.

<u>What We Learn About Nehemiah from these Vignettes</u>
    a. Nehemiah organizes to maintain the renewal effort by providing a strong Jerusalem.
    b. Nehemiah values centralized worship and provides finances for temple workers.

Observations Drawn From An Overall Analysis of All Vignettes
Nehemiah was an accomplished leader—probably the best at organizing that we see in the whole Old Testament. Here are some summary observations about his leadership drawn from an overall view of the various leadership vignettes.

Observation 1. Civil Leader Who Was Spiritual
Nehemiah was a new breed of leader. He was not only a civil leader who organized well, he was a spiritual man who was sensitive to God. The first strong lay leader type in the Bible. Prophets do not play a role in the book of Nehemiah (except a small negative one) which Nehemiah rejects.

Observation 2. Used Teamwork
Nehemiah valued other leader's contributions and teamed with them to get tasks accomplished.

Observation 3. Utilized Change Dynamics
Nehemiah was a catalyst and process helper in the change process. He knew how to stir people up and he knew the overall process to move them toward his final objectives.

Observation 4. Long Term Goals for His Leadership
Nehemiah's leadership was much bigger than just building a wall—that was only a first step in movement toward a renewed people obeying God with Jerusalem providing the spiritual impetus in centralized worship.

Observation 5. Continuing Renewal
Nehemiah organized so as not only to bring in renewal but continue it over the long haul.

What Can We Surmise About Nehemiah

From a study of these vignettes how can we describe Nehemiah as a person?[67] Nehemiah was most likely a strong leader who viewed God as the God of Heaven, a supreme God who could intervene in daily affairs and bring about His purposes. He is a man of prayer who entreats this God of Heaven. Note Nehemiah's prayers in this regard. And note to whom Nehemiah gives the credit when things are accomplished. Nehemiah centered his life around serving this God.

Nehemiah, being in the court of Artaxerxes, knew the value of networking. He is politically astute and works to get ownership across a wide variety of individuals[68] and groups.[69] At the same time he is a person of integrity. This is seen in his accountability efforts and in his own personal handling of finances.

He is a generous person. He expects loyalty from his followers and he is loyal to them. He serves God and his followers—an early prototype of a servant leader. He is a leader who can motivate others. But most of all he is a leader of integrity who is sensitive to God. He also knows and uses God's Word in his leadership. And at the same time he is a very practical man.

In summary what are the words that capture Nehemiah as a person?

Leader
Spiritual
Prayerful
Practical
Generous
Integrity
Detailed
Anticipator

Macro Lessons Illustrated in Nehemiah's Leadership

More macro lessons are observed in Nehemiah's leadership than any other single leader in the Old Testament. Some are seen explicitly in his leadership. Some are strongly implied. And then many are seen in seed form—that is, there are intimations of the core idea seen though certainly not known by Nehemiah.

Table Ne 19-3 Macro Lessons Overtly Seen In Nehemiah's Leadership

Number	First Seen-Leadership Era	Label/Statement of Macro Lesson
3	Patriarchal	Timing/ God's timing is crucial to accomplishment of God's purposes.
5	Patriarchal	Integrity/ Integrity is the essential character trait of a spiritual leader.
6	Patriarchal	Faith/ Biblical Leaders must learn to trust in the unseen God, sense His presence, sense His revelation, and follow Him by faith.

[67] In Myers-Briggs terminology, Nehemiah was a natural leader type: An ESTJ.

[68] See **Article,** *21. Nehemiah, Change Participants*, to get a feel for who were the important individuals in the change process he was working with.

[69] See **Article,** *30. Nehemiah, Peoples and Places*, to get a feel for the complexity of working relationally with the remnant folks in Jerusalem and Palestine.

7	Patriarchal	Purity/ Leaders must personally learn of and respond to the holiness of God in order to have effective ministry
8	Pre-Kingdom	Intercession/ Leaders called to a ministry are called to intercede for that ministry.
9	Pre-Kingdom	Presence/ The essential ingredient of leadership is the powerful presence of God in the leader's life and ministry.
10	Pre-Kingdom	Intimacy/ Leaders develop intimacy with God which in turn overflows into all their ministry since ministry flows out of being.
11	Pre-Kingdom	Burden/ Leaders feel a responsibility to God for their ministry.
13	Pre-Kingdom	Challenge/ Leaders receive vision from God which sets before them challenges that inspire their leadership.
14	Pre-Kingdom	Spiritual Authority/ Spiritual authority is the dominant power base of a leader and comes through experiences with God, knowledge of God, godly character and gifted power.
17	Pre-Kingdom	Continuity/ Leaders must provide for continuity to new leadership in order to preserve their leadership legacy.
19	Kingdom	Stability/ Preserving a ministry of God with life and vigor over time is as much if not more of a challenge to leadership than creating one.
20	Kingdom	Spiritual Leadership/ Spiritual leadership can make a difference even in the midst of difficult times.
21	Kingdom	Recrudescence/ God will attempt to bring renewal to His people until they longer respond to Him.
27	Post-Kingdom	Perseverance/ Once known, leaders must persevere with the vision God has given.
30	Pre-Church	Focus/ Leaders, to be effective, must move toward an increased focus on their calling and ultimate contribution.
35	Shepherd	Shepherd/ Leaders must preserve, protect, and develop God's people.
41	All Eras	Complexity/ Leadership is complex, problematic, difficult and fraught with risk—which is why leadership is needed.

An amazing thing is that a number of macro lessons, which are discovered explicitly in later leadership eras, are seen in early seed form in Nehemiah's leadership.

Table Ne 19-4 Macro Seen In Seed Form in Nehemiah's Leadership

Number	First Seen-- Leadership Era	Label/Statement of Macro Lesson
4	Patriarchal	Destiny/ Leaders must have a sense of destiny.
25	Post Kingdom	Modeling/ Leaders can most powerfully influence by modeling godly lives, the sufficiency and sovereignty of God at all times, and gifted power.
26	Post Kingdom	Ultimate Goal/ Leaders must remember that the ultimate goal of their lives and ministry is to manifest the glory of God.
28	Pre-Church	Selection/ The key to good leadership is the selection of good potential leaders which should be a priority of all leaders.
31	Pre-Church	Spirituality/ Leaders must develop interiority, spirit sensitivity, and fruitfulness in accord with their uniqueness since ministry flows out of being.
32	Pre-Church	Servant/ Leaders must maintain a dynamic tension as they lead by serving and serve by leading.
36	Pre-Church	Movement/ Leaders recognize that movements are the way to penetrate society though they must be preserved via appropriate ongoing institutions.
39	Church	Giftedness/ Leaders are responsible to help God's people identify, develop, and use their resources for God.
40	Church	Word Centered Ministry/ God's Word is the primary source for equipping leaders and must be a vital part of any leaders ministry.

Closure

As leaders, we can learn directly via our own experience or indirectly, that is, vicariously from the lives of others. Nehemiah is a leader whose legacy goes on today because he was careful to preserve his story. And because he told his story, we can benefit today in our leadership. Nehemiah is one who fits the leadership mandate.

> Remember your former leaders. Imitate those qualities and achievements
> that were God-Honoring, for their source of leadership still lives—Jesus!
> He, too, can inspire and enable your own leadership today.
> Hebrews 13:7,8 Clinton Interpretive Paraphrase

Nehemiah left a legacy both in tangible form in his day—a centralized worshipping community who were following God in a renewed centralized worship center in a protected Jerusalem—and for us, his written record. Nehemiah has a revered place in the history of God's people. His book is one of the most often referred to sources of biblical leadership in terms of preaching, teaching, seminars. He is worthy to be imitated, especially in his dependence upon God and his practical efforts to do what God wanted.

20. Nehemiah, Calendar and Dating

Introduction

It is helpful when studying any of the restoration era books—Haggai, Zechariah, Malachi, Ezra, Nehemiah—to recognize the order in which they occur. Table Ne 20-1 puts these books in order.[70] Note below when Nehemiah's leadership occurs.

Table Ne 20-1. Restoration Books and Miscellaneous Information

Item	539 B.C.	536 B.C.	520-516 B.C.	486-465 B.C.	465-424 B.C.	430 B.C.[71]
Restoration Activity	Daniel Prays	Work on Temple Begun	Work on Temple begun again and Completed	Israelites Preserved due to Esther and Mordecai's activities	Wall constructed Ezra and Nehemiah, restoration. Nehemiah, governor, 446-433.	Malachi again engenders restoration movement
Bible Indication	Daniel 9	Ez 3:12	Ez 6:13-15 Haggai Zechariah	Esther	Nehemiah; latter part of Ezra	Malachi
Left Hand of God	Cyrus		Darius	Xerxes	Artaxerxes	
Restoration Leaders	Daniel		Haggai, Zechariah, Zerubbabel, Joshua	Mordecai, Esther,		

Table Ne 20-2 correlates Nehemiah's ministry with Ezra's. Ministry.

---

[70] There is disagreement by scholars on the dating given. I have comparatively studied I.S.B.E., the CEV, and **Wilmington's Complete Guide to Bible Knowledge—Volume 1 Old Testament People** to arrive at the dates above. These dates may not be provable exactly, but they are plausible and helpful as one studies the leadership of Ezra and Nehemiah.

[71] Scholars differ as to when Malachi prophesied. Most agree it is in the Persian era. The things he describe about the Jewish people and their need for renewal agrees with the kinds of things that Ezra and Nehemiah attempted to correct. However, Malachi is not mentioned in either Nehemiah or Ezra as prophesying during this time. This is probably a mystery that won't be clarified till we reach heaven.

Table Ne 20-2 Nehemiah and Ezra—Timing and Overlap in Ministry

Order	Date[72] (using modern calendar)	Prophetic Message/ Or Other Activity	Bible Passage (or other reference to dating)
1	538 B.C.	Cyrus had defeated Babylon in 539 B.C. He probably made his proclamation about this time. Zerrubabel, the appointed Governor and Joshua, the Priest, takes a group back into the land. They set up the altar and began worshipping God. They also began work on the temple foundation. But this work was stopped.	Ezra 1-6;
2	Sep 21, 520 B.C.	Work begun again on temple. Opposed or hindered from 536-530 B.C. Stopped altogether from 530 to 520 B.C.	Ezra 3ff (see especially 3:12) Ez 4:1-5, 24
3	519-518 B.C.	Tattenai's letter to Darius; about rebuilding the temple	Ez 5:3-6:14)
4	Mar 12, 516 B.C.	Dedication of the temple[73]	Ez 6:15-18
5	458 B.C.[74]	Ezra comes to Jerusalem[75]	Ez 7:1
6	446 B.C.	Nehemiah comes to Jerusalem.	Ne 1:1
7	446-433	Nehemiah exercises political rule in Jerusalem.	Ne 5:14

Conclusion

The books of Ezra and Nehemiah when taken together vindicate God's activity with His people. They show that God fulfilled His promise, or prophecy, to restore his exiled people back into the land. He uses both non-Jewish and Jewish leaders to do this. On the one hand, these books reveal how God's Left Hand,[76] his providential overshadowing of foreign rulers, like Cyrus, Darius, and Artaxerxes, accomplishes His purposes of getting His people back into their promised inheritance. On the other hand, they reveal God's right hand working through leaders within the Jewish community such as Joshua and Zerubbabel, Haggai and Zechariah and Ezra and Nehemiah. Cyrus, Darius, and Artaxerxes sponsored the return of Jews to the promises land and provided various kinds of resources. Joshua and Zerubbabel re-instated the Altar and worship of God and laid the foundation for the building of the temple. Haggai and Zechariah stirred up the hearts of the people to rebuild the temple. Ezra and Nehemiah built the protective wall around Jerusalem, repopulated Jerusalem, and reestablished worship and ceremony of the traditional Jewish

---

[72] Modern dating suggested by NIV study Bible and corroborated in other study Bibles.

[73] One wonders if Haggai was around for this. If I am right about Haggai's Afterglow ministry, then he probably wasn't.

[74] If this is Artaxerxes I the year is 458 B.C. according to the CEV.

[75] If this dating is roughly correct then Ezra was probably in his mid 30s when he came to Jerusalem. He would be in his late 40s when he preached and taught the word of God in the great revival of Ne 8.

[76] Dr. Arthur Glasser, formerly Professor Emeritus in the School of World Mission of Fuller Theological Seminary, uses the phrase, the *Left Hand of God*, to call attention to God's use of non-believers to accomplish His purposes. This *Left Hand of God* is seen numerous times in the Old Testament. See **Article**, *15. Left Hand of God*.

religion. They left behind a renewed people who were separated from foreign admixtures, customs and idolatry with religious observations purified.[77]

This work of God to get His people back into the land and worshipping and following Him did not take place overnight. Time was involved. When reading the various passages about Nehemiah's restoration activity, keep in mind the overall timing of what was going on. Remember, the wall was built fairly rapidly. But Nehemiah made a trip back to Artaxerxes and then returned later. He had a about 12 years, total, of ministry back in Jerusalem. His ministry was in collaboration with Ezra and his well-trained team.

---

[77] Perhaps Malachi was part of this renewal effort. It is clear that renewal is a necessary on-going effort of leadership. Though Nehemiah and Ezra left behind a renewed people, it doesn't take long for them to stray away from God again.

21. Nehemiah, Change Participants

Introduction

The book of Nehemiah, more than any other leadership situation in the Bible,[78] illustrates a leader who implemented change effectively. In fact, Nehemiah as a leader, is one who illustrates every facet of a well-thought-out bridging strategy.[79] This article will overview that bridging strategy[80] with a specific focus on the change participants that were involved in Nehemiah's change situation. I will first introduce the notion of a bridging strategy and the preliminary definitions necessary to understand it. This will provide a framework for viewing Nehemiah's change situation. I will give a cursory treatment of three of the four stages involved in a deliberate bridging strategy. Then I will focus more on one of those stages—the people involved in the change, something amply illustrated in the book. This will emphasize to us, present day leaders, the importance of knowing the people involved in our change situations.[81] One of the most important things that we do as leaders is to introduce change. Knowing the change participants is essential if leaders are to bring about change with the best probability of success and the least amount of trauma. Nehemiah knew his change participants and worked to bring about as much ownership as possible.

Some Preliminary Definitions Involving Change Dynamics

Deliberate change introduced into a situation, whether reactive or proactive, involves the notion of *anticipation*. A person bringing about change must anticipate where he/she would like to be some time later after the changes are introduced and working. Such a

---

[78] Two possible exceptions are the Moses-Joshua leadership transition and Jesus institution of a movement, which eventuated in an ongoing institution for change, the church. Nehemiah's change situation is succinct enough and takes place in a relatively short time period—making it much easier to evaluate as a change situation than the other two.

[79] Nehemiah strikes me as an ESTJ, using Myers-Briggs terminology. But more than just an ESTJ—He was a very-spiritual-and-sensitive-to-God ESTJ. An ESTJ personality is one who plans well considering various details and researching them (S), analyzes situations well and plans (T), and moves to accomplish those plans in a specific way that allows for evaluations and accountability (J). The E part is seen in is working with people, one of the foci of this article. His prayer life and his concern for God's work, including realized-holiness, mark him as a very spiritual person. He is an unusual person of change and well worth studying from a change dynamics standpoint.

[80] The theoretical material in this paper comes from years of teaching a course on implementing change in Christian organizations and the research associated with that course. See Clinton, **Bridging Strategies**, Barnabas Publisher. This change dynamics manual goes into details in all the change theory that I introduce in this article in a cursory manner.

[81] This is preliminary to getting ownership—a necessary component of a successful implementation of change with a view toward eventual stabilization with the change in place and also with a view toward the least amount of trauma in the process. I deal with the concept of ownership later in this article. See *ownership*, **Glossary**.

change person is applying the adage,[82] *Begin with the end in mind.* Think of yourself as a change person. Having recognized the end, then you are almost ready to think how to get there. You have only to first assess where you are now. Knowing the **Now** and the anticipated **Then** you are ready to devise a strategy to get from where you are **Now** to where you want to be **Then**. Such a strategy is called a bridging strategy and is one approach to proactively implementing change. You bridge from the **Now** to the **Then**. Pictorially then, this key idea is seen as shown in Figure Ne 16-1.

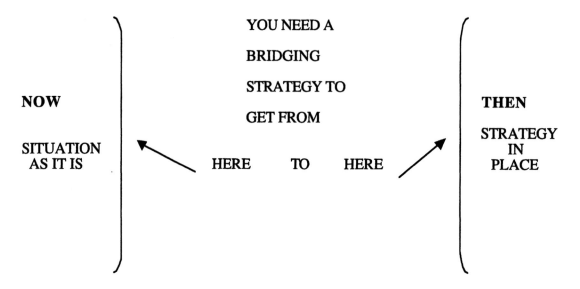

Figure Ne 21-1. The Notion of a Bridging Strategy Diagrammed

It is not enough to have the end result in mind. You must know how you are going to get there. Your bridging strategy helps you understand the complexity of getting your changes accepted by people, getting the structures in place, and changing the values that are necessary if the new changed situation is to arise. Careful analysis will have to be done. Resulting steps of action will have to be sequenced in order to bring about implementation.

Definition   A <u>bridging strategy</u> is the resulting plan of action for implementing a given strategy so as to transition the group, organization, or structure from the present situation to the anticipated situation.

Lets explore briefly the notions of now and then as implied in Ne Figure 22-1.

The Now Situation
Understanding where we are at the present is a preliminary must for thinking about introducing change. One way of doing this is to formulate a list of the items that seem intuitively to be significant in the system if change is to be considered. We call this list the raw factors. From this list certain of the items will be more crucial and carry more weight if change is to be implemented. We call these the critical factors. This will give us an overall outline to modify, clarify, and add to when we do our careful analysis.

---

[82]This notion has been popularized by Stephen Covey in his book, **The 7 Habits of Highly Effective People**. But it is well known in leadership literature in many other forms as well, think ahead, forewarned is forearmed, etc.

Description   The <u>NOW situation</u> refers to an intuitive pre-analysis of the system before any changes are introduced.

Example from Nehemiah
Ne 1:3 describes it succinctly.

> 3 They said to me, "Those who survived the exile and are back in the province are in great trouble and disgrace. The wall of Jerusalem is broken down, and its gates have been burned with fire.

Description   <u>Raw factors</u> refer to a list of items, which pinpoint important facets of the system into which change is to be introduced and definitely affect analysis of the situation.

Examples from Nehemiah
Further study of the book of Nehemiah and other restoration books (Ezra, Nehemiah, Haggai, Zechariah, Esther), along with some applied imagination, results in a list of raw factors. Probably others could be added. But this certainly illustrates the point of raw factors. Some raw factors include:

- a remnant of people have returned to the land,
- Jerusalem is under populated,
- Haggai, Joshua, and Zechariah have rebuilt the temple,
- there are priests and Levites in the land, though not necessarily functioning well,
- the people back in the land are discouraged,
- Jerusalem is undefended, no protective wall,
- Nehemiah is aware of the situation,
- Nehemiah senses a call from God to do something about the situation,
- Nehemiah has access to resources that can be used to rebuild the defensive protection in Jerusalem,
- the remnant people of God back in the land are not wholeheartedly following God,
- the remnant are basically unaware of God's revelation and its impact on their conduct,
- there is no centralized worship emanating from Jerusalem which is a testimony to God,
- the Priest-Scribe, Ezra, and a team of well trained associates, know the Word of God and long to see a revival among this remnant,
- there are various factions of people who returned to the land,
- there are leaders of various kinds among the remnant who have returned, including in Jerusalem itself and in the surrounding villages and towns.
- There is a strong anti-Jewish faction of people in the land—some in prominent appointed leadership positions (Persian appointed governor).

Description   <u>Critical factors</u> refer to a list of items selected from the raw factors which must be considered and addressed in the change situation if change is to be implemented.

Examples from Nehemiah
Further study of the book of Nehemiah (with some hindsight help) results in a list of the more important critical factors, which Nehemiah did address.

- the people back in the land are discouraged,
- the remnant people of God back in the land are not wholeheartedly following God,
- Jerusalem is under populated,

- there are priests and Levites in the land, though not necessarily functioning well,
- the remnant are basically unaware of God's revelation and its impact on their conduct,
- there is no centralized worship emanating from Jerusalem which is a testimony to God,
- Jerusalem is undefended, no protective wall,
- there are various factions of people who returned to the land,
- there are leaders of various kinds among the remnant who have returned, including in Jerusalem itself and in the surrounding villages and towns.
- There is a strong anti-Jewish faction of people in the land—some in prominent appointed leadership positions (Persian appointed governor).

The Then Situation

Not only must you as a change person understand intuitively where you are at the present time, the NOW situation but you must also have an intuitive grasp of what your changed situation might be like. You must not just know that there are problems to be solved. But you must look down the road as if those problems were already solved. And if so what does the situation look like? Again this is an intuitive ideal, which may not hold water with careful analysis. But it gives you something to shoot at as you do your bridging analysis.

Definition   The <u>THEN situation</u> refers to an intuitive pre-analysis of the system after needed changes have been introduced and the system is stable.

Definition   <u>Ideal factors</u> refer to a list of items, which reflect the essential good points of the new system with problems solved that prompted the changes.

Some ideal factors for Nehemiah's hoped-for THEN situation include the following:

- the remnant people of God back in the land are wholeheartedly following God,
- they are aware of God, their own history with God, His demands on their lives,
- Jerusalem is well populated and has defensive protection (a wall in place with strong gates and a security system in place),
- there are priests, Levites, and worship leaders in Jerusalem, who are functioning well,
- these priests, Levites, and worship leaders are provided for financially,
- there is a powerful centralized worship emanating from Jerusalem which is a testimony to God,
- there is a united people of God in Jerusalem and the surrounding area,
- there is leadership in place which can maintain the renewed momentum of a spiritual renewal brought about by Nehemiah, Ezra, and others.

The Clinton 4 Stage Bridging Model

Clinton's 4 stage bridging model can give further perspective that can help us as we evaluate Nehemiah's change situation. Figure Ne 21-2 includes the following four elements of a bridging strategy. We will be focusing on Stage 1 in this article.

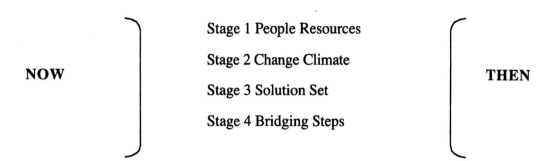

Figure Ne 21-2. Clinton's 4 Stage Bridging Model

Table Ne 21-1 gives a brief overview of each of these stages in the change process with a cursory overview of Nehemiah's situation. This article is concerned primarily with Stage 1 People Resources.

Table Ne 21-1 The Four Stage Model Explained

Stage	Name	Essence of Stage	Comments on Nehemiah
1	People Resources	An analysis of the change agents involved, the individual change participants involved, the various groups involved, and the relationships between these various change participants with a view toward a strategy for developing as positive as possible **RELATIONSHIPS** that will enhance change.	The following section will deal in detail with this stage.
2	Change Climate	An analysis of the situation **NOW** with its critical factors; This analysis includes problems, opportunities and the system as a whole. How has the system responded to change in the past and how is it likely to respond to change at present?	See previously given list of raw and critical factors for the NOW situation. This is a very cursory treatment of this. Much more is required of a full analysis.
3	Solution Set	An analysis of the possible **THEN** situation including inside and outside resources, idealistic solutions, formation of the solution set, identification of the bridging profile for a selected solution.	See previously given list of ideal factors for the THEN situation. Again this is a very cursory treatment of this. Much more is required of a full analysis.
4	Bridging Steps	An application **BRIDGING IDEAS** in order to form action alternatives for individuals, structure, and philosophical values. This analysis includes time analysis, adaptation of solutions, ethical analysis, and conceptualization for continuity or stabilization.	Some steps seen in Nehemiah's situation. Step 1. Get approval of Artaxerxes and his authoritative backing and promise of resources. Timing critical in when to do this. Step 2. Survey the actual situation in Jerusalem and build credibility with the present leadership in Jerusalem and surrounding areas. Step 3. Motivate toward ownership of the whole project by first concentrating

			on a felt need by the people—the wall for defense. Do this with leaders first. Step 4. Organize the people into a strong work force with a plan to simultaneously work on all portions of the wall. Provide material resources. Step 5. Deal with contingencies. Step 6. Model loyalty to the people. Step 7. Celebrate completion of the wall. Step 8. Use spiritual resources to bring about a mass renewal. Step 9. Organize for continued renewal. A centralized worship out of the Temple. Step 10. Repopulate Jerusalem to make it strong. Step 11. Continue to Hold People Accountable for continued testimony to God.

The Change Participants in Nehemiah's Change Situation

The two main groupings of people involved in the change are those deliberately bringing about the changes, the change agents (Nehemiah, Hanani, Ezra and his team), and those who are part of the system being changed (see the lists in ch 3, 7, 10, 12 and individual passages scattered throughout). The ones in the system being changed, called change participants, will significantly be involved in reacting to these changes. Figure Ne 21-3 represents the two main groupings of people involved in the change. Note that the larger portion of change participant types are neutral or favorable.

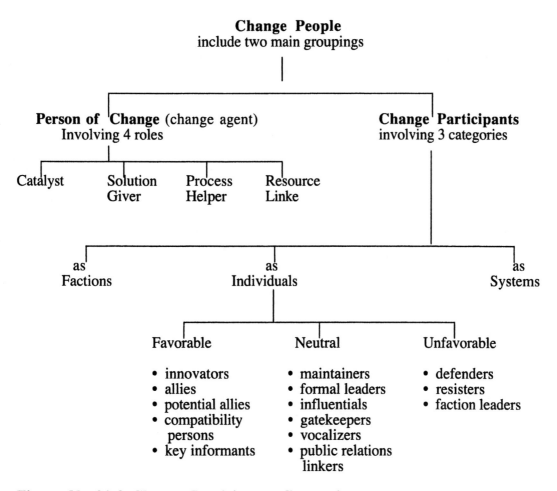

Figure Ne 21-3 Change Participants Categories

I will give definitions for the Person of Change (change agents) and examples from Nehemiah. Then I will give a Table, which summarizes the Change Participants that can be seen in Nehemiah.

Person Of Change synonym: change agent
The person of change is the euphemism for change agent. The concept of agent has negative connotations in many parts of the world. So I prefer to use the term person of change to mean a person who is deliberately thinking about introducing change into some movement, organization, or institution. Here are definitions apropos to those who are deliberating influencing the change.

Definition   The <u>person of change</u> represents a person who wants to deliberately introduce change into a situation.

A person who sees something wrong in a system and wishes to correct it. This person will usually call attention to what is wrong. Nehemiah and Ezra were such people.

Definition   A <u>catalyst</u> is a person of change who initiates the change process by expressing dissatisfaction with the status quo and actively stimulating discontent in others as well.

Nehemiah was the main catalyst in this change situation.

Definition   A <u>process helper</u> is a person of change with overall perspective on the system and its needs and of change processes in general who thus focuses on the entire change process for the client's benefit and facilitates change at every stage.

The process helper is the type of person who sees the overall picture, recognizes the importance of the catalyst's pressure to change, and coordinates or facilitates the change process throughout all its stages. This person of change sees the needs for solution givers and resources linkers and utilizes their contributions in the change process in order to build upon the initial work of the catalyst. Nehemiah was also the dominant process helper. Usually a person of change will be dominant in one or more of the four change agent roles. There will be a primary role and secondary role. Nehemiah's primary role was that of catalyst and secondary role as process helper.

Definition   A <u>solution giver</u> is a person of change who clearly sees the situation for the present and the future and forms and communicates a plan that could work to solve the system's current problems.

While Nehemiah was the initial solution giver (saw the necessity for the wall and a repopulated Jerusalem) it is more likely that the total solution was a team effort involving Nehemiah, his brother Hanani, and Ezra—along with some of the leaders in and around Jerusalem. The Jewish people of the remnant were given over to rigorous discussion and even argument. The total solution probably emerged from a group of people though Nehemiah had the positional authority to back a solution.

Definition   The <u>resource linker</u> is a change agent who keeps the process of change going by matching needs and resources, which are material, financial, educational and personnel, at any stage of the process but particularly in the diagnosis, search for solutions, and application stages.

Nehemiah was the initial resource linker, particularly with regards to finances and needed materials. He was able to get Artaxerxes to agree to help in this regard. But linking overall was a cooperative effort. Linking to the work force for building the wall was a cooperative effort of many of the leaders in Jerusalem and surrounding towns and villages. Linking to resources for religious leadership was probably a function that Ezra and his team were involved with along with the Jerusalem priests and Levites. They would be knowledgeable about worship leaders, for example.

Usually deliberate change introduced into a system will need all four types of examples listed in order to bring in the changes and stabilize them. It is these kinds of people who will work with the various change participants, hopefully energizing the favorable participants, recruiting neutral participants toward the favorable, and minimizing the opposition of the unfavorable.

Table Ne 21-2 defines some of these types, particularly those that can be identified in Nehemiah. I am not going to list all the factions but only the more important ones. I also am not going to deal with the change participants in terms of systemic analysis, which is beyond the scope of this article.

Table Ne 21-2 Change Participants in Nehemiah—Possible Factions

Type	Who	Comments
Political Faction Against the Change	Sanballat, Tobiah, and Geshem	Frequently the introduction of change, like Nehemiah was doing, will alienate people who have vested interests in the system the way it is. Tobiah, Sanballat, and Geshem and their coalition were outsiders (non-Jewish) who had vested interests threatened by Nehemiah's changes. These men formed a political coalition, which was strongly opposed to Nehemiah's building of the wall; they threatened military intervention; they threatened to send a report to Artaxerxes describing Nehemiah's leadership as sedition.
Religious Faction Against the Change	Eliashib and Joiada (who were insiders) also had vested interests which would be upset by Nehemiah's changes.	Eliashib and Joiada (who were insiders) also had vested interests which would be upset by Nehemiah's changes. They were probably typical of other priests and Levites in the system. These two were also allied to the coalition of Tobiah, Sanballat, and Geshem.
Prominent Rich People in Jerusalem--neutral	Not named individually.	While the large majority of craftsmen of various ilk were largely behind Nehemiah's changes, there were at least two indications that some of the richer people of status (nobles) were not entirely behind the project (one indication to some nobles who would not do practical work on the wall; a group of rich nobles were charging large interest on loans to poorer people; Nehemiah corrected this). It should also be pointed out on the positive side, that some rich people also provided heavily into the funds for backing religious workers.

Table Ne 21-3 Change Participants in the Book of Nehemiah—Individuals

Type	Who	Comments
Favorable-- allies	Hanani, Hananiah, Ezra and his team	See Ne 1:2; 7:1-4; ch 8.
Favorable—potential allies	The remnant, particularly the poorer classes	Nehemiah champions the case of the poor people. It is clear that he was loyal to them and could expect them to be loyal in return.

Favorable—Innovator	Nehemiah, Ezra	Nehemiah wanted to bring about change that would have a lasting impact. He knew that a strong centralized worship in a strong Jerusalem would do this. Ezra was a priest who studied the word and obeyed it personally and taught others. He trained a team of people who could interpret the word to the common people.
Neutral—Maintainers	City officials	See Ne 2:16. Nehemiah moved these toward becoming allies; these folks are helpful in keeping the change going once it is in place.
Neutral—Potential allies	Tribal and clan leaders	Several of these are mentioned in the listing of those who pitched in and worked on the wall. It is clear then that Nehemiah converted many of these to allies.
Neutral—formal leaders	City officials; those in mayor like positions in surroundings towns	Numerous of these are mentioned in the listing of those who pitched in and worked on the wall. It is clear then that Nehemiah converted many of these to allies.
Neutral—influentials	Nobles	See Ne 2:16; see ch 5:6ff
Neutral—gatekeepers	Religious workers	Priests and Levites; these folk could kill the spiritual renewal easily if not converted to favorable or at least neutral.
Unfavorable—defenders	Some prophets Noadiah et al	See Ne 6:14. Noadiah was a prophet and was apparently connected to a group of other prophets.
Unfavorable—resisters	Shemaiah	See Ne 6:10
Unfavorable—faction leaders	Already mentioned	See Table Ne 21-2

Nehemiah and Ownership

Consider this, you are a change agent like Nehemiah. But you are working in a modern situation where communication is so much more readily available to all the people in your situation. If everybody in your situation really knew about the changes that you have in mind, how would they feel about them? Would they be eagerly awaiting them, generally receptive to them, neutral toward them, against them generally, or very much opposed to them? Knowing the answer to your own change participants can make a difference in your getting ownership for your changes.

Definition A person in a change situation is said to have <u>ownership</u> for the changes when he/she is not only for the changes but is willing to cooperate in the change process.

This is what Nehemiah did so well on. Getting ownership is crucial. Nehemiah got ownership. In general, what a change agent must do is to move the unfavorable people over at least to the neutral category. Move as many of the neutral category participants as possible over to the favorable category. And then you must get the favorable folks really turned on to change so as to proactively help in it. Nehemiah got an overwhelming majority of people over to the favorable category. See the folks who celebrated with him in ch 12 the completion of the wall. See the list of folks who signed the covenant in ch 10. He at least countered the efforts of those who were opposed to the changes, such as Noadiah, Shemaiah, the rich banker types, and the outside political coalition headed by Sanballat and Tobiah.

In general there are four approaches to bringing about changes with regard to participants. Most change participants represent forces for or against change. Those people and other entities for the change are said to be driving forces. Those people or other entities against the change are said to be resisting forces. To move the influences so that the change has a better probability to happen, you can,

1. **increase** the driving forces,
2. **decrease** the restraining forces,
3. **do a combination** involving both increasing the driving forces and decreasing the resisting forces, or
4. take a restraining force and **turn it around** so that it becomes a driving force (this is possible especially with a person opposing some change).

Nehemiah worked on the combination described in 3.

Most Important Insights on Nehemiah's Dealing with Change Participants
Here are some summary observations about Nehemiah as a change agent:

1. Nehemiah was knowledgeable about the change participants. He also had some excellent records that had been kept from the early time of return of some of the remnant.
2. Nehemiah cultivated his allies. Note especially his work on the behalf of worship leaders and other religious leaders.
3. Nehemiah cultivated the neutrals. Notice his work for the poor.
4. Nehemiah countered his unfavorable participants. Note his hitting conflict head on.
5. Nehemiah got ownership.
6. Nehemiah got committal (see the signing of the covenant).
7. Nehemiah selected leaders to maintain the change. These were men of character and were allies.
8. Nehemiah modeled what a good change agent should model. He was a person of character—integrity was a top quality.
9. Nehemiah was a Bible centered leader. He used the Bible well to reinforce his position, especially on renewal issues like separation and adherence to covenant.
10. Nehemiah was a spiritual civil leader. His heart for God comes through in all that he does.

Closure
Nehemiah's godly leadership involved careful planning to get ownership of as many of the change participants as he could. Nehemiah is not about building a wall. It is about a comprehensive change strategy to build a strong Jerusalem out of which a centralized worship center would be a grand testimony to God. It is about seeing God's people renewed and worshipping God and following Him so that His testimony would go out. Nehemiah is a Hebrews 13:8 leader who should be emulated, especially with regard to careful planning to implement significant change. Nehemiah left behind a legacy—a strong Jerusalem with a centralized worship bring honor to God and a book that tells us about his leadership. We do well to learn from him about leadership.

22. Nehemiah—Civil Leadership With A Spiritual Twist

Introduction

To have impact on a society, a broad spectrum is needed which includes civil leadership, mainstream religious leadership, and peripheral religious leadership. Nehemiah was a civil leader. But more than that, Nehemiah was an excellent civil leader who had a strong spiritual bent to his life and ministry. Synergistic leadership is needed. The three types of leadership will be defined below—Civil, mainstream religious, and peripheral religious. Each has important functions to accomplish. But note, when you have a civil leader who is spiritual you have an additional thrust complementing the triad of leadership needed. This article will define the three kinds of leadership needed.[83] Then I will speak a moment about Nehemiah's civil leadership, with a spiritual twist.

Definition   Civil leadership refers to followers of God, sold out on following God, yet impacting the society via two types of roles often needed—1. Governmental or political roles sanctioned by the society and 2. Military roles sanctioned by the society.[84]

They are not considered religious workers.

Definition   Mainstream religious leadership refers to officially recognized religious roles sanctioned by the society and religious structures.

Priest and various ordained ministry roles (e.g. a pastor in today's world) would be mainstream religious roles. They maintain the need for worship of God and provide the necessary mediation between God and the people.

---

[83] See also the **Article**, *11. Haggai—Coalition Leadership* which explores the need for synergistic leadership between the three types.

[84] I do not talk about the military role in this article since it is missing for the most part. Nehemiah, in a pseudo manner did some of the military role. The military role is seen especially in the Kingdom Leadership Era.

Definition   <u>Peripheral religious</u> leadership refers to those roles, mostly outside the
                  mainstream religious structures, which attempt to speak for God to bring
                  about change in religious groups, structures, and society in general.

They were needed to correct lapses in the functions of the other two types of leaders. These
sometimes fringe leaders are frequently needed because mainstream religious leaders go
nominal in their pursuit of God. Or the civil leaders do not follow God. God raises these
types of leaders up in an *ad hoc sort of manner*, as and when needed. The oral and writing
prophets of the O.T. and those exercising prophetic ministries and some apostolic
ministries in the present *Church Leadership Era* typically would be examples of peripheral
religious leaders.

Typically, all three of the above types of leadership are needed to accomplish God's
work in our world. Table Ne 22-1 lists the six Biblical leadership eras and shows how
these roles played out in the various eras.

Table Ne 22-1 Civil, Religious, and Peripheral Religious Leaders

Leadership Era	Civil a. political b. military/ Example	Mainstream Religious/ Example	Peripheral Religious/ Example
I. Patriarchal	The family head served as civil political, and military when needed. / Abraham	The family head served to interceded in a priestly way with God for the family. / Abraham, Job	The family head received revelation from God for situations. / Abraham, Job
2. Pre-Kingdom a. Desert	Civil done by an apostolic type leader raised up by God for the time/ a. political—Moses (supported by Miriam as adviser) b. Military—Joshua under Moses control.	God initiated a specific religious role the Priesthood (supported by the Levites)/ Aaron	Moses served to receive revelatory word for the people.
2. Pre-Kingdom b. Conquering the Land	Civil done by succession leader appointed by Moses/ a. political— Joshua b. Military —Joshua	Aaron's successor was appointed by Moses/ Eleazar, head priest	Joshua served to receive revelatory word (less frequently than Moses)
2. Pre-Kingdom b. Conquered by the Land	No overall civil head; Joshua did not appoint a successor; Military heads were the Judges who were raised up according to need.	Not clear who was the head priest; none apparently coordinating priestly effort for all the tribes; Eli had some sphere of influence but not clear how wide his range of influence. Samuel performed this function toward the end of the Judges era.	Occasional prophets arose like Deborah; Samuel performed this function toward the end of the Judges era.

3. Kingdom	Civil done by the King; kings generally by succession—oldest family member or one appointed by king; Various advisory posts supplemented civil leadership (Nathan and Gad); Military appointed by king	Priests; not clear how head priest was chosen;	Oral prophets raised up by God outside the normal priestly structures to correct civil and military leadership/ Elijah and Elisha are typical examples. Writing prophets raised up to correct both Northern and Southern Kingdoms/ Amos, Micah, et al
4. Post-Kingdom a. As Kingdom was crumbling	None; the people were subservient to conquerors	Not clear how priestly families survived or a head priest appointed; Impact of leadership unknown; Ezekiel was a priest;	Jeremiah and Ezekiel were typical of those who received revelatory information and corrective information for civil and military leadership as the kingdom was being dismantled;
b. In exile	Not clear;	None mentioned;	Daniel would be typical of one getting revelation.
c. Return to Land	Civil: leaders like Zerubbabel and Nehemiah Military: none	Joshua and Ezra were priests who impacted	Haggai, Zechariah, and Malachi
5. Pre-Church Leadership Era	None; Sanhedrin some influence; ruled by appointed leadership from Rome; Roman military garrisoned Palestine	There were high priests and a priestly line; not sure how succession was done	John the Baptist; Jesus
6. Church	Civil missing; No military leadership	Pastors, elders, deacons were formally appointed by formal Apostolic leadership or local church leadership	Apostolic leaders and prophets (itinerant leaders)

Nehemiah's Civil Leadership—An Organizational Leader with A Spiritual Twist

The thesis of this article is that coalition leadership is greatly strengthened in its synergistic leadership when the civil leader is not only good in organizational things but also a very spiritual person. Nehemiah was such a person. Let me suggest four different ways that Nehemiah's spirituality is seen:

1. He was a man of prayer. Prayers interweaves throughout his whole ministry.
2. He was concerned with the people's needs—both material and spiritual. He was concerned about spiritual renewal of the people, not just their protection in a strong Jerusalem

3. He was concerned with a spiritually revitalized mainstream religious corps of workers. Such a group of leaders would continue the renewal effort.
4. He collaborated with Ezra, a spiritually alive mainstream religious worker with a peripheral religious worker's bent, to push hard for renewal.

Let me elaborate on each of the four.

1. He was a man of prayer.
I have already written about Nehemiah's prayer life in two other leadership articles, *24. Nehemiah, Desperate Praying* and *18. Nehemiah—And Daniel, A Comparison of Vicarious Praying*. So I won't comment, except briefly in this article. Nehemiah was a man of prayer. Table Ne 22-2 lists references to Nehemiah's prayers.

Table Ne 22-2 References to Nehemiah's praying.

Number	Verse(s)	Label	Description
1	Ne 1:4, 5, 6, 8, 11	Burdened Prayer for Jerusalem	Vicarious confession by Nehemiah seen here. Remember prayer Type I[85].
2	Ne 2:4-8	Spontaneous Praying	Nehemiah in a desperate situation before the King flings up a thought prayer to God right on the spot before he answers the King.
3	Ne 4:4,9	Spontaneous Prayer	Prayed for protection as they guarded the city.
4	Ne 5:19	Spontaneous Prayer	Remember prayer Type III. Nehemiah asking God to remember himself.
5	Ne 6:9	Spontaneous Prayer	Nehemiah asks for strength to continue the work in light of the threats received
6	Ne 6:14	Spontaneous Prayer	Remember prayer Type II. Nehemiah asking God to punish enemies.
7	Ne 9:5-38	Spontaneous Prayer	Vicarious confession occurs here. Nehemiah a part of this but not only one praying.
8	Ne 13:14	Spontaneous Prayer	Remember prayer Type III. Nehemiah asking God to remember himself.
9	Ne 13:22	Spontaneous Prayer	Remember prayer Type III. Nehemiah asking God to remember himself.
10	Ne 13:29	Spontaneous Prayer	Remember prayer Type II. Nehemiah asking God to punish enemies.
11	Ne 13:31	Spontaneous Prayer	Remember prayer Type III. Nehemiah asking God to remember himself.

It is clear that Nehemiah illustrated the important macro lesson[86] on prayer.

---

[85] Type I. Remember God, an exhortation for the people to remember in the past what God had done (both in blessing and punishing) or to remind God of what He has said; Type II. Remember enemies—an imprecatory prayer asking God to punish the enemies. Type III. A personal request for God to remember Nehemiah for what he had done in his leadership.

[86] A macro-lesson is a high level generalization of a leadership observation (suggestion, guideline, requirement), stated as a lesson, which repeatedly occurs throughout different leadership eras, and thus has potential as a leadership absolute. Macro lessons even at their weakest provide strong guidelines describing leadership insights. At their strongest they are requirements, or absolutes, that leaders should follow.

8.[87] Intercession[88]
Leaders called to a ministry are called to intercede for that ministry.

Nehemiah prayed for his people and the various leadership situations he faced. Many were crisis situations. But many also were for his people to be renewed and follow God.

2. He was concerned with spiritual renewal of the people.
Two macro lessons are seen in Nehemiah's ministry, which illustrate this characteristic of Nehemiah's leadership. The stability macro, stated as, *Preserving a ministry of God with life and vigor over time, is as much, if not more of a challenge to leadership, than creating* one is definitely demonstrated at several points in the book, including Prayer Items 9, 10, and 13 given in Table Ne 22-2 above.

3. Concerned for spiritually revitalized mainstream religious   workers.
Another macro lesson is alluded to in ch 13 and seen in Item 8 of the prayer table. Nehemiah wants adequate financial backing for the mainstream religious workers. They will need it if they are to devote themselves to their spiritual task. Another indication of Nehemiah's concern for the mainstream religious workers is Nehemiah's is careful attention to purification. He has the Priests and Levites purify and cleanse things—wherever some omission or sinful thing has been taking place. This occurs several times during Nehemiah's leadership—see especially ch 13 vs 9, 22. The purity macro lesson, first identified in the Patriarchal Leadership Era and repeated in other eras, is stated as, *Leaders must personally learn of and respond to the holiness of God in order to have effective ministry*. Nehemiah sees to be deeply impressed with God's holiness. Prayer items 10 and 13 also refer to Nehemiah's efforts to bolster the mainstream religious workers.

4. Collaboration with Ezra
Frequently a high level leader is threatened by a co-worker and will make attempts to restrain such a worker. Just the opposite is the case with Nehemiah. He supports Ezra's ministry wholeheartedly. The Ne ch 8 passage is one of the great revival passages in the Bible. And Nehemiah is right there with a coalition of leaders, civil, mainstream religious and peripheral, to support this revival effort. Ezra functions here as both a mainstream religious leader and as a peripheral religious leader (does the prophetic function).

In fact, Nehemiah not only worked with Ezra, he actually is part of a coalition of leaders of which Ezra is one.

Coalition is a French word that originated from a Latin participle having to do with growing together. Having crossed over into English its meaning is as follows:

Leaders ignore them to their detriment. 41 Macro Lessons have been identified. These macro lessons are numbered.

[87]The prayer macro lesson is number 8. See **Article**, *17. Macro Lessons: List of 41 Across Six Leadership Eras*.

[88]This macro lesson was seen first in the Pre-Kingdom Leadership Era. Study across the Bible has identified six leadership eras: (1) Patriarchal; (2) Pre-Kingdom; (3) Kingdom; (4) Post-Kingdom; (5) Pre-Church; (6) Church. Macro lessons have originated in each of the eras. At least they were first identified in an era and then checked backwards and forwards for occurrences in other eras.

Definition   Coalition refers to an alliance, especially a temporary one, of people, factions, parties, or nations.

Taking this definition a bit further, we arrive at our Biblical leadership definition,

Definition   A leadership coalition in Biblical literature refers to

- a partnership, whether formal or informal,
- which exists between civil leaders, mainstream religious leaders and/or peripheral religious leaders,
- for a temporary period of time

in order to accomplish some God-directed task(s).

The more formal and deliberate is the coalition and the more specifically the task is defined, the more effective is the leadership.

Some Observations About Coalition Leadership

The two most effective coalitions were that of Haggai, Zechariah, Joshua and Zerubbabel and that of Ezra and Nehemiah. Some commonalities include:

1. Both of these coalitions were for relatively short times.
2. Both of these collations were very specific, one to rebuild the temple, the other to rebuild the wall around Jerusalem.
3. In both cases, all of the leaders were spiritually alive—civil, formal religious, and peripheral religious.

Some differences include:

1. Ezra operated in the role of formal religious (was a priest) and informal religious leader (calling for reform and renewal). Haggai, the major motivator was a peripheral religious leader. The religious leader, Joshua, was supplementary to Haggai's leadership.
2. Ezra's informal religious ministry was focused on renewal—via the revealed word of God—getting people back to knowing and obeying God's word. Haggai's informal religious ministry was focused on motivating the people to rebuild the temple.
3. Nehemiah was the inspirational leader, though a civil leader. He was the practical, get it done kind of person, yet also a very spiritual leader. Haggai was the inspirational leader, though not in the formal religious structure.
4. Nehemiah, though very practical, was a man of dependence upon God in prayer. Haggai was the practical point person in the rebuilding of the temple. Zechariah was probably the spiritual motivator.
5. The obstacles that Nehemiah and Ezra faced were primarily external (coming from opposition from without though there were some internal obstacles in terms of resources). The obstacles that Haggai, Zechariah, Joshua, and Zerubbabel faced were dominantly internal—in the hearts and minds of the followers.
6. Nehemiah's connections into the power structure provided a source of resources. Zerubbabel had to raise resources from the people themselves, who were going through major times of depression.

Civil Leadership An Important Key

Remember, I am asserting that Nehemiah offered something special to his civil leadership. He was a tremendously spiritual man. Some observation on synergistic functioning of civil, military, formal religious and peripheral religious leadership include the following[89]:

1. When civil and priestly leadership were spiritually strong there was little need for peripheral religious leadership.
2. Civil leadership that is spiritual is needed to control military. Only two military leaders in O.T. were strong spiritually—David and Joshua (who both wore two hats—civil as well; and David had weak moments in which prophetic leadership exercised corrective action).
3. The strongest synergistic efforts are seen in the Post-Kingdom leadership era in two different times: a. Rebuilding the temple—Haggai, Zechariah, Joshua, and Zerubbabel; b. Building the wall around Jerusalem—Nehemiah, Ezra (who wore two hats—priestly and prophet's) and bringing a renewed centralized worship to a strong Jerusalem.
4. In the church leadership era the emphasis, structure wise, is units, local churches, which will fit into any culture or society anywhere as a religious influence on the society (correcting wrongs of society and bringing people in the society into relationship with God). The place of military and civil leadership is not directly related to the religious structure. The peripheral religious function occurs both within these local churches (apostolic, prophetic and exhortive ministries) and without (apostolic, prophetic and exhortive ministries).
5. Civil leadership is exercised outside the jurisdiction of local church structures.
6. Military leadership is exercised outside the jurisdiction of local church structures.
7. Priestly leadership that was spiritual directly affected civil leadership for the good several times in the kingdom era.
8. Kingly leadership which was spiritual directly affected the whole nation several times.
9. Spiritual leadership, whether kingly, priestly, or peripheral religious prolonged the life of the southern Kingdom well beyond that of the northern kingdom which had no spiritual leadership throughout. Spiritual leadership makes a difference.

Closure

Coalitions worked because various leadership functions were needed to pull off the accomplishments that God was challenging them to. And leaders who were gifted in the various areas (civil, main stream religious, military, and peripheral religious) were willing to work together and respect the necessary leadership of the others in the coalition. It is the cooperative effort and respect for others leadership that made the two most effective coalitions so successful (Nehemiah's—the building of the wall; Haggai's—the rebuilding of the temple).

The coalition in which Nehemiah worked, benefited from a civil worker who was very good in organizing, well connected, an inspirational task oriented leader, and yet a very spiritual leader. His spiritual leadership is a model for us today. Certainly, this model of Nehemiah ought to bring hope and courage to lay leaders today.

---

[89] Note that I have added some remarks here to the present day situation, in which civil leadership acts very different than a civil leader like Nehemiah.

23. Nehemiah, Contextual Flow—Seeing the Presentation

Introduction
It is helpful to see the general flow of the information Nehemiah gives about the building of the wall and the reformation efforts to move the followers back to worshipping and obeying God.

Below is given the flow of the contextual statements through out the book.

The book of Nehemiah is logically structured. Understanding its structure will make the difference in seeing its meaning—denotation and connotation. I will use the outline and theme given in the General Reference section of the commentary. I will use my own contextual breakdown. Read the interweaving statement given below of the theme of Nehemiah. Then as you move through the actual outline with the given contextual statements, notice how each major part of the structure builds this theme.

Theme   **NEHEMIAH'S ORGANIZATIONAL LEADERSHIP**
- was the result of God's initiation,
- made itself felt in the face of obstacles to rebuild the wall,
- was inspirational in bringing about reform and a covenant in Jerusalem, and
- included drastic steps of separation in order to insure an on-going meaningful religious atmosphere.

The Plan for Developing this theme:

I.	(ch 1)	Receiving Direction to Rebuild in Jerusalem
II.	(ch 2-7:3)	Organizing to Rebuild the Wall
III.	(ch 7:4-10:39)	Organizing for Reform
IV.	(ch 11-13)	Organizing for Continuation

NEHEMIAH: CONTEXTUAL FLOW OF BOOK

I. (ch 1) Receiving Direction to Rebuild in Jerusalem

Chapter 1
1:1-4   Nehemiah hears a report of what has happened to the exiles in Jerusalem, which moves him deeply to want to help the exiles in the city.

1:5-11a   Nehemiah prays, vicariously confessing to God the sins of his people, and asks for God's help to do something about the situation in Jerusalem and specifically asking God to give him favor with Artaxerxes the King of Persia, his boss.

1:11b   Nehemiah mentions that he is the cupbearer, a trusted position, to King Artaxerxes.

II. (ch 2-6) Organizing to Rebuild the Wall

Chapter 2
2:1-10   Nehemiah interacts with Artaxerxes about the Jerusalem situation and gets his permission and backing to go to Jerusalem and do something about.
2:11-16   Nehemiah, in Jerusalem, surveys the state of the wall around Jerusalem
2:17-20   Nehemiah exhorts the exiled Jews in Jerusalem—including the priests, nobles, rulers, and others who are needed—to rebuild the defensive wall and gates.

Chapter 3
3:1-16   Nehemiah lists 22 important individuals and 3 groups of people (men of Jericho, men of Gibeon and Mizpah, inhabitants of Zanoah) who built part of the wall and 4 gates (sheep gate, fish gate, valley gate, dung gate) probably along the northern part of Jerusalem.

3:17-21   Nehemiah singles out some Levites, naming seven specifically who worked on the next section of the wall.

3:22-26   Nehemiah singles out some Priests , naming six individually and two groups (Priests, Nethinims dwelt in Ophel) men of the plain and who worked on an wall that bordered their houses, presumably a section of the wall to the east which contained the water gate.

Chapter 4
4:1-3   Sanballat, and Tobiah the Ammonite oppose the rebuilding of the defensive wall and gates and stir up opposition to this project.

4:4-6   Nehemiah responds to this opposition by an intercessory prayer against the opposition and and continues to rebuild the wall, making progress on it.

4:7-9   The progress on the wall angers Sanballat and Tobiah further and they conspired with Arabians, Ammonites, and Asdodites, all nearby groups to fight and against Jerusalem and to hinder this rebuilding effort which motivates group prayer to God and setting a watch night and day.

4:10-23   Discouragment at the threat of Sanballat and Tobiah and their coalition temporarily paralyzes the workers on the wall but Nehemiah inspires them to fight if necessary and organizes them to have half the workers building and half ready with swords, bows, and spears to be ready for instant defense and the rebuilding of the wall goes on.

Chapter 5
5:1-13   Loans to some of the poorer people involved in building the wall have put them into bondage to the lenders and threaten the wall project; Nehemiah brings justice to the situation by having the lenders cancel their unfair financial (usury) practices.

5:14-19   Nehemiah models financial integrity, way above the norm, in his own life by unselfishly funding his administration (governorship) out of his own pocket and does not tax the people as previous governors had.

Chapter 6

6:1-14 Sanballat, Tobiah, and Geshem, the Arabian leader, now try other tactics to dissuade the wall project which has now been completed except for the hanging of the gates; their strategem included repeatedly seeking to have meetings with Nehemiah (which he refused to do) and then starting rumors about Nehemiah wanting to become king of Jerusalem and hence rebelling against Artaxerxes. Nehemiah stands solidly against this new form of opposition and resorts to prayer for God to stop this opposition.

6:15-19 The wall is completed after 52 tension-filled days and even opposition from within the city by many who are linked to Tobiah in various ways; those in opposition perceive that God, indeed, has enabled this project to succeed.

II. (ch 7:1-10:39) Organizing for Reform

Chapter 7

7:1-4 Nehemiah appoints Hanani and Hananiah to leadership over Jerusalem and orders the gates to be watched carefully as well as appoints religious and worship leaders

7:5-60 Nehemiah registers those who were the first exiles to return who had proof of their ancestry.

7:61-65 Nehemiah lists those who could not prove their ancestry.

7:66-73 Nehemiah sums up the total of all of the lists given previously and some of the financial resources that were given to back Nehemiah's efforts.

Chapter 8

8:1-13 At a celebration and completion service, all the people gather and hear Ezra and his team read the law of Moses. The people respond, greatly convicted, with a desire to turn back to God and follow the law of Moses.

8:14-18 The feast of the tabernacles, which the people had heard about in the reading of the law of Moses, is restored and people from all around invited to participate in it.

Chapter 9

9:1-3 The people listen to the word of God being read and respond by fasting and confessing their sins and repenting of their connections to aliens and then worshipping the Lord their God

9:4-38 The Levites publicly vicariously confess to God, remembering all that He had done for His people, in one of the longest prayers in the Bible. This long prayer motivates the Levites and Priests to make a covenant with God to obey God's law.

Chapter 10

10:1-27 The Priests and Levites and leaders seal the covenant. Many (some 82) are listed individually as signing the covenant.

10:28-39 All the people now who had earlier repented also seal the covenant. Many of the requirements of the covenant are listed so that people know what it is that they are agreeing to.

III. (ch 11-13) Organizing for Continuation

Chapter 11

11:1-19 Provision is made to populate Jerusalem with some folks living outside of Jerusalem. Those selected agree to move into Jerusalem.

11:20-35 Those living outside of Jerusalem in various villages and on farms are listed and instructions are given for them to help financially support those leading worship in Jerusalem.

Chapter 12

12:1-9 Priests and Levites who went back to Jerusalem with Zerubbabel and Joshua (official restoration leaders) are listed (including the prominent one Ezra).

12:10-21 The descendants of the Priest, Jesua, are listed.

12:22-26 The descendants of the Levites during the days of Elisahib, Joiada, and Johanan, and Jaddua are recorded (those up to the reign of Darius the Persian).

12:27-43 A description of the celebration of the completion of the wall, which was a parade around the wall led by Levites and singers, is given.

12:44-47 The ministry of the Levites, singers, and Priests is established again, as in the day of David. Provision to support them financially is made and kept all during the days of Zerubbabel and Nehemiah.

Chapter 13

13:1-3 The law is read concerning separation from the Ammonites and Moabites and prohibiting of them to worship in the congregation of God, which caused the people to separate from the same.

13:4-9 The temple is cleansed and Elisahib the priest in alliance with Tobaiah was ousted. Nehemiah was absent for a while being back with King Artaxerxes.

13:10-14 The financial pledges to support the Levites had not been kept, so Nehemiah restores this function and appoints priests to be responsible for the accounting of the finances that would come in.

13:15-22 Nehemiah reinstates the Sabbath, which was being violated by some in various commercial activity.

13:23-31 Nehemiah reinforces the ban against intermarriage with other races (Ammonittes, Moabites).

Closure—Summarizing What We Have Seen

Nehemia's leadership is clearly spelled out in the book of Nehemiah. His first order of priority was rebuilding the wall, gates, and towers to provide defensive measures for the security of Jerusalem. Section I of the book,

I. (ch 1-7:3) Organizing to Rebuild the Wall,

details this organizational leadership effort of Nehemiah.

After providing for the security of the city, Nehemiah next focuses on religious reforms to move the people to worship God and obey His law. Nehemiah knows that the wall and gates and towers are not the real defense of Jerusalem but God, Himself. So he wants to motivate the people to turn back to God and obey Him and have a dependent relationship. Section II of the book,

II. (ch 7:4-10:39) Organizing for Reform,

details this crucial organizational effort by Nehemiah.

Finally, Nehemiah recognizes that on-going efforts must be made over time to continue to inspire people to keep the covenants they make. Section III,

III. (ch 11-13) Organizing for Continuation,

shows this effort by Nehemiah.

The interweaving subject and major ideas of the book are easily linked to the structural outline. It is summarized as,

Theme   **NEHEMIAH'S ORGANIZATIONAL LEADERSHIP**
- was the result of God's initiation,
- made itself felt in the face of obstacles to rebuild the wall,
- was inspirational in bringing about reform and a covenant in Jerusalem, and
- included drastic steps of separation in order to insure an on-going meaningful religious atmosphere.

The contextual flow as given in this article, clearly relates to these major ideas.

24. Nehemiah, Desperate Praying

Introduction

Nehemiah illustrates more macro lessons[90] than any other Old Testament leader. It is clear that Nehemiah demonstrated a very important macro lesson.

8.[91] Intercession[92]
Leaders called to a ministry are called to intercede for that ministry.

Table Ne 24-1 List references to Nehemiah's praying.

Table Ne 24-1 References to Nehemiah's praying.

Number	Verse(s)	Label	Description
1	Ne 1:4, 5, 6, 8, 11	Burdened Prayer for Jerusalem	Vicarious confession by Nehemiah seen here. Remember prayer Type I[93].
2*	Ne 2:4-8	Spontaneous Praying	Nehemiah in a desperate situation before the King flings up a thought prayer to God right on the spot before he answers the King.
3*	Ne 4:4,9	Spontaneous Prayer	Prayed for protection as they guarded the city.

[90] A macro-lesson is a high level generalization of a leadership observation (suggestion, guideline, requirement), stated as a lesson, which repeatedly occurs throughout different leadership eras, and thus has potential as a leadership absolute. Macro lessons even at their weakest provide strong guidelines describing leadership insights. At their strongest they are requirements, or absolutes, that leaders should follow. Leaders ignore them to their detriment. 41 Macro Lessons have been identified. These macro lessons are numbered. See **Article,** *16. Macro Lessons—Defined*

[91] The prayer macro lesson is number 8. See **Article,** *17. Macro Lessons: List of 41 Across Six Leadership Eras.*

[92] This macro lesson was seen first in the Pre-Kingdom Leadership Era. Study across the Bible has identified six leadership eras: (1) Patriarchal; (2) Pre-Kingdom; (3) Kingdom; (4) Post-Kingdom; (5) Pre-Church; (6) Church. Macro lessons have originated in each of the eras. At least they were first identified in an era and then checked backwards and forwards for occurrences in other eras.

[93] Type I. Remember God, an exhortation for the people to remember in the past what God had done (both in blessing and punishing) or to remind God of what He has said; Type II. Remember enemies—an imprecatory prayer asking God to punish the enemies. Type III. A personal request for God to remember Nehemiah for what he had done in his leadership.

4*	Ne 5:19	Spontaneous Prayer	Remember prayer Type III. Nehemiah asking God to remember himself.
5*	Ne 6:9	Spontaneous Prayer	Nehemiah asks for strength to continue the work in light of the threats received
6*	Ne 6:14	Spontaneous Prayer	Remember prayer Type II. Nehemiah asking God to punish enemies.
7	Ne 9:5-38	Spontaneous Prayer	Vicarious confession occurs here. Nehemiah a part of this but not only one praying.
8*	Ne 13:14	Spontaneous Prayer	Remember prayer Type III. Nehemiah asking God to remember himself.
9*	Ne 13:22	Spontaneous Prayer	Remember prayer Type III. Nehemiah asking God to remember himself.
10*	Ne 13:29	Spontaneous Prayer	Remember prayer Type II. Nehemiah asking God to punish enemies.
11*	Ne 13:31	Spontaneous Prayer	Remember prayer Type III. Nehemiah asking God to remember himself.

This article concentrates on Nehemiah's moments of spontaneous prayer. Some of them were arrows shot to God on the spot in moments of desperation. The asterisk marked prayers are those I want to focus in on this article. Items 2, 3, 4, 5, 6, 8, 9, 10, and 11 represent spontaneous prayers worth observing and learning lessons from.

I am using the two following definitions as I focus on Nehemiah's prayer as a leader in this article.

Definition   Spontaneous prayer is the willful directing of a silent thought prayer to God, usually as prompted by a situation.

Definition   Desperation prayers refer to spontaneous prayers shot upward to God in a crisis moment of time in which God must answer or the leader faces defeat and failure.

This article will analyze Nehemiah's prayers from these two foci with a view to identifying any leadership observations that will help present day leaders. For each item, I will refer to the item, print the scriptural context in which the item occurs, and then give observations on the spontaneous prayer, in its context. I will bold face the actual spontaneous prayer phrases.

Item 2 Spontaneous Prayer, Ne 2:1-8

Chapter 2
1 In the month of Nisan in the twentieth year of King Artaxerxes' reign, I was serving the king his wine. I had never appeared sad in his presence before this time. 2 So the king asked me, "Why does your face look so sad when you are not ill? You look like a man with deep troubles."
Then I was badly frightened, 3 but I replied, "Long live the king! Why shouldn't I be sad? For the city where my ancestors are buried is in ruins, and the gates have been burned down."
4 The king said to me, "Well, how can I help you?"

With a prayer to the God of heaven,[94] 5 I replied, "If it please
Your Majesty and if you are pleased with me, your servant, send me to Judah to rebuild
the city where my ancestors are buried."

6 The king, with the queen sitting beside him, asked, "How long will
you be gone? When will you return?" It pleased the king to send me, and I set a date for
my departure and return.

7 I also said to the king, "If it please Your Majesty, may I have letters to the
governors of the province west of the Euphrates River, instructing them to let me travel
safely through their territories on my way to Judah? 8 And may I have a letter to Asaph,
the manager of the king's forest, instructing him to give me timber? I will need it to
make beams for the gates of the Temple fortress, for the city walls, and for a house for
myself."

Observations On This Spontaneous Prayer.

From this one incident it is evident that spontaneous prayers—short and sweet, and to
the point—are just the tip of the iceberg. A life of prayer and integrity underlie a given
desperate prayer.

Observation 1. Timing and Previous Prayer

Nearly three months have transpired between the time Nehemiah received the news
about Jerusalem and this moment. Nehemiah has fasted and prayed. He is waiting for an
intervention moment to approach the king about it. All of that to say that this spontaneous
prayer has been backed by lots of previous prayer over a period of three months.

Observation 2. A Risk Taking Situation

This prayer bolsters a courageous effort by Nehemiah. Obviously Nehemiah was one
who showed his emotions. His empathetic identification with his people in Jerusalem
showed in his outward demeanor. In one sense it was a desperate prayer, for absolute
rulers of empires like Assyria, Babylon, and Persia were capricious and at a whim could
have those around them put to death. Nehemiah is hoping he hasn't displeased Artaxerxes.
This is a critical time, a pivotal point[95] in the life of Nehemiah. He can be put to death for
displeasing the king or he can petition the king for help, be backed, and be on his way to
accomplishing something great for God.

---

[94] The *God of heaven* is a title that is used 21 times in the Old Testament—two times in Genesis, once in
the Psalms, once in Jonah, and the rest in the times of exile or restoration leadership. Its common thread in
these usages is a title that would be recognized by people other than God's people. It is a popular term for
God by the leaders in exile and restoration times. Nehemiah uses it 4 times: Ne 1:4 And it came to pass,
when I heard these words, that I sat down and wept, and mourned several days, and fasted, and prayed before
the **God of heaven**; Ne 1:5 And said, I beg you, O LORD **God of heaven**, the great and terrible God,
that keeps your promises and shows mercy to them that love you and observe your commandments;
Ne 2:4 Then the king said unto me, What do you really want to ask of me? So I prayed to the **God of
heaven**; Ne 2:20 Then answered I them, and said unto them, The **God of heaven** will prosper us.
Therefore we his servants will arise and build. But you have no claim, nor right, nor memorial, in
Jerusalem. Nehemiah's uses all see God as the God above all others who has ultimate power to intervene,
especially in his own situation.

[95] A pivotal point is a critical time in a leader's life in which something happens, sometimes inadvertently,
or a decision is made which can: 1. curtail further use of the leader by God or at least curtail expansion of
the leader's potential; 2. limit the eventual use of the leader for ultimate purposes that otherwise could have
been accomplished, 3. enhance or open up the leader for expansion or contribution to the ultimate purposes
in God's kingdom or 4. serve as a guidance watershed which forever changes the direction of the life. See
Article, *Pivotal Points—Illustrated in Habakkuk and Jonah.*

Observation 3. A Life of Integrity

This prayer was backed by a life of integrity. It is obvious that Nehemiah had credibility with the king. In a desperate moment a leader, whose life has been one demonstrating integrity, can expect his/her spontaneous prayers to be honored by God.

Item 3 Spontaneous Prayer, Ne 4:1-9 (especially vs 4,9)

Chapter 4

When Sanballat heard that we were rebuilding the wall, he became angry and was greatly incensed. He flew into a rage and mocked the Jews, 2 saying in front of his friends and the Samarian army officers, "What does this bunch of poor, feeble Jews think they are doing? Do they think they can build the wall in a day if they offer enough sacrifices? Can they bring the stones back to life from those heaps of rubble—burned as they are?"

3 Tobiah the Ammonite, who was standing beside him, remarked, "That stone wall would collapse if even a fox walked along top of it!"

4 Then I prayed, "Hear us, O our God, for we are being mocked. May their scoffing fall back on their own heads, and may they themselves become captives in a foreign land! 5 Do not cover up their guilt or blot out their sins from your sight, for they have provoked you to anger before the builders."

6 So we rebuilt the wall to half its original height all around the city, for the people had worked with all their heart. 7 But when Sanballat and Tobiah and the Arabs, Ammonites, and Ashdodites heard that work was going ahead and gaps in the wall were being repaired, they became furious. 8 They plotted to come and fight against Jerusalem and to bring about confusion there. 9 **But we prayed to our God and guarded the city day and night to meet this threat.**

Observations On This Spontaneous Prayer.

Sometimes the way forward is blocked by enemies of God's purposes.[96] Perhaps the only way forward is to pray them out of the situation or counter their efforts by asking God to block them. Imprecatory prayers are not always easy to understand. But seen in the light of asking God to thwart efforts that block His will, we can see how a leader could use imprecatory prayers. Such is the case with Nehemiah's efforts in this desperate prayer. At its heart it is not a selfish prayer but one that puts God's testimony and honor first.

Observation 1. A Valid Use of Imprecatory Praying

Nehemiah is praying to thwart the efforts of opponents of God's plan to rebuild a strong Jerusalem. He therefore asks God to block their efforts and have them sense the desperate feelings that the remnant itself is feeling in their oppressive situation.

Observation 2. Emotions Sometimes a God-Used Stimulus

Obviously Nehemiah was one who showed his emotions. God used this in the previous instance of spontaneous prayer with Artaxerxes. I think too, that here, God uses this display of righteous anger to prompt Nehemiah's prayer. See **Article**, *Transparency With God*.

---

[96] Paul certainly does this in the Corinthian situation. See 1 Co 5:3-5 commentary notes. See *spiritual warfare*, **Glossary**.

Item 4 Spontaneous Prayer, Ne 5:19

Chapter 5
14 I would like to mention that for the entire twelve years that I was governor of Judah—from the twentieth until the thirty-second year of the reign of King Artaxerxes—neither I nor my officials drew on our official food allowance. 15 This was quite a contrast to the former governors who had laid heavy burdens on the people, demanding a daily ration of food and wine, besides a pound of silver. Even their assistants took advantage of the people. But because of my fear of God, I did not act that way. 16 I devoted myself to working on the wall and refused to acquire any land. And I required all my officials to spend time working on the wall. 17 I asked for nothing, even though I regularly fed 150 Jewish officials at my table, besides all the visitors from other lands! 18 The provisions required at my expense for each day were one ox, six fat sheep, and a large number of domestic fowl. And every ten days we needed a large supply of all kinds of wine. Yet I refused to claim the governor's food allowance because the people were already having a difficult time.

19 Remember, O my God, all that I have done for these people, and bless me for it.

Observations On This Spontaneous Prayer.

Again this little prayer flows out of a context in which Nehemiah is taking up the cause of poor people of the remnant who are being exploited my fellow Jews who have lent them money at high interest. Nehemiah contrasts his own leadership style with former Governors who have taxed the people severely to line their own pockets and pay their own expenses. Nehemiah has not done that. This testimony illustrates very strongly his financial integrity.

Observation 1. A Life of Integrity

This prayer was backed by a life of integrity. It is obvious that Nehemiah had credibility with the people. His testimony demonstrates integrity. He can admonish the rich bankers with a clear conscience. His spontaneous prayer seeks that assurance from God of his righteous behavior as a leader.

Observation 2. Rewards

This prayer also shows how leaders can expect God to reward them. Here the prayer is one of the *Remember Prayers* on the behalf of Nehemiah, himself. As mentioned elsewhere there are three kinds of remember prayers: 1. Remember God, an exhortation for the people to remember in the past what God had done (both in blessing and punishing); 2. Remember enemies—an imprecatory prayer asking God to punish the enemies. 3. A personal request for God to remember Nehemiah for what he had done in his leadership. This last type seems to imply that Nehemiah was a eunuch who wanted God to mercifully include him with God's people (De 23:1), because he had so faithfully served God. It is legitimate for a leader to expect God to reward them. Rewards are not the dominant motivation for leadership. But they are certainly one motivating factor.

Item 5 Summary of Spontaneous Prayers, Ne 6:9

Chapter 6
1 When word came to Sanballat, Tobiah, Geshem the Arab and the rest of our enemies that I had rebuilt the wall and not a gap was left in it—though up to that time I had not set the doors in the gates—2 Sanballat and Geshem sent me this message: "Come, let us meet together in one of the villages on the plain of Ono."

But they were scheming to harm me; 3 so I sent messengers to them with this reply: "I am carrying on a great project and cannot go down. Why should the work stop while I leave it and go down to you?" 4 Four times they sent me the same message, and each time I gave them the same answer. 5 The fifth time, Sanballat's servant came with and open letter in his hand, 6 and this is what it said:

"Geshem tells me that everywhere he goes he hears that you and the Jews are planning to rebel and that is why you are building the wall. According to his reports, you plan to be their king. 7 He also reports that you have appointed prophets to prophesy about you in Jerusalem, saying, 'Look! There is a king in Judah!' You can be very sure that this report will get back to the king, so I suggest that you come and talk it over with me."

8 My reply was, "You know you are lying. There is no truth in any part of your story." 9 They were just trying to intimidate us, imagining that they could break our resolve and stop the work. **So I prayed for strength to continue the work.**

Observations on this Item

Notice Nehemiah's reply. He first denies the truth of the claims in the letter. He sees through their attempt to intimidate. He then prays and continues building the wall. Note the phrase *imagining that they could break our resolve and stop the work*. Resolve is a key word. Leaders must have this quality if they want to carry out a vision from God. Resolve is perseverance, which is based on dependence upon God. I think Nehemiah was worn down by their continual repeated haranguing. I think he was near giving up. And I think this prayer is not the actual prayer but the bottom line of the spontaneous prayers he sent up to God. Nehemiah depended on God to encourage him to continue.

Observation 1. Stamina to Go On

This statement probably sums up a batch of spontaneous prayers, which we do not have in the text. The opponents were continually putting pressure on Nehemiah over time. He was nearly worn out and ready to give up. But the bottom line is, that he prayed to God for strength to continue. His resolve was strengthened.

Observation 2. Focus

Nehemiah's prayers helped him focus on the main task, in this case continuing to build the wall, and not be deterred by the opponents repeated pressures. Lies tearing down one's reputation are a major way that opponents discourage the work of God.

Item 6 Summary of Spontaneous Prayers, Ne 6:14

Chapter 6

10 Late I went to the house of Shemaiah son of Delaiah and grandson of Mehetabel, who was shut in at his home. He said, "Let us meet in the house of God, inside the temple, and let us close the temple doors, because men are coming to kill you—by night they are coming to kill you."

11 But I replied, "Should someone in my position run away from danger? Should someone in my position enter the temple to save his life? No, I won't do it!" 12 I realized that God had not spoken to him, but that he had uttered this prophecy against me because Tobiah and Sanballat had hired him. 13 They were hoping to intimidate me and make me sin by following his suggestion. Then they would be able to accuse and discredit me.

14 **"Remember, O my God, all the evil things that Tobiah and Sanballat have done. And remember Noadiah the prophet and all the prophets like her who have tried to intimidate me."**

Observations on this Spontaneous Prayer

This is another incident of imprecatory praying—that is, prayers to counter the enemies of God. This incident reveals that there is opposition from within. Shemaiah, an insider, is in alliance with the outside coalition. This is another attempt to get Nehemiah, this time based on a religious principle. Safety within the temple. See also 13:4-9; 28 for other insiders (Eliashib and Joiada) in alliance with Tobiah. Also opposition is coming from prophetical leaders, Noadiah.

Observation 1. Sensitivity To God

Notice the phrase, sin by following his suggestion. Sin in what way? Showing a lack of trust in God to protect, or what? Nehemiah is very sensitive to God. Holiness, the purity macro lesson is real for Nehemiah. To fail to do what God wanted was sin for Nehemiah.

Observation 2. A Valid Use of Imprecatory Praying

This is one of the *remember prayers* of the imprecatory type. Nehemiah is praying to thwart the efforts of opponents of God's work. He therefore asks God to block their efforts. He particularly asks God to remember their evil ways. And he prays against a female prophetess, Noadiah, and other prophets, who were bringing pressure to bear on Nehemiah by falsely prophesying.

Item 8 Summary of Spontaneous Prayers, Ne 13:14

Chapter 13

10 And I saw that the money promised to support the Levites had not been given them. For the Levites and the singers, that did the work, had all returned to their own farms. 11 Then I reprimanded the leaders, and said, Why is the house of God forsaken? And I got the Levites and singers to come back to the temple and put them to work again. 12 Everyone started giving again to finance the temple work—the tithe of the corn and the new wine and the oil. 13 And I appointed several to be accountable for the financial resources being given into the temple. These included: Shelemiah the priest, and Zadok the scribe, and of the Levites, Pedaiah. Others in charge included: Hanan the son of Zaccur, the son of Mattaniah. These men were trustworthy and would honestly distribute the supplies to their fellow temple workers.

14 Remember me, O my God, concerning these good things I have done for the house of my God, and for the leadership of the Temple and for the worship there.

Observations on this Spontaneous Praying

Nehemiah was definitely a sponsor mentor. He raises support for the religious leaders who will head up the centralized worship center in Jerusalem.

Observation 1. Centralized Worship Important

Nehemiah knows of the importance of centralized worship in keeping a work of God alive (one of the strong para-messages of 1,2 Ch). The budget for this is crucial. He gets right on this problem. This reflects his intuitive sense of the stability macro lesson. *Preserving a ministry of God with life and vigor over time is as much if not more of a challenge to leadership than creating one.* He prays for the leadership of the Temple. If they are not spiritual, the renewal movement will not continue. If they are not financially taken care of then they will not be devoting their energy to the renewal effort.

Observation 2. Reward for Supporting Financially

Raising money for others in ministry is not always recognized or appreciated. Nehemiah wants or needs God's affirmation on this.

Observation 3. Prayer Represents a Righteous Cause

This prayer follows hard on the heels of Nehemiah's defense of his righteous cause. Confrontation is always tough. But it is much easier when the one confronting is assured of the rightness of his/her cause. Nehemiah has a neat effective methodology for confronting—especially with Jewish people who had some knowledge of the O.T. He uses a number of rhetorical questions in this chapter: vs 11, vs 17, vs 18, vs 21, vs 26, vs 27. A rhetorical question is a figure of speech in which a question is not used to obtain information but is used to indirectly communicate an affirmative or negative statement, the importance of some thought by focusing attention on it, and/or one's own feeling or attitudes about something. All of these rhetorical questions used by Nehemiah are devices to couch a strong reprimand. Here in verses 17 and 18 the three questions are interpreted as: You have broken the Sabbath and invited God to punish us again like he did when our ancestors did this. He destroyed Jerusalem. One of Nehemiah's conflictual techniques is to use rhetorical questions to emphasize Biblical precedence and principles which almost shames the people into obedience.

Observation 4. Leadership Selection, Men of Character

Financial integrity is important to Nehemiah. He appoints multiple people to oversee finances—people of character. That is one of the things especially included in the phrase of this spontaneous prayer—**concerning these good things I have done for the house of my God, and for the leadership of the Temple.**

Item 9 Spontaneous Prayer, Ne 13:22

Chapter 13

19 So I commanded that the gates of Jerusalem be closed at the beginning of each Sabbath. Don't open them till after the Sabbath is over. I put some of my own men to oversee the shutting of the gates. I did not want the Sabbath profaned. 20 A couple of times merchants and various sellers of all kind spent the night before the Sabbath outside of Jerusalem. 21 But I warned them. Don't hang around here overnight. If you do this again I will forcibly remove you. From then on they didn't return to sell on the Sabbath. 22 I ordered the Levites to purify themselves and to insure the gates were closed in order to make sure the Sabbath day was kept holy.

Remember me, O my God, concerning this also, and spare me according to the greatness of your mercy.

Observations On This Spontaneous Prayer.

Again this is a *remember prayer* primarily for Nehemiah himself.

Observation 1. Sensitivity To God

Keeping the Sabbath was important to Nehemiah who is very sensitive to God and God's commands. Holiness, the purity macro lesson is real for Nehemiah. To fail to do what God wanted, in this case, keeping the Sabbath, was sin for Nehemiah.

Observation 2. Personal Remember Prayer

Here the prayer is one of the *Remember Prayers* on the behalf of Nehemiah, himself. This type of *remember prayer* seems to imply that Nehemiah was a eunuch who wanted God to mercifully include him with God's people (De 23:1). The *spare me* phrase is one of the strong indicators of this. Nehemiah faithfully served God. It is legitimate for Nehemiah to want God to reward him and fully accept him.

Item 10   Spontaneous Prayer, Ne 13:29

Chapter 13

23 In those days also saw I Jews that had married wives from Ashdod, Ammon, and Moab. 24 And the children were raised to speak their mother's tongue and not the Jewish language. 25 And I quarreled with the men, calling them despicable. I punished some with beating. I embarrassed some by pulling out their hair. I forced them to make an oath to God that their children would not intermarry with foreigners. 26 Did not Solomon king of Israel sin by these things? God made him king over all Israel. There was there no king like him among all the surrounding nations. But note, these foreign women caused him to sin. 27 Shall we then follow his example and do this great evil? Shall we disobey our God by marrying foreign wives?

28 Joiada was the son of Eliashib, the high priest. One of Joiada's sons married Sanballat the Horonite's daughter. I banished him from Jerusalem.

29 Remember them, O my God, because they have defiled the priesthood. They have broken, the covenant that all the priests and Levites signed.

Observations on this Spontaneous Prayer

I have mentioned before Nehemiah's use of the Old Testament scriptures in his ministry. This prayer context includes that. Spiritual leaders who do not serve God are a tremendous detriment to the work of God. Nehemiah knows this. Religious leaders have tremendous sway with the people. He prays against this happening. This imprecatory prayer wants these religious leaders banished from their ministry.

Observation 1. Scripture Based Praying

When a leader's prayers are backed by Scriptural truth, that leader can pray with increased expectation. Again we see Nehemiah's knowledge of the Scriptures informing his leadership. Further we see a second component of a Bible Centered Leader being illustrated, the dynamic application of past Scripture to a current situation.

Observation 2. Corporate Integrity At Stake Here

Notice how Nehemiah uses the commitment of the covenant (as described generally in vs 23-27) to give backing for the strong leadership exercised in verse 28. The keeping of promises in the O.T. is one of the major indicators of integrity. Nehemiah knows this. Notice his inclusion of the phrase, broken the covenant, in his imprecatory prayer. This is a Type III Remember Prayer—imprecatory. He prays against these religious leaders who are not doing God's will.

Observation 3. Purity Macro

Note the prayer itself deals with the purity macro. Nehemiah is defending God's purity in the priesthood. The purity macro lesson, first identified in the Patriarchal Leadership Era and repeated in other eras, is stated as, *Leaders must personally learn of and respond to the holiness of God in order to have effective ministry.* Nehemiah sees to be deeply impressed with God's holiness.

Item 13   Spontaneous Prayer, Ne 13:31

Chapter 13

30 Thus I purified the people from foreign influence. I organized the priests and the Levites concerning their duties. 31 I made sure that people brought the wood for burnt offerings at the proper time. I made sure that first offerings of grain and fruit were brought in.

Remember me, O my God, for the good I have done.

Observations on this Spontaneous Prayer
Nehemiah is concerned with maintaining the centralized worship in the Temple. This remember prayer emphasizes that.

Observation 1. Emphasizing Commitment to Temple
Nehemiah closes off these special memoirs by restating how important it is to keep centralized worship going. He has solved problems that will keep the Temple worship going. A final reminder to us of the stability macro, *Preserving a ministry of God with life and vigor over time is as much if not more of a challenge to leadership than creating one.*

Observation 2. Purity Macro Stressed
Again the purity macro is stressed. Nehemiah is very sensitive to God's demands of holiness (here seen—purified people; organized the priests and Levites for their duties).

Observation 3. Repetition Stresses Importance of A Thing
This is the last *remember prayer*. All leaders need affirmation. Nehemiah has shot personal Remember Prayers to God in this book. Over a lifetime of leadership, affirmation is one of the factors God uses to keep a leader in ministry. What is important to note about Nehemiah's need for affirmation is that he goes to God for it and expects God to give it.

Observation 4. Closing With His Strength
It seems fitting to me that Nehemiah, a man of prayer, closes off these special memoirs with another prayer, a *remember prayer*. This is a personal remember prayer recognizing that God does reward good leadership. See Hebrews 11:6 But without faith it is impossible to please him, for he that comes to God must believe that He is, and that He is a rewarder of them that diligently seek Him. Nehemiah is a great Old Testament leader who sought God. We, leaders today, benefit from the model this great leader left for us.

Observation 5. Answered Prayer—My Thoughts
I think God answers this final prayer for Nehemiah. Each time some present day leader reads Nehemiah's memoirs and sees what great leadership he exemplified and seeks to emulate Nehemiah's leadership values in his/her own leadership.

Summary of Important Observations
Here is a brief summary of the more important things seen in these spontaneous prayers.

Observation 1. Basis for Spontaneous Prayers
Spontaneous prayers, especially the desperate ones, flow out of a life backed by integrity, out of a life involved in habitual disciplines of prayer, and have scriptural truth underlying their requests.

Observation 2. Place for Imprecatory Prayers
Personal revenge is not a motive for imprecatory prayers. But prayers which thwart the opponents of God, which promote God's honor and character, and which defend God are a legitimate part of a leader's arsenal.

Observation 3. God Hears Spontaneous Thought Prayers
We should be encouraged by what Nehemiah accomplished. Each of his thought prayers were answered. We too can shoot spontaneous thought prayers, sometimes even

desperate ones, if our lives are models of integrity and if we habitually long for God's will to be done in our lives, and if we habitually depend upon God.

Closure

Nehemiah was a civil leader. But more, he was a civil leader who modeled a strong spirituality. All throughout the book, his prayer life is referred to. He depended upon God. He planned. He took practical steps to carry out his plans. And he prayed all throughout. He is worthy to be emulated. Nehemiah demonstrated a very important macro lesson.

8.[97] Intercession[98]
Leaders called to a ministry are called to intercede for that ministry.

And we see a new kind of prayer involved in intercession for ministry, that of spontaneous prayers. So, send your thought prayers God-ward. And make sure they have a solid basis underlying them.

---

[97]The prayer macro lesson is number 8 of the 41 macros. See **Article**, *17. Macro Lessons: List of 41 Across Six Leadership Eras.*

[98]This macro lesson was seen first in the Pre-Kingdom Leadership Era. Study across the Bible has identified six leadership eras: (1) Patriarchal; (2) Pre-Kingdom; (3) Kingdom; (4) Post-Kingdom; (5) Pre-Church; (6) Church. Macro lessons have originated in each of the eras. At least they were first identified in an era and then checked backwards and forwards for occurrences in other eras.

25. Nehemiah, Eight Important Ideas to Communicate

Introduction

G. Campbell Morgan, in his book, **Living Messages of the Books of the Bible**, studied each book of the Bible for its contribution to the flow of truth in the Bible as a whole. He specifically identified truth from each book, which was applicable to present day situations. I have capitalized on that notion for Habakkuk, Jonah, and Nehemiah. These books have some important ideas for leaders today. Nehemiah, especially deals with crucial change dynamic ideas.

Today, we live in the Church Leadership Era.[99] It is difficult to place ourselves back hundreds of years into the 4th leadership era—Post-Kingdom Leadership. God has taken a people and made them into a kingdom. But the kingdom has split into a northern segment, Israel, and a southern segment, Judah.[100] God's program using the nation of Israel has come to a halt. Both kingdoms were destroyed and the people were taken into exile. After 70 years in exile a remnant has come back into the land. Most modern day pastors and parachurch leaders do not bother to go back and study this period of time in the Bible.[101] What does this small remnant in the land have to do with anything, anyway? Why is this book of Nehemiah included in the Bible, you say? Well at least one reason is that it is an example of inspirational/motivational leadership for us. As present day leaders, we need to know how to motivate people. We can study a leader who knew how to organize to accomplish a task, Nehemiah. We can learn how God uses a leader to motivate followers.[102] We can learn how a leader carefully prepares to implement significant change

---

[99] See **Articles**, *13. Leadership Eras In The Bible, Six Identified; 35. Six Biblical Leadership Eras, Approaching the Bible with Leadership Eyes*. This is probably an important prerequisite for you before approaching the commentary.

[100] See **Article**, *1. Biblical Framework—The Redemptive Drama*. This is another important prerequisite giving important background information within which Nehemiah's wall-building incident happens. See also **Article**, *33. Prophetic Crises, 3 Major Biblical Times*, which pinpoints the crisis Nehemiah was facing.

[101] Nehemiah is an exception. If folks teach on leadership from the Bible, Nehemiah is the favorite book to teach from—usually the only one.

[102] See **Articles**, *14. Learning Vicariously From Other Leaders' Lives; Nehemiah, Biographical Sketch*.

involving a whole range of different followers. Nehemiah got ownership[103] in bringing about change.

In addition, Nehemiah illustrates more macro lessons[104] in his leadership than any other leader in the Old Testament.

In order to identify those ideas, we need to know the background of the book. We need to know the situation of the leader, Nehemiah. We need to know the message of the book. We need to know the structure of the book that develops that message. We need to know the purposes of the book. From such an understanding, we can transfer the truth implied in that situation to similar situations today. From such an analysis, we can then pinpoint several ideas worth communicating today. We have noted 8 ideas from the book of Nehemiah. But first the background analysis needed to see the basis for getting the 8 ideas.

Understanding Nehemiah—The Story Line

The time is a little more than a decade after the events in the first part of the book of Ezra. Nehemiah, who serves in the court of Artaxerxes, hears of the need of the remnant which has returned to Jerusalem to rebuild the temple. After a period of fasting and prayer, seeking God on behalf of the people, he asks permission of the king to return and provide organizational oversight to the situation there. He organizes the people to build the wall. There is opposition to this by people who have vested interests in the land. Nehemiah overcomes every obstacle and builds the wall in a short time. He then goes on to bring about reform as the city itself is being repopulated. He leaves behind a strong Jerusalem, defensible, and a center of worship, with leaders in place who want to maintain the renewal that he and Ezra have brought about.

Understanding Nehemiah—The Structure of the Book

The book naturally breaks up into 4 sections as it weaves its story.

Structure			
	I.	(ch 1)	Receiving Direction to Rebuild in Jerusalem
	II.	(ch 2-7:3)	Organizing to Rebuild the Wall
	III.	(ch 7:4-10:39)	Organizing for Reform
	IV.	(ch 11-13)	Organizing for Continuation

---

[103] A person in a change situation is said to have <u>ownership</u> for the changes when he/she is not only for the changes but is willing to cooperate in the change process. See **Article**, *27. Nehemiah, Getting Ownership*.

[104] A <u>macro-lesson</u> is a high level generalization of a leadership observation (suggestion, guideline, requirement), stated as a lesson, which repeatedly occurs throughout different leadership eras, and thus has potential as a leadership absolute. Macro lessons even at their weakest provide strong guidelines describing leadership insights. At their strongest they are requirements, or absolutes, that leaders should follow. Leaders ignore them to their detriment. 41 Macro Lessons have been identified. These macro lessons are numbered. This faith macro is number 6 one of the early macro lessons discovered in the Bible. See the list of macro lessons. See **Articles**, *16. Macro Lessons—Defined; 17. Macro Lessons: List of 41 Across Six Leadership Eras; Nehemiah, Biographical Sketch*.

Understanding Nehemiah—The Theme of the Book

The overall message of the book can easily be synthesized from analysis of its structure. One way of integrating the overall message flowing from the four major sections is as follows:

Theme   **NEHEMIAH'S ORGANIZATIONAL LEADERSHIP**
- was the result of God's initiation,
- made itself felt in the face of obstacles to rebuild the wall,
- was inspirational in bringing about reform and a covenant in Jerusalem, and
- included drastic steps of separation in order to insure an on-going meaningful religious atmosphere.

Understanding Nehemiah—Some Purposes of the Book

While it is not easy to derive purposes for a book, when they are not stated explicitly by the author, some purposes can tentatively be identified. Some purposes of the book include the following. God wanted:

- to tell of the rebuilding of the walls around Jerusalem,
- to show the importance of networking power,
- to introduce a new kind of leader (a lay leader who is Bible-centered and who models task-oriented and organizational behavior),
- to describe task-oriented inspirational leadership that implements significant change, and which keeps organizational issues central,
- to illustrate motivational techniques,
- to show the importance of prayer in leadership,
- to show the importance of the Word in leadership,
- to illustrate perseverance in leadership the midst of opposition and obstacles,
- to show dynamic balance between dependence upon God and activity for God.

Implications for Us Today

A new order of leadership is seen in this book. Kings have come and gone and still God's work needs accomplishing. God raises up a lay person who is willing to walk by faith in the midst of darkness and opposition. Nehemiah illustrates the basic message of Habakkuk 2:4, "My righteous one shall live by faith." His attitude of persevering faith, his continued activity on the wall, and his completion of the task illustrate what leadership that mixes faith with obedience can do. Nehemiah lived out the advice of the old Bible teacher who told his students, "Pray as though everything depended on God, and act as though everything depended on you." Nehemiah was a spiritual lay leader who accomplished much for God. Today, no church will prosper well without strong lay leadership. Nehemiah emphasizes strong lay leadership working carefully with full time religious workers to accomplish God-given tasks.

Identifying Ideas From Nehemiah for Present Day Leadership Situations
When we teach the book of Nehemiah, we first give the information that we have written above. When folks understand Nehemiah's situation and God's leadership through him, then they can see how the following 8 ideas are transferable to present day times. We usually choose 3 or 4 of these ideas to use in a short series. Table Ne 25-1 lists the ideas and gives a brief explanation about each one. We are applying these ideas directly to leaders since that is the thrust of this commentary.

Table Ne 25-1. 8 Key Ideas From the Book of Nehemiah

Idea	Topic	STATEMENT/Discussion
1.	Importance of Biographical information in the Bible	**EFFECTIVE LEADERS LEARN VICARIOUSLY FROM OTHER LEADERS' LIVES.** Biblical leaders' biographical information should be studied to learn lessons vicariously (see Hebrews 13:7,8; 1 Co 10:6, 11; Ro 15:4). Vicarious learning refers to the method of learning from someone else's life. The principle of intentional selectivity plays a vital role here. That something of a biographical nature, dealing with leadership, is included in Scripture, out of all that could be included, signifies something special about the entry. You can learn negative lessons, hard lessons, without going through the deep processing or tragic things the leader you are studying did to learn them. You can learn through the positive things, the blessings, the gains that leader experienced. You can gain valuable long-term perspective that you cannot get until you have lived a whole lifetime. In fact, as a leader, you will never learn enough leadership lessons, just from what you experience personally, to have an effective and successful ministry. You need to learn from other leaders. See **Articles**, *2. Biographical Study in the Bible, How To Do; 19. Nehemiah, Biographical Sketch.*
2.	Macro Lessons	**BIBLICAL MACRO LESSONS GIVE PERSPECTIVE THAT EVERY LEADER TODAY NEEDS TO KNOW.** Nehemiah illustrates more macro lessons in his leadership than any other Old Testament leader. Eighteen macro lessons are clearly seen and another nine in seed form are alluded to. See **Article**, *19. Nehemiah, Biographical Sketch.*
3.	Change Dynamics	**NEHEMIAH WAS AN EFFECTIVE PERSON OF CHANGE.**

		Nehemiah illustrates better than any other Old Testament leader the notion of implementing change via a careful well thought out plan. Today we would call this plan a *bridging strategy*. An important facet of a bridging strategy is working with change participants to get ownership. Nehemiah got ownership. See **Article**, *21. Nehemiah, Change Participants.*
4.	Dependence Upon God	**DEPENDENCE UPON GOD IS FUNDAMENTAL TO ALL EFFECTIVE LEADERSHIP.** Nehemiah was very practical. And he was also very spiritual. Nehemiah's prayer life can be studied to see his dependence upon God. Nehemiah lived out the advice of the old Bible teacher who told his students, "Pray as though everything depended on God, and act as though everything depended on you." See **Articles**, *18. Nehemiah, And Daniel—comparison of Vicarious praying; 24. Nehemiah, Desperate Praying.*
5.	God at Work	**GOD ADVANCES HIS PURPOSES, EVEN IN TIMES THAT SEEM DARK AND BLEAK.** Nehemiah lived in such a time. God worked through Nehemiah in spite of the times. Lets trace redemptive history and watch this above idea taking place. The Introduction to the story of redemption, narrated in Genesis 1-11, records why God's redemptive work was needed—humanity's relationship was broken with Him because of sin. In Part One of the story, chapter one (Genesis 12-1 Kings 10), God creates a nation through whom He could reconcile humanity to Himself. While unrecorded numbers of followers put their trust in God throughout a number of centuries, the overall track record of God's people was poor. In spite of prophetic messengers and divine interventions in the life of His people, they continued to turn away from Him and to prostitute themselves to idols. Thus, God destroyed the nation, as chapter two of Part One recounts (1 Kings 11-Malachi)— Samaria was sacked and Israel was exiled in 722 B.C.; Jerusalem was reduced to rubble and Judah/Benjamin was exiled, finally, in 586 B.C. Those taken into exile in Babylon and those left in the land in the southern kingdom were shattered. Many questioned whether His reach extended beyond the borders of their country and whether they still had a future as His people. God had finally exercised the curses clause of His covenant with them (see Deuteronomy 28:36-37ff). This was probably the bleakest of times. Yet God was at work. Notice, for example:

		1. As early as 605 B.C. Jeremiah had prophesied that the Lord would send the southern kingdom into exile for a period of 70 years (Jeremiah 25:1-14). 2. While there, Jeremiah said they were to prosper and multiply, that God continued to think good thoughts for them and would one day remove their reproach and bring them back to Judah (Jeremiah 29:1-23). 3. While exiled in Babylon, Daniel rose to prominence in the courts of Nebuchadnezzar, Belshazzar, Darius the Mede, and Cyrus the Persian. Daniel was a leader of remarkable integrity and stature. As he learned while reading the scroll of Jeremiah (Daniel 9), the time of the end of the exile was nearing. His prayer in Daniel 9 reveals his grasp of how God was working on behalf of His people. 4. In 538 B.C., the first year of Cyrus' reign, the Lord moved upon him to permit the exiles to return to Jerusalem (2 Chronicles 36:22ff). 5. The temple was rebuilt between 520 and 518. Zerubbabel, Joshua, Haggai, and Zechariah were key figures through whom the Lord worked (Ezra 1-7). 6. Esther became queen and helped bring about God's providential deliverance of His people (c. 474-473 B.C., book of Esther). 7. In 458 B.C. a second group returned to Jerusalem with Ezra. Then, beginning in 445 B.C., Nehemiah and Ezra worked together to institute a number of civic and religious reforms. So, while Nehemiah's time of ministry was probably the second bleakest time, behind the Babylonian exile, God was still at work. In fact, Nehemiah is a most excellent book to demonstrate this important idea of God at work in dreary times. Notice specifically: God sent Nehemiah to rebuild the walls of the city and make it defensible again. He worked through him to repopulate the city. Leaders were appointed over the city, the citadel by the temple and the storerooms for the temple. Religious festivals and assemblies were reinstated and religious fervor was renewed. All of this was God at work, even in areas that at first glance appear primarily practical vs. spiritual, and even in the darkest of times. See **Article,** *1. Biblical Framework—The Redemptive Drama.*
6.	Importance of Godly Leadership	**GODLY LEADERS CAN TURN THE TIDE.** See the important macro lesson 20: *Spiritual leadership can make a difference even in the midst of difficult times.* What seemed to concern Nehemiah most was the overall shame and disgrace that characterized the plight of God's people. He did not stop his work and return to King Artaxerxes once the walls were rebuilt. Nehemiah worked with Ezra and other faithful leaders,

		leaders of character and integrity, to institute reforms in the civic and covenantal practices of the Jews of his day. Through their godly leadership, the people were moved from shame and disgrace into a populated and defensible city where the worship of the LORD was resumed and the people were instructed in the statutes and ordinances of the book of the Law. See **Article,** *15. Left Hand of God, The; 34. Restoration Leaders; Spiritual Leadership—Prolonging the Life of God in a Work; 16. Macro Lessons—Defined; 17. Macro Lessons: List of 41 Across Six Leadership Eras*
7.	Leadership in Action	What does leadership look like? Nehemiah's memoirs paint a picture for us. Notice that Nehemiah: 1) Walks with God and maintains commitment to the Lord (godly character is part of his capacity to lead) 2) Sees through the ploys of his adversaries and can testify to the gracious hand of the Lord upon him (spiritual authority is part of his capacity to lead, as well as one of his primary forms of influence) 3) Inspires a shared vision; organizes a plan and the people; delegates the work; confronts opposition and solves problems (as surely as Bezalel and Oholiab were gifted in the arts of craftsmanship—Exodus 35:30-35—Nehemiah was gifted for visionary, organizational, and strategic leadership; this giftedness was also part of his capacity to lead) 4) Works with a number of key opinion leaders and influentials to institute significant changes and reforms for a small, frequently rebellious, and seemingly insignificant province of the vast Persian empire (drew upon positional authority, expertise, spiritual authority, and the force of his own character and example to influence followers) 5) Continually interacts with the Lord on behalf of the Lord's people (he felt a sense of burden for the people) To put it another way, we see leadership in action when we study Nehemiah as he: 1) walked with God 2) heard from God 3) developed a plan 4) inspired a shared vision 5) organized the people 6) delegated the work 7) solved problems 8) overcame problems 9) celebrated progress 10) and maintained his focus.

		See **Articles,** 27. *Nehemiah, Getting Ownership; 29. Nehemiah, Leadership Functions.*
8.	Focused Living	Nehemiah models focused living for his readers. In short, a focused life is a life dedicated exclusively to carrying out God's purposes.

Nehemiah models focused living in two primary time periods that we're aware of: short-term, in the 52 days of intensive work on the wall; long-term, for the duration of his 12-year assignment on behalf of Jerusalem.

Through the power of focused living he was able to zero in on a handful of key assignments from the Lord and devote his leadership to their ongoing accomplishment: rebuilding the walls, repopulating the city, reforming religious practices, suppressing social injustices, and removing the shame and disgrace of God's people.

See Dr. Clinton's **Focused Lives: Inspirational Life Changing Lessons from Eight Effective Christian Leaders Who Finished Well**, available through Barnabas Publishers. |

Conclusion

There are great lessons in the book of Nehemiah; lessons, which apply today. Nehemiah is a relatively short book. You can easily construct a short series on this book, which will challenge both full time and lay leaders in your situation. If you are thinking of instituting major change in your situation, here is a book that is worthy of a series dealing with change dynamics. We have not exhausted all the ideas that can be applied today from Nehemiah. But the ones listed above are certainly important ones. And they can make a difference in a leader who wants to his/her leadership to count.

26. Nehemiah, Financial Integrity

Introduction

At least six obstacles stand in the way of the leader who would finish well:[105] 1) the use and abuse of power; 2) **the use and misuse of finances**; 3) pride; 4) sexual misconduct; 5) family problems; and 6) plateauing. It only takes one of these obstacles to torpedo a leader's influence, and numerous leaders have fallen due to some issue related to the use and misuse of finances.

Leaders, particularly those who have power positions and make important decisions concerning finances, can be tempted to engage in practices that encourage financial improprieties. They can be tempted by greed, a deeply rooted negative character trait. They can be tempted to let down their guard on what are seemingly small matters, but in the long-term be establishing negative habits and nursing dangerous attitudes that in the end will lead to their demise.

So leaders, consider carefully how you will think about and relate to money (and related resources). In this article we will identify three features that characterized Nehemiah's approach to finances.

Nehemiah's Approach to the Use of Finances (and Related Resources)

1. Openness

Nehemiah was open with the king, asking for timber to use in his residence. He could easily have overlooked this "detail." He could have taken timber from the overall allotment without asking the king for permission for this resource for his personal use. He chose, instead, to be open with the king about his intentions (Ne 2:8).

2. Exemplary Living

Nehemiah's life set a standard for the people. He refused to acquire land or go beyond what was needed in the procurement of food for his table (Ne 5:17-18).

He loaned money and grain to help people, but did not charge additional interest, which the book of the Law forbade (see Exodus 22:25-27). Nehemiah lived out of reverence for the Lord and for the good of the people, which set boundaries for his perspectives on and use of finances and other resources (5:10-11; 14-16).

3. Providing for the Needs of Centralized Worship

Nehemiah 10:32-34, which is part of the covenant the people made with the Lord in response to Ezra's reading from the book of the Law, spells out the commitment of the people to support the work at the temple. This covenant signing was a result of Nehemiah's

---

[105] See **Articles,** 4. *Finishing Well—Five Enhancements; 5. Finishing Well—Six Characteristics; 6. Finishing Well—Six Major Barriers.*

and Ezra's leadership. Nehemiah was one of several leaders of the people who sealed the covenant.

He also enforced the commitments the people made. Upon returning to Jerusalem from his trip back to King Artaxerxes, Nehemiah found that the covenant stipulations were not being followed (13:6-13). For Nehemiah this meant the house of the Lord was being neglected and the priority of centralized worship was in peril. So he immediately took action to restore the proper collection and disbursement of funds and other resources.

From Nehemiah to Today

To sum up, if a leader is to finish well, she or he can learn aspects of financial integrity from leaders like Nehemiah. Nehemiah modeled openness, exemplary practices, and provided for the needs of the house of the Lord. What possible applications can we make from his example to leadership today? Here are a few observations.

What are some leaders doing today to insure financial openness?
1. Conducting monthly and quarterly financial reviews.
2. Delegating check signing to people other than the senior leader.
3. Providing for annual audits by qualified outside accounting firms.
4. Joining organizations such as the Evangelical Council on Financial Accountability.

What are some leaders doing today to practice exemplary living?
1. Tithing their income or giving even more.
2. Contributing "free will" offerings to their local churches and/or supporting other Christian leaders or nonprofit agencies.
3. Simplifying their lifestyles and scaling back on personal possessions.
4. Helping their adult and/or married children (or parents) during times of financial difficulty.
5. Attending stewardship and financial management courses offered through their churches—and putting into practice principles learned.
6. Meeting with accountability partners who ask them weekly about their use, personally and in ministry, of money and related resources.

What are some leaders doing today to provide resources for centralized worship?
1. In addition to regular tithing and offering contributions, giving sacrificially to capital fundraising campaigns.
2. Responding to personal appeals from other leaders to give sacrificially to help fund new staff roles in church or parachurch ministries.
3. Expanding their understanding of what the Bible teaches about money so they can more effectively equip followers for a lifestyle of stewardship and biblical giving.
4. Linking followers to resources designed to help them eliminate debt and free more resources for God's kingdom.

Closure

And what about your relationship to money and related resources? To what extent are you open about your giving and spending patterns? What about the openness of the organization you lead? To what extent would your followers say that you modeled an exemplary lifestyle in your use of money? To what extent would they say that your organization provides for centralized worship, or for the funding of its primary purpose?

We can tell you how they would have answered for Nehemiah. Nehemiah was exemplary in all these financial issues.

27. Nehemiah, Getting Ownership

Introduction
Why do some change initiatives succeed while others fail or achieve only minimal success? In some cases they fail because the change leader (or leaders) failed to gain ownership for the change. For the change initiative to succeed in the short-term and long-term, people must embrace the change, that is, "own it", mentally and emotionally. They must feel the need for the change and believe in the better way that it promises in order for them to actively support the new way. Nehemiah illustrates one of the important principles of instituting successful change—that of getting ownership. What can we learn about ownership from Nehemiah's experience? Lets define ownership and then look at eight important ownership principles from Nehemiah's substantial work to get ownership.

What Is Ownership?
Ownership is certainly a strange word—one not usually seen in our everyday conversation. Yet it is a crucial concept when thinking of change dynamics.

Definition   Ownership refers to the willing acceptance and support, by followers, of changes being proposed by a leader.

When followers "own" the change, they participate wholeheartedly because they think it is right to do so. Follower ownership is imperative for accomplishing overwhelming tasks.

What Can Nehemiah Teach Us About Ownership?—Eight Observations
Chapter 3 of the book of Nehemiah lists an impressive number of people whom Nehemiah motivated to help him with his task. At least 48 people or groups of people are named. These include priests, Levites, goldsmiths, other businessmen, leaders of towns, and common people. Nehemiah was able to motivate all kinds of people to willingly be a part of rebuilding the wall.

He was undoubtedly successful because he was partnering with God in the work God wanted done (the gracious hand of God was upon him). And he also had the king's permission and resources. But further, Nehemiah was also successful because of the approach he took to initiating the change and gaining the ownership of the people. His approach leads us to identify eight observations. And we give these observations as recommendations to change leaders today.

1. Appeal to what the followers see as a better way.

The inhabitants of Jerusalem were well aware of their plight. They recognized the shame and disgrace of their condition. Thus Nehemiah could appeal to them in 2:17 with these words: "'You know full well the tragedy of our city. It lies in ruins, and its gates are burned. Let us rebuild the wall of Jerusalem and rid ourselves of this disgrace!'" Notice the current condition—tragedy... ruins... burned... disgrace—and how Nehemiah contrasts that with the better way—rebuild and rid ourselves.

Leaders today will be well served by explaining how their change initiatives will lead to a better way of life, ministry, leadership, funding, etc., for their followers. If the change initiatives do not lead to a better way, then obtaining ownership will be even more difficult for the leader. This is not to say that the change should be manipulated or contrived in some manner to *appear* like a better way when in fact it is not, but to point out that if the change is from the Lord, in some way it *will* result in a better way for His people or for a particular community or country, even though initially it may seem otherwise.

2. Keep it simple so that people can easily grasp the picture of the preferred way.

What did Nehemiah say to them? *Rebuild the wall and rid ourselves of this disgrace.* Surely that was an overwhelming undertaking and would require intensive focus, dedication, and hard work. But Nehemiah stated the better way succinctly and memorably—rebuild and rid.

Even complex, overwhelming projects can be stated in simple terms that followers can understand and embrace. Scripture provides other examples: multiply and fill the land; build an ark; get Israel out of Egypt; possess Canaan; make disciples. Leaders can too often become emotionally attached to how their lofty aspirations are worded and described in detail than to what their aspirations actually achieve.

3. Include yourself and work you've done in the ownership of and solution to the problem.

Nehemiah came to Jerusalem as a Jew but as an outsider to the established civic and religious leaders. His outsider status probably cut two ways. On the one hand, people could have been hesitant to trust him ("Who is he? Why is he here? What is his real agenda? What if the king really sent him here to spy on us or to somehow set us up for further oppression?"). On the other hand, they could have fully welcomed him ("This man is one of us, and cupbearer to the king at that! He can really help us. He has access to the throne. Finally, someone who has our well-being at heart!").

Nehemiah's word selection identifies him <u>with</u> the people and their plight. His word selection, which reflects his self-perception, begins in his prayer in chapter 1, but notice specifically what he says in chapter 2:

- to the key leaders in verse 17 (emphasis ours)—"'You know full well the tragedy of <u>our</u> city. Let <u>us</u> rebuild...and rid <u>ourselves</u> of this disgrace!'"
- to his adversaries in verse 20 (emphasis ours)—"The God of heaven will give <u>us</u> success. <u>We his servants</u> will start rebuilding this wall. <u>But you</u> have <u>no stake</u> or claim in Jerusalem."

Nehemiah also reports on work he's already accomplished on behalf of the people and their need. He is on site, fully present, and ready to continue the work that he began in Susa:

- (verse 18)—"Then I told them about how the gracious hand of God had been on me, and about my conversation with the king."

Leaders today need to be careful that they're not perceived as condescending, that they alone have a "corner" on the market of what is best for a particular group. If leaders today have not cultivated authority with followers to lead a major change, or even a minor one, ownership will be diminished. Leaders can cultivate authority through their prayer and fasting; through their prior work on behalf of the people; by taking time to survey the need firsthand, for themselves; and by including themselves with the people and their condition.

4. Influence the opinion leaders first.

Once he had heard from God, most likely during his time of prayer and fasting in chapter 1, Nehemiah had to approach King Artaxerxes. He needed the king's permission and release of resources in order to accomplish his work. So he prays to the Lord for favor with the king, then prays again as he approaches the king, and then asks for permission and support. Once he has the king's support he can meet with the influentials in Jerusalem. Once he has their support the change message can extend further to those who will be doing the work. Nehemiah influenced the opinion leaders first. With their support he could lead the change successfully.

Leaders today should take note of this process. Too many times we have noted how leaders short-circuit their change initiatives by appealing first to the masses instead of those who actually shape opinion and control the flow of resources. In our experience pastors often make the mistake of going directly from the prayer room—where they feel "envisioned" by God for some bold new venture—to the pulpit, where they announce that bold new initiative, bypassing a number of opinion leaders and influentials who could have helped refine, improve, and secure ownership for it.

Leader, sharing first with the opinion leaders, and taking the time to process their thoughts and feelings, will serve you and God's work better, in the long-term, than taking the initiative directly to the people and then feeling resentful when they don't get as excited about it as you have. Perhaps their reluctance is not rebellion but misunderstanding. Perhaps you have failed to consider that your bold venture is not just a bold venture, but a high-level order of change with a number of significant implications for the followers. In our opinion you would be better served by first influencing the opinion leaders.

5. Do your homework by developing a plan.

When Nehemiah made his request of King Artaxerxes, the king had questions: How long would Nehemiah be gone? When would he return? Note that Nehemiah was not taken off-guard by these questions. His answer was ready, as were his follow-up requests, because he had taken time to think through what the work would require and how long it would take.

Leaders can more effectively gain the support of influentials when they have done their homework by thinking through what a particular change initiative will require, how much it will cost, how long it will likely take, and a general plan of action for getting from the way things are today to the way they see them (with the change implemented) tomorrow.

6. Practice strategic delegation.

Nehemiah delegated the work of rebuilding to a significant number of people. But notice that his delegation was not random or haphazard but strategic—he had families, for example, work on the parts of the wall closest to their homes. By doing so, he increased their ownership by appealing to their desire to have a sturdy wall, especially, next to their own abode.

Leaders today can follow this example. They can increase ownership of a change project by allowing people to work on areas of the change about which they feel passionate. Maybe their area of interest is children or funding or facility development, so instead of arbitrarily assigning them to some area, invite them to contribute in the area of their interest. Then their buy-in and enthusiasm for the work will be greater, and the work itself will be of a higher quality. Lets define the basic concept involved here.

Definition   <u>Strategic delegation</u> means the assignment of groups or individuals to pieces of the change project to which they are naturally drawn or have some vested interest in.

Nehemiah used strategic delegation.

7. Model the vision by the way you live.
   It was Gandhi who said we must "become the change we wish to see." But Gandhi could easily have derived this lesson from Nehemiah. For twelve years Nehemiah put his heart and soul into the renewal and well-being of God's people in Jerusalem. His life was aligned with his God-given assignment. How?

- Through his own prayer and fasting over the condition of the city and the people
- By going to the king and requesting permission and resources
- By facing down his adversaries
- By modeling a lifestyle of character and faith for the people
- By devoting himself to the work on the wall
- By following up the work on the wall with work on the repopulation of the city, restoration of centralized and vibrant worship, and renewal of obedience to the book of the law

8. Persevere and Celebrate Progress.
   Once you have gained ownership, <u>persevere</u> through the obstacles to the completion of the change initiative. By persevering, and celebrating progress along the way, you can maintain the ownership you worked so hard to obtain. Maintaining ownership, throughout the change, is just as important as gaining it initially. When ownership stalls, the project will likewise stall or slow down.

Closure
   All of these eight observations on getting ownership in a change situation are helpful. By way of summarizing and forcing you to think through these eight observations again we will restate them in the form of questions. Think back to the last important change you sought to bring about in your ministry and reflect on these questions in light of that change.

Question 1. Did you appeal to the change participants in terms of the better way possible?

Question 2. Did you state your change situation in simple terms?

Question 3. Did you use wording to include yourself with the change participants in the situation?

Question 4. Did you identify the opinion leaders and begin to influence them before going to the rest of the change participants?

Question 5. Did you have a well thought out plan (even alternate scenarios) before you started influencing ownership?

Question 6. Did you identify groups and individuals and strategically work with them to assign them to a part of the change about which they were passionate?

Question 7. Are you modeling what the change is all about so that people can see that you are heart and soul involved in the change situation and that you are following God in it?

Question 8. Did you persevere through to see the change happen? And along the way did you celebrate significant benchmarks in the process?

Nehemiah has a lot to say to us about the crucial ownership principle involved in successfully bringing about change. More than just a wall was involved. But that was an excellent starting place. And its success was a stepping-stone to the overall change process of a renewed people worshiping God in a strong centralized worship center. Seeing the wall finished was a pivotal point in getting ownership for the whole renewal emphasis that Nehemiah and Ezra longed for.

28. Nehemiah, In the Trenches

Introduction

Where does the work of leadership most often occur? In our experience aspiring leaders often equate leadership with a position of glamour. They sense that the work of leadership most often takes place:

- when the spotlight is beaming down upon the gifted orator in the pulpit,
- when the board chair is persuasively convincing the board to adopt the upcoming five-year vision and plan, with its accompanying budget,
- when the small group members hang on every word of the small group leader, and
- when signs and wonders are operating in the crusade-sized gathering of hungry worshipers.

And while leadership does happen in these instances, at least to some extent, the book of Nehemiah illustrates that leadership happens most often in the trenches. Nehemiah was in the trenches with the people. We will introduce five trench-like observations on the What and Where of leadership as seen in Nehemiah's leadership.

Where Leadership Occurs in the Book of Nehemiah

The text illustrates the following leadership venues, some of which were preparatory to actual leadership acts[106] themselves:

- A question and answer session with some family members and probable acquaintances who had recently arrived from a despair-stricken city,
- A prayer closet,
- At the royal throne of King Artaxerxes,
- At the headquarters of the leaders of provinces west of the Euphrates river,
- On a donkey's back and by foot on a nighttime trip around Jerusalem,
- At an outdoor gathering of civic and religious leaders,
- Face-to-face with adversaries,
- In the outspoken ridicule and intimidation of adversaries,
- In the outcry of people who had been treated unfairly,
- In the fearful anticipations of the workers,

---

[106] A leadership act is a technical leadership term, which describes a leader influencing a specific group of followers toward some purpose of God in an actual situation. The leadership style can be studied. A result can be observed. Principles can be derived.

- Elbow to elbow with other workers,
- In dumpster loads of rubble, rubble, rubble,
- In the square and courtyards of the city and temple,
- In the face of slander and false prophecies.

What We Can Learn from Where Leadership Occurs in Nehemiah— Five Observations

1. Leadership is work.

Work is the application of energy to a specified task. The primary task of leadership is to influence followers toward fulfillment of God's purposes for the group. The followers may be younger or older than the leader, less mature or more mature, able to competently perform a task, or in need of training to perform a task. The followers are related to the leader in some type of context, and in leadership the context is more often than not one that requires some degree of change.

Nehemiah sought to change not only the physical condition of Jerusalem, but the actual living conditions and mental perspectives of the residents—he sought to move them out of shame and disgrace. Changing internal perspectives is typically more complex than changing physical conditions. The people could have replied, "Sure, Nehemiah, we can rebuild the walls, but forget calling us back to our covenant with the LORD. Forget putting an end to Sabbath violations and intermarriage transgressions."

But because of the work he put in on the front end of his assignment—the prayer and fasting, seeking the support and resourcing of the king, his preliminary planning, how he started with the city's defenses (an area of felt need)—Nehemiah's challenges to the people met with success.

But notice the overall context within which his work took place. The context was charged with more than open support (as in 2:17). Nehemiah faced opposition and intimidation from outspoken opponents. Some of the nobles refused to take place in the work. Others were oppressing their fellow Jews, and some were still in violation of covenant requirements.

So yes, Nehemiah heard from God. God put the restoration and renewal work in his heart. And the implementation of that ministry served the Lord and His people. But Nehemiah's leadership was work not play; ongoing effort and attention to detail not thoughtless delegation; heartfelt prayer, ongoing inspiration of the people, steadfast faith, and relentless focus. He served the people and the Lord by working on his assignment until he saw it through to completion.

2. What leaders work on gets done.

Nehemiah received direction from the Lord, then he took action. Ultimately a vision from God will lead to work. Without work the leader only has a dream or inspiration.

But not just any work. Specific work. Vision-focused work. In our mentoring of leaders through the years we have watched them hear from God. We have encouraged them to draft a personal life mandate, articulating in writing what they sensed God leading them to do. Then we have also seen them take on projects and become distracted with other items that were not related to their vision or assignment from God.

What leaders work on will get done, but they need to work on the right things. Following the example of Nehemiah, they need to say no to meetings and appointments, to projects and involvements, that will take them away from the primary purpose God has called them to achieve. Increasingly throughout their lives they need to say no to the good in order to say yes to the better, then no to the better in order to say yes to the best.

3. When leaders persevere, they can see the completion of their God-given assignments.

Through God's grace, the king's support, and the help of at least forty people, Nehemiah was able to lead the rebuilding of Jerusalem's wall in 52 days—a monumental achievement that was completed, in his words, with the help of the Lord. His overall ministry, however, as narrated in his memoirs, lasted for at least 12 years. The troubles he experienced in the 52 days probably typified, at least to some extent, the totality of his ministry.

On several occasions Nehemiah must have been tempted to lose hope and give up—to quit. He chose, however, to pray and persevere. His character was proved solid by the adversity he encountered. Because he did not quit but followed through with his assignment, he saw the completion of what God had put in his heart to do.

Leaders today need to take heart from his experiences and perseverance. In many cases they, too, are tempted to give up—a key leader leaves the church; a solid supporter becomes an adversary; funding dries up; conversions cease; squabbles at home intensify; volunteers don't deliver on their commitments; their board votes against them; or they themselves yield to some sinful temptation. Focus is lost. Hope fades. Courage evaporates. The opposition seems too strong, the rubble endless. They choose the path of least resistance and fall back from the full completion of their God-given purpose.

To these leaders Nehemiah would say: "Face your adversaries. Stand firm in biblical faith. Ask the Lord to strengthen your hands. Ask the Lord to deal with your opponents. Summon your courage and keep on working. The work can be done. The work is of God. The end is in sight."

4. When leaders persevere, it can work out for the well-being of God's people.

Because Nehemiah stayed on the wall, the work got done. The walls were rebuilt. Jerusalem's natural defenses were established. The enemies of the Jewish people were put to shame.

Because he and Ezra called the people back to the Law of Moses, their hearts were turned to the Lord. They experienced and celebrated the goodness and joy of the Lord. They experienced life under the oversight of leaders of character and integrity.

Had Nehemiah (and Ezra) not persevered, had he succumbed to the threats and intimidation of Sanballat and Tobiah, the situation of the people would have worsened. Their morale would have diminished even further. Their hope would have turned to despair.

When leaders persevere and follow through on their God-given assignments, when they stay on the wall and don't stop short of what God has set before them, when they remain faithful and don't quit, God's people reap the rewards. God's people end up better off than before. And God's leaders are more likely to hear Him say, "Well done."

5. When leaders start the work, they need to know that God has called them to the work.

Nehemiah's experience with conflict and problems, as noted specifically in chapters 2, 4, 5, 6, and 13, could have derailed his work. He could have surrendered his leadership to his opponents. The conflict was external and internal, outspoken and whispered. False prophets were solicited to prophesy against him. Traps were set to ensnare him. Sound foreboding? Can you believe it—here he is on an assignment from God, **and he no sooner arrives in Jerusalem** than Sanballat and Tobiah confront him, angry that someone had come to promote the welfare of the Israelites.

He was possibly tempted to despair and to give up, but he did neither. Nehemiah turned to the Lord, resolved the conflicts, solved the problems, and faced down his opponents. What kept him going?

He kept going, in large part, because he knew God had called him. Through his time of fasting and prayer he had heard from God. He had felt the needs of the people and their condition. He could start the work, and stay with the work, because he was sure of his call.

Leaders today need this same certainty, same solid foundation for fueling their ministry during seasons of darkness and distress. Conflict does not limit itself to stories of biblical leaders. Conflict arises against any who promote the well-being of God's people and the advancement of His purposes.

Closure

If we were to order these five observations chronologically they could probably be arranged in the order shown in Table Ne 28-1.

Table Nehemiah 28-1. Priortizing the Observations Chronologically

Observation	Statement	Comment
5	When leaders start the work, they need to know that God has called them to the work.	If a leader does not have a strong call then that leader will not really work on anything.
2	What leaders work on gets done.	With a strong calling a leader can prioritize toward work agreeing with that calling.
1	Leadership is work.	However you cut it, leadership is work. Our symbol of the trench in this article is focusing on this notion—leadership is work.
3	When leaders persevere, they can see the completion of their God-given assignments.	Having a calling, prioritizing work toward that calling, really doing the work of that calling and persevering in it will see accomplishment of the task.
4	When leaders persevere, it can work out for the well-being of God's people.	The task completed will almost always have broader ramification than the leader knew of as God accomplishes His purposes in the work.

Trench work takes place where the work is. And it is hard work. Nehemiah had a call. He prioritized what he did. He worked hard at the task. He accomplished it. His work stands today as one of the fine Biblical treatises on leadership.

29. Nehemiah, Leadership Functions

Introduction

The central ethic of biblical leadership is *influencing toward God's purposes*. That is, the prime function of leadership is the influencing of groups so that they accomplish *God's purposes* for the group. This requires vision from God, and this dynamic of *external direction* is one of the features that distinguishes Christian from secular leadership.

But what, specifically, do leaders *do* to exert influence, as *leaders*? In other words, while each leader will have some measure of direct ministry based on giftedness,[107] what are the actual *functions* they fulfill in their role as *leaders*? In this article we will define some key leadership terms, identify three categories of leadership functions and their related behaviors, look at Nehemiah's leadership in terms of these functions, then consider how we may apply these insights today.

Basic Leadership Definitions

I will give definitions for leadership act, leadership, and leadership functions. Then I will describe the three high level leadership functions.

Definition   A <u>leadership act</u> occurs when a given person influences a group, so that the group acts or thinks differently than it did before the instance of influence.

While any given act of leadership may have several persons of the group involved in bringing about the process, and while the process may be complex and difficult to assess, leadership can, nevertheless, be seen to happen and be composed essentially of influencer, group, influence means, and the resulting change of direction by the group—the four major parts of a leadership act.

A leadership <u>act</u>, then, is the specific instance at a given point in time, of the leadership influence process between a given influencer (person said to be influencing) and follower(s) (person or persons being influenced), in which the followers are influenced toward some goal.

We differentiate between a momentary instance of leadership, which we call a leadership <u>act</u>, and leadership as an ongoing process, which we call leadership. A significant difference between one who influences momentarily in a group and one who influences persistently over time is the emergence of vision and the sense of responsibility for seeing that vision fulfilled.

---

[107] For example, leaders gifted with the gift of teaching will probably do some level of teaching, and those with the gift of apostleship will probably do some form of starting new churches or organizations.

Leadership is essentially the ongoing persistence of leadership acts by one person. One who consistently exerts influence over a group is said to manifest leadership. Leadership is then seen to be an ongoing process involving several complex items.[108]

Definition   <u>Leadership</u> is a dynamic process over an extended period of time, in which a leader utilizing leadership resources, and by specific leadership behaviors,[109] influences followers toward accomplishment of aims mutually beneficial for the leader(s) and followers.

Definition   <u>Leadership functions</u> are those general activities that leaders must do and/or be responsible for in their influence responsibilities with followers.

Three Primary Categories of Leadership Functions

High level Christian leaders perform many leadership functions. In addition to direct ministry functions based on giftedness, noted in the introduction above, there are those additional functions that typify their role as leaders, that is, people responsible for influencing specific groups of God's people. The Ohio State model[110] reported that most leadership functions could be grouped under two major categories: <u>consideration</u> functions (relationships) and initiation of <u>structure</u> functions (task). In addition to these two there are the <u>inspirational</u> functions that typify those gifted with one or more word gifts.[111]

<u>Consideration</u> is the Ohio State term for all activities a leader does to affirm followers, to provide an atmosphere congenial to accomplishing work, and to give emotional and spiritual support to followers so that they can mature and grow. In other words, consideration refers to those functions a leader performs in order to act <u>relationally</u> with followers in order to enable them to develop and be effective in their contribution to the organization.

Initiation of <u>structure</u> is the Ohio State term for activities a leader does to accomplish the <u>task</u> or vision for which the structure (organization, ministry or group) exists. Task behaviors involve clarifying goals, setting up structures to help reach them, holding people accountable, and disciplining where necessary—in short, influencing followers to act responsibly and to accomplish goals.

Since Christian leadership is *externally directed*, goals result from vision from God. Such leadership must therefore <u>inspire</u> followers toward recognition and ownership of the vision. <u>Inspirational</u> is our term for activities a leader does to lead followers toward recognizing and accepting God's vision, to obtain goal ownership, to participate in the accomplishment of the vision and goals, and to renew support for the vision and goals during those occasions when morale may be slipping.

Leadership Behaviors Related to Leadership Functions

The three categories of leadership functions may be studied further by noting the primary behaviors related to each function.

---

[108] This observation, and the definition that follows, emerged from a research project conducted by Dr. Clinton in which he studied the development of leadership theory from 1841 through 1986.

[109] The leadership behaviors are subsets of the leadership functions described in this article.

[110] See Dr. Clinton's **Leadership Perspectives: How to Study the Bible for Leadership Insights**, page 27 (available through Barnabas Publishers).

[111] Word gifts refer to a category of spiritual gifts used to clarify and explain about God. These help us understand about God including His nature, His purposes and how we can relate to Him and be part of His purposes. These include: teaching, exhortation, pastoring, evangelism, apostleship, prophecy, ruling, and sometimes word of wisdom, word of knowledge, and faith (a word of). All leaders have at least one of these and often several of these.

Relationship Behaviors
Christian leaders:
1. must be involved in the selection, development and release of emerging leaders
2. are called upon to solve crises involving relationships between leaders
3. will be called upon for decision making focusing on people
4. must do routine problem solving related to interpersonal dynamics
5. will coordinate with people—subordinates, peers, superiors
6. must facilitate leadership transition—their own and those of other leaders
7. must do some level of direct ministry related to people (extent depends on giftedness)

Task Behaviors
Christian leaders:
1. must provide structures for the accomplishment of vision
2. will be involved in crisis resolution related to structural issues
3. must make decisions involving structures
4. will do routine problem solving related to structural dynamics
5. will adjust structures as needed to facilitate leadership transitions
6. must do some level of direct ministry related to maintaining and changing structures (extent depends on giftedness)

Inspirational Behaviors
Christian leaders:
1. must motivate followers toward God's vision
2. must encourage the faith and perseverance of the followers
3. are responsible for the corporate integrity of the structures and organizations of which they are part
4. are responsible for developing and maintaining the welfare of the corporate culture of the organization
5. are responsible for promoting the public image of the organization (especially higher level leaders)
6. are responsible for the financial welfare of the organization (especially higher level leaders)
7. are responsible for some level of direct ministry along the lines of their giftedness, as it relates to inspirational behaviors
8. must model a personal relationship with God (holistically—knowing, being and doing) so as to inspire followers toward the reality of God's intervention in their lives
9. have corporate accountability to God for the organization or structures in which they operate

Illustrations of Leadership Functions and Behaviors in the Book of Nehemiah

Relationship Behaviors
1. Selecting and releasing leaders:
   a. Hanani in charge of Jerusalem, 7:2
   b. Hananiah as commander of the citadel, 7:2. Note the descriptor phrase—"because he was a man of integrity and feared God more than most men do."
   c. In 12:44-47, appointing leaders to oversee the temple storerooms
2. Solving crises involving relationships between leaders:
   a. See chapter 5, the resolution of the crisis between the poorer people of the land and the leaders who were oppressing them.

3. Making decisions focusing on people:
    a. See also chapter 5.
4. Solving problems related to interpersonal dynamics:
    a. Again, see chapter 5.
5. Coordinating with people—subordinates, peers, superiors:
    a. 2:1-9, coordinating with King Artaxerxes, the governors of Trans-Euphrates, the army officers and cavalry. Some of this would have been structural and some more relational.
    b. 2:17-18, his challenge to the leaders to rebuild the wall was set in relational language (the use of we and our) and delivered as more of a challenge/invitation than an edict or mandate.
6. Facilitating leadership transition—their own and those of other leaders:
    a. 7:2, putting the city and citadel under the care of Hanani and Hananiah. These men and other leaders likely carried on his work during the time period that he returned to King Artaxerxes.
7. Doing some level of direct ministry related to people (extent depends on giftedness):
    a. Throughout the book we see Nehemiah relating to people, especially in the context of the work to be done.
    b. He was gifted to lead, to organize, to exhort and to encourage. He probably had additional gifts of faith and discernment (discernment may have been a natural talent or acquired skill). He worked with people, as far as we can tell, primarily through these gifts.

Task Behaviors
1. Providing structures for the accomplishment of vision:
    a. All of chapter 3, where work is organized for rebuilding the wall
    b. 7:3, setting policies for when and how the gates of Jerusalem were to be opened and closed; providing for the appointment of city guards
    c. 7:4, registering the people by families and later selecting among them for populating the city (ch 11)
    d. Chapters 8-11, provisions for religious renewal
    e. 12:27ff, arrangements for the wall dedication ceremony
    f. Chapter 13, further policies related to covenant faithfulness
2. Resolving crises related to structural issues:
    a. Responding to adversarial conflict and averting the threat of attack in chapters 4 and 6
    b. Commanding obedience the covenant in chapter 13
3. Making decisions involving structures:
    a. Each chapter in 2-11 is based to some extent on decisions Nehemiah made to provide for some type of civic, military or religious structure.
4. Solving routine problems related to structural dynamics:
    a. Nehemiah solves problems throughout the book, but given the context and the nature of his work they are not what we would consider "routine" problems.
5. Adjusting structures as needed to facilitate leadership transitions:
    a. 6:1-15, making adjustments to how the work was initially designed
6. Doing some level of direct ministry related to maintaining and changing structures (extent depends on giftedness):
    a. Throughout the book we see Nehemiah setting structures and guidelines in place to get the work done.
    b. He was gifted to lead, to organize, to exhort and to encourage. He probably had additional gifts of faith and discernment (discernment may have been a natural talent or acquired skill). Each of these was brought to bear in his direct ministry.

Inspirational Behaviors
1. Motivating followers toward God's vision:
    a. With the king in 2:1-9
    b. With leaders from Jerusalem in 2:17
2. Encouraging the faith and perseverance of the followers:
    a. Especially in chapters 4 and 6 when confronted by the opposition coalition
3. Providing for the corporate integrity of the structures and organizations of which they are part:
    a. Nehemiah is concerned for the welfare of God's people, which he sees as directly related to their understanding of and obedience to the book of the Law. We see this connection in various places in the book, but first in his prayer in chapter 1.
    b. Note also his wording in 5:9, as he confronts those guilty of oppressing their fellow Jews—"'What you are doing is not right. Shouldn't you walk in the fear of our God to avoid the reproach of our Gentile enemies?'"
    c. His wording is similar in 13:17-18 where he rebukes those guilty of Sabbath violations—"'What is this wicked thing you are doing—desecrating the Sabbath day? Didn't your forefathers do the same things, so that our God brought all this calamity upon us and upon this city? Now you are stirring up more wrath against Israel by desecrating the Sabbath.'"
4. Developing and maintaining the welfare of the corporate culture of the organization:
    a. Jewish corporate culture was based on the covenantal relationship between the LORD and his people. See comments under #3 above.
5. Promoting the public image of the organization:
    a. See #3 above.
6. Looking out for the financial welfare of the organization:
    a. See **Article,** *26. Nehemiah, Financial Integrity.*
7. Doing direct ministry along the lines of their giftedness, as it relates to inspirational behaviors:
    a. Nehemiah's probable gifts of leadership and exhortation are in use in direct ministry, especially in chapters 4 and 6 where he rallies the workers to keep on working and prepare to fight for their brothers and families.
8. Modeling a personal relationship with God (holistically—knowing, being and doing) so as to inspire followers toward the reality of God's intervention in their lives:
    a. His response to outside opposition in 2:20 illustrates his knowledge of the Lord: "I answered them by saying, 'The God of heaven will give us success. We his servants will start rebuilding, but as for you, you have no share in Jerusalem or any claim or historic right to it.'"
    b. His spontaneous prayers portray his relationship with God. See **Articles,** *18. Nehemiah, And Daniel—Comparison of Vicarious Praying; 24. Nehemiah, Desperate Praying.*
    c. His encouragement to the builders in the face of intimidation points to his relationship with God, 4:14b—"'Don't be afraid of them. Remember the Lord, who is great and awesome, and fight for your brothers, your sons and your daughters, your wives and your homes.'"
9. Having corporate accountability to God for the organization or structures in which they operate:
    a. Notice Nehemiah's "remember" prayers, such as 13:14—"'Remember me for this, O my God, and do not blot out what I have so faithfully done for the house of my God and its services.'"

b. See our comments on *Prayerful Spirit* in the General Reflection section of the commentary.

Closure

Even a cursory review of leadership functions illustrated in the book of Nehemiah points to what we said in the Definitions section of this article: *Leadership is essentially the ongoing persistence of leadership acts by one person. One who consistently exerts influence over a group is said to manifest leadership. Leadership is then seen to be an ongoing process involving several complex items.* These items involve the dynamic interplay of behaviors related to one or more of three primary categories of functions: relational, task and inspirational. Nehemiah's memoirs illustrate several of these functions.

So how does your leadership look to you? How does it look to those you lead? In which of the three categories of functions are you strongest? Weakest? What do you see in Nehemiah's leadership that can strengthen your own? Think of the last major project you led, or a current initiative you're leading, and use the table that follows to note specific areas that may need your attention.

Table Ne 29-1 Application of Leadership Functions

Category of Function	Sub-set Behaviors	How You Are Doing or May Need to Do This Behavior
Relational	1. Selecting, developing, and releasing emerging leaders	
	2. Solving interpersonal crises	
	3. Decision making that is focused on people	
	4. Routine problem solving related to people issues	
	5. Coordinating with subordinates, peers, and superiors	
	6. Facilitating leadership transition	
	7. Doing direct ministry	
Task	1. Providing structures to accomplish the vision	

Task, continued	2. Resolving crises related to structures	
	3. Making decisions involving structures	
	4. Solving routine problems related to structures	
	5. Adjusting structures where necessary to facilitate leadership transition	
	6. Doing direct ministry	
Inspirational	1. Motivating toward vision	
	2. Encouraging perseverance and faith	
	3. Maintaining corporate integrity	
	4. Providing for the welfare of the corporate culture	
	5. Promoting the public image of the organization	
	6. Looking out for the financial welfare of the organization	
	7. Doing direct ministry	
	8. Modeling a relationship with God that inspires followers	
	9. Having corporate accountability to God for the organization	

30. Nehemiah, Peoples and Places

Introduction

Four important hermeneutical principles for studying a book of the Bible are listed below in Table Ne 30-1:[112]

Table Ne 30-1. Hermeneutical Laws

LAW	Dealing With	Statement
1	Book and Books	**In The Spirit, Prayerfully Study The Book As A Whole In Terms Of Its Relationship To Other Books In The Bible** (i.e. the Bible as a whole) **To Include:** a. its place in the progress of revelation, b. its overall contribution to the whole of Bible literature, and c. its abiding contribution to present time.
2	Historical Background	**In The Spirit, Prayerfully Study The Historical Background Of The Book Which Includes Such Information As:** a. the author of the book and the *historical perspective* from which he/she wrote. b. the *occasion* for the book c. the *purpose* for the book including where pertinent the people for whom it was intended and their situation. d. any geographical or cultural factors bearing on the communication of the material.
3	Structure of the Book	**In The Spirit, Prayerfully Study The Book As A Whole Until You See The Author's Plan Or Structure Or The Way He Relates His Parts To The Whole Book To Accomplish His Purpose Or Develop His Theme.**
4	Theme of the Book	**In The Spirit, Prayerfully Study The Book As A Whole Until You Can Identify And State Concisely The Author's Theme Of The Book.**

We have previously given at least a superficial tip of the hat to Laws 1, 3, and 4 in the **Preface Section** and the **General Reflection Section** of this commentary. But Law 2 dealing with historical background gets attention basically only in occasional comments on the text itself.[113] Because Nehemiah is such an important leadership book in terms of

---

[112] See Appendix G, **Having A Ministry That Lasts**, for the complete listing of the 7 General Laws of Hermeneutics and the 7 Special Language Laws.

[113] We are especially focusing on part d of the law.

change dynamics it behooves us to treat this historical law in some depth. This article does that, especially in terms of peoples and places mentioned in the book.[114] Change participants are crucial to any major leadership implementation of a bridging strategy. Nehemiah's overall change strategy involved people surrounding Jerusalem as well as the city itself. Hence, a knowledge of the peoples and places helps us grasp the difficulty of the change process that Nehemiah was dealing with.

This article will list the peoples (ethnic groups, tribes, clans) and places (surrounding regions, towns, sections of Jerusalem and other towns) mentioned in Nehemiah along with some descriptive information.

Review
Let us hurriedly mention what we have already said about each of these laws. And then we will move on to the listing of peoples and places, part d of the Historical Background Law.

Law 1. Book and Books
The Bible is a unique book made up of 66 books. Each of the 66 contribute something to the story of the Bible as a whole. Law 1 deals with this emphasis.

In The Spirit, Prayerfully Study The Book As A Whole In Terms Of Its Relationship To Other Books In The Bible (i.e. the Bible as a whole) **To Include**:
   a. its place in the progress of revelation,
   b. its overall contribution to the whole of Bible literature, and
   c. its abiding contribution to present time.

In the redemptive drama Nehemiah occurs at the close of chapter 2 Destruction of a Nation. One way to overview the redemptive drama in the Bible is as follows:

   Introduction
   Chapter 1 The Making of a Nation
   Chapter 2 The Destruction of a Nation
        a. A United Kingdom
        b. A Divided Kingdom
        c. The Southern Kingdom
        d. Back in the Land
   Chapter 3. Messiah
   Chapter 4. Church Around the World
   Chapter 5. Kingdom

Nehemiah occurs in Chapter 2, part d, Back in the Land. The Israelite nation has been taken away in exile due to their disobedience to God. Now God brings back a remnant, which will build a base for Messiah to come in Chapter 3. Nehemiah deals with God's building a foothold in the land, which will eventuate, when the time is right, in Messiah's coming.

In the leadership commentary series, we are viewing books not only from the framework of what they contribute to the redemptive drama but also in terms of a leadership framework. We have identified the following Leadership Eras.

---

[114] Here we give the names and descriptions. In the **Article**, *21. Nehemiah, Change Participants*, we treat the more important individual people in the change process in terms of their relationship to the changes Nehemiah was implementing.

I. **Patriarchal Era**

II. **Pre-Kingdom Era**
  A. Desert Years
  B. The War Years
  C. The Tribal Years

III. **Kingdom Era**
  A. United Kingdom
  B. Divided Kingdom
  C. Southern Kingdom

IV. **Post-Kingdom Era**
  A. Exilic
  B. A Foothold Back in the Land

V. **Pre-Church Era**

VI. **Church Era**

Nehemiah occurs in Leadership Era IV, entitled Post-Kingdom Leadership. More specifically the happenings of the book of Nehemiah occur in Part B, the Post Exilic subphase, or as titled above, *A Foothold Back in the Land*. It is a time when the work and plans of God seem minor. The people of God are few—their spirits low. They need inspirational leadership. Nehemiah provides task-oriented leadership, which inspires the people. A new order of leadership is seen in this book. The kings have come and gone and still God's work needs accomplishing.[115] God raises up a lay person, a Civil Leader who is a spiritual man and who is willing to walk by faith in the midst of darkness and opposition. Nehemiah illustrates the basic message of Habakkuk 2:4, "My righteous one shall live by faith." His attitude of persevering faith, his continued activity on the wall, his completion of that task, and his renewal leadership illustrate what leadership that mixes faith with obedience can do. Nehemiah lived out the advice of the old Bible teacher who told his students, "Pray as though everything depended on God, and act as though everything depended on you." Nehemiah's special contribution leadership-wise is the demonstration, a case study, if you will, of how to bring about change which will result in renewal. Nehemiah planned well and carried out his plan. He illustrates many of the change dynamics principles we have identified in organizational change.[116] Nehemiah's abiding contribution to the Bible as a whole is a case study of leadership, one of only a few Bible books dealing with a strong leadership focus. See the leadership topics listed in the General Reflection section of this commentary for the very helpful and abiding contribution of Nehemiah to leadership information in the Bible. Nehemiah, the person, is one of those *Hebrews 13:7,8 characters*, whose faith and exploits need to be emulated.

Law 3. Structure of the Book
This general principles is usually not done well by most exegetical commentary writers. Particularly is that true of identifying the major ideas being promulgated by each structure.

---

[115] Prophets still exist but have no kings to prophesy against. Priests and Levites still exist but have not yet established centralized worship. Haggai has helped by getting the temple built. Both Haggai and Zechariah were prophets who stimulated restoration. But Nehemiah is different, being neither Prophet, Priest, or King. He is a Tirshatha (Persian appointed Governor). This is a different breed of leadership. But through this appointment he will implement spiritual renewal.

[116] See **Article**, *21. Nehemiah, Change Participants*. See also Clinton and Clinton, **Bridging Strategies**.

In The Spirit, Prayerfully Study The Book As A Whole Until You See The Author's Plan Or Structure Or The Way He Relates His Parts To The Whole Book To Accomplish His Purpose Or Develop His Theme.

Nehemiah got his directions from God at the right time. His personal testimony before Artaxerxes was well established. This allowed him to use networking power very well. He gets a vision from God and plans to implement it. The book shows how that plan worked out. In chapter 1 the long term vision and plan is planted in Nehemiah's heart. Then steps one and two occur. In part II of the book, Nehemiah gets a secure base. By building the wall to make Jerusalem a walled city, defensible. In part III of the book he organizes central worship in Jerusalem and makes sure there are resources for it to happen. And finally in part IV of the book he seeks to implement long term follow-up from the renewal movement. A breakdown of the book in terms of this planning by Nehemiah and his implementing his plan would be:

Structure   I.   (ch 1)   Receiving Direction to Rebuild in Jerusalem
                 II. (ch 2-7:3)   Organizing to Rebuild the Wall
                 III. (ch 7:4-10:39)   Organizing for Reform
                 IV. (ch 11-13)   Organizing for Continuation

In each of these sections of the book, peoples and places are sprinkled throughout. We need to understand them to see the complexity facing Nehemiah's leadership.

Law 3. Theme of the Book
In The Spirit, Prayerfully Study The Book As A Whole Until You Can Identify And State Concisely The Author's Theme Of The Book.

Usually each part of the book contributes some major idea to the overall theme of the book. Such is the case with Nehemiah.[117] Then a synthesis of these major ideas along with other repeated emphases throughout the book help to identify the subject of these major ideas. Here is the way we have organized the thematic intent of the book.

Theme   **NEHEMIAH'S ORGANIZATIONAL LEADERSHIP**
                 • was the result of God's initiation,

                 • made itself felt in the face of obstacles to rebuild the wall,
                 • was inspirational in bringing about reform and a covenant in Jerusalem, and
                 • included drastic steps of separation in order to insure an on-going meaningful religious atmosphere.

Again, peoples and places are crucial to understanding each of the major ideas of this theme, which interweaves and unites the message of the book as a whole.

Law 2. Historical Background
Read again the hermeneutical principle dealing with historical background and note carefully part d. That is what we are focusing on in this article. But we will also give a brief summary of parts a, b, and c.

---

[117] This assumption of logical thought weaving through a book occurs for what I call the left brain books of the Bible. There are some right brain books (less than 10) which don't follow this logical organization. There theme is found differently.

In The Spirit, Prayerfully Study The Historical Background Of The Book Which Includes Such Information As:
   a. the author of the book and the *historical perspective* from which he/she wrote.
   b. the *occasion* for the book
   c. the *purpose* for the book including where pertinent the people for whom it was intended and their situation.
   d. any geographical or cultural factors bearing on the communication of the material.

We are not certain of the authorship of the book Nehemiah. Most likely it was Nehemiah himself, in old age as he reflected back on his leadership. But it could have been someone to whom he related these things and gave access to his journal and other records. We prefer to believe it was Nehemiah himself.[118] In any case, the author was familiar with much detail of the time period and Nehemiah's thoughts and prayers.

As to occasion, who knows what prompted the writing. Perhaps an old man, Nehemiah, felt that future generations should know of the struggles it took to rebuild Jerusalem and preserve the temple and centralized worship. It is certainly a legacy to Nehemiah's ministry and captures leadership principles that brought renewal. As leaders, we need to capture our moments of God's special working and use them as celebrations honoring God and passing on our experience to help others. Nehemiah does that. But the actual occasion, which prompted the writing of the book remains unknown.

We have previously suggested several purpose. While we cannot say for certain that these purposes were in the mind of the author, we can see that the book does shed light on them. Here are the purposes we listed in the General Reflection Section of the commentary.
   * to tell of the rebuilding of the walls around Jerusalem,
   * to show the importance of networking power,
   * to introduce a new kind of leader (a lay leader who is Bible centered and who models task oriented and organizational behavior),
   * to describe task oriented inspirational leadership which has organizational issues central,
   * to illustrate motivational techniques,
   * to show the importance of prayer in leadership,
   * to show the importance of the Word in leadership,
   * to illustrate perseverance in leadership the midst of opposition and obstacles,
   * to show dynamic balance between dependence upon God and activity for God.

This article is primarily attempting to shed light on part d of this hermeneutical principle—d. any geographical or cultural factors bearing on the communication of the material. Tables Ne 30-2 and Ne 30-3 give the basic information dealing with peoples and places. By peoples we are specifically thinking of people groups—ethnically bound together as tribes or clans or religious groups.[119] By places we are describing surrounding towns, geographical terms, regions, and sections of Jerusalem.

Table Ne 30-2 Peoples Referred To in the Book of Nehemiah
Section 1 of the Book (chapter 1)
None

Section 2 of the Book (chapters 2-7:3)

---

[118] Other scholars might not agree with this.
[119] In the **Article**, *21. Nehemiah Change Participants*, we also deal with specific individuals. Here we are focusing on people groups which a reader of Nehemiah might otherwise not know.

Location	Item	Comments
2:10	Horonite	A descriptive phrase for Sanballat--Sanballat the Horonite, indicating that Sanballat came from Beth-Horon. Sanballat held some post in the Persian government. Beth-Horon is located north of Jerusalem.
2:10	Ammonite	A descriptive phrase for Tobiah--Tobiah the Ammonite. Ammonites, traditionally, were said to descend from Lot. Ammonite territory was at one time, east of the Dead Sea and Jordan, between the Arnon and the Jabbok. Amorites took much of Ammonite land even before the Israelites came into the land. They formed the Kingdom of Sihon.
2:16	City Officials	KJV ruler (SRN 5461); a subordinate civil leader
2:16	Religious Leaders	Priests and perhaps Levites formally associated with the temple in Jerusalem. Haggai had inspired the building of the temple. These religious leaders were those associated with the temple.
2:19	Arab	A descriptive phrase for Gesham—Gesham the Arab indicating his original home was Arabia. Arabs were nomadic tribes which inhabited the Syrian desert or the peninsula of Sinai surrounded on the south side by the Indian Ocean, the red Sea on the west and the Persian Gulf on the east. Bands of them marauded various regions throughout Palestine.
3:1	The Priests	Formal religious leaders descended from Aaron. They were duly authorized to perform the sacrifices in the Temple. They mediated between the people and God.
3:5	Tekoites	People from Tekoa, a village probably outside of Bethlehem and on the edge of the wilderness. Amos was from here as was Ira one of David's mighty men. A wise woman unnamed who confronted David was from here. This might be the city Rheoboam fortified.
3:5	Nobles	See 2:16; 4:14; 6:17. A person born free and usually upper class with wealth or status. Exercised influence with civil leader or even had civil leadership posts.
3:7	Gibeonite	A person from Gibeon, one of the royal cities of the Hivites (Josh 9:7). Later a part of the tribe of Benjamin. A city given to the Levites. The Gibeonites were the people who avoided annihilation by deceiving Joshua.
3:7	Meronothite	Descriptive term for Jadon probably indicating location of origin. But no place Meronothite has ever been identified.
3:8	Goldsmiths	A guild of workers who refined gold and shaped it into all kinds of decorative objects. First mentioned in connection with the tabernacle (Ex 31:4; 36:1). Obviously craftsmen of ability.
3:8	Apothecaries	KJV (SRN 07546) Another guild of special workers who made ointments and perfumes.
3:13	inhabitants of Zanoah	Describes a group of people from a town in Judah grouped with Eshtaol, Zoral, and Ashnah (Josh 15:34). The folks helped repair the wall near the valley gate.
3:17	Levites	Descendants of the tribe of Levi. They were religious leaders who helped the priests by preparing sacrifices and cleaning the holy place in the Temple.

3:22	Priests, Men of the Plains	A person duly authorized to offer sacrifices at the altar in the temple—a mediator between people and God. These were priests who lived outside of Jerusalem in the Jordan Valley. They probably farmed for their living and provided priestly services as well, maybe on some rotational basis.
3:26	Nithinims	Temple slaves assigned to the priests and Levites for temple service. CEV translates as temple workers. Where they came from or how they became indentured is not known.
3:32	Merchants	Shopkeepers and traveling salesmen.
4:1	Army of Samaria	Probably a militia force or some mercenary outfit hired by Sanballat to protect his administration.
4:7	Ashodites	Inhabitants of Ashdod, one of the five chief cities in territory once ruled by the Philistines. These people intermarried with the Israelites.
4:14	Rulers	Literally one who superintends. Described lesser civil leaders in the prefects. See 3:5 also; 4:19 nobles, rulers, and rest of people. In large group meetings these are the three breakdowns: nobles (wealthy influential people); civil rulers and everyone else.
5:14	Governor of Judah	tsavah KJV (SRN 06346). An appointed position (by Persian rulers); Nehemiah held this appointment.
6:14	The Prophets	Noadiah is mentioned by name as a prophet and others are alluded to. This shows that prophets still were influential religious leaders. This group was opposed to Nehemiah's rebuilding in Jerusalem.
7:1	Porters	Porters, KJV (07778). The CEV identifies these as Gate Keepers. Probably, some sort of security guards for the Temple.
7:2	Singers	These were men (and probably women) who functioned like our modern day worship leaders. David had instituted this kind of leadership long ago.

Section 3 of the Book (chapters 7:4-10:39)

Location	Item	Comments
7:8-63	Numerous Clans	Some named after men; others from locales.
7:60	Descendants of Solomon's Servants	These people are named as a special group, similar to a guild.
8:9	Tirshatha; Governor	A foreign word, probably of Persian origin, Tirshatha; KJV and CEV use governor (08660). The title used by the Persian governor in Judea

Section 4 of the Book (chapters 11-13)

Location	Item	Comments
11:1-36	Numerous clans	Too many to list. Most of descendants of someone—many named; some are identified from an area which they populated.
13:1	Moabites	A district east of the Dead Sea and extending from a point some distance north of it to its southern end. The eastern boundary is desert. About 30 x 50 miles in extent. People here were descended from Lot. Ruth was a Moabite.

Table Ne 30-3 Places Referred To in the Book of Nehemiah

Section 1 of the Book (chapter 1)

Location	Item	Comments
1:1	Fortress of Susa	This was the capital of Elam Province, a part of the Persian empire. It was the winter home of Persian kings. It lies slightly northeast of the northern tip of the Persian Gulf.

Section 2 of the Book (chapters 2-7:3)

Location	Item	Comments
2:7	Province West of the Euphrates	Beyond the river, KJV. The Euphrates is implied. This would be a Persian administered territory. Nehemiah would have knowledge of the various provinces and rulers appointed by Persians to administer them.
2:8	Kings Forest	Nehemiah knows the name of the person (Asaph) who is in charge of a large forest area which supplied timber to Artaxerxes. He has done his homework. He will need lumber to get his job done.
2:13	Valley Gate	According to the CEV the Valley Gate was probably the main gate in the western wall. Probably opened toward the Tyropoeon Valley.
2:13	Dragon's Spring	KJV Dragon's Well. A well that supplied part of the city's water. Probably on the western edge of the city.
2:13	Dung Gate	An opening in the wall that led to the garbage dump probably in the Hinnom Valley.
2:14	Fountain Gate	Probably on the southeastern part of the city where the city water supply pools were located.
2:14	King's Pool	CEV suggests that this pool was a collection place for water from the Gihon Spring, which helped supply the city with water.
2:15	Kidron Valley	The valley forming the city's eastern boundary.
3:1	Sheep Gate	Probably located at the northeastern part of the wall. Sheep were sold there. John 5:2 mentions this gate.
3:3	Fish Gate	Named because it was the site of the city's fish markets. Probably located at the northwest corner of the city. A road led from this location to the Mediterranean Sea.
3:6	Old Gate	Located at the western part of the wall.
3:9	Half Part of Jerusalem	Jerusalem had two major civil districts. Rephaiah was the mayor of this part of the city.
3:11	Tower of the Furnaces	A place where ovens were located (pottery? Or metal works? Or bread?). This tower was a lookout tower on the wall. CEV suggests that it could have been built by Uzziah.
3:12	Half Part of Jerusalem (other half)	This is the second of Jerusalem's major civil districts. Shallum was mayor of this part of the city.
3:14	Part of Bethhaccerem	
3:15	Part of Mizpah	Used to describe Shallam, son of Colhozeh, whose group worked on the wall near the Fountain Gate. He was a leader

		in a district of Mizpah, under Ezer or in our terms a councilman. It is probably the town identified in Jos 13:26. It is the place where Jacob and Laban parted. Jephthah was from Mizpah. It lies north of Mahanaim. It was east of the Jordan on the borders of Gad and Manasseh's territories. Or as the CEV suggests Mizpah could be a town eight miles north of Jerusalem near the border of Samaria.
3:15	Pool of Siloah	A small reservoir in the southeast portion of Jerusalem probably supplied via an aqueduct.
3:16	Half part of Bethzur	Mentioned in Jos 15:58 as near Halhul and Gedor in the hill country of Judah. Was probably that city fortified by Rehoboam (2 Ch 11:7). Used to describe the district ruled over by Nehemiah, the son of Azbuk.
3:17	Half part of Keilah	Describes the district over which Hashabiah was leader. Keilah was a city in the strip of hill country that runs along the western base of the mountains of Judah, terminating in the north at the valley of Aijalon and perhaps extending westward to Philistine country.
3:18	Other Half of Keilah	Describes the district over which Binnui (KJV Bavai) was leader. These men worked on the wall near where the Levites repaired, just past the royal cemetery, artificial pool, and the army barracks (CEV).
3:19	Mizpah	Same place as described above in 3:15. Here used to describe Ezer who was the chief leader of Mizpah.
3:26	Wall of Ophel	Ophel named a section of Jerusalem where the temple workers lived. This was near the Water Gate and the tower guarding the Temple.
3:28	Horse Gate	Probably located near where the Priests lived. Most likely on the east wall between the temple and the royal palace.
3:29	East Gate	A gate on the eastern part of Jerusalem.
6:2	Plain of Ono	The place where Tobiah, Sanballat and Geshem wanted to have Nehemiah meet and talk over Nehemiah's plans for Jerusalem. It was occupied by Benjamites after the return from exile. Lod is the city that is prominent in the Plain of Ono. This lies near the hill country described above when talking of Keilah.

Section 3 of the Book (chapters 7:4-10:39)

Location	Item	Comments
7:63	Gileadite	A branch of the tribe of Manasseh. Also describes the natives of the district of Gilead near Mizpah.
9:7	Ur of the Chaldees	The original home of Abraham. This was a town in what later came to be Babylonian territory. This territory was far to the east of Jerusalem, all the way across the Arabian desert.
9:8	Canaanites	A more general term describing people inhabiting Palestine with a long history. Subjugated for a long time by Egypt and then by Babylon. Became Baal worshippers.
	Hittites	Descendants of Heth. An ancient people probably inhabiting northeastern Palestine (Syria). Another ancient people. Finally associated with Sihon, king

	Amorites	of the Amorites, who had conquered the northern half of Moab and ruled on the east side of Jordan. The Israelites destroyed the majority of this group. The Gibeonites were said to be a remnant of the Amorites.
	Perizzites	Probably people who inhabited scattered villages throughout Palestine. These were unwalled towns and country villages.
	Jebusites	A people who were a mountain tribe in Jerusalem and surrounding region, probably not populous. Their capital Jebus was taken by the men of Judah and burned with fire (Jdg 1:8).
	Girgashites	Little is known at all about this group of people. Maybe located on the east side of the Sea of Galilee.
9:13	Mt. Sinai	The mountain where Moses received revelation from God which impacted Israelite culture. Included in this prayer to reinforce the notion of God's commands which the Israelites had repeatedly disobeyed.
9:22	Land of Sihon	Describes the geographical area east of the Jordan river ruled over by Sihon King of the Amorites. He and his armies were destroyed by the Israelites before they crossed over the Jordan and went into the lad.
9:22	Land of Heshbon	The name of the royal city of Sihon, king of the Amorites. Lies on the southern border of the land of the tribe of Gad.
9:22	Land of Bashan	Describes the land of the kingdom of Og, the most northerly part of the land east of the Jordan. It stretched from the border of Gilead in the south to the slopes of Mt. Hermon in the north.

Section 4 of the Book (chapters 11-13)

Location	Item	Comments
11:35	Lod, and Ono, the valley of craftsmen.	This adds a descriptor to the previous wording about the Plains of Ono. Evidently there are people with special abilities. What the crafts were is not known.
12:29	fields of Geba and Azmaveth	A town on the northeast border of the territory of Benjamin. It was in the past a Levite town. Probably a village nearby Jerusalem.

Closure
We have included this article for two main reasons.

Reason 1. We want to stress how important it is to do good work in assessing the overall importance of a Bible book. Hermeneutical laws 1, 3,4 look at a book in the Bible from its overall emphasis. Most exegetical commentaries do not do this very well. They concentrate more of the details of the text. But assessing the overall importance of the book is a necessary foundational analysis that will then allow one to go on and apply insights from the book to leadership issues.

Reason 2. We wanted to stress the peoples and places mentioned in Nehemiah in order to show just how complex was the task that Nehemiah undertook. A tremendous variety of peoples were involved. There were craftsmen, goldsmiths, perfumers, leaders of cities or districts, religious leaders including prophets, priests, Levites, Temple Guards and all kinds of tribal and clan groups as well as peoples from surrounding towns in Palestine. Nehemiah had a mighty task to motivate these people to unite and rebuild Jerusalem. Nehemiah's task as a leader was complex. There were lots of diverse peoples that he had to work with. They were scattered all around. He did his homework. He knew the peoples and the surrounding region well enough to unite the people into a renewal effort that had a chance for ongoing impact.

Nehemiah accomplished much. His task in bringing about change was enormously complex.

31. Nehemiah, Strategic Timing

Introduction

Leaders must learn to be sensitive to God's timing. God's direction includes *What, How, and* **When**. All are important. Effective leaders are increasingly aware of the timing of God's interventions in their lives and ministry. They move when he moves. They wait. They confidently expect. One of the major macro lessons first seen in *the Patriarchal Leadership Era* and then in every leadership era thereafter states:

> **God's timing is crucial to the accomplishment of God's purposes.**[120]

This is a leadership lesson that all leaders must learn. Strong leaders, such as apostolic leaders, desperately need to learn this. Such leaders usually have a strong sense of destiny and a strong vision they want to accomplish. Often these strong leaders tie their vision to some prophecy or other revelatory word. While they may know the *what* and even the *how* of the vision they may well be off in the *when*. They often move ahead of God's timing. *God's timing is crucial.*   Less bold and forceful leaders also need to learn about God's timing. Frequently they lag behind it.

In this article we will identify two levels of timing issues and make seven recommendations about timing that can help leaders deepen their sensitivity to the *when* of God's direction.

Two Levels of Timing Issues

We see two levels of timing issues in the book of Nehemiah, the **strategic** and the **micro**. Strategic level timing issues point to the need for leaders to be sensitive to the times within which they live and minister. Micro level issues point to the importance of a consistent sensitivity to the Lord's leading and to sensing appropriate times for patience and action in following through on the vision God has called them to fulfill.

At the strategic level, Nehemiah leads a rebuilding and renewal initiative within the larger renewal work of God on behalf of His people. The exile has ended, two companies of people have returned to the land, and the previous work of Ezra, Haggai and Zechariah has paved the way. The temple has been rebuilt and priests and Levites are present who can conduct the temple ministry. In this sense, Nehemiah's ministry is consistent with the larger, or strategic level, work of the Lord.

This was also the case with the men of Issachar and the leadership of David. The men of Issachar, we're told, understood the times and knew what Israel should do. They lived during the early days of the establishment of the monarchy within Israel and during the

---

[120] See **Articles**, *16. Macro Lessons—Defined; 17. Macro Lessons—List of 41 Across Six Leadership Eras.*

transition of leadership from the house of Saul to the house of David. They discerned the strategic timing for making David king over all Israel (1 Chronicles 12:32). Likewise David, according to Acts 13:36, served the Lord's purposes *in his generation*. He defeated the enemies of the Lord's people, extended the borders of the country, and prepared for the construction of the temple.

At the micro level we see Nehemiah's sensitivity in waiting for the right time to approach the king and waiting for the right time to challenge Jerusalem's leaders to rebuild the wall. First, at least *five months* passed from the time of Nehemiah's initial prayer on behalf of Jerusalem (1:4) to his request of the king for permission to return to the land (2:5). Nehemiah had no doubt prayed about the right timing for approaching and making his request of King Artaxerxes, for he concludes his prayer in chapter 1 with these words: *Please grant me success now as I go to ask the king for a great favor. Put it into his heart to be kind to me* (1:11b, NLT).

Second, Nehemiah was also discerning in the timing of his challenge to Jerusalem's leaders to rebuild the wall. He had developed a tentative plan for the reconstruction work, but he confirmed or modified his plan through an on-site assessment of the status of the wall—his nighttime reconnaissance mission—so that he had firsthand knowledge of the situation prior to addressing the leaders and informing them of why he had come to the city. Notice the surveillance-like character of his words: *I slipped out during the night...I had not told anyone about the plans...I went out...to inspect...the city officials did not know...for I had not yet said anything to anyone about my plans...But now I said to them...* (see 2:11-18).

Perhaps Nehemiah took time to rest and refresh himself during the three days following his long journey, as well as to greet various leaders and officials, but surely their interest was piqued by the arrival of this fellow Jew, this cupbearer to the king no less, who had arrived with army officers and cavalry in his company. And while Nehemiah could have addressed them from the outset of his arrival, he waited for the right time.

Seven Timing-Related Recommendations for Leaders Today

What can we learn about deepening our sensitivity to God's timing from studying the book of Nehemiah? Consider these seven recommendations, each of which can help you discern strategic and micro level indicators of God's timing.

1. Listen to people.
   Nehemiah asked Hanani in chapter one about the condition of the people living in Judah, then he listened. His listening moved him to respond with weeping, prayer and fasting.

2. Listen to God.
   In his time of prayer and fasting he heard from God. He came to understand God's purposes for the city and his role in God's plans. Nehemiah referred to rebuilding the wall as what "God had put in my heart to do for Jerusalem" (2:12). He later reports that God also "put it into my heart" to assemble the leaders and common people for registration by families (7:5).

3. Listen to the Scriptures.
   Because Nehemiah listened to the Scriptures he knew how God wanted His people to live. He was no doubt schooled in the stipulations of the covenant and also was aware of the history of Israel. His zeal for reverencing God and living above reproach was fueled by his insights into the Scriptures (see especially the prayer in chapter 9, how the festivals

were celebrated in chapter 8, how the dedication ceremony was organized in chapter 12, and the reforms listed in chapter 13).

4. Listen to those around you.

Some leaders are too insecure to listen to those around them, but Nehemiah listened to Hanani, listened to the people report on the threat of attack, listened to those suffering financial oppression, listened to Ezra, and even listened to the impact of what his opponents were saying.

5. Listen to the circumstances.

What we mean here is that leaders should watch what is happening around them and look for the implications of what they see. Nehemiah listened to the circumstances described in by Hanani and was moved to pray. He listened to the threat of attack and counteracted it. He listened to what he saw in Hanani and Hananiah, observed that they were men of integrity who feared God more than most other men, and put them in charge, respectively, of the city and the citadel. He listened to the population of the city and was moved by God to lead the repopulation initiative.

6. Improve your listening skills.

Communication is a fundamental interpersonal relational skill, and it involves sending and understanding messages. Understanding messages is the listening part, and listening is a skill that can be improved. Strong leaders are often talkers. They have strong word gifts. They are convinced of their God-given vision. They want others too follow and can often be seen exhorting and communicating verbally. As public communicators they put a lot of work into increasing the effectiveness of sending (primarily talking) messages—and rightly so.

But all leaders can also increase their effectiveness by working on their listening skills. As they improve at listening to the Lord, to people, to circumstances, and to the Scriptures, etc., they will find that others seek them out for counsel and advice; that others will feel more cared for by them; that others will feel more valued and honored by them; that they will see different sides to an issue of problem that may have had them stumped; and that others will then feel more inclined to listen to them and be supportive of their change initiatives.

We encourage leaders to improve listening skills by:

- reading Covey's chapter on seeking first to understand, then to be understood[121]
- listening to tapes such as those available through Fuller Seminary's continuing education department on active listening[122]
- attending a seminar or workshop on active listening, then practicing the skills that were taught with people at home or at work
- taking one day per month for a personal prayer retreat to listen in a more intensive manner to the Lord and the Scriptures, especially to practice listening prayer[123]
- reading local newspapers
- prayer walking in different parts of the city or community to listen to the circumstances[124]

---

[121] See Covey's Habit 5 in **The Seven Habits of Highly Effective People**.

[122] Two that we have found helpful are "Improving Your Listening Skills" by Joan Sturkie and "Overcoming Seven Communication Barriers" by Gary Sweeten.

[123] Bill Hybels discusses the importance of listening in chapter 10 of **Too Busy Not to Pray**. A helpful book on listening to God is Loren Cunningham's **Is That Really You, God?**

[124] A helpful videocassette on this topic is "Prayerwalking Your City" featuring Pastor Ted Haggard.

- meeting with leaders outside their local organizations to for a cross-pollinization of perspectives

7. Evaluate your ministry philosophy.[125]

Ministry philosophy refers to ideas, values, and principles that a leader uses as guidelines for decision making, for exercising influence, and for evaluating his or her ministry. Three basal factors comprise the effective ministry philosophy:

- Scripture—as a leader experiences life he or she will see more truth in the Scriptures than at previous times. These new insights will shape and refine the ministry philosophy.

- Giftedness—Discovery of giftedness set and the prominence of certain gifts will affect ministry philosophy. Since effective leaders minister out of being, and giftedness is part of being, the effective philosophy of ministry will reflect the gifts of the leader.

- Situation—No two leadership situations are the same, and situation is affected by timing, both strategic and micro. At the strategic level, a ministry philosophy will be most effective when it reflects the larger work and purposes of God for a particular era or time period. At the micro level, it will flex somewhat depending on local organizational issues.

Closure

Let me repeat in closing:

- God's timing is crucial in the accomplishment of God's purposes.

- God's timing is noticeable at two levels, the strategic and the micro.

- Effective leaders will be increasingly aware of the level of the timing of God's interventions in their lives and ministry.

- Their sensitivity to His timing can deepen by practicing the seven recommendations discussed in this article.

So what do you understand about God's timing in your life and ministry at this point? Are you in alignment with His strategic level purposes? Are you sensitive to timing indicators on the micro level? Is it time to move forward or to wait? How would your colleagues, followers, and family members rate your listening skills?

We know we can say of Nehemiah that he sensed and took action in harmony with God's strategic level and micro level timing indicators in his life. He was sensitive to the *what, how, and **when*** of God's direction for his life and for Jerusalem.

---

[125] See Dr. Clinton's **The Making of a Leader**, chapter 8.

32. *Promises of God, The*

Introduction

Paul makes the following wonderful statement in the midst of a challenge to the Corinthians to give to a relief fund to help out Jerusalem Christians.

> 8 And God is able to provide more than you need. You will have what you need with some left over for giving. 2Co 9:8

I believe this to be a **promise** from God that is broader than just the Corinthians. When believers give cheerfully and generously and to meet God-directed needs, I believe they can expect God to enrich them to give. The right kind of attitude is crucial however. They don't give to get. They give because God gives them grace to give and gives them liberal and joyous hearts to give. And they surrender themselves to God for this giving ministry through them. When this is done, I believe this promise is as good as gold.

I also believe the equalizing principle is in effect.

> 13 I don't intend that you should give so much that you suffer for it. But there is an equalizing principle here. Right now you have more than you need and can help them out. Later you may have need and they may help you out.

If they give out of their surplus they can expect help when they have need. A Pauline leadership value occurs here.

> **Financial Equality Principle: Christian leadership must teach that Christian giving is a reciprocal balancing between needs and surplus.**

This equalizing principle, giving when we have abundance and others have need, and in turn receiving when we have needs and others have abundance, must be recognized, embraced, and then applied very carefully so as to not create dependencies.[126]
What I have just done is introduce you to the notion of a promise from God, but one that has conditions. God will supply. But we must generously give. We can give out of our surplus. Later there will be times when we don't have enough. Others will give to us.

---

[126] This principle is difficult for western Christians to see. For the most part western Christians don't realize just how wealthy they are when in comparison with many other non-western Christians. With no exposure to missions and churches around the world, Christians will rarely ever really embrace this principle. Leaders must raise awareness levels about needs around the world as well as teach this principle (and model it in their own lives).

Some promises are unconditional and are for all who want to appropriate them. Others promises are for a special group or person. Other promises have conditions. A leader must be able to discern promises of God, both for himself/herself, for the leadership situation, and for followers within his/her influence. This article defines a promise and gives some general guidelines about promises and introduces the image of God as *The Promise Keeper*.

Promises of God

When I was a little boy my friends and I would often say, "I promise." And the other person would say, "Cross your heart and hope to die?" The meaning was, "Do you really mean it?" Now little boys make and break promises about as fast as can be. But with God it is not so. One, He does not promise helter skelter like. And when He does promise He can be trusted. Our problem is learning to hear Him promise and being sure what we heard was a promise from Him, for us.

Definition   A <u>promise from God</u> is an assertion from God, specific or general or a truth in harmony with God's character, which is perceived in one's heart or mind concerning what He will do or not do for that one and which is sealed in our inner most being by a quickening action of the Holy Spirit and on which that one then counts.

There are three parts to the promise:

1. the cognitive part which refers to the assertion and its understanding, and
2. the affective part which is the inner most testimony to the promise, and
3. the volitional act of faith on our part which believes the assertion and feelings and thereafter counts upon it.

A leader can err in three ways, concerning promises. One, the leader may misread the assertion. That is, misinterpret what he/she thinks God will do or not do. Or two, the leader may wrongly apply some assertion to himself/herself which is does not apply. It may even be a true assertion but not for that leader or that time. Or the leader may misread the inner witness. It may not be God's Spirit quickening of the leader.

Sometimes the assertion comes from a command, or a principle, or even a direct statement of a promise God makes. The promise may be made generally to all who follow God or specifically to some. It may be for all time or for a limited time. Commands or principles are not in themselves promises. But it is when the Holy Spirit brings some truth out of them that He wants to apply to our lives that they may become promises. Such truths almost always bear on the character of God.

One thing we can know for certain, if indeed we do have a promise from God, then He will fulfill it. For Titus 1:2 asserts an important truth about God.

God can not lie.

He is the promise keeper. This is an image of God that all leaders need. God keeps his promises. He is the Promise Keeper. Table Ne 32-1 gives some examples to shore up our faith in **The Promise Keeper**. I could have chosen 100s of promises.[127]

---

[127] Over the years I have kept a listing of promises I felt God has made to me and my wife. Many of these have been fulfilled. In December of 1997 I reviewed all of these—an encouraging faith building exercise.

Table Ne 32-1. God The Promise Keeper—Examples

To Whom	Vs	Basic Promise/ Results
Abraham	Gen 12:1,2	Bless the world through Abraham. Give descendants. Spawn nations. Give a land. / This has happened and continues to happen.
Nahum	Whole book	Judgment on Nineveh/ Assyria. Promises fulfilled.
Obadiah	Whole book	Judgment on Edom. Promises fulfilled.
Habakkuk	Ch 2	Judgment on Babylon. Promises fulfilled. See Da 5.
Zechariah	Lk 1:13	Birth of John the Baptist. Promise fulfilled.
Mary	Lk 1:35	Birth of Jesus. Promise fulfilled.
Hezekiah	Isa 39:1ff, especially vs 5-7	Babylonian captivity. Royal hostages taken (Daniel was one of these). Promise fulfilled.
Daniel	Ch 2	The broad outlines of history/ nations and God's purposes. Promise fulfilled in part with more to come.
Daniel	Ch 9	Messiah and work of cross. Promise fulfilled.
Daniel	Ch 10-11:35	Again the broad outline of history particularly with reference to Israel. Everything up to 11:35 has taken place in detail as promises. The rest is yet to come.

Conclusion

The dictionary defines a promise as giving a pledge, committing oneself to do something, to make a declaration assuring that something will or will not be done or to afford a basis for expectation. Synonyms for promise include: covenant, engage, pledge, plight, swear, vow. The central meaning shared by these verbs is *to declare solemnly that one will perform or refrain from a particular course of action.* God is **The Promise Keeper**. As children of His we should learn to hear His promises and to receive them for our lives. As a leader you most likely will not make it over the long haul if you do not know God **as The Promise Keeper**.

One of the six characteristics[128] of a leader who finishes well is described as,

> **Truth is lived out in their lives so that convictions and promises of God are seen to be real.**

A leader who has God's promises and lives by them will exemplify this characteristic. Paul did. Paul, the model N.T. church leader knew God as **The Promise Keeper**. Do you?

See cognitive, affective, volitional; **Glossary**. See **Article**, *Principles of Truth*

---

[128] The six characteristics include: 1. They maintain a personal vibrant relationship with God right up to the end. 2. They maintain a learning posture and can learn from various kinds of sources—life especially. 3. They manifest Christ-likeness in character as evidenced by the fruit of the Spirit in their lives. 4. Truth is lived out in their lives so that convictions and promises of God are seen to be real. 5. They leave behind one or more ultimate contributions. 6. They walk with a growing awareness of a sense of destiny and see some or all of it fulfilled.

33. Prophetic Crises, 3 Major Biblical Times

Introduction
Years ago, when I took the class on prophets by James (Buck) Hatch, each of us was assigned a major project—do a chart on the prophets. Professor Hatch knew that the historical background was crucial to understanding the writing prophets. I still have that chart today and use it whenever I introduce any of the prophetic books. I am thankful to Professor Hatch for that project and his course that introduced me to each of the prophetic books. Getting perspective, on the times these books address, was a great leap forward in understanding them. Most of the writing prophets cluster around three major crises in the life of God's people. It is these prophetic crises, which prompted the rise of the prophetic ministry as reflected in the writing prophets.

1. The Assyrian Crisis
2. The Babylonian Crisis
3. The Restoration Crisis

Let me briefly describe each of these and identify the books, which speak to them.

General Background And Some Basic Definitions
Samuel's leadership ministry transitioned the commonwealth into a kingdom that Saul ruled over. This was followed by David's rule and then his son Solomon's rule. This sets the stage for God's disciplinary work among His people.

The Assyrian and the Babylonian Crises
The story line leading to the Assyrian crisis and the Babylonian crisis hinges around the following major events:
1. Solomon goes away from the Lord providing a great warning to all leaders—He had the best start of any king yet did not finish well. A good start does not insure a good finish.
2. Rehoboam (1 Kings 12) makes an unwise decision to increase taxes and demands on people—kingdom splits as prophecy said. 10 tribes go with the northern kingdom, Judah with the southern. A poor start might not be overcome.
3. The northern kingdom under Jereboam quickly departs from God. Jereboam is used as the model of an evil king to whom all evil kings are likened; He had a good start also—God would have blessed him. Abuse of power is a major barrier to finishing well.

4. The southern kingdom generally is bad with occasional good Kings and partially good kings: Asa, Jehoshaphat, Joash, Amaziah, Uzziah, Jotham, Hezekiah, Josiah. But the trend was always downward. The extended length of life of the southern kingdom more than the northern kingdom is directly attributed to the spiritual life of the better kings. Spiritual leadership does make a difference. Lack of spiritual leadership speeds up deterioration and leads to God's bypassing of the leadership structures and even destruction of the wayward people.

5. During both the northern and southern kingdoms God sent prophets to try and correct them—first the oral prophets (many—but the two most noted were Elijah and Elisha) and then the prophets who wrote.

Now in order to understand this long period of history you should know several things:
1. The History books that give background information about the times.
2. The Bible Time-Line, need to know when the books were written.
3. Need to know the writing prophets: northern or southern kingdom, which crisis, direct or special.

The History Books
    The history books covering the time of the destruction of a nation include 1, 2 Samuel, 1,2 Kings, and 1,2 Chronicles. The following chart helps identify the focus of each of these books as to major content.

Chart Neh 33-1 The History Books—Major Content

1 Samuel	2 Samuel 1 Chronicles	1,2 Kings 2 Chronicles
Samuel, Saul, David	David	1,2 Kings: Solomon to Zedekiah (gives time oriented details on northern and southern kingdoms) 2 Chronicles exclusively on line of Judah (southern kingdom)

    There are four categories of prophetical books. Prophetical books deal with three major crises: the Assyrian crisis which wiped out the northern kingdom; the Bablonian crisis which wiped out the southern kingdom; the return to the land after being exiled. There are also prophetical books not specifically dealing with these crises but associated with the time of them. The prophetical books dealing with these issues are:

Category 1. Northern—Assyrian Crisis
    Jonah, Amos, Hosea, Nahum, Micah

Category 2. Southern—Babylonian Crisis
    Joel, Isaiah, Micah, Zephaniah, Jeremiah, Lamentations, Habakkuk, Obadiah

Category 3. In Exile
    Ezekiel, Daniel, Esther

Category 4. Return From Exile—The Restoration Crisis

Nehemiah, Ezra, Haggai, Zechariah, Malachi

In addition, to knowing the crises you must know the prophets that wrote:

- A. Direct to the Issue of the Crisis either Assyrian, Babylonian, or Return To The Land—The Restoration Crisis. These were:
  Amos, Hosea, Joel, Micah, Isaiah, Jeremiah, Ezekiel, Haggai , Zechariah, Malachi

- B. Special-These were:
  Jonah, Nahum, Habakkuk, Obadiah, Zephaniah, Daniel.

The special prophets, though usually associated with one of the crisis times, wrote to deal with unique issues not necessarily related directly to the crisis. The following list gives the special prophets and their main thrust.

1. Jonah—a paradigm shift, pointing out God's desire for the nation to be missionary minded and reach out to surrounding nations. Assyria is the nation God uses to teach Jonah this important lesson.
2. Nahum—vindicate God, judgment on Assyria.
3. Habakkuk—faith crisis for Habakkuk, vindicate God, judgment on Babylon.
4. Obadiah—vindicate God, judgment on Edom for treatment of Judah.
5. Zephaniah—show about judgment, the Day of the Lord.
6. Daniel—give hope, show that God is indeed ruling even in the times of the exile and beyond, gives God's plan for the ages.

Having overviewed the story line that threads through the *Assyrian Crisis* and the *Babylonian Crisis* and briefly listed the Biblical books (both history and prophetical) that apply to these crises, we can move on to the *Restoration Crisis*.

The Restoration Crisis Overviewed

Several Bible books are associated with the return to the land from the exile. After a period of about 70 years (during which time Daniel ministered) Cyrus made a decree, which allowed some Jews (those that wanted to) to return to the land. Some went back under Zerubbabel, a political ruler like a governor. A priest, Joshua, also provided religious leadership to the first group that went back. This group of people started to rebuild the temple but became discouraged due to opposition and lack of resources. They stopped building the temple. Two prophets, after several years, 10-15, addressed the situation. These two, Haggai and Zechariah, were able to encourage the leadership and the people to finish the temple.

Another thirty or forty years goes by and then we have the events of the book of Esther, back in Persia. Her book describes the attempt to eradicate the Jewish exiles—a plot which failed due to God's sovereign intervention via Esther, the queen of the land and a Jewish descendant going incognito, and her relative Mordecai.

Still another period of time passes, 20 or so years and a priest, Ezra, directs another group to return to the land. The spiritual situation has deteriorated. He brings renewal.

Another kind of leader arrives on the scene some 10-15 years later. Nehemiah, a lay leader, and one adept at organizing and moving to accomplish a task, rebuilds the wall around Jerusalem. He too has to instigate renewal.

Finally, after another period of 30 or so years we have the book of Malachi which again speaks to renewal of the people. The Old Testament closes with this final book.

A recurring emphasis occurs during the period of the return. People are motivated to accomplish a task for God. They start out, become discouraged, and stop. They must be renewed. God raises up leadership to bring renewal.

Let me now introduce some important definitions before giving further detail on the *Restoration Crisis*.

Some Definitions

In my leadership literature I define two restoration terms that are important. They have some overlap but also need to be seen as distinct.

Definition   <u>Restoration</u> (individual leader) is the process whereby a fallen leader is transitioned back into leadership. It usually involves repentance, restitution where appropriate, correction of the aberrant leadership dysfunctions, and recognition by other leaders of the restoration process and their stamp of approval for the leader to renew ministry.

Definition   <u>Corporate restoration</u> refers to God's attempts to restore the people of God as a viable channel through whom He can work to carry out His Biblical purposes.

It is this latter definition that is important to the third major crisis—the *Restoration Crisis*.

Description   The <u>restoration crisis</u> refers to the period of time from 539 B.C. to 430 B.C. and which covers the activity of God in bringing His people back into the land and establishing a testimony there. His providential care of His people (both in the land and outside it) is also shown.

The Restoration Crisis—Further Details

While it is true that God attempts restoration efforts throughout almost all the leadership eras in both the O.T. and N.T., I define the *Restoration Crisis* as the time specifically dealing with the return of the exiles to the land and the aftermath activities that occurred. This means the time from 539 B.C. when Daniel initiated the time with his great intercessory prayer in Daniel 9 to around 430 B.C. when Malachi made a major thrust at restoration. Table Ne 33-1 gives a brief overview of this time. The major Biblical books dealing with the *Restoration Crisis* include: Ezra, Haggai, Zechariah, Ezra, Nehemiah, Esther, and Malachi.

Table Ne 33-1. The Restoration Era Crises And Related Biblical Material

Item	539 B.C.	536 B.C.	520-516 B.C.	486-465 B.C.	465-424 B.C.	430 B.C.
Restoration Activity	Daniel Prays	Work on Temple Begun	Work on Temple begun again and Completed	Israelites Preserved due to Esther and Mordecai's activities	Wall is constructed around Jerusalem—Ezra and Nehemiah bring about restoration movement	Malachi again engenders restoration movement
Biblical Material	Daniel 9	Ez 3:12	Ez 6:13-15 Haggai Zechariah	Esther	Nehemiah; latter part of Ezra	Malachi
Crises	1. God's Timing	2. Public Testimony Needed	3. Public Testimony Needed—Work	4. People of God Outside of	5. Protection of Jerusalem/ Public Testimony of	6. Leadership Nominality;

	and Faith	Back in the Land	Stopped	Land—Danger of being Destroyed	People	follower nominality

The themes of each of the biblical books dealing with the restoration crises should be seen in terms of the crises given above in Table Ne 33-1.

Table Ne 33-2 gives the theme of the relevant books along with the crisis that most likely prompted the activity of the book.

Table Ne 33-2. The Restoration Era Crises And Book Thematic Emphasis

Crisis	Book	Theme/ Brief Explanation Relating to Corporate Restoration
1. God's Timing and Faith	Daniel	**THE MOST HIGH** (sovereign God) **RULES** in the affairs of individuals, nations, and history. **Brief Explanation:** Daniel shows how God is sovereignly working out his purposes and lays out a time table for God's future work. Included in that book is the crucial identification of the 70 years in captivity and the time to begin the restoration effort in Jerusalem.
2. Public Testimony Needed Back in the Land	Ezra	See below for explanation of Ezra theme.
3. Public Testimony Needed—Work Stopped	Ezra	See below for Ezra Theme
	Haggai	**God's Work in Rebuilding the Temple** (Under Haggai's Prophetic Impact) began when His people back in the land were renewed and reprioritized their lives in response to God's Word, initially brought discouragement and was counteracted by God's promise of His presence and blessing as the rebuilders obeyed God's Word, continued to be fueled by a God-given vision of what it could be, not what it was, and carried with it God affirmation and promise of power to the leadership inspiring this work, in an overwhelming time.
	Zechariah	**THE WORKING OF THE LORD ALMIGHTY** involves encouragement in the present to leaders, brings correction and hope to sincere followers, and reveals His future plans so as to cause anticipation and encouragement. **Brief Explanation:** Corporate restoration is an on-going process. Hope along with restoration comes when we get perspective on what God is doing and will do in the future.
4. People of God Outside of Land—Danger of being Destroyed	Esther	**THE PROVIDENTIAL WORKING OF GOD** involves foresight which includes His use of apparently natural events and responses behind the scenes in *anticipation* of later events, will test leadership in the crisis, will have timely intervention in unusual yet natural events to protect, and will accomplish His purposes in the end. **Brief Explanation:** This shows that God is still working both outside the land as well as in the land. The left hand of God is seen in the affairs of preservation that Mordecai and Esther take part in. The Left Hand of God is an important concept in the whole restoration era.
5. Protection of Jerusalem/ Public	Ezra	**EFFECTIVE LEADERSHIP IN JERUSALEM UNDER EZRA** built on a foundation of that done by Haggai, Zechariah, Zerubbabel, and Joshua, and involved a call back to Biblical standards for the people in Jerusalem.

Testimony of People		**Brief Explanation:** The heart of corporate restoration is to have people understand God's revelation for them and to obey it. Ezra's ministry did this.
	Nehemiah	**NEHEMIAH'S ORGANIZATIONAL LEADERSHIP** made itself felt in the face of obstacles to rebuild the wall, was inspirational in bringing about reform and a covenant in Jerusalem, and included drastic steps of separation in order to insure an on-going meaningful religious atmosphere. **Brief Explanation:** This book emphasizes the importance of civil leadership working with religious leadership in bringing about corporate restoration.
6. Leadership Nominality; follower nominality	Malachi	**NOMINALITY**, religious form without power and meaning, reflects a lack of understanding of God's love, is manifested by half-hearted obedience which hinders God's purposes, is perpetuated by nominal leadership, and ultimately will be corrected by God. **Brief Explanation:** The heart of corporate restoration is to have people understand God's revelation for them and to obey it. Malachi, like Ezra's ministry, did this. Both Ezra and Malachi's ministries show that the people of God will tend toward nominality over time and need intervention ministries that will call them back to God.

The important macro lessons that are illustrated in the restoration crisis era include the following (numbers refer to a list of 41 macro lessons seen in the Bible):

19.	**Stability**	**Preserving a ministry of God with life and vigor over time is as much if not more of a challenge to leadership than creating one.**
20.	**Spiritual Leadership**	**Spiritual leadership can make a difference even in the midst of difficult times.**
21.	**Recrudescence**	**God will attempt to bring renewal to His people until they no longer respond to Him.**
22.	By-pass	God will by-pass leadership and structures that do not respond to Him and will institute new leadership and structures.
23.	Future Perfect	A primary function of all leadership is to walk by faith with a future perfect paradigm so as to inspire followers with certainty of God's accomplishment of ultimate purposes.
24.	**Perspective**	**Leaders must know the value of perspective and interpret present happenings in terms of God's broader purposes.**
25.	Modeling	Leaders can most powerfully influence by modeling godly lives, the sufficiency and sovereignty of God at all times, and gifted power.
26.	Ultimate	Leaders must remember that the ultimate goal of their lives and ministry is to manifest the glory of God.

27. Perseverance   Once known, leaders must persevere with the vision God has given.

Of these, macro lessons 19, 20, 21, 24 and 27 directly relate to corporate restoration.

General Lessons Learned From Perspective on The There Major Crises
In observing the length of time of the northern kingdom leading to the Assyrian Crisis as compared to the length of time of the southern kingdom leading to the Babylonian Crisis, a much longer time, one can emphasize strongly the spiritual leadership macro lesson.

20. Spiritual Leadership   Spiritual leadership can make a difference even in the midst of difficult times.

In observing the intervention times in all three prophetic crises, one cannot but help notice the crucial sense of timing involved in God's activity through the prophets.

3. Timing Macro-Lesson   God's Timing Is Crucial To Accomplishment Of God's Purposes.

We should also be warned. God has by-passed leadership and structures in the past, which did not respond to His warnings. This can happen again to us in our church leadership eras. We should be warned.

22. By-pass   God will by-pass leadership and structures that do not respond to Him and will institute new leadership and structures.

In general, we note that if we are to be Bible Centered leaders who apply O.T. scriptures appropriately in our N.T. Church leadership era, we must study carefully the details of the historical background surrounding these O.T. writing. We must adhere carefully to the General Hermeneutical principle involved with historical background.

Historical Background Hermeneutical Principle
In The Spirit, Prayerfully Study The Historical Background Of The Book Which Includes Such Information As:
   a. the author of the book and the *historical perspective* from which he/she wrote.
   b. the *occasion* for the book
   c. the *purpose* for the book including where pertinent the people for whom it was intended and their situation.
   d. any geographical or cultural factors bearing on the communication of the material.

Closure
Perspective makes a difference. The difference between leaders and followers is perspective. The difference between leaders and more effective leaders is better perspective. Leaders today need perspective on how God has worked. To understand the writing prophets, the three major crises detailed in this article become very significant. Bible centered leaders who want to apply concepts from the writing prophets to today's ministry must understand the historical background associated with these major crises.

34. Restoration Leaders

Introduction

In my leadership literature I define two restoration terms that are important. They have some overlap but also need to be seen as distinct.

Definition	Restoration (individual leader) is the process whereby a fallen leader is transitioned back into leadership. It usually involves repentance, restitution where appropriate, correction of the aberrant leadership dysfunctionalities, and recognition by other leaders of the restoration process and their stamp of approval for the leader to renew ministry.
Definition	Corporate restoration refers to God's attempts to restore the people of God as a viable channel through whom He can work to carry out His Biblical purposes.

It is this latter definition that is important to the third major crisis—the *Restoration Crisis*, which has to do with our notion of restoration leaders.

Description	The restoration crisis refers to the period of time from 539 B.C. to 430 B.C. and which covers the activity of God in bringing His people back into the land and establishing a testimony there. His providential care of His people (both in the land and outside it) is also shown.
Definition	Restoration leaders refer to the important leaders—civil, religious, and prophetical—who worked during the restoration crisis years to bring some kind of recrudescence to God's people.

This article will list several of these leaders and give an overall evaluation of their restoration leadership.

The Restoration Crisis Overviewed

Several Bible books are associated with the return to the land from the exile. After a period of about 70 years (during which time Daniel ministered) Cyrus made a decree, which allowed some Jews (those that wanted to) to return to the land. Some went back under **Zerubbabel,** a political ruler like a governor. A priest, **Joshua,** also provided religious leadership to the first group that went back. This group of people started to rebuild the temple but became discouraged due to opposition and lack of resources. They stopped building the temple. Then two prophets, after several years, 10-15, addressed the situation. These two, **Haggai** and **Zechariah**, were able to encourage the leadership and the people to finish the temple.

Another thirty or forty years go by and then we have the events of the book of Esther, back in the land. Her book describes the attempt to eradicate the Jewish exiles—a plot which failed due to God's sovereign intervention via **Esther**, the queen of the land and a Jewish descendant going incognito, and her relative **Mordecai**.

Still another period of time passes, 20 or so years and a priest, **Ezra**, directs another group to return to the land. The spiritual situation has deteriorated. He brings renewal.

Another kind of leader arrives on the scene some 10-15 years later. **Nehemiah**, a lay leader, actually a civil leader, and one adept at organizing and moving to accomplish a task, rebuilds the wall around Jerusalem. He too has to instigate renewal.

Finally, after another period of 30 or so years we have the book of **Malachi**, which again speaks to renewal of the people. The Old Testament closes with this final book.

A recurring emphasis occurs during the period of the return. People are motivated to accomplish a task for God. They start out, become discouraged, and stop. They must be renewed. God raises up leadership to bring renewal.

Restoration Leaders
Restoration leaders are listed along with times and the basic restoration activity and crisis involved.

Table Ne 34-1 The Restoration Era Crises And Restoration Leaders

Item	539 B.C.	536 B.C.	520-516 B.C.	486-465 B.C.	465-424 B.C.	430 B.C.
Restoration Activity	Daniel Prays	Work on Temple Begun	Work on Temple begun again and Completed	Israelites Preserved due to Esther and Mordecai's activities	Wall is constructed around Jerusalem—Ezra and Nehemiah bring about restoration movement	Malachi again engenders restoration movement
Restoration Leader	Daniel	Joshua Zerubbabel	Haggai Zechariah	Esther Mordecai	Nehemiah; Ezra	Malachi
Crises	1. God's Timing and Faith	2. Public Testimony Needed Back in the Land	3. Public Testimony Needed—Work Stopped	4. People of God Outside of Land—Danger of being Destroyed	5. Protection of Jerusalem/ Public Testimony of People	6. Leadership Nominality; follower nominality
Results	Cyrus gives decree; God's Restoration activity begins.	People go back to the land; they establish homes and lay the foundation for the	People start again on building God's temple; eventually it is completed.	Jewish people in exile are preserved.	Nehemiah sees walls rebuilt; Ezra sees revival and folks following God's word.	Not sure; but people are certainly made aware of God's desires for

		temple				them.

Macro Lessons Emphasized By Restoration Ministry

The important macro lessons that are strongly illustrated in the ministry of these restoration leaders include the following (numbers refer to a list of 41 macro lessons seen in the Bible):

19. Stability	Preserving a ministry of God with life and vigor over time is as much if not more of a challenge to leadership than creating one.

All of the restoration leaders (probably apart from Esther and Mordecai) illustrate this.

21. Recrudescence	**Kingdom God will attempt to bring renewal to His people until they no longer respond to Him.**

This is certainly a conviction of Ezra, Haggai, and Zechariah who ministered to bring spiritual renewal.

22. By-pass	God will by-pass leadership and structures that do not respond to Him and will institute new leadership and structures.

The inclusion of civil leaders like Zerubbabel and Nehemiah, along with priests like Ezra and Joshua and prophetic leaders like Haggai, Zechariah and Malachi, certainly demonstrate this macro lesson. The kingdom structure was bypassed. What the new structures will be is not clear from this part of Biblical history. But leaders and leader functions necessary are seen.

27. Perseverance	**Once known, leaders must persevere with the vision God has given.**

Haggai and Nehemiah particularly emphasize this macro lesson.

Closure

Leaders attentive to God and who want to see vital relationships renewed between God and His people can be used to see this happen, no matter how bleak the situation around them. God is still the Lord Almighty. Further, no work of God is small if God is in it. The general restoration activity back in the land took part with a small remnant. Compared to the earlier days of the kingdom, the work seemed very small. But God was in it and used it as a foundation later for Messiah to come. Restoration leaders are needed especially in our Church Leadership Era where so many Christian groups have become nominal. We need to study these restoration leaders in the O.T. to be inspired by what they did and to know the Lord Almighty they knew.

See **Article**, *Haggai—Calendar and Dating; Restoration Leaders; Civil Leadership, The Missing Ingredient; 15. Left Hand of God; 1. Biblical Framework, The Redemptive Drama; 35. Six Biblical Leadership Eras—Approaching the Bible With Leadership Eyes; 16. Macro Lesson, Defined; Macro Lessons, 17. List of 41 Across Six Leadership Eras.*

35. Six Biblical Leadership Eras
Approaching the Bible with Leadership Eyes

Introduction

In my opinion, the Bible provides one of the richest resources that Christian leaders have on leadership. The Bible is full of leadership insights, lessons, values and principles about leaders and leadership. It is filled with influential people and the results of their influence... both good and bad.

Three assumptions undergird what I will say in this article.

1. I have a strong **conviction** that the Bible can give valuable leadership insights.
2. I have made a **willful decision** to study the Bible and use it as a source of leadership insights.[129]
3. To study the Bible for leadership insights, you need **leadership eyes** to see leadership findings in the Bible. That is, there are many leadership perspectives, i.e. paradigms, that help stimulate one to see leadership findings. I have been discovering and using these in my own study.

I want to do three things in this keynote overview. I want to introduce two most helpful perspectives for studying the Bible for leadership findings: 1. Seeing Leadership Eras; 2. Recognizing Leadership Genre. I will give more space to *the Six Leadership Eras*. These two concepts will help give one *leadership eyes*. And then I want to talk about the impact of the two most important boundary times between leadership eras, Moses desert leadership and Jesus' foundational work instigating a major movement. Both of these were fundamental and foundational times of Biblical leadership. They introduced radical macro lessons that deeply impact our own leadership today.

The Six Leadership Eras

A first step toward having *leadership eyes*, for recognizing leadership findings in the Bible involves seeing the various leadership eras in the Bible. These time periods share common leadership assumptions and expectations. These assumptions and expectations differ markedly from one leadership time period to the next. Though, of course, there are commonalties that bridge across the eras.

Definition   A <u>leadership era</u> is a period of time, usually several hundred years long,[130] in which the major focus of leadership, the influence means, basic

---

[129] I have been doing this deliberately for ten years at this writing.

[130] There is one exception. Though technically, the N.T. Pre-Church Era includes the inter-testamental time, I only really focus on Jesus' ministry which lasted a short period of time. But it is so unique and so radically different from what preceded and followed it that I treat it as the essential time in this era.

leadership functions, and followership have much in common and which basically differ with time periods before or after it.

Table Ne 35-1 contains the outline of the six eras I have identified.

Table Ne 35-1. Six Leadership Eras Outlined

Era	Label/ Details
I.	**Patriarchal Era** (Leadership Roots)—Family Base
II.	**Pre-Kingdom Leadership Era**—Tribal Base A. The Desert Years B. The War Years—Conquering the Land, C. The Tribal Years/ Chaotic Years/ Decentralized Years—Conquered by the Land
III.	**Kingdom Leadership Era**—Nation Based A. The United Kingdom B. The Divided Kingdom C. The Single Kingdom—Southern Kingdom Only
IV.	**Post-Kingdom Leadership Era**—Individual/ Remnant Based A. Exile—Individual Leadership Out of the Land B. Post Exilic—Leadership Back in the Land C. Interim—Between Testaments
V.	**New Testament Pre-Church Leadership**—Spiritually Based in the Land A. Pre-Messianic B. Messianic
VI.	**New Testament Church Leadership**—Decentralized Spiritually Based A. Jewish Era B. Gentile Era

The three overarching elements of leadership include: the *leadership basal elements* (leader, follower, situation which make up the **What** of leadership); *leadership influence means* (individual and corporate leadership styles which make up the **How** of leadership); and *leadership value bases* (theological and cultural values which make up the **Why** of leadership).[131] It was this taxonomy which suggested questions that helped me see for the first time the six leadership eras of the Bible. It is these categories that allow comparison of different leadership periods in the Bible. Later I will apply the taxonomy to each of the eras and give my preliminary findings.

Using these leadership characteristics I studied leadership across the Bible and inductively generated the six leadership eras as given above. Table Ne 35-2 adds some descriptive elements of the eras.

---

[131] See the **Article**, *Leadership Tree Diagram*, which explains in details these three elements of leadership.

Table Ne 35-2. Six Leadership Eras in the Bible—Definitive Characteristics

Leadership Era	Example(s) Leader(s)	Definitive Characteristics
1. Foundational (also called Patriarchal)	Abraham, Joseph	Family Leadership/ formally male dominated/ expanding into tribes and clans as families grew/ moves along kinship lines.
2. Pre-Kingdom	Moses, Joshua, Judges	Tribal Leadership/ Moving to National/ Military/ Spiritual Authority/ outside the land moving toward a centralized national leadership.
3. Kingdom	David, Hezekiah	National Leadership/ Kingdom Structure/ Civil, Military/ Spiritual/ a national leadership—Prophetic call for renewal/ inside the land/ breakup of nation.
4. Post-Kingdom	Ezekiel, Daniel, Ezra, Nehemiah	Individual leadership/ Modeling/ Spiritual Authority.
5. Pre-Church	Jesus/ Disciples	Selection/ Training/ spiritual leadership/ preparation for decentralization of Spiritual Authority/ initiation of a movement.
6. Church	Peter/ Paul/ John	decentralized leadership/ cross-cultural structures led by leaders with spiritual authority which institutionalize the movement and spread it around the world.

When we study a leader or a particular leadership issue in the Scripture, we must always do so in light of the leadership context in which it was taking place. We cannot judge past leadership by our present leadership standards. Yet, we will find that major leadership lessons learned by these leaders will usually have broad implications for our leadership.

Second Major Perspective for Getting Leadership Eyes—The Seven Leadership Genre

Further study of each of these leadership eras resulted in the identification of seven leadership genre which served as sources for leadership findings. I then worked out in detail approaches for studying each of these genre.[132] These seven leadership genre are shown in Table Ne 35-3.

Table Ne 35-3. Seven Leadership Genre—Sources for Leadership Findings

Type	General Description/ Example	Approach
1. Biographical	Information about leaders; this is the single largest genre giving leadership information in the Bible/ **Joseph**	Use biographical analysis based on leadership emergence theory concepts.
2. Direct Leadership Contexts[133]	Blocks of Scripture which are giving information directly applicable to leaders/ leadership; relatively few of these in Scripture/ **1 Peter 5:1-4**	Use standard exegetical techniques.
3. Leadership Acts[134]	Mostly narrative vignettes describing a leader influencing followers, usually in some crisis situation; quite a few of	Use three-fold leadership tree diagram as basic source for suggesting what areas of leadership to look for.

[132] See **Leadership Perspectives—How To Study the Bible for Leadership Findings**. Altadena: Barnabas Publishers.
[133] I have identified many of the direct leadership texts and exegetically analyzed the important ones.
[134] Many leadership acts have been identified and more than 20 have been analyzed. There is much work to do on analyzing leadership acts.

	these in the Bible/ **Acts 15 Jerusalem Council**	
4. Parabolic Passages[135]	Parables focusing on leadership perspectives: e.g. stewardship parables, futuristic parables; quite a few of these in Matthew and Luke./ **Luke 19 The Pounds**	Use standard parable exegetical techniques but then use leadership perspectives to draw out applicational findings; especially recognize the leadership intent of Jesus in giving these. Most such parables were given with a view to training disciples.
5. Books as a Whole	Each book in the Bible[136]; end result of this is a list of leadership observations or lessons or implications for leadership/ **Deuteronomy**	Consider each of the Bible books in terms of the leadership era in which they occur and for what they contribute to leadership findings; will have to use whatever other leadership genre source occurs in a given book; also use overall synthesis thinking.
6. Indirect Passages	Passages in the Scripture dealing with Biblical values applicable to all; more so to leaders who must model Biblical values/ **Proverbs; Sermon on the Mount**	Use standard exegetical procedures for the type of Scripture containing the applicable Biblical ethical findings or values.
7. Macro Lessons[137]	Generalized high level leadership observations seen in an era and which have potential for leadership absolutes/ **Presence Macro**	Use synthesis techniques utilizing various leadership perspectives to stimulate observations.

The Criteria For Evaluating An Era

What Are the Distinguishing Characteristics We Are Looking For? I have used the following categories:

1. Major Focus—

Here we are looking at the overall purposes of leadership for the period in question. What was God doing or attempting to do through the leader? Sense of destiny? Leadership mandate?

2. Influence means—

Here we are describing any of the power means available and used by the leaders in their leadership. We can use any of Wrong's categories or any of the leadership style categories I define. Note particularly in the Old Testament the use of force and manipulation as power means.

3. Basic leadership functions—

We list here the various achievement responsibilities expected of the leaders: from God's standpoint, from the leader's own perception of leadership, from the followers. Usually they can all be categorized under the three major leadership functions of task, relational, and inspirational functions. But here we are after the specific functions.

---

[135] I have studied every parable, exegetically, in Matthew, Mark and Luke for its central truth and applicable leadership lessons.

[136] I have done this for each book in the Bible over the past 10 years. My findings are included in **The Bible and Leadership Values** (and in the commentary series). Though I have made a good start, there is much more to be done here. I am intending other Handbooks which include all of the top 25 Bible books on leadership.

[137] This area needs the most research. Several PhD research projects are now focused on this.

4.Followers—
Here we are after sphere of influence. Who are the followers? What are their relationship to leaders? Which of the 10 Commandments of followership are valid for these followers? What other things are helpful in describing followers?

5. Local Leadership—
In the surrounding culture: Biblical leaders will be very much like the leaders in the cultures around them. Leadership styles will flow out of this cultural press. Here we are trying to identify leadership roles in the cultures in contact with our Biblical leaders.

6. Other:
Miscellaneous catch all; such things as centralization or decentralization or hierarchical systems of leadership; joint (civil, political, military, religious) or separate roles.

Thought Questions—
In addition to the above categories, I try to synthesize the questions that I would like answered about leaders and leadership if I could get those answers. With these thought questions I am considering such things as the essence of a leader (being or doing), leadership itself, leadership selection and training, authority (centralized or decentralized), etc.

My preliminary findings for these categories for each leadership era follows.

1st Leadership Era: Patriarchal Leadership
1. **Major Focus—**Pass on the promise and heritage of the Most High God to the family; priestly role (regularity)—intercede, sacrifice, and worship the Most High God;
2. **Influence means—**apostolic style, father-initiator, father-guardian, full range of Wrong's typology: force, manipulation, authority (coercive, inducive, positional—fatherly head, competence, personal), spiritual authority
3. **Five basic leadership functions—**(1) Godly/ priestly functions:- demonstrate absolute loyalty to God; - demonstrate reality of the unseen God; - pass on heritage of what is known (revelatory) of God and His ways and desires, very little revelation, animistic; - pass on sense of destiny; —God's prophetic promises; (2) Primarily performing the inspirational function—largely through modeling; the relational function consisted primarily of keeping the family together and obedience to the patriarch. Inspirational function -Creating hope in God -Creating sense of God's intervention in life; (3) Mediate Blessing of God: - contagious blessing; - heritage blessing; (4) Military head—protection of family; (5) Civil—judge/ justice
4. **Followers—**family members: (1) Age/masculine-oriented; (2) Almost all of 10 Followership Laws in force; (3) Oldest to receive blessing and birthright; (4) The one receiving blessing and birthright passes it on to next generation
5. **Local Leadership—**in the culture around the Patriarchs: - tribal heads; - City States / Regional heads (called kings);
   - local priests (practitioners/ animistic); - local military
6. **Other:** Highly Decentralized; each given family responsible to God

Thought Questions—1. How did other families relate to God (Melchezidek's, Labin's, etc.)? 2. What were expectations of Patriarchs as leaders? by followers? by God? by surrounding culture? 3. What was the foundational aspect of character? What was integrity to the Patriarchs? 4. What was the birthright? What was the blessing? 5. If modeling was the primary training methodology, what were the most important positive leadership qualities modeled by Abraham? by Isaac? by Jacob? by Joseph? by Job? 6. Using a modified form of the six characteristics of finishing well, how did the Patriarchs finish? Abraham? Isaac? Jacob? Joseph? Job?

2nd Leadership Era: Pre-Kingdom Leadership

1 .**Major Focus**—Uniting of a people, preparing them to follow God, preparing them to invade the promised land, settling them in the land. The Desert leadership is one of discipline, a heavy time of revelation, and supernatural events backing leadership. The Challenge Era is one of stretching of faith to overcome the many obstacles involved in capturing the land. The Judges Era has the major challenge of how to unite disparate peoples, survive attacks, and correct degeneration of relationship to God. In each there is Charismatic Leadership: You lead because of spiritual authority, personal authority or competence not because of nepotism or birth; a formal priestly role is secondary—there is an inheritance with this role—and this leadership is weak, probably because of that.

2 .**Influence means**—apostolic style, father-initiator, father-guardian, full range of Wrong's typology: force, manipulation, authority (coercive, inducive, positional—fatherly head, competence, personal), spiritual authority

3 .**Seven basic leadership functions** seen include: (1) Centralize Authority/ Develop Authority Structures:- military, political, religious;- tribal/ trans-tribal (elders); (2) Primarily performing the inspirational function: -Creating hope in God; -Creating sense of God's intervention in life. (3) Revelatory (Desert)/Inscribe and pass on the basic revelation of God as given in the law/how to live separated lives; (4) Military head—protection/ mobilize an on-call army distributed over the tribes; (5) Civil—judge/ justice/ set up legal system for interpreting and applying the law; (6) Fulfill Promise of Taking the Land; settling it; (7) Call to renewal; recrudescence; see God work anew.

4 .**Followers**—12 large tribes:(1) Age/ masculine-oriented leadership; (2) Almost all of 10 Followership Laws in force; centralization out of balance; leadership more nepotistic than functional; reciprocal commands a legalistic thing carried by enforcement of law.

5 .**Local Leadership**—in the surrounding culture:- tribal heads; - City State / Regional heads (called kings); - local priests (practitioners/ animistic); - local military

6. **Other**: Highly centralized during desert and capturing of land; highly decentralized during Judges era/ continuity of leadership a major problem except for the first transition from Moses to Joshua

Thought Questions:
1. How were leaders selected and developed? 2. What did they do at the different levels? 3. What is missing from the Judges Era that was the driving force of the Warfare Era? 4. What has happened to the Abrahamic mandate? Which of the eras, if any, are concerned with that mandate? 5. How does this era compare with the Patriarchal, spiritually?

3rd Leadership Era: Kingdom Leadership

1. **Major Focus**—The Kingdom united the dispersed tribal groups into a more cohesive nation which could provide government and military protection. The Davidic covenant was part of an on-going means to bring about Abraham's promise and to manifest the concept of God's rule on earth as well as provide resources to bring others into relationship with God. It never lived up to its ideals.

2. **Influence means**—the full range of Wrong's typology : **force, manipulation, authority** (coercive, inducive, positional)—fatherly head; competence, personal, spiritual authority.

3. **Six basic leadership functions** seen include:(1) Centralize Authority/ Develop Authority Structures:- military, political, religious; - tribal/ trans-tribal (elders); (2) Revelatory (Particularly in the Divided Kingdom and the Single Kingdom)/ Much of the corrective revelation done by the prophets was oral. But there was also the Prophetic revelation which was inscribed. Often these writings were a call to repentance, renewal, and a return to kingdom ideals; (3) Military head—protection/ have a standing army that

could defend against the attacks that were coming more frequently from the expanding empires or ambitious kings. They would also mobilize an on-call army distributed over the tribes to go along with the standing army in big crises. (4) Civil—judge/justice/set up legal system for interpreting and applying the law; (5) Call to renewal; recrudescence; see God work anew (prophetic function); (6) Persevere as a people of God; maintain a base from which God could work. Major Problems: communication and control; followership scattered over large area; -large empires on the rise

4. Followers—a. United Kingdom-12 large tribes, also the many surrounding small kingdoms that were conquered

b. Divided Kingdom—Northern-10 1/2 Large Tribes c. Southern—About 1 1/2 tribes—mostly Judah; Leadership (1) Age/ masculine oriented; (2) Almost all of 10 Followership Laws in force; centralization out of balance; leadership more nepotistic than functional;

5. Local Leadership—in the surrounding cultures: - tribal heads; - kings of territories with a number of cities; usually one dominated and was walled; - local priests (practitioners/ animistic); - military.

6. Other: Large Empires are vying for world dominion or at least for large influence: Assyria, Egypt, Babylon

Thought Questions:1. Why were the prophets raised up? 2. According to Deuteronomy what was the place of the law for the Kings? Was it followed? 3. Was the central religious function (the three yearly treks) carried out? 4. Why was the nepotistic approach to leadership selection used? Was it successful? 5. How does this era compare spiritually with the Pre-Kingdom era?

4th Leadership Era: Post-Kingdom Leadership

1. Major Focus—The nation no longer exists. It has been disciplined by God. Leadership during this time must do several things: analyze what happened and why; bring hope during this time; demonstrate the importance of godliness under oppressive conditions; demonstrate the importance of God's sovereignty; point to the future in which God is going to work.

2. Influence means—largely by modeling, spiritual authority, toward latter time in the time of the return, Jewish leaders again take up roles: political, religious, quasi-military for the Jewish people.

3. Basic leadership functions seen include: The inspirational function is dominant. The need for community in little pockets brings out the need for the relational function of leadership. The rise of the synagogues—small communities upholding their Jewish origins and religion bring about the need for scribes, and those who interpret the written scriptures.

4. Followers—Pockets of scattered Jewish people

5. Local Leadership—in the surrounding cultures: - tribal heads; - City States / Regional heads (called kings); - local priests (practitioners/ animistic); - local military; - emperors/ kings/ heads of powerful international groups formed by conquering vast territories and kingdoms/ various administrative leaders under these

6. Other: ?

Thought Questions: 1. Why did Jewish leaders prosper during these oppressive days? 2. What kinds of leadership did they participate in? 3. What has happened to the Abrahamic promise? How did the Jewish people feel about it in these days? 4.   How were religious leaders selected (e.g. for the synagogues)?

5th Leadership Era: Pre-Church Leadership

1. Major Focus—Galatians 4:4. This is the acme of charismatic leadership. Jesus models servant leadership and ideal spiritual authority—all aspects of it. The end result of this leadership is revelation, redemption, and a movement to universalize the redemption to all humankind.

2. Influence Means—the entire range of Pauline leadership styles are demonstrated. The whole range of Wrong's Typology is seen.

3. Leadership Functions: (1) Provide the redemptive base reconciling God and humankind and its major ramifications, the revelation and enabling power for human beings to realize their idealized human potential.

(2) Provide a leadership mandate that will utilize all three major leadership functions in its fulfillment. Task, relational, and inspirational functions are essential to the accomplishment of the mandate. (3) Create a movement that will institutionalize the leadership functions for on-going effective leadership. (4) Provide a call for renewal to Israel. (5) Present the Kingdom of God in concept and power. (6) Provide a revelatory base, model, and standards for future revelation.

4. Followers—In the land there were remnants of the tribes, mixed ethnic groups (like Samaritans), religious leadership like the Pharisees, Saducees, and the political leaders of the Roman empire along with garrisons of Roman Military to give authority as well as the Jewish Religious leaders the Sanhedrin.

5. Local Leaders: Sanhedrin, Saducees, Pharisees, Lawyers, Roman Military, Synagogues/ elders, Rabbis.

6. Other: This is a mixed era of centralized and decentralized means and authority. Jerusalem provided some means of religious centralization. There was political centralization in a number of centers. But Jesus leadership was not centralized.

Thought Questions:1. What renewal aims did Christ specifically focus on? 2. What were the leadership selection and development processes in existence in the culture? 3. What were Jesus' leadership selection and development processes? How different? 4. How does Christ leadership compare or contrast with essential characteristics of each of the previous eras?

6th Leadership Era: Church Leadership

1. Major Focus—When Barnabas and Paul give their report to the elders back in Jerusalem at the Jerusalem conference described in Acts 15, there is much discussion. Finally, James summarizes the essence of the major focus of the Church leadership era, "Simon has declared how God at the first did visit the Gentiles, to take out of them a people for his name (Acts 15;14)." The central message of the book of Acts emphasizes this thrust in more detail. THE GROWTH OF THE CHURCH which spreads from Jerusalem to Judea to Samaria and the uttermost parts of the earth is seen to be of God, takes place as Spirit directed people present a salvation centered in Jesus Christ, and occurs among all peoples, Jews and Gentiles. During this leadership era, God is developing an institution that will carry His salvation to all cultures and all peoples. The development of this decentralized institution which can be fitted to any culture and people, the church, with its nature its leadership and its purposes for existing will be at the heart of this leadership era. Paul is a major architect of this leadership era. The book of 2 Corinthians is especially helpful to give us insights into early church leadership.

2. Influence Means—My past leadership studies have identified a number of leadership styles. In particular, I have categorized ten Pauline leadership styles. The entire range of Pauline leadership styles are demonstrated during the Church Leadership Era. The whole range of Wrong's Typology is seen including force, manipulation, authority, and persuasion power forms.

3. Leadership Functions—All three of the generic leadership functions are prominent: task oriented leadership, relationship oriented leadership and inspirational leadership. The major models for this era include Peter, John, and Paul with much more information given about Paul. Paul is dominantly a task-oriented leader with a powerful inspirational focus. He sees the necessity of relationship oriented leadership but that is not his strength. John is more of a relationship-oriented leader who also has a powerful inspirational thrust. Peter is dominantly a task oriented leader with inspirational thrust. As each matures they become more gentle—that is, relational leadership begins to come to the front. But always they are dominantly inspirational. God is creating new forms through which to reveal Himself to the world and followers must be inspired to participate and carry it all over the world in the face of persecution and obstacles.

4. Followers—The beauty of the church lies in its ability as an institutional form to fit into any culture. Since leadership in a given culture is defined in part by the followers expectations of what a leader is, we will have distinctive differences in various cultures as to leadership and followership. Each cultural situation will be different and hence have its unique demands. But there are commonalties in Biblical church leadership across cultures. This is seen especially in the values which determine why leaders operate and the standards by which they are judged. The book of 2 Corinthians helps us understand key leadership values.

5. Local Leaders—Various kinds of models of leadership existed in the various cultures. Paul, the main architect of local church leadership, gives us various descriptions of qualitative characteristics of leaders in his various epistles. The essential trait that flows throughout all of them is integrity. But Paul having described key character traits recognizes that these will manifest themselves differently in different cultures and situations.

6. Other—The church leadership era is a highly decentralized period of time. Churches are to exist in all cultures and peoples. They will be spread far and wide. Because of the decentralized nature of the church it is especially important to ask what unites it? What is common? Particularly is this important for leadership. And one of the answers is leadership values. 2 Corinthians helps us see some of the values that Paul modeled.

The Findings—The Best of Each Era

Table Ne 35-4 summarizes the more important aspects of each of the leadership eras.

Table Ne 35-4. Six Leadership Eras, On-Going Impact Items, Follow-Up

Era	On-Going Impact Items And Areas For Follow-Up Study
1. Patri-archal	Destiny leadership; Introduction of biographical study of leadership (Abraham, Isaac, Jacob, Joseph, Job); God's shaping processes introduced; intercession macro lesson introduced; character strength highlighted (Abraham, Jacob, Joseph); leadership responsibility to God instigated (accountability); leadership responsibility to followers introduced (blessing); leadership intimacy with God introduced (Abraham—friend of God, Job—trusting in deep processing). **Key Macro Lesson**: Destiny—Leaders must have a sense of destiny.
2. Pre-Kingdom	Seven Macro lessons from Moses' desert leadership (Timing; Intimacy; Intercession; Burden; Presence; Hope; Transition); Spiritual authority highlighted in Moses' and Joshua's ministries; pitfalls of centralized leadership seen; pitfalls of decentralized leadership seen; roots of inspirational leadership seen (Moses, Joshua, Caleb, Deborah, Jephthah, Samuel, David); outstanding biographical genre material. **Key Macro Lesson**: Presence—The essential ingredient of leadership is the powerful presence of God in the leader's life and ministry.
3. Kingdom	Five macros carry a warning for all future leadership (Unity; Stability; Spiritual Leadership; Recrudescence; By-Pass). Excellent biographical material both positive and negative examples (Saul, David, Asa, Josiah, Uzziah, Hezekiah, Elijah, Elisha, Jonah, Habakkuk, Ezekiel, Jeremiah and many others). **Key Macro Lesson**: Spiritual leadership can make a difference in the midst of difficult times.
4. Post-Kingdom	All five macros stress revelational perspective (Future Perfect; Perspective; Modeling; Ultimate, Perseverance). Excellent biographical genre available (Ezekiel, Daniel, Ezra, Nehemiah). **Key Macro Lesson**: Future Perfect—A primary function of all leadership is to walk by faith with a future perfect paradigm so as to inspire followers with certainty of God's accomplishment of ultimate purposes.

5. Pre-Church	Selection/ Training/ spiritual leadership/ preparation for decentralization of Spiritual Authority/ initiation of a movement. Major Biographical— Jesus' and his movement leadership. **Key Macro Lesson**: Focus—Leaders must increasingly move toward a focus in their ministry which moves toward fulfillment of their calling and their ultimate contribution to God's purposes for them.
6. Church	Decentralized leadership/ cross-cultural structures led by leaders with spiritual authority, which institutionalize the movement and spread it around the world. Excellent biographical (Peter, Barnabas—a bridge leader, Paul, John); numerous leadership acts. **Key Macro Lesson**: Universal—The church structure is universal and can fit any culture. It must be propagated to all peoples.

The Foundational Transitions—Moses' And Jesus' Leadership Eras

Three figures give perspectives on Biblical leadership. Figure Ne 35-1 illustrates the relative time involved in the six leadership eras. Figure Ne 35-2 pinpoints distinctive features of leadership across the time-line. Figure Ne 35-3 focuses on the two major transitions—Moses' Desert Leadership; Jesus' Movement Leadership.

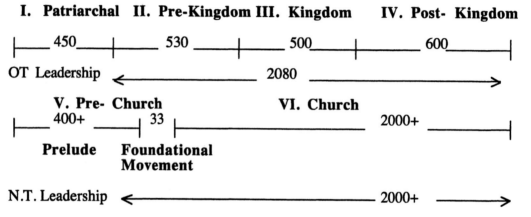

Figure Ne 35-1. Leadership Eras— Rough Chronological Length In Years

I. Patriarchal Leadership Roots	II. Pre-Kingdom Leadership	III. Kingdom Leadership	IV. Post-Kingdom	V. N.T. Pre-Church Leadership	VI. Church Leadership

```
|——————|——————|——————|——————|——————|——————|
```

I. Patriarchal Leadership Roots	II. Pre-Kingdom Leadership	III. Kingdom Leadership	IV. Post-Kingdom	V. N.T. Pre-Church Leadership	VI. Church Leadership
A. Abraham B. Isaac C. Jacob D. Joseph E. Job	A. Desert B. Conquering The Land C. Conquered By the Land	A. United B. Divided C. Single	A. Exile B. Post Exile C. Interim	A. Pre-Messianic B. Messianic	A. Jewish B. Gentile
Family	Revelatory Task Inspirational	Political Corrective	Modeling Renewal	Cultic Spiritual Movement	Spiritual Institutional
Blessing Shaping Timing Destiny Character Faith Purity	(Timing) Presence Intimacy Burden Hope Challenge Spiritual Authority Transition Weakness Continuity	Unity Stability Spiritual Leadership Recrudescence By-Pass	Hope Perspective Modeling Ultimate Perseverance	Training Focus Spirituality Servant Steward Shepherd Movement	Structure Universal Giftedness Word Centered Harvest

Figure Ne 35-2. Overview Time-Line of Biblical Leadership

In Figure Ne 35-2 above, macro lesson labels occur at the bottom in the six columns. Just above the macro lesson labels are given distinctive characteristics of each of the eras. Finally, above that occurs the outline of the sub-time periods and the major time-line with the six eras.

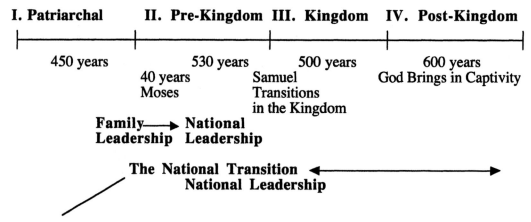

I. Patriarchal   II. Pre-Kingdom III. Kingdom   IV. Post-Kingdom

450 years   530 years   500 years   600 years
                   40 years   Samuel   God Brings in Captivity
                   Moses   Transitions
                                    in the Kingdom

Family———▶ National
Leadership   Leadership

The National Transition ◀————————————▶
National Leadership

Crucial Macro Lessons: 3. Timing, 8. Intercession, 9. Presence, 10. Intimacy, 11. Burden, 12. Hope, 13. Challenge, 14. Spiritual Authority, 15. Transition.

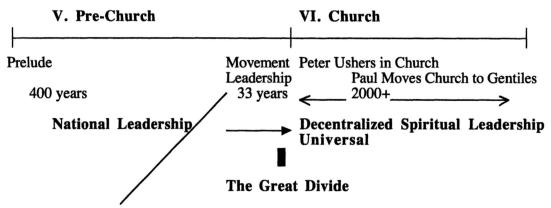

V. Pre-Church   **VI. Church**

Prelude   Movement Peter Ushers in Church
                           Leadership   Paul Moves Church to Gentiles
400 years   33 years ◀———— 2000+————————▶

National Leadership ———————▶ **Decentralized Spiritual Leadership Universal**

The Great Divide

Crucial Macro Lessons: 28. Selection, 29. Training, 30. Focus, 31. Spirituality, 32. Servant, 33. Steward, 34. Harvest, 37. Shepherd, 36. Movement.

Figure Ne 35-3. Two Major Transitions—The National Transition and The Great Divide

Note two things. These major transition times were short. God brought in major changes in a short period of time. Both transition times contain a large number of important macro lessons. For such short periods of time these are relatively large numbers of important leadership lessons.

Table Ne 35-5 lists the transitions and key figures and the result of the transition.

Table Ne 35-5. Transitions Along the Biblical Leadership Time-Line

Transition	Eras Involved	Key Figure/ Results
To God Directed Leadership	Begin Patriarchal Era	Abraham/ a God directed destiny involving an ethnic group and leaders from that group hearing God, getting revelation from Him, and obeying God.
Tribal to National	From the Patriarchal Era to the Pre-Kingdom Era	Moses/ A nation is established. God established concept of influential leader with spiritual authority to direct the nation; God reveals truth about Himself, life, and destiny for this nation. Major leadership guidelines

		(important macro lessons) flow through this transitional leadership.
Federation to Kingdom	Pre-Kingdom to Kingdom	Samuel/ A dispersed geographical/tribal society, each doing its own thing and basically not following God-given truth, is moved toward a centralized, unified national entity directed by one major leader—a king, who is to direct the nation with God's direction.
Babylonian Captivity	From Kingdom to Post-Kingdom	God/ God dismantles the kingdom structure. He disperses the followers. God by-passes the kingdom leadership altogether and begins a long preparation that will eventually emerge in spiritual leadership. In this era, individual spiritual leadership is highlighted in which God's perspective is crucial.
The Great Divide	From Post-Kingdom to Pre-Church. From a defunct national leadership to spiritual leadership which can be decentralized anywhere.	Jesus/ Jesus re-established God-directed leadership—the concept of the Kingdom of God. God by-passes the Jewish national leadership when they reject Him—i.e. His message through Jesus. Jesus at the same time of offering the kingdom also builds the foundational roots of a movement which will eventually contextualize the Kingdom of God in an institutional church form which can move into any culture on earth.
Universal Invitation	From Pre-Church to Church	Peter, Paul/ Peter ushers in the church to the Jewish followers of Jesus. Paul takes the church to the Gentiles. God's invitation of salvation and His truth for living God-directed lives become available (decentralized) to any people on the earth.

Note that that there are transition times between all the eras. Each of these are important in themselves but two stand out: Moses' Desert-Leadership; Jesus' Movement-Leadership. As is sometimes the case crucial transitions in the Bible are foundational. God focuses intently in these times and usually reveals foundational truth. Such is the case with all the transitions.

Tables Ne 35-6 and Ne 35-7 give the macro lessons discovered in these key transition times with suggested implications for today.

Table Ne 35-6. Moses' Transition/ Lessons/ Implications

Timing— God's timing is crucial to accomplishment of God's purposes. **Implication**(s): Leaders today, especially in their complex ministries involving multi-cultural settings, must be more sensitive to the timing of God than ever before.
Intercession— Leaders called to a ministry are called to intercede for that ministry. **Implication**(s): Various prayer movements have gained tremendous momentum in our day testifying to the fact that God sees this as a very important aspect of leadership in our day.
Presence— The essential ingredient of leadership is the powerful presence of God in the leader's life and ministry. **Implication**(s): Much present day leadership misses the balance of this—God both in powerful ministry and in powerful life changing impact in the leader himself/herself.
Intimacy— Leaders develop intimacy with God which in turn overflows into all their ministry since ministry flows out of being. **Implication**(s): Doing and achievement dominate present day leadership. God through the various spirituality movements is

calling leaders back to spirituality and beingness as the core of their ministries.
Burden— Leaders feel a responsibility to God for their ministry. **Implication**(s): Accountability is missing altogether in most cultures. This is true of Christian leadership as well. Sensitivity to this needed ingredient would avoid many of the leadership gaffes that are seen.
Hope— A primary function of all leadership is to inspire followers with hope in God and in what God is doing. **Implication**(s): This is especially true for leaders trying to reach Xers—generally without hope. But it is needed in all ministries as complex situations tend to take away hope for most Christians.
Challenge— Leaders receive vision from God which sets before them challenges that inspire their leadership. **Implication**(s): A leader must hear from God if that leader is to influence specific groups of people toward God's purposes—the basic definition of a leader. This is deeply needed especially in the many small churches which are floundering in our day.
Spiritual Authority—Spiritual authority is the dominant power base of a spiritual leader and comes through experiences with God, knowledge of God, godly character and gifted power. **Implication**(s): Abuse of power is one of the five major barriers facing leaders today. There are lots of leaders with all kinds of authority but few who exercise spiritual authority as a primary power base (with all its implications).
Transition—Leaders must transition other leaders into their work in order to maintain continuity and effectiveness. **Implication**(s): Every work of God is just one generation away from failure if it does not transition emerging leaders into its decision-making influential positions.

Table Ne 35-7. Jesus' Transition/ Lessons/ Implications

Selection— The key to good leadership is the selection of good potential leaders which should be a priority of all leaders. **Implication**(s): Leadership selection is desperately needed in church and parachurch organizations. Recruitment is often haphazard at best, especially in local church situations.
Training—Leaders should deliberately train potential leaders in their ministry by available and appropriate means. **Implication**(s): If emerging new leaders are not developed they will exit organizations and go somewhere else, depriving churches and parachurch organizations of on-going leadership. Leading with a developmental bias is the key to seeing on-going recruitment and longevity in organizational life.
Focus— Leaders should increasingly move toward a focus in their ministry which moves toward fulfillment of their calling and their ultimate contribution to God's purposes for them. **Implication**(s): Focused leaders are few and far between. Most leaders are faddish leaders jumping on the bandwagon of other apparently successful leaders. What is needed is leaders, knowing their own focus, and following it. Focused leaders are the need of the hour.
Spirituality— Leaders must develop interiority, spirit sensitivity, and fruitfulness in accord with their uniqueness since ministry flows out of being. **Implication**(s): As previously seen with the intimacy lesson from Moses' era, spirituality is crucial to leadership. And what is true of intimacy, one aspect of spirituality, is true as leaders develop balanced spirituality. Doing and achievement dominate present day leadership. God through the various spirituality movements is calling leaders back to spirituality and beingness as the core of their ministries.
Servant— Leaders must maintain a dynamic tension as they lead by serving and serve by leading. **Implication**(s): Servant leadership is not naturally found in any culture. It requires a paradigm shift for any leader to move into this leadership model—which is what Jesus intended for leaders he developed. Because of accepted leadership patterns in some cultures (great power distance) this is really difficult for emerging leaders to see or

accept.
Steward— Leaders are endowed by God with natural abilities, acquired skills, spiritual gifts, opportunities, experiences, and privileges which must be developed and used for God. **Implication**(s): Accountability is greatly needed in our generation where successful leaders dominantly self-authenticate their own ministries and heed little or nothing from outside resources which could hold them accountable.
Harvest— Leaders must seek to bring people into relationship with God. **Implication**(s): The outward aspect of the Great Commission must be carried out. God is focusing on this as He continues to raise up missionary movements from all over the world. The impetus of the missionary movement has already moved from the western world to the non-western world. We need to support this while at the same time bringing about renewal of missionary thinking in the western world.
Shepherd— Leaders must preserve, protect, and develop God's people. **Implication**(s): God still gets most of the leadership business done at local church level. Leaders who hold to the shepherd model concepts must in fact carry local church ministries—especially as cultures become more radically opposed to Gospel values. This means that more pastoral work will be necessary if we are winning those from deteriorating cultures.
Movement— Leaders recognize that movements are the way to penetrate society though they must be preserved via appropriate on-going institutions. **Implication**(s): New life can be instilled in parachurch organizations and churches when movement ideals are focused on. We see all around us movement leaders being raised up by God who are creating new ministries which God is blessing. This can be done more deliberately and proactively when movement dynamics are heeded.

Conclusion

The Six Leadership Eras and the seven leadership genre provide major perspectives for studying leadership in the Bible. The leadership commentary series analyzes Bible books and applies these perspectives. Of particular importance are two of the leadership genre—the *macro lessons* across each leadership era and the Bible *books as a whole*. The macro lessons flowing from Moses' desert leadership and Jesus' movement foundations are particularly instructive. They apply with great force to today's leadership challenges.

See **Articles**, *2. Biographical Study in the Bible—How To Do*; *Bible Centered Leader; Leadership Act;13. Leadership Eras in the Bible—Six Identified; Leadership Genre—Seven Types; 16. Macro Lessons Defined;17. Macro Lessons—List of 41 Across Six Leadership Eras; Principle of Truth.*

36. Vanishing Breed

Introduction

The concept of a vanishing breed is a relatively modern idea. For example, in the latter third of the 19th century, the buffalo became so hunted as to become an endangered species—a vanishing breed. As applied to the Christian scene the concept of a vanishing breed, in one sense, is a modern concept but in another is quite old concept. Until the mid 19th century and the proliferation of printed materials only a relatively few leaders were very familiar with the entire Bible. But with the Bible becoming a perennial best seller as has been the case in the 20th century, you would expect that many leaders would be Bible Centered leaders. But actually that is not the case. And it is growing worse, relatively speaking, because a rising generation of leaders is basically a non-reading group of people. But the notion of being a *Bible Centered Leader* is as old as the N.T. Church Leadership Era. Paul, the Apostle, stressed it to Timothy his younger co-worker. His two epistles, 1Ti and 2 Ti fairly bristle with Bible Centered Leadership insights. I suppose that you are not really surprised when I say the endangered specie I am concerned about is a little known animal—*A Bible Centered Leader*. Let me stress some ideas about that concept that I want to cover in this article:

We need Bible centered leaders.
You can become one.
Here are some helpful suggestions to become a Bible centered leader.

Shortly I will define for you a Bible centered leader. Let me first give my credentials.

I have been studying and using the Bible for 34 years. I have some deep convictions about that Bible. And I have learned some things about how to habitually ground oneself in this Bible. Three of my fundamental convictions are simple. They are captured in the following Biblical references.

A Lasting Source

The grass withers, the flower fades; but the Word of our God will stand forever. Isaiah 40:8

Fads, helpful as they may be, will come and go.[138] Effective leaders will recognize and use fads which are appropriate to the times and situations in which they lead. But there is

---

[138] I consider a fad as a fashion that is taken up with great enthusiasm for a brief period of time; a craze. Frequently, behind a fad is some dynamic principle. If we can identify the dynamic underlying principle we can re-engineer other *fads* which will work later after the original fad dies out (e.g. seeker sensitive churches, various church growth fads, etc.) But the Word of God will always be eternally fresh for any time if its dynamic principles are unlocked.

more. My personal conviction about lasting effective ministry flows from the following two verses.

2 Timothy 3:16,17 The Guarantee About That Source

Every Scripture inspired of God is profitable for teaching, for setting things right, for confronting, for inspiring righteous living, in order that God's leader be thoroughly equipped to lead God's people.

2 Timothy 2:15 The Proper Response to the Guarantee

Make every effort to be pleasing to God, a Bible Centered leader who is completely confident in using God's Word with impact in lives.

In my opinion we have only one guarantee for an effective life time experience as a leader. We must be people of the Word. Seminaries are good. But a seminary degree does not guarantee an equipped leader. Short term training in leadership institutes are good and helpful. But institutes that offer various leadership emphases can not guarantee equipping. Retreats, workshops, seminars, and conferences, all good in themselves and helpful in our development, can not guarantee equipping. But God does guarantees it. He insures us that this unfading Word which will stand forever can equip us. If we center our lives and ministry in the Word we have a guarantee from God that it will equip us to lead. Our job is to respond and make every effort to please God in our mastery and use of this Word for our own lives and for those we serve. Let me suggest then, that,

> Effective leaders should have an appropriate, unique, lifelong plan for mastering the Word in order to use it with impact in their ministries.

I want to share with you four discoveries I have personally learned in my own thirty-four year pilgrimage of mastering the Word and using it with impact in my ministry.

1. A Guiding Paradigm Helps

Few leaders master the Word without a proactive, deliberate approach which plans to do so. I was challenged early on, shortly after my *Lordship committal* in 1964, to begin a lifelong mastery of the Word of God—an overwhelming task I thought at that time. Pastor L. Thompson, the challenger, had been in the Word almost 30 years at that time. He was my model that it could be done. My Navigator trained friend, Harold Dollar, gave me my first paradigm for doing that. The Navigators were using an illustration called *The Hand* to challenge people to study and use God's Word. The little finger represented listening to God's Word. The ring finger stood for reading God's Word. The middle finger indicated studying God's Word. The index finger reminded of memorizing God's Word. The thumb represented Meditating on God's Word. I immediately set out to use this paradigm. I learned to listen well (using *Sermon Listening Sheets*). I started to get tapes from Bible teachers. I started my yearly read through the Bible program. I began to memorize three verses per week. I set a goal to study one book thoroughly each year (if a long book or more if shorter books). I learned techniques for analyzing verses and doing word studies which helped me learn how to meditate. In short, I made this paradigm really work for me. I used this paradigm for 15 years with one or more of the components having more prominence from time-to-time.

During the next 10 years I found that not all the components were important to me. By this time I was well into my leadership research and was not actively teaching the Bible in a local church context. I did continue to use several of *The Hand* components as guidelines. Essentially I was struggling for a better paradigm that both fit me and my ministry.

During the last seven years I have been working from my new paradigm. And that is what I want to share with you. It has given me new life. Every where I go I try to share it—one on one, in groups, in seminars, and in classes. I find that people really respond to it. They react with a fresh new excitement about studying the Bible. I know that some of my readers have really plateaued in their mastery of the Word. I know that some of you are not seeing the Word impacting your leadership. Some of you are probably seeing impact, but are looking for more. Maybe what I have found may help you.

But even if my new paradigm may not work for you, I still contend that you need some plan to move toward life long mastery.

2. The Breakthrough Insight—The Notion of Core

I stumbled on to this new paradigm as I studied giftedness of leaders.[139] In my research of leaders developing over a lifetime, I found that:

(1) all leaders have at least one word gift; most have a set of word gifts. Word gifts include teaching, exhortation, prophecy, pastoring, evangelism, apostleship, and ruling (leadership). Sometimes either word of knowledge, word of wisdom, discernings of spirits or word of faith functions as a word gift.

(2) all leaders have core items in the Bible which are important to them.

It was this last item that was the *breakthrough insight*. This observation can prove extremely valuable to one who has a desire to establish a life long habit of mastering the Word and wants to use it impactfully in ministry. The observation, expanded a bit:

> **Leaders usually have favorite Bible books, or special passages, which God has used mightily in their own lives to spur their growth or solve their problems or otherwise meet them. It is these books or special passages which form the basis for much of what they share with others in their ministry.**

And they usually do so with added impact since these core items have meant something to them personally. This interest in and repetitive use of core items suggests a selection criterion. We can limit what should be mastered in-depth over a life time to our core items. These core items provide a definite starting place for mastery of the Bible. From this observation I have drawn two important definitions.

Definition   A <u>Core Set </u>is a collection of very important Bible books, usually from 5-20, which are or have been extremely meaningful to you in your own life and for which you feel a burden from God to use with great power over and over in your ministry in the years to come.

Definition   A <u>Core Selection</u> refers to important passages, important biographical characters, special psalms, special values or key topics which are or have been extremely meaningful to you in your own life and for which you feel a burden from God to use with great power over and over in your ministry in the years to come.

It is this breakthrough insight which makes mastery of the Bible a realizable potential for word gifted leaders. The *Equipping Formula* suggests one paradigm a leader can use to focus his/her mastery of the Bible.

---

[139] These first three observations which follow came as a result of 10 years research in giftedness among contemporary leaders at the School of World Mission. See **Unlocking Your Giftedness** from Barnabas Publishers which gives the results of studies of giftedness among leaders.

3. The Equipping Formula—four components
My new paradigm, which I call the *Life Long Bible Mastery Paradigm*, has four components.

Component 1. **Mastery** of one's Core Books or other core material,
Component 2. **Devotional Input** (from Core Books and other Bible portions as well)
Component 3. When needed, **Familiarity Reading** of weak Bible Portions.
Component 4. **Situational Study**

The first two components are obligatory and should be going on all the time. The next two are contingent upon need.

All leaders need to be working on mastering core material continually. All leaders need to have God speak to them personally through the Word. All leaders need to have some minimum familiarity with the whole Word, even though they are moving toward mastery of a limited number of core items in the Bible. From time to time leaders will have situations in their leadership setting which demand a searching study of the Bible for special findings. These will come and go as prompted by situations. The *Equipping Formula* takes in to account these various needs. Its four components form the basis for planning, short term and long term.

4. Impact Communication—Studying for Ideas that Change Lives
Core items are important to a leader. They have already impacted that leader personally. Because of this, a leader can usually use the core items in ministry to impact others. I teach those who want to use this *Life Long Bible Mastery Paradigm* to identify the key ideas in a core book, a core Psalm, a core passage, a core topic, core biographical characters or core values. Then as part of the plan of mastering that core item, I teach them to design communication events to present these key ideas.

Effective leaders should have an appropriate, unique, lifelong plan for mastering the Word in order to use it with impact in their ministries. We need Bible centered leaders. The *Life Long Bible Mastery Paradigm* is simply one of many that can be used. You may use others. I am happy if you do. The real questions are, "Do you have a Bible centered ministry? Are you a Bible Centered leader." Well, I promised earlier to define this endangered specie.

Definition   A <u>Bible Centered leader</u> refers to a leader whose leadership is informed by the Bible, who has been shaped by Biblical leadership values, who has grasped the intent of Scriptural books and their content in such a way as to apply them to current situations and who uses the Bible in ministry so as to impact followers.

Join the *Save the Bible Centered Leaders Association*! At least save one of them. You! Be a Pauline fan and appropriate 2 Ti 3:16,17 for your life and ministry. Don't *let Bible Centered Leaders* become a vanishing breed!

(This page deliberately blank.)

Nehemiah

Focused Leadership

Glossary and Bibliography

Glossary—Leadership Definitions

The following leadership related definitions occur throughout the **Nehemiah Leadership Commentary**. They are listed here alphabetically for convenience in referencing. SRN stands for Strong's Reference Number. These numbers can be used to look up the definitions of these words in the **Strong's Exhaustive Concordance** containing Hebrew and Greek dictionaries. These numbers are now also used by many other Bible study aids.

Item	Definition
Absolutes	*Absolutes* refer to replicated truth in leadership situations across cultures without restrictions. Failure to follow or use will normally result in some stirrings of conscience.
Affect	a learning domain, that is, a term describing learning which primarily moves the feelings and emotions.
Affirmation	the process in which a leader gives approval to a follower in such a way as to empower or inspire that follower to want to follow more strongly.
Authority	Authority refers to the right to exercise leadership influence by a leader over followers with respect to some field of influence.
Authority Insights	from leadership emergence theory. One of 51 process items that God uses to shape a leader. Authority insights describe those instances in ministry in which a leader learns important lessons, via positive or negative experiences, with regards to: submission to authority, authority structures, authenticity of power bases underlying authority, authority conflict, how to exercise authority.
Bent of Life	An ultimate testimony concept which refers to the overall general evaluation of a life, usually highlighted by summary passages. E.g. see Acts 2:25; 13:36 for David's bent of life. Usually the bent of life puts the most positive spin it can on the character. David had many flaws in his life and ministry but his bent of life is good.
Bible Centered Leader	a leader (1) whose leadership is being informed by the Bible and (2) who personally has been shaped by Biblical values, (3) who has grasped the intent of Scriptural books and their content in such a way as to apply them to current situations and (4) who uses the Bible in ministry so as to impact followers.
Biographical Data	Biographical data refers to that large amount of information in the Scriptures which is made up of small narrative slices of life about a person.
Bridging Strategy	A bridging strategy is the resulting plan of action for implementing a given strategy so as to transition the group, organization, or structure from the present situation to the anticipated situation.
Capture	a technical term used when talking about figures of speech being interpreted. A figure or idiom is said to be captured when one can display the intended emphatic meaning of it in non-figurative simple words. e.g. not ashamed of the Gospel = captured: completely confident of the Gospel.

Catalyst

A <u>catalyst</u> is a person of change who initiates the change process by expressing dissatisfaction with the status quo and actively stimulating discontent in others as well. This is one of 4 change agent roles defined in Clinton's change dynamics book—**Bridging Strategies**. This is the person who stimulates change by calling attention to the need for it. This is a motivator type person, a challenging type persons, and frequently a person with a prophetical bent.

Certainty Continuum

a horizontal line moving from suggestions on one extreme to requirements on the other extreme which attempts to provide a grid for locating a given statement of truth in terms of its potential use with others and the degree of authority with which it can be asserted.

Change Participants

a technical term from Clinton's change dynamics theory, which indicates the set of people involved in the change situation including the three basic categories of factions, individuals (favorable, neutral, unfavorable) and systems.

Civil Leadership

refers to followers of God, sold out on following God, yet impacting the society in which they exercise two types of roles often needed in society—1. Governmental or political roles sanctioned by the society and 2. Military roles sanctioned by the society.

Coalition

<u>Coalition</u> refers to an alliance, especially a temporary one, of people, factions, parties, or nations.

Coalition Leadership

A <u>leadership coalition</u> in Biblical literature refers to a partnership, whether formal or informal, which exists between civil leaders, mainstream religious leaders and/or peripheral religious leaders, for a temporary period of time in order to accomplish some God-directed task(s).

Cognitive

a learning domain, that is, a term describing learning which primarily focuses on the transmittal and understanding of knowledge and ideas.

Conflict

from leadership emergence theory. One of 51 process items that God uses to shape a leader. The <u>conflict process item</u> refers to those instances in a leader's life-history in which God uses conflict, whether personal or ministry related to develop the leader in dependence upon God, faith, and inner-life.

Core Set

A <u>Core Set</u> is a collection of very important Bible books, usually from 5-20, which are or have been extremely meaningful to you in your own life and for which you feel a burden from God to use with great power over and over in your ministry in the years to come.

Core Selection

A <u>Core Selection</u> refers to important passages, important biographical characters, special psalms, special values or key topics which are or have been extremely meaningful to you in your own life and for which you feel a burden from God to use with great power over and over in your ministry in the years to come.

Crisis	from leadership emergence theory. One of 51 process items that God uses to shape a leader. <u>Crisis process items</u> refer to those special intense situations of pressure in human situations which are used by God to test and teach dependence.
Critical Incident Source	A type 1 biographical source of leadership information is labeled a <u>Critical Incident Source</u> when its source material is comprised of a single incident or series of incidents taking place in a very short time. That is, there is limited information (span wise over a leader's entire life) available about the leader being studied.
Desperation Prayers	refer to spontaneous prayers shot upward to God in a crisis moment of time in which God must answer or the leader faces defeat and failure.
Destiny Item Type I	a destiny experience which is an awe-inspiring experience in which God is sensed directly as acting or speaking in the life. Example: Moses at the burning bush.
Destiny Item Type II	a indirect destiny experience in which some aspect of destiny is linked to some person other than the leader and is done indirectly for the leader who simply must receive its implications. Example: Hannah's promise to give Samuel to God.
Destiny Item Type III	the build up of a sense of destiny in a life because of the accumulation of providential circumstances which indicate God's arrangement for the life. See Apostle Paul's birth and early life situation.
Destiny Item Type IV	the build up of a sense of destiny in a life because of the sensed blessing of God on the life, repeatedly. Seen by others and recognized by them as the Hand of God on the life. See Joseph.
Destiny Pattern	a leadership pattern. The development of a sense of destiny usually follows a three fold pattern of destiny preparation, destiny revelation, and destiny fulfillment. That is, over a period of time God shapes a leader with experiences which prepare, reveal, and finally brings about completion of destiny.
Destiny Processing	refers to the shaping activities of God in which a leader becomes increasingly aware of God's Hand on his/her life and the purposes for which God has intended for his/her leadership. This processing causes a sense of partnership with God toward God's purposes for the life and hence brings meaning to the life. See also Type I, II, III, IV destiny items.
Divine Affirmation	a concept from leadership emergence theory. The shaping activity of God whereby God makes known to a leader his approval of that leader. This is a major motivating factor to keep one serving the Lord.
Divine Contact	from leadership emergence theory. One of 51 process items that God uses to shape a leader. A <u>divine contact</u> is a person whom God brings in contact with a leader at a crucial moment in a development phase in order to accomplish one or more of the following: to affirm leadership potential, encourage leadership potential, give guidance on a special issue, give

insights which may indirectly lead to guidance, challenge the leader God-ward, open a door to a ministry opportunity, other insights helping the emerging leader to make guidance decisions.

Double Confirmation	from leadership emergence theory. One of 51 process items that God uses to shape a leader. Double confirmation refers to the unusual guidance in which God makes clear His will by giving the guidance directly to a leader and then reinforcing it by some other person totally independent and unaware of the leader's guidance.
Experiental	an integrative learning domain which involves cognitive, affect, and conative domains so that the things being learned are put into the life and used—they are understood (cognitive), appreciated or valued (affect) and have affected the desires to use (conative). Jesus consistently taught so as to move people toward experiential learning.
Faith Challenge	from leadership emergence theory. One of 51 process items that God uses to shape a leader. A faith challenge refers to those instances in ministry where a leader is challenged to take steps of faith in regards to ministry and sees God meet those steps of faith with divine affirmation and ministry affirmation and often with guidance into on-going ministry leading to a focused life.
Faith Check	from leadership emergence theory. One of 51 process items that God uses to shape a leader. A faith check is a process item God uses to shape a leader so that the leader can learn to trust God, by faith, to intervene in his/her life or ministry.
Figure	the unusual use of a word or words differing from the normal use in order to draw special attention to some point of interest. The more important figures (100s used in Bible) include: metaphor, simile, metonymy, synecdoche, hyperbole, irony, personification, apostrophe, negative emphatics (litotes and tapenosis), rhetorical question. See individual definitions for each of these. See **For Further Study Bibliography**, **Figures and Idioms** by Dr. J. Robert Clinton.
Flesh Act	from leadership emergence theory. One of 51 process items that God uses to shape a leader. A flesh act refers to those instances in a leader's life where guidance is presumed and decisions are made either hastily or without proper discernment of God's choice. Such decisions usually involve the working out of guidance by the leader using some human manipulation or other means and which brings ramifications which later negatively affect ministry and life. See Genesis 16 for an example in Abraham's life. See Joshua's treaty with Gibeonites in Jos 9. See Isa 39:4 for Hezekiah's action with Babylonian envoys.
Gifted Power	refers to the empowerment of the Holy Spirit when using giftedness; 1Pe 4:11 gives the basic admonition for this to the use of word gifts. It is naturally extended to other areas of giftedness.
Giftedness Discovery	from leadership emergence theory. One of 51 process items that God uses to shape a leader. Giftedness discovery refers to instances in which a leader becomes aware of natural abilities, or acquired skills, or spiritual gifts so as

to use them well in ministry. This is a significant advance along the giftedness development pattern.

guidance

from leadership emergence theory. One of 51 process items that God uses to shape a leader. <u>Guidance</u> is the general category which refers to the many ways in which God reveals information that informs a leader about decisions to be made.

Guidelines,

a term used to define a position on the Certainty Continuum. *Guidelines* are truths that are replicated in most leadership situations and should only be rejected for good reasons though there will be no loss of conscience.

Hyperbole

A <u>hyperbole</u> is the use of conscious exaggeration (an overstatement of truth) in order to emphasize or strikingly excite interest in the truth. Example—1 Co 4:14-16, ten thousand instructors.

Ideal Factors

A technical term from Clinton's change dynamics theory. <u>Ideal factors</u> refer to a list of items, which reflect the essential good points of the new system with problems solved that prompted the changes.

Idiom

the use of words to imply something other than their literal meanings. People in the culture know the idiomatic meaning of the words. Example: *I smell a rat.* Some idioms are patterned in which case you can reverse the pattern to get the meaning. Others must simply be learned in the culture from contextual usage of them.

Imprecatory Prayer

a special prayer against something or someone in which negative wishes for that situation are prayed. Sometimes the imprecatory prayer is like a curse. God is beseeched to act in a harmful way in the situation or against the person.

Influentials

a technical term from Clinton's change dynamics theory, which indicates any of the change participants who have special influence over individuals or groups. These people are those often searched out and asked for their opinion about matters. Often the natural leaders in a group.

Inspirational Leadership

a description of one of three major high level generic leadership functions that a leader of an organization is responsible for producing. It describes the motivational force for developing the relational base and for achieving the task. The ability to get and motivate toward vision, the ability to see God's presence in a work, and to believe and challenge toward hope—God's future working in the organization—are all part of inspirational leadership. Whereas some leaders are by personality either task-oriented or relationally-oriented in their leadership, inspirational leadership appears both in task and relationally oriented leaders. All three functions are necessary for healthy ministry. Haggai's ministry was dominantly task and inspirational leadership.

Integrity

the top leadership character quality. It is the consistency of inward beliefs and convictions with outward practice. It is an honesty and wholeness of personality in which one operates with a clear conscience in dealings with self and others.

Integrity Check	from leadership emergence theory. One of 51 process items that God uses to shape a leader. The <u>integrity</u> check refers to the special kind of process test which God uses to evaluate heart–intent, consistency between inner convictions and outward actions, and which God uses as a foundation from which to expand the leader's capacity to influence. The word check is used in the sense of test—meaning a check or check-up. See also testing patterns.
Intervention Time	a technical term from Clinton's change dynamics theory, which indicates the proper time to implement some change due to circumstances, God's prompting or whatever. It is a time when the change being introduced has the highest probability of being accepted.
isolation	from leadership emergence theory. One of 51 process items that God uses to shape a leader. <u>Isolation processing</u> refers to the setting aside of a leader from normal ministry involvement in its natural context usually for an extended time in order to experience God in a new or deeper way.
Leader	A <u>leader</u> in the Biblical sense that we use in the leadership commentaries is a person with God-given capacity and God-given responsibility who is influencing a specific group of people toward God's purposes.
Leadership	<u>Leadership</u> is a dynamic process over an extended period of time, in which a leader utilizing leadership resources, and by specific leadership behaviors, influences followers toward accomplishment of aims mutually beneficial for the leader(s) and followers.
Leadership Act	A leadership <u>act</u> occurs when a given person influences a group, so that the group acts or thinks differently than it did before the instance of influence.
leadership backlash	from leadership emergence theory. One of 51 process items that God uses to shape a leader. The <u>leadership backlash process</u> item refers to the reactions of followers, other leaders within a group, and/or Christians outside the group, to a course of action taken by a leader because of various ramifications that arise due to the action taken. The situation is used in he leader's life to test perseverance, clarity of vision, and faith.
Leadership Challenge	from leadership emergence theory. One of 51 process items that God uses to shape a leader. It is a leadership emergence theory term referring to the shaping process God uses to give a leader an on-going renewal experience about leadership and to direct that leader to some new leadership task.
Leadership Coalition	A *leadership coalition* in Biblical literature refers to a partnership, whether formal or informal, which exists between civil leaders, mainstream religious leaders and/or peripheral religious leaders, for a temporary period of time in order to accomplish some God-directed task(s).
Leadership Committal	a special shaping activity of God observed in leadership emergence theory, which is usually a spiritual benchmark and produces a sense of destiny in a leader. It is the call to leadership by God and the wholehearted response by the leader to accept and abide by that call. Paul's Damascus road experience, the destiny revelation given by Ananias, and Paul's response to it as a life calling provide the New Testament classic example of leadership committal.

Leadership Era | A <u>leadership era</u> is a period of time, usually several hundred years long, in which the major focus of leadership, the influence means, basic leadership functions, and followership have much in common and which basically change with time periods before or after it.

Leadership Functions | Leadership <u>functions</u> are those general activities that leaders must do and/or be responsible for in their influence responsibilities with followers. This is a technical term, which refers to the three major categories of formal leadership responsibility: task behavior (defining structure and goals), relationship behavior (providing the emotional support and ambiance), and inspirational behavior (providing motivational effort).

Left Hand of God | in contradistinction to the phrase *the right hand of God* which refers to an evident manifestation of God's power in a situation, usually through His people or His leaders, this phrase, *the left hand of God*, refers to God's use of people, nations, events not necessarily recognizing Him or what He is doing for His own purposes (e.g. Cyrus). See also Jn 11:49-51.

life crisis | from leadership emergence theory. One of 51 process items that God uses to shape a leader. A <u>life crisis process item</u> refers to a crisis situation characterized by life threatening intense pressure in human affairs in which the meaning and purpose of life are searched out with a result that the leader has experienced God in a new way as the source, sustainer, and focus of life.

Macro-Lesson | a high level generalization of a leadership observation (suggestion, guideline, requirement), stated as a lesson, which repeatedly occurs throughout different leadership eras, and thus has potential as a leadership absolute. Macro lessons even at their weakest provide at least strong guidelines describing leadership insights. At their strongest they are requirements, that is absolutes, that leaders should follow. Leaders ignore them to their detriment. Example: *Prayer Lesson: If God has called you to a ministry then He has called you to pray for that ministry.*

Mainstream religious Leadership | <u>Mainstream religious</u> leadership refers to officially recognized religious roles sanctioned by the society and religious structures.

Metonymy | a figure of speech in which one word is substituted for another word to which it is related. This is to emphasize both the word and call attention to the relationship between the two words. e.g. Philemon *6 communicate your faith* to *communicate what you believe and on which you have strong convictions.*

Ministerial Formation | the shaping activity in a leader's life which is directed toward instilling leadership skills, leadership experience, and developing giftedness for ministry.

Ministry Affirmation | a concept from leadership emergence theory. The shaping activity of God whereby God makes known to a leader his approval of that leader's ministry efforts. This is a major motivating factor to keep one serving the Lord.

Ministry Conflict | from leadership emergence theory. One of 51 process items that God uses to shape a leader. The ministry conflict process item refers to those instances in a ministry situation, in which a leader learns lessons via the positive and negative aspects of conflict with regards to: 1. the nature of conflict, 2. possible ways to resolve conflict, 3. possible ways to avoid conflict, 4. ways to creatively use conflict, and 5. perception of God's personal shaping through the conflict.

Ministry Task
one of 51 process items that God uses to shape a leader. A ministry task is an assignment from God which primarily tests a person's faithfulness and obedience but often also allows use of ministry gifts in the context of a task which has closure, accountability, and evaluation. e.g. Barnabas trip to Antioch; Titus had 5 ministry tasks.

Negative Preparation
from leadership emergence theory. One of 51 process items that God uses to shape a leader. Negative preparation refers to the special guidance process involving God's use of events, people, conflict, persecution, or experiences, all focusing on the negative, so as to free up a person from the situation in order to enter the next phase of development with a new abandonment and revitalized interest.

Networking Power
a leadership emergence theory term. One of 51 processing items used by God to shape a leader's ministry. It describes how God can connect a leader to resources of all kinds which can come from contacts with people. People provide a bridge, connecting a given leader with other persons or needed resources.

Obedience Check
from leadership emergence theory. One of 51 process items that God uses to shape a leader. An Obedience check refers to that special category of process item in which God tests personal response to revealed truth in the life of a person.

Ownership
A person in a change situation is said to have ownership for the changes when he/she is not only for the changes but is willing to cooperate in the change process.

Paradigm
a controlling perspective in the mind which allows one to perceive and understand REALITY.

Paradigm Shift
from leadership emergence theory. One of 51 process items that God uses to shape a leader. It is a change of a controlling perspective so that one perceives and understands REALITY in a different way than previously.

Pattern
pattern is the term used in leadership emergence theory to describe a repetitive cycle of happenings (observed in comparative analysis of case studies on leaders) and may involve periods of time, stages of something happening, combinations of process items, or combinations of other identifiable leadership concepts, all of which serve to give perspective. 23 identifiable patterns have been described.

Peripheral Religious Leadership
Peripheral religious leadership refers to those roles, mostly outside the mainstream religious structures, which attempt to speak for God to bring about change in religious groups, structures, and society in general.

Person of Change	A technical term from Clinton's change dynamics theory. The person of change represents a person who wants to deliberately introduce change into a situation.
Pivotal Point	A *pivotal point* is a critical time in a leader's life in which processing going on will be responded to in such a way that one of three typical things may happen: The response to this processing can: 1. curtail further use of the leader by God or at least curtail expansion of the leader's potential. 2. limit the eventual use of the leader for ultimate purposes that otherwise could have been accomplished, 3. enhance or open up the leader for expansion or contribution to the ultimate purposes in God's kingdom, that is, it may be a springboard to future expanded use by God of the leader.
Power Base	a term referring to the means which enable a leader's influence. Force, manipulation, authority, and persuasion enfold various power means. It is the source of credibility, power differential, or resources, which enables a leader (*power holder*) to have authority to exercise influence on followers (*power subjects*).
Power Encounter	A phrase first defined by a missiological anthropologist, A. R. Tippett, which identifies a situation in which the power of God is tested over against some other god's power. Several elements that should be present in classical power encounters: a) A crisis between people representing god and other people must be differentiated clearly. b) There must be recognition that the issue is one of power confrontation in the supernatural realm. c) There must be public recognition of the pre-encounter terms (If...Then...). d) There is an actual crisis/ confrontation event (the more public usually the better will be the aftermath). e) There must be confirmation that God has done the delivering as the power encounter resolves. f) Celebration to bring closure and insure continuation of God's purpose in the power event. Examples: Jephthah, Jdg 11:12-32. Da 3.
Prayer Power	from leadership emergence theory. One of 51 process items that God uses to shape a leader. Prayer power refers to the specific instance in which God uses the situation to answer prayer and demonstrate the authenticity of the leader's spiritual authority.
Principle (of truth)	refers to generalized statements of truth which reflect observations drawn from specific instances of leadership acts or other leadership sources.
Process Helper	A process helper is a person of change with overall perspective on the system and its needs and of change processes in general who thus focuses on the entire change process for the client's benefit and facilitates change at every stage. One of 4 change agent roles defined in Clinton's change dynamics book—**Bridging Strategies**. This is the person who recognizes the entire change process and can facilitate what is needed. This is a person who can use the catalyst to stimulate change. This person recognizes the place of the resource linker and the solution giver and can help them become part of the change process.
Process Item	a technical name in leadership emergence theory describing actual occurrences in a given leader's life including providential events, people,

circumstances, special divine interventions, inner-life lessons and other like items which God uses to develop that leader by shaping leadership character, leadership skills, and leadership values. These shaping things indicate leadership capacity and/or potential; they expand this potential; they confirm appointment to roles or responsibilities using that leadership capacity; they direct that leader along to God's appointed ministry level for realized potential. Some 51 different shaping activities (process items) have been identified in leadership emergence theory. Synonym: shaping activities of God.

Progressive Calling

the recognition that most leaders will receive on-going leadership challenges from God throughout their lifetimes and not just some initial call; such challenges will bring renewal, divine affirmation, ministry affirmation and will continue to give strategic guidance to a leader's ministry.

Promise

or more specifically, a *promise from God* is an assertion from God, specific or general or a truth in harmony with God's character, which is perceived in one's heart or mind concerning what He will do or not do for one, and which is sealed in that one's inner most being by a quickening action of the Holy Spirit, and on which that one then counts. See Jn 14 where six such promises are used to inspire the disciples in a crisis moment.

Prophecy

one of the 19 spiritual gifts. It is in the *Word Cluster* and *power cluster*. A person operating with the gift of prophecy has the capacity to deliver truth (in a public way) either of a predictive nature or as a situational word from God in order to correct by exhorting, edifying or consoling believers and to convince non-believers of God's truth. **Its central thrust is To Provide Correction Or Perspective On A Situation.**

Prophecy (genre)

refers to the genre of Scripture in which the thrust of the passage is an authoritative revelation from God usually through a spokesperson, called a prophet or prophetess, to correct a given historical situation or to warn of a future situation.

Recruitment

refers to the deliberate efforts to challenge potential leaders and to engage them in on-going ministry so that they will develop as leaders and move toward accomplishment of God's destiny for them.

Relationship Insights

from leadership emergence theory. One of 51 process items that God uses to shape a leader. Relationship insights refers to those instances in ministry in which a leader learns lessons via positive or negative experiences with regard to relating to other Christians or non-Christians in the light of ministry decisions or other influence means: such lessons are learned so as to significantly affect future leadership.

Relational Oriented Leadership

a description of one of three major high level generic leadership functions that a leader of an organization is responsible for producing. It describes those activities which a leader does to affirm followers, to provide an atmosphere congenial to accomplishing work, to give emotional and spiritual support for followers so that they can mature, in short, to act relationally with followers in order to enable them to develop and be effective in their contribution to the organization. All three functions are necessary for healthy ministry.

Religious leadership, Mainstream	refers to officially recognized religious roles sanctioned by the society and religious structures.
Religious leadership, Peripheral	refers to those roles, mostly outside the mainstream religious structures, which attempt to speak for God to bring about change in religious groups, structures, and society in general.
Resource Linker	The <u>resource linker</u> is a change agent who keeps the process of change going by matching needs and resources, which are material, financial, educational and personnel, at any stage of the process but particularly in the diagnosis, search for solutions, and application stages. One of 4 change agent roles defined in Clinton's change dynamics book—**Bridging Strategies**.
restoration (corporate)	refers to God's attempts to restore the people of God as a viable channel through whom He can work to carry out His Biblical purposes.
restoration (crisis)	refers to the period of time from 539 B.C. to 430 B.C. and which covers the activity of God in bringing His people back into the land and establishing a testimony there. His providential care of His people (both in the land and outside it) is also shown.
Restoration (individual)	the process whereby a fallen leader is transitioned back into leadership. It usually involves repentance, restitution where appropriate, correction of the aberrant leadership dysfunctions, and recognition by other leaders of the restoration process and their stamp of approval for the leader to renew ministry.
Restoration Leaders	refer to the important leaders, civil, religious, and prophetical, who worked during the restoration crisis years to bring some kind of recrudescence to God's people.
Rhetorical Question	a figure of speech in which a question is <u>not</u> used to obtain information but is used to indirectly communicate an affirmative or negative statement, the importance of some thought by focusing attention on it, and/or one's own feeling or attitudes about something. 1 Tim 3:5 "For if anyone knows not how to rule his own house, how shall that one take care of the church of God." Captured: A person who can not lead his/her own family can't lead people in a church.
Sense of Destiny	an inner conviction arising from an experience or a series of experiences in which there is a growing sense of awareness that God has His hand on a leader in a special way for special purposes. See destiny pattern.
Sentness	a term capturing the divine backing of Jesus' intervention in the world to represent and reveal God to our world. It carries the notion of anointing and appointment by God for a mission, but in Jesus' case—more since it was the incarnation of God in human form. The closest functional equivalent for leaders today is divine appointment.

Solution Giver	A <u>solution giver</u> is a person of change who clearly sees the situation for the present and the future and forms and communicates a plan that could work to solve the system's current problems. One of 4 change agent roles defined in Clinton's change dynamics book—**Bridging Strategies**.
Sovereign Guidance	a general process item category which refers to any guidance a leader gets which is attributed to God's special intervention.
Sovereign Mindset	an attitude demonstrated by the Apostle Paul in which he tended to see God's working in the events and activities that shaped his life, whether or not they were positive and good or negative and bad. He tended to see God's purposes in these shaping activities and to make the best of them. Haggai demonstrates this when He sees God's Hand involved in the setbacks of the people.
Sphere of Influence	refers to the totality of people being influenced and for whom a leader will give an account to God. The totality of people influenced subdivides into three domains called direct influence, indirect influence, and organizational influence. Three measures rate sphere of influence: 1. Extensiveness—which refers to quantity; 2. Comprehensiveness—which refers to the scope of things being influenced in the followers' lives; 3. Intensiveness—the depth to which influence extends to each item within the comprehensive influences. Extensiveness is the easiest to measure and hence is most often used or implied when talking about a leader's sphere of influence.
Spiritual Authority	from the standpoint of the follower, Spiritual authority is the right to influence, conferred upon a leader by followers, because of their perception of spirituality in that leader. Technically this is called extrinsic spiritual authority (ESA). From the leader's perspective Spiritual Authority is that characteristic of a God-anointed leader, developed upon an experiential power base (giftedness, character, deep experiences with God), that enables him/her to influence followers through persuasion, force of modeling, and moral expertise. Technically this is called intrinsic spiritual authority (ISA).
Spiritual Authority Insights	from leadership emergence theory. One of 51 process items that God uses to shape a leader. Spiritual authority insights refers to any discovery a leader learns about his/her own spiritual authority—its existence or its use.
Spiritual Formation	the shaping activity in a leader's life which is directed toward instilling godly character and developing inner life.
Spiritual Warfare	refers to the unseen opposition in the spirit world made up of Satan and his demons and their attempts to defeat God's forces, including believers. It also involves the response by believers to these attempts.
Spontaneous Prayers	those prayers, like those demonstrated in the book of Nehemiah, which involve the willful directing of a silent thought prayer to God, usually as prompted by a situation.
Strategic Delegation	<u>Strategic delegation</u> means the assignment of groups or individuals to pieces of the change project to which they are naturally drawn or have some vested interest in.

Strategic Formation	the shaping activity in a leader's life which is directed toward having that leader reach full potential and achieve a God-given destiny.
Suggestions	a term used to describe a position on the Certainty Continuum. It refers to truth observed in some situations and which may be helpful to others but they are optional and can be used or not with no loss of conscience.
Task Oriented Leadership	a description of one of three major high level generic leadership functions that a leader of an organization is responsible for producing. It describes the thing to be accomplished by the organization, its raison d'être, reason for being. Some leaders by personality and processing are highly task oriented and tend to prioritize everything in terms of getting the task done; this means frequently using people. All three functions are necessary for healthy ministry (task, relational, inspirational.
THEN Situation	A technical term from Clinton's change dynamics theory. The <u>THEN situation</u> refers to an intuitive pre-analysis of the system after needed changes have been introduced and the system is stable.
Ultimate Contribution Set	From focused lives theory, this phrase denotes the lasting legacy that a leader leaves behind which can include specific being or doing achievements unique to the person and/or any of the 13 standard ultimate contribution categories: saint, stylistic practitioner, family, mentor, public rhetorician, pioneer, change person, artist, founder, stabilizer, researcher, writer, promoter. See **Articles**, *Leaving Behind a Legacy*; *Ultimate Contribution* for details on these standard legacy categories.
Vicarious Confession (Vicarious Prayer)	a process involving the confession of past sins, even many generations ago, by a present day leader as if he/she had committed those sins. The confession is done on the behalf of people in the past who did not confess these sins. The result is the on-going work of God, which may have been blocked in some way or other due to this unrepentant sin.
Vicarious Learning	<u>Vicarious learning</u> refers to the method of learning from someone else's life.
Volitional	a learning domain, that is, a term describing learning which primarily focuses willful decisions that are made in response to learning. Haggai's ministry focuses on this very strongly.
Word Check	from leadership emergence theory. One of 51 process items that God uses to shape a leader. A <u>word check</u> is a process item which tests a leader's ability to understand or receive a word from God personally and to see it worked out in life with a view toward enhancing the authority of God's truth and a desire to know it.
Word Gifts	a category of spiritual gifts used to clarify and explain about God. These help us understand about God including His nature, His purposes and how we can relate to Him and be a part of His purposes. These include: teaching, exhortation, pastoring, evangelism, apostleship, prophecy, ruling, and sometimes word of wisdom, word of knowledge, and faith (a word of). All leaders have at least one of these and often several of these.

Word of Knowledge | one of the 19 spiritual gifts. It is primarily in the *Power Cluster* but can be in the Word Cluster and Love Clusterde depending upon what is revealed. The *word of knowledge gift* refers to the capacity or sensitivity of a person to supernaturally perceive revealed knowledge from God which otherwise could not or would not be known and apply it to a situation. **Its central thrust is Getting Revelatory Information.**

Word of Wisdom | one of the 19 spiritual gifts. It is primarily in the Power Cluster but can be in the Word Cluster and Love Cluster depending upon what is revealed. The **word of wisdom gift** refers to the capacity to know the mind of the Spirit in a given situation and to communicate clearly the situation, facts, truth or application of the facts and truth to meet the need of the situation. **Its central thrust is Applying Revelatory Information.**

Nehemiah Bibliography

American Bible Society, General Editors
   2001   **The Learning Bible, contemporary English Version.** New York: American Bible Society.

(Bratcher, Robert G. et al)
   n.d.   **Good News Bible—Today's English Version.** New York: American Bible Society.

Bullinger, E. W.

Clinton, Dr. J. Robert
   1977   **Interpreting The Scriptures: Figures and Idioms.** Altadena, Ca: Barnabas Publishers.

   1983   **Interpreting The Scriptures: Hebrew Poetry.** Altadena, CA: Barnabas.

   1986   **Coming to Conclusions On Leadership Styles.** Altadena,Ca: Barnabas Publishers.

   1986   **Short History of Leadership Theory,** 1986, by Dr. J. Robert Clinton. Altadena, CA: Barnabas Publishers.

   1989   *The Ultimate Contribution.* Altadena,Ca: Barnabas Publishers.

   1989   **The Making of A Leader.** Colorado Springs: NavPress.

   1989   **Leadership Emergence Theory.** Altadena,Ca: Barnabas Publishers.

   1992   **Bridging Strategies—Leadership Perspectives for Introducing Change.** Altadena,Ca: Barnabas Publishers.

   1993   **The Bible and Leadership Values.** Altadena,Ca: Barnabas Publishers.

   1993   **Leadership Perspectives.** Altadena,Ca: Barnabas Publishers.

   1995   **Focused Lives—Inspirational Life Changing Lessons From Eight Effective Christian Leaders Who Finished Well.** Altadena,Ca: Barnabas Publishers.

   1995   *The Life Cycle of a Leader.*   Altadena,Ca: Barnabas Publishers.

   1997   **Having A Ministry That Lasts.** Altadena,Ca: Barnabas Publishers.

   2000   **Clinton's Biblical Leadership Commentary CD.** Altadena,Ca: Barnabas Publishers.

   2001   **Titus—Apostolic Leadership.** Altadena,Ca: Barnabas Publishers.

   2002   **Habakkuk—Hope For A Leader In Troubled Times.** Altadena,Ca: Barnabas Publishers.

   2002   **Haggai—Restoring a Work of God, Inspirational, Task-Oriented Leadership.** Altadena,Ca: Barnabas Publishers.

Clinton, Dr. J. Robert and Dr. Richard W.

1993   **Unlocking Your Giftedness—What Leaders Need To Know To Develop Themselves and Others**. Altadena,Ca: Barnabas Publishers.

Covey, Stephen
    The 7 Habits of Highly Effective People.

Cunningham, Loren
    Is That Really You, God?

Davis, Stanley B. Davis,

1987   **Future Perfect**. New York: Addison-Wesley, 1987.

Ebor, Donald (Chairman of the Joint Committee)
1970   **New English Bible**. Oxford: Oxford University Press.

Ellison, H.L.,
1985   "Jonah." *The Expositor's Bible Commentary*. Vol. 7. Edited by Frank E. Gæberlien. Grand Rapids, MI: Zondervan Publishing.

Haggard, Ted
    Prayerwalking Your City. (video cassette).

Hersey Paul, and Blanchard, Ken
1977   **Management of Organizational Behavior—Utilizing Human Resources**. New York: Harper and Row.

Hybels, Bill
    Too Busy Not to Pray.

InterVarsity Press, General Editors
1996   *The New Bible Dictionary*, 3rd edition, InterVarsity Press: Downers Grove, IL.

Kraft, Charles
2002   p 177 dealing with identificational repentance

Kuhn, Thomas
1970   **The Structure of Scientific Revolution**s. Chicago: University of Chicago Press.

Mickelsen, A. Berkley
1963   **Interpreting The Bible**. Grand Rapids: Eerdmans Publishing Company.

Morgan, G. Campbell
    Living Messages of the Books of the Bible.

Phillips, J.B.
1958   **The New Testament in Modern English.** USA: The Macmillan Company.

Pusey, E. B. D.D.,
1907   **The Minor Prophets With a Commentary, Vol. VI, Habakkuk and Malachi,** London: James Nisbet and Co.

Sturkey, John
        Improving Your Listening Skills.
Strong, James
    1890   **The Exhaustive Concordance of the Bible** (with Dictionaries of the Hebrew and
            Greek Words). Nashville: Abingdon Press.

Sweeten, Gary
        Overcoming 7 Communication Barriers.

(Taylor, Ken did original version; other Bible scholars the new version)
    1996   **Holy Bible—New Living Translation**. Wheaton, Il: Tyndale house Publishers, Inc.

Terry, Milton S. (2nd edition)
    1964   **Biblical Hermeneutics**. Grand Rapids: Zondervan.

Trebesch, Shelley
    1997   **Isolation—A Place of Transformation in the Life of A Leader**. Altadena,Ca:
            Barnabas Publishers.

Trible, Phyllis,
    1996   "The Book of Jonah." *The New Interpreter's Bible: A Commentary in Twelve Volumes*. Vol.
            VII. Nashville, TN: Abingdon Press.

Willard, Dallas
        The Spirit of the Disciplines.

Wilmington's Complete Guide to Bible Knowledge—Volume 1 Old Testament People

Wrong, Dennis
    1979   **Power—Its Forms, Bases, and Uses**. San Francisco, CA: Harper and Row.

BARNABAS PUBLISHER'S MINI CATALOG

Approaching the Bible With Leadership Eyes: An Authoratative Source for Leadership Findings — Dr. J. Robert Clinton

Barnabas: Encouraging Exhorter — Dr. J. Robert Clinton & Laura Raab

Boundary Processing: Looking at Critical Transitions Times in Leader's Lives — Dr. J. Robert Clinton

Connecting: The Mentoring Relationships You Need to Succeed in Life — Dr. J. Robert Clinton

The Emerging Leader — Dr. J. Robert Clinton

Fellowship With God — Dr. J. Robert Clinton

Finishing Well — Dr. J. Robert Clinton

Figures and Idioms (Interpreting the Scriptures: Figures and Idioms) — Dr. J. Robert Clinton

Focused Lives Lectures — Dr. J. Robert Clinton

Gender and Leadership — Dr. J. Robert Clinton

Having A Ministry That Lasts: By Becoming a Bible Centered Leader — Dr. J. Robert Clinton

Hebrew Poetry (Interpreting the Scriptures: Hebrew Poetry) — Dr. J. Robert Clinton

A Short **History of Leadership Theory** — Dr. J. Robert Clinton

Isolation: A Place of Transformation in the Life of a Leader — Shelley G. Trebesch

Joseph: Destined to Rule — Dr. J. Robert Clinton

The Joshua Portrait — Dr. J. Robert Clinton and Katherine Haubert

Leadership Emergence Theory: A Self Study Manual For Analyzing the Development of a Christian Leader — Dr. J. Robert Clinton

Leadership Perspectives: How To Study The Bible for Leadership Insights — Dr. J. Robert Clinton

Coming to Some Conclusions on **Leadership Styles** — Dr. J. Robert Clinton

Leadership Training Models — Dr. J. Robert Clinton

The Bible and **Leadership Values:** A Book by Book Analysis— Dr. J. Robert Clinton

The Life Cycle of a Leader: Looking at God's Shaping of A LeaderTowards An Eph. 2:10 Life — Dr. J. Robert Clinton

Listen Up Leaders! — Dr. J. Robert Clinton

The Mantle of the Mentor — Dr. J. Robert Clinton

Mentoring Can Help—Five Leadership Crises You Will Face in the Pastorate For Which You Have Not Been Trained — Dr. J. Robert Clinton

Mentoring: Developing Leaders...Without Adding More Programs — Dr. J. Robert Clinton

The Mentor Handbook: Detailed Guidelines and Helps for Christian Mentors and Mentorees — Dr. J. Robert Clinton

Moses Desert Leadership—7 Macro Lessons

Parables—Puzzles With A Purpose (Interpreting the Scriptures: Puzzles With A Purpose) — Dr. J. Robert Clinton

Paradigm Shift: God's Way of Opening New Vistas To Leaders — Dr. J. Robert Clinton

A Personal Ministry Philosophy: One Key to Effective Leadership — Dr. J. Robert Clinton

Reading on the Run: Continuum Reading Concepts — Dr. J. Robert Clinton

Samuel: Last of the Judges & First of the Prophets–A Model For Transitional Times — Bill Bjoraker

Selecting and Developing Those Emerging Leaders — Dr. Richard W. Clinton

Social Base Processing: The Home Base Environment Out of Which A Leader Works — Dr. J. Robert Clinton

Starting Well: Building A Strong Foundation for a Life Time of Ministry — Dr. J. Robert Clinton

Strategic Concepts: That Clarify A Focused Life – A Self Study Guide — Dr. J. Robert Clinton

The Making of a Leader: Recognizing the Lessons & Stages of Leadership Development — Dr. J. Robert Clinton

Time Line —Small Paper (What it is & How to Construct it) — Dr. J. Robert Clinton

Time Line: Getting Perspective—By Using Your Time-Line, Large Paper — Dr. J. Robert Clinton

Ultimate Contribution — Dr. J. Robert Clinton

Unlocking Your Giftedness: What Leaders Need to Know to Develop Themselves & Others — Dr. J. Robert Clinton

A **Vanishing Breed:** Thoughts About A Bible Centered Leader & A Life Long Bible Mastery Paradigm — Dr. J. Robert Clinton

The Way To Look At Leadership (How To Look at Leadership) — Dr. J. Robert Clinton

Webster-Smith, Irene: An Irish Woman Who Impacted Japan (A Focused Life Study) — Dr. J. Robert Clinton

Word Studies (Interpreting the Scriptures: Word Studies) — Dr. J. Robert Clinton

(Book Titles are in Bold and Paper Titles are in Italics with Sub-Titles and Pre-Titles in Roman)

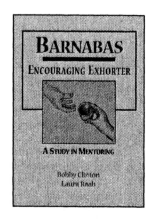

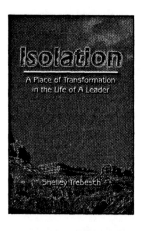

Printed in the United States
53502LVS00002B/79-126